Brecht in Context

Comparative Approaches

Revised Edition

15

John Willett was born in London in 1917 and educated at Winchester and Christ Church, Oxford. His books include *Popski*, a life of Vladimir Peniakoff D.S.O., M.C., *The Theatre of Bertolt Brecht*, *Art in a City* (about Liverpool), *Expressionism*, *The Theatre of Erwin Piscator*, *The New Sobriety: Art and Politics in the Weimar Period*, *The Weimar Years*, *Caspar Neher: Brecht's Designer*, *The Theatre of the Weimar Republic* and *Heartfield versus Hitler*. His compilation, *Brecht on Theatre*, remains a standard work on both sides of the Atlantic. He is co-editor (with Tom Kuhn and the late Ralph Manheim) of Brecht's *Collected Plays* as well as his *Poems 1913–1956*, *Short Stories 1921–1946* and other writings by Brecht. John Willett's Brecht–Kipling show *Never the Twain* (1970) was performed in England, Australia, Jamaica and the US; his translation of *Mother Courage* was broadcast in 1990 with Sheila Hancock as Courage; and his translation of the Brecht–Eisler *The Decision* was performed and broadcast under Robert Ziegler in 1987/88 when it was still blocked elsewhere. His translation with Manheim of *The Threepenny Opera* was staged by Richard Foreman in New York in 1976, and he has collaborated on Robyn Archer's two records of Brecht songs for EMI. After serving two terms on the Arts Council's Art Panel, in 1985 he selected the first exhibition of Caspar Neher's stage designs to be seen outside German-speaking countries and devised the cabaret show *Lulu and After* to accompany the Royal Academy's exhibition of 20th-century German art. He lives in London and Normandy.

Also by John Willett

Popski: A Life of Vladimir Peniakoff D.S.O., M.C.
Art in a City
The Theatre of Bertolt Brecht
Expressionism
The Theatre of Erwin Piscator
The New Sobriety: Art and Politics in the Weimar Period
The Weimar Years: A Civilisation Cut Short
The Theatre of the Weimar Republic
Caspar Neher, Brecht's Designer
Heartfield versus Hitler

Edited by John Willett

Brecht on Theatre
Brecht: Diaries 1920–1922
Brecht Then and Now (Brecht Yearbook, no. 20)
Brecht: Bad Time for Poetry
Brecht: Journals 1934–1955
Brecht: War Primer

Edited by John Willett and Ralph Manheim

Brecht: Poems 1913–1956
Brecht: Short Stories 1921–1946
Brecht: Collected Plays (*in progress*)
Brecht: Letters
Brecht: Songs and Poems from the Plays

Brecht
in Context

Comparative Approaches

Revised Edition

JOHN WILLETT

Methuen

Published by Methuen 1998

1 3 5 7 9 10 8 6 4 2

Copyright © 1984, 1998 by John Willett

John Willett has asserted his right
under the Copyright, Designs and Patents Act, 1988
to be identified as the author of this work

First published in the United Kingdom in 1984 by Methuen London Ltd
This revised edition published in 1998 by Methuen London Ltd
Random House, 20 Vauxhall Bridge Road, London SW1V 2SA

Random House Australia (Pty) Limited
20 Alfred Street, Milsons Point, Sydney,
New South Wales 2061, Australia

Random House New Zealand Limited
18 Poland Road, Glenfield,
Auckland 10, New Zealand

Random House South Africa (Pty) Limited
Endulini, 5A Jubilee Road, Parktown 2193, South Africa

Random House UK Limited Reg No. 954009

A CIP catalogue record for this book is available at the British Library
ISBN 0–413–72310–0

Chapter 5 'The role of Elisabeth Hauptmann' is a revised version of
'Bacon ohne Shakespeare?: The Problem of Mitarbeit'
reprinted from the *Brecht Yearbook*, vol. 12, 1983
by permission of Wayne State University Press
Copyright © 1985 Wayne State University Press
Chapter 13 (d) 'Brecht for the media, 1981–82' is reprinted from
the *Brecht Yearbook*, vol. 11, 1982
by permission of Wayne State University Press
Copyright © 1983 Wayne State University Press

Typeset by Deltatype Ltd, Birkenhead, Merseyside
Printed and bound in Great Britain
by Mackays of Chatham PLC, Chatham, Kent

Contents

Preface

This book first appeared in 1984, nearly a quarter of a century after my *The Theatre of Bertolt Brecht* had set out to give a basic account of Brecht's dramatic work, along with a discussion of its main aspects. By the end of the seventies he had become a recognised factor in European, if not world theatre, radically influencing plays and productions in many countries. His poetry had at last been discovered, as had the scope of his theoretical writings. Once seen as an outsider by Germanists and drama departments alike, he was now, for better or worse, a fertile subject for academic study and dissertation.

I incidentally contributed to this by making an English version of his German publisher's selection of the writings *Über Theater*, but even as I was translating them the picture was changing, as more and more of the unpublished work came to light. Since we were not allowed to publish anything until it had appeared in German, I summarised a lot of the more important new material in my linking notes. The result appeared in 1964 as *Brecht on Theatre*.

Meantime the focus was widening, and when Methuen wanted to make a further book of the various articles and lectures which I had been writing I thought I should do something to offset the still rather narrow view of Brecht as primarily a theatrical practitioner and theoretician. I hoped therefore to place him in a wider context, first of all that of his own poetry (of which Ralph Manheim and I edited a 628-page selection in English translations in 1976); then that not just of comparative literature, but of the arts as a whole and their socio-political background. This meant going further into some of the 'eight aspects' covered in *The Theatre of Bertolt Brecht*, and looking at them from new angles. The result was to set him in relation to Kipling, to Auden, to Erwin Piscator, to Expressionism and to his musical and visual collaborators.

I also wrote a general account, centring on the history of Europe from the First World War to the establishment of the Third Reich, which appeared in 1978 under the title *The New Sobriety: Art and Politics in the*

Weimar Period. This was the background to my calling the new Brecht book *Brecht in Context: Comparative Approaches*. The comparison was not to be restricted to literature. But there was still one major lacuna which I had to fill, concerning the role of his chief literary and dramaturgical collaborator, Elisabeth Hauptmann, who worked closely and productively with and for him from 1925 to 1933, and from 1949 until after his death in 1956. The result was an article for the *Brecht Yearbook* a year or so later, unfortunately too late for the first edition of this book.

In the new edition I have added it (with minor amendments) as chapter 5, between Auden and the Expressionists. Elsewhere there are corrections and small amplifications at many points, notably with regard to Isherwood (in the Auden chapter), where we now have that writer's own diary entries, and to Carola Neher's death in the USSR. Here her son had been able in the 1990s to establish that she died from typhus; she was not shot. I have kept the evidence of Hannah Arendt's intellectual dishonesty, but refrained from any detailed probing of John Fuegi's *Life and Lies*[1] book with this particular bargepole. Interested readers can find that work dissected by several hands in the *Brecht Yearbook*, no. 20. I have also added a slightly revised account of my experience with Brecht and the media, originally published in the *Brecht Yearbook*, no. 11.

John Willett
1998

I

An Englishman
looks at Brecht

I started to get interested in Brecht before the Second World War, when some vestiges of Weimar culture were still surviving in conservative Austria. I had left school early to go to Vienna and spend six months studying the cello with Hans Czegka and stage design with Josef Gregor. Gregor, an eminent theatre historian, was the director of the theatre collection of the Austrian National Library and had written the libretto for Richard Strauss's late opera *Friedenstag*; we worked on a long table among piles of books and portfolios. Almost incidentally I became fluent in the language; the critical moment, I remember, came when I was having my hair cut and reading a translation of Edgar Wallace, and suddenly realised that I no longer needed to look up words I didn't know. From that point on I could start buying and exploring books in German, including some of those by my teacher. His awe-inspiring *Weltgeschichte des Theaters* admittedly only served me for reference; and to this day I have never read it right through. But two of his lesser works were eye-openers, for his volume on Russian theatre introduced me to such great Soviet productions of the 1920s as the Meyerhold–Popova *Magnificent Cuckold*, while his little book on the cinema showed how film related to a whole range of modern works from *Ulysses* and the German Expressionist drama to the political theatre of Piscator and to what he termed 'a perfectly composed sound film six years before the introduction of sound'. This was a play called *Drums in the Night*, and the extracts which he gave (which I quote on p. 121) struck me as the work of a dramatist of great imaginative power.

In the autumn of 1936 I moved on to Oxford to learn politics, philosophy and economics, three useful but never entirely congenial subjects. There I one day ran into Humphrey Searle, composer and tympanist of our school orchestra, who was then a scholar of New College, and heard from him of an erudite refugee, seemingly some kind of musician or – a new word to me – musicologist, whom he had met in Isaiah Berlin's rooms and who bore the euphonious name of Doctor Theodor Wiesengrund-Adorno. This Teddy Wiesengrund, as he was then called, is remembered as charming, clever, amusing and, in the old sense of the term, gay; later he surprised his Oxford friends by emerging as a major international pundit. He had a decisive influence on Searle by arranging for him to go to Austria at the end of the academic year and study with his friend Anton von Webern, and incidentally at some point played him the old (1931 Telefunken) *Dreigroschenoper* recording. This Searle described to me so infectiously that I went out to the record shops and bought it. Thereafter I listened carefully to what he said about *Lulu*, *Mahagonny* and other operas that English critics, like the Nazis, considered 'degenerate', and back in Vienna again the next summer was impelled by him to go to a 'studio' performance of the Milhaud–Cocteau *Le Pauvre Matelot*: a revelation of what a modern opera could be like. Only a few months later the Nazis moved in and took the country over, but in Prague Wieland Herzfelde's Malik publishing house had managed to bring out the first two volumes of what was meant as a comprehensive Brecht edition. These the incomparable Blackwells' bookshop quickly got for me, and I read them from cover to cover, from *The Threepenny Opera* to *Señora Carrar's Rifles*: eleven plays all told.

And that was it. Prague fell, no third volume appeared, Brecht records were already banned. But from then on I was sold, sold to the gentleman in the cloth cap. Everything I could find of, by or to do with him I got hold of: secondhand 78 rpm records, the music of Kurt Weill and Hanns Eisler, the grey-bound *Versuche* booklets in which he used to bring out his writings before 1933, the exiled publications like his second book of poems and his *Threepenny Novel*, the *Dreigroschenroman*, the Moscow-based magazines in which he wrote like *Das Wort* and the German edition of *International Literature*, early rarities like *Trommeln in der Nacht* (the play from which Gregor had quoted) and his first book of poems, *Die Hauspostille*. I found them wherever I could: scattered in English bookshops who had got them from anti-Nazi refugees, in Prague, in Budapest, in Basel, even in Braumüller's bookshop in occupied Vienna among a pile of books which the Gestapo was supposed to come back and collect. Aside from the somewhat uncharacteristic *Señora Carrar's Rifles*, which Unity Theatre were touring round England (including the old Oxford Playhouse, where I saw it), I had not heard of anything of Brecht's being currently staged; while the author himself, so I learned, was living obscurely in Denmark. But my curiosity and, in due course, my familiarity with his special world quickly fanned out to embrace everything that might touch it: the theatre of Piscator, the designs of Caspar Neher, Eisler's political ballads and film music, the singing of Ernst Busch and Lotte Lenya, even a rare short story of his shadowy editor-collaboratrix Elisabeth Hauptmann who, it turned out, had once lodged a friend of mine in Berlin.

The impact which Brecht came to make on me in such ways could be felt, I suppose, on four different levels. First in point of time was the (to me) entirely new combination of music, performance and sharp sense in the songs: something that will perhaps always constitute his most immediate appeal. But secondly, just because I had grown up fairly resistant to poetry in any language, the words of the songs and the poems were an absolute revelation to me. Here was poetry which changed the German language and, through it, might change ours; and did so not in order to strike 'poetic' attitudes or to explore and express the self but from an urgent concern with a world being driven to war. Thirdly, then, came the political element in Brecht's work which seemed to me both revealing and realistic, for instance in its sensitivity to the social factors linking political enemies (as in the 'Song of the SA Man' or the 'Report on the Death of a Comrade') and its awareness that uniting to change that world might leave all concerned with pretty messy hands.

Finally, there was the question of the theatre, where I had been hoping to work as a designer. What had rather stunned that ambition, aside from the war's steady encroachment from the Munich Agreement onwards, was my allergy to the English theatre as it then was, likewise to its practitioners or would-be practitioners whom I met in Oxford. Brecht's plays and theoretical notes were something I could at last fall on with relief. More radically though less spectacularly than the productions of Meyerhold and Piscator, works like *Mahagonny* and *Die Mutter* (*The Mother*) conjured up a theatre as far removed as possible from Shaftesbury Avenue, from Messel, Beaton and Motley; way out beyond the Unity and Group Theatres of the English Left. Instead it could seriously build on such real Anglo-American achievements as the music-hall, the Christmas pantomime, jazz music, *Waiting for Lefty* and *The Cradle Will Rock*.

* * *

The war came, as we knew it would, and for five and a half khaki-clad years all I was left with was my addiction. During that time I read a lot, including a lot of German; learned to digest contradictory masses of information and write intelligible reports; forgot almost entirely about any theatre except the Mediterranean theatre of war, and became so engaged in the social and political world around me that I began to see its reform and reconstruction as the overriding task. Then in the autumn of 1946 I found myself back in Vienna once more with the rump of Eighth Army HQ, fulfilling the largely self-imposed role of encouraging cultural links both between the allies and with the Viennese: this on behalf of our level-headed and much-liked commander Sir Richard McCreery. Here for a few months till I finally got discharged I met for the first time people who could talk illuminatingly about Brecht, notably Oskar Fritz Schuh, then directing at the Opera, and the Austro-Soviet poet Hugo Huppert, subsequently best known perhaps for his translations of Mayakovsky. With Huppert I could also discuss the problems of translating Brecht, something that I had begun to do for my own amusement, improvement and frequent exasperation. I saw a makeshift Viennese performance of some scenes from *Furcht und Elend des Dritten Reiches* (*Fear and Misery of the Third Reich*), picked up whatever information I could about Brecht's own activities since 1939 (tantalising snippets about such unpublished plays as *Mutter Courage, Galileo, Der gute Mensch von Sezuan* and *Puntila*) and went unauthorisedly to Prague, where E.F. Burian was directing a stunning, if somewhat high-handed production of the *Dreigroschenoper* (*The Threepenny Opera*) in Czech. Soon after seeing this I returned to England to be demobilised, my interest as keen as ever though I had little idea how I was going to pursue it in my new civilian suit, or reconcile it with what I felt to be more urgent obligations.

In the event I became a foreign correspondent, then primarily a leader-writer for the *Manchester Guardian*. It had never occurred to me to make any contact with Brecht or to join his effort to set up his own theatre in East Berlin, where I might even then have been a useful, though perhaps not an entirely reliable disciple. But in the course of a number of foreign trips I did manage to see the Brecht–Engel 1949 *Mutter Courage* in that city as well as Hans Schweikart's *Puntila* production in Munich, which had a memorable performance by Erni Wilhelmi as Eva; and the notes which I made on these (and on the Burian *Dreigroschenoper*) will follow in the last chapter of this book. Having long sworn that I would never become a critic, I thereafter in a small and sporadic way joined the growing band of people writing about Brecht. Perhaps it was this that made me start looking critically, not at the work itself so much as at the way in which it was being presented to the English and to a lesser extent the American publics. For here the writing, the poetry and the actual theatrical realisation of the plays were coming to take second place to a preoccupation with theoretical principles which, while fascinating in itself, seemed only too likely to confuse those wishing to stage and perform Brecht's work, or even in extreme cases to scare them off the whole business. Though I myself certainly had never gone all that deeply into Brecht's theories, I felt that I had a better idea of many other aspects and implications of his work which I now saw were in some danger of being neglected. So I thought I should try to map them out in a book.

I envisaged this as a short basic study of the kind that my friends Bernard Wall and Iris Murdoch had written for a series called 'Studies in Modern European Literature and Thought' on Léon Bloy and Jean-Paul Sartre respectively. I haven't kept my letter to Bowes and Bowes, its publishers, but I could hardly throw away the reply from their London office, dated 9 November 1954. They were only accepting further titles, they said,

> where these fill the more obvious gaps left in the series so far. Bertolt Brecht, not being one of the better known figures in modern European Thought does not, unfortunately, come into this category . . .

Such was the climate of those times, when no one was yet thinking of Berlin as a major theatrical city. Impelled however by the enthusiasm of Kenneth Tynan and other theatre critics who had seen *Mutter Courage* in Paris in the Berliner Ensemble's second production or in the French version at the TNP, some readers were even then anxious to know more about Brecht. Moreover outside insular England, though much of his work was still unperformed and unpublished, he was already set on the road to classical status. It was no doubt in view of this, and of the handful of Brecht productions which were then current or impending, that *The Times Literary Supplement* allowed me in the winter of 1955/56 to write a long account of his work, in so far as it was then available in German (the collected plays were up to vol. 4, the poems and prose not yet started) along with *Theaterarbeit* and some early critical accounts in other languages. Admittedly it was only recently that the editor, my former Vienna colleague Alan Pryce-Jones, had seen me more as an authority on military adventure stories about escapes and spying, private armies and liaison with the European resistance. However, he was a kind-hearted man as well as a far-sighted and most un-insular editor, and he let me go ahead. The publication of this essay was important for me, in that it turned me henceforward into the paper's regular writer on Brecht; I went on to shrug off my military burdens and become its authority also on concrete poetry, Evelyn Waugh, Frans Masereel and

Michael Frayn; later I joined the regular staff. But I think it was also important for Brecht, in that it defined his boundaries much more widely than had previously been done. It showed how the playwright struck us at the start of a politically and theatrically crucial year – the year of Suez and Budapest, of *Look Back in Anger* and the Berliner Ensemble's first London visit – and I am not ashamed of it now. 'Eine einzige Lobeshymne', a West German paper called it: an undiluted hymn of praise. Well, why not? The first job was surely to convey his significance and direct people to his work.

Five months later Brecht was dead, and I wrote a sonnet in memory of him in the same paper. Meant to suggest Brecht's own 'literary sonnets' (of which four are now included in *Poems 1913–1956*, pp. 214 and 311–12), it contains allusions to various of his poems, the essay on rhymeless verse and the magazine *Das Wort* as well as, obviously, to *Hamlet*, a play which meant much to him and stimulated one of the sonnets in question. Unthinkingly I signed it 'J.W.' and thereby prompted John Wain to write to the paper disclaiming authorship: it was, he later told me, in a style he had himself once used but discarded. Here it is; I have slightly retouched it:

> No bitterness could put out that cigar
> Or stop the stubborn twisting of its smoke.
> Confronted with the facts, he saw the joke.
> The moral of the play? 'That's how things are'.
>
> Language to him was a conductor's stick:
> He used it for the sense, not for the rhyme
> To mark the fierce divisions of our time
> The inconsistencies that make it tick.
>
> He spread the word, he did the awkward thing
> Upset the state, the church, was not polite
> Made trouble, got the theatre arguing . . .
>
> Our theatre, like our time, is out of joint
> And he is dead who tried to set them right.
> Those who come after him will see his point.

*　　*　　*

I am not sure exactly when it had become known that Peter Daubeny, that irreplaceable impresario who for some years sponsored a World Theatre season in London, had invited the Berliner Ensemble to the

Palace Theatre in August 1956, the very month of Brecht's death. But this news had combined with the publication of my essay to cause various effects. Partly through my old friend Hans Hess, her ex-lodger, I met Elisabeth Hauptmann who had come over to see Blitzstein's Off-Broadway version of *The Threepenny Opera*, now being staged by Sam Wanamaker for the Royal Court Theatre. I wrote her a critique of that version, and she and her close friend Margaret Mynatt, a leading Communist whose responsibilities included publishing and (I inferred) the relations between the German and British parties, became in effect my guides to the matriarchy which then ran the Brecht collective: I liked them both very much indeed. Through Hauptmann I learnt that Brecht had been intrigued and impressed by the (in those days) unsigned *TLS* article, not least perhaps because it appeared in so impeccably Establishment a paper, and wished me to arrange some kind of supervision of the English translation of his plays in the hope of eliminating bad versions. My first effort in this direction concerned George Devine's proposed production of *The Good Woman* [*sic*] *of Sezuan*, one of Brecht's two least unsentimental plays which I felt had been rendered too sugary in Eric and Maya Bentley's published translation. With this in view I wrote to Arthur Waley, whom I had met once or twice, in the hope of getting his help as an adviser, if not as an actual translator.

I had in mind Brecht's own debt to Waley's Chinese and Japanese translations, one of which had been taken bodily into this particular play. What I didn't then realise was that Waley's family had actually come from Frankfurt, so that he might well have been an ideal translator for Brecht. His undated response from 50 Gordon Square was starkly professional:

> I think it would be useful if we could meet again and talk about the Brecht translations. In the case of 'Der gute Mensch aus Sechuan' [*sic*] it occurs to me (as it has probably occurred to you) that the only published translation, the American one, may have been published by the American publishers (Univ. of Minneapolis [actually Minnesota] Press) after purchase of all rights in English-speaking countries. In that case, there would be no alternative to using the American translation, though of course the actors could discreetly adapt it a little. That (so far as I know) is still the position with regard to Pirandello's plays. How about tea on Wednesday May 2, 4.30?

Tea at Gordon Square, so far as I remember, was inconclusive, though I recall Waley's damning verdict on one of Brecht's 'Buckow Elegies' which I had rashly compared with his own oriental translations. 'Oh?' he

said. 'I thought it was more like Ernest Bramah' – Bramah being no god
but the author of some once popular exercises in British Chinoiserie
entitled *Kai Lung Unrolls His Mat*. Anyhow Waley rejected the idea of
translating the play, and the upshot was that I decided to do this myself,
and in due course sent the result off to Devine. Probably Peggy
Ashcroft, who was to play the part, had already by then got the 'good
woman' (rather than the non-committal *gute Mensch* or 'good person')
irretrievably into her mind; at all events my submission was politely
turned down, and that autumn we saw a (to my mind) over-sweet
production in a too pretty set by Teo Otto, relieved by Devine's own
performance as the barber and notable for an angry carpenter played by
John Osborne in a rasping voice.

I saw various publishers before Methuen, in the amiable person of
John Cullen, decided to publish two first volumes of Brecht plays and
also to commission my book *The Theatre of Bertolt Brecht*. Brecht had
wanted me to come out to Berlin to help prepare material for the
Ensemble's London season – which would also allow me to fill some of
the many gaps in the notes which I was already getting together with the
book in view. So Anne and I set out in our small French car that June on
the first of numerous journeys from Dieppe to Berlin, avoiding the
autobahns and taking the old German highway number 1 across
beautiful parts of Westphalia. Living close to the still un-Walled sector
boundary in an excellent if somewhat abandoned hotel, we spent much
of our time watching rehearsals at the Theater am Schiffbauerdamm,
talking with Elisabeth Hauptmann or looking up persons, publications
and illustrations related to Brecht's life and work. Now and again with
Carl Weber, an assistant director who spoke excellent English and had
had a somewhat traumatic experience trying to advise on Joan
Littlewood's Barnstaple production of *Mother Courage* a year earlier, I
would repair to the Schiffbauerdamm's *Turmzimmer*, an isolated upper
room where Brecht used to work when in Berlin, and go over the
translation of the programme and publicity material being prepared for
the London performances. Armed with permits arranged by the
Ensemble's 'cadre leader' Lili Salm, a greying crop-haired Communist
who had lived in Ulan Bator in the 1930s and spent the Second World
War in Kazakhstan, we drove up to Rostock to see *The Good Person of
Szechwan*, to Leipzig with Peter Palitzsch and Manfred Wekwerth of the
Ensemble to see *Lucullus* and then on to Frankfurt by largely deserted
roads for the first production of *The Visions of Simone Machard*. There
we spent some time with Brecht's publishers Suhrkamp-Verlag –

Suhrkamp himself being in hospital – before parting company with the two young Ensemble members and returning to France.

Brecht himself had been out of Berlin all this while, living quietly at his house in Buckow and trying to regain strength after a spell in hospital that spring. But Elisabeth Hauptmann had said that he wanted to see me, and on 17 June I drove her out there to stay the night. The notes which I made following that visit are included later in this book; but I also retain other vivid if not so immediate memories of the occasion. There were two houses at Buckow: the older, bigger one (which has since been made into a museum) contained the main living room and kitchen, as well as the small room where I slept, more or less encased by the paperbound English and American crime stories which were stored there. The second, less pretentious building was where Brecht lived and worked. I was taken to him in the garden tended by his wife, Helene Weigel, and described in the second of the Buckow Elegies (also in Eisler's beautiful song 'The Flower Garden'), where I found an unexpectedly awkward figure with a crooked cap and an unwell, slightly puffy face. He was extremely courteous in a now rare way. We talked in the garden, then in his room where he broke off for a phone conversation about getting a National Prize for someone he (doubtless for my benefit) called 'B' – I thought this was Ernst Busch, but now realise it was probably the novelist Willi Bredel. The talk was easy. I had already sent a copy of my *Szechwan* translation, which he seemed to think passable, though he said that my first effort at the gods' concluding trio ('Leider können wir nicht bleiben/Mehr als eine flüchtige Stund') missed its self-conscious, almost parodistic beauty. We went on to talk about Goethe, not a favourite of his; about style in Latin prose – when I mentioned Tacitus he approvingly said 'ah' – and about French literature, where I was struck by the fact that he didn't know Musset's *On ne badine pas avec l'amour* but pricked up his ears at what I told him about Zola's *Le Roman expérimental*, that early blueprint for the 'literature of the scientific age', which I had lately been reading. We swapped information about crime stories – two Scandinavians whom he recommended to me must, I think, have been that brilliant pair Sjöwall and Wahloo – and I was relieved and a little surprised to find that he admired the novels of Ignazio Silone without apparent political reservations. There was in fact only one point of sharp conflict between us, when I said I thought war between Communist states was by no means inconceivable. That, he snapped, was 'eines Gymnasiasten Ansicht', a schoolboy's view.

'Once we get down there,' Elisabeth Hauptmann had told me in Berlin, 'we'll see if we can get Brecht to open the chest. Your visit might

just put him in the right mood.' *Die Truhe*, the chest, was a box which
had arrived from Sweden containing some of the papers which he had
left there in 1940, and nobody had yet seen what they were. Accordingly
when we went into the main house to join her and Weigel for supper – I
cannot now remember who else was there – Hauptmann with one of her
funny squint-eyed looks said 'Why don't we have a look at *Die Truhe*,
Brecht?' and so we did. Together they rummaged in the close-packed
box and pulled out half-forgotten items. I didn't have the sense (or
effrontery) to get out a notebook and jot them down, but I do remember
early sketches for the settings of the *Threepenny Opera* songs – I think
they must have been those by F.S. Bruinier – and also one of the
polemical essays of the late 1930s against Lukács's definitions of realism.
Brecht seized on this with a most impressive mixture of detachment and
curiosity, read it through and said 'This isn't at all bad. Why don't we
publish it?'

Driving away through the sandy Buckow landscape the following day
I found myself giving a lift to Peter Palitzsch, who at some point had
turned up there, along with the actress Katarina Tüschen and her half-
sister. Palitzsch, later the head of the Frankfurt city theatre and a lifelong
friend of ours, told me that Brecht approved of me. I for my part took
away strong impressions of Brecht's slightly awkward reserve, of his
intellectual restlessness and of the self-critical detachment which could
allow him to shelve and forget his work, then regard it anew. Fortunate
and useful as these insights might be, however, they were only secondary
when compared with my overall awareness that the whole Brecht inner
entourage – that mixture of family, harem and producers' co-op – was
very close to me, that I had known them for a long time. Superficially of
course our acquaintanceship had been limited to three or four months of
1956, but it didn't feel like that. For it had developed out of twenty
eventful and frequently dark years during which I had not only been
absorbing Brecht's own work but getting to know the same background,
making many of the same judgements and fighting some of the same
enemies as they. Of course there was no reason why the feeling should be
reciprocated, yet at moments over the ensuing years it seemed to me that
it was. Despite disagreements – and there were certainly to be a number
of these – from now on I felt that with these people Anne and I were in
some intangible sense at home.

*   *   *

I was lucky in the timing of my book, not so much because of the growing interest in Brecht (for it appeared in small editions and the publishers were content that it should sell slowly) but because in the late 1950s the available knowledge about him could still be encompassed and digested. There was not even a Brecht Archive yet into which researchers like myself could plunge blissfully and lose their way; the wood could still be seen, not just a proliferation of individually intriguing trees. So I was in a position to try and look at the subject as a whole and establish various aspects of it in such a way, I hoped, that they would not be overlooked when future scholars came to explore it in greater detail. More immediately relevant perhaps was the task which this now gave me in the general propagation of Brecht's work to the English-speaking world. This included not only editing, translating, teaching, lecturing and public reading but also, thanks in the first place to Wal Cherry (who reviewed my book for the Melbourne *Age*), some more practical work with directors and performers ranging from Californian students to Robyn Archer and David Bowie. The most important part of all this in the long run will surely have been the making and publication of a proper English selection of Brecht's poetry, which had then been only partially – and that often inadequately – translated. It was hair-tearing work, and it dragged out over many years to the despair of all concerned, who expected the poems at best to sell much less than the plays, then found that the rights for the expected American publication still had to be negotiated. The negotiations slowly ground to a halt (for reasons which I still have not understood) till finally John Cullen, bless him, decided to go it alone and bring the book out at all costs. He did this with a success which surprised everyone and later, after his untimely death, spread to the United States. He told me that since 1945 his firm had published nothing of which he was so proud.

Today the Germanists, who as late as the 1950s used, with rare exceptions, to think Brecht beyond the pale of serious *Literaturwissenschaft*, have changed their mind with a vengeance; there is now a special branch of scholarship called *Brecht-Forschung* or Brecht Research as well as an International Brecht Society run from America; and both East and West Germans came round to accepting him as part of that national 'cultural heritage' which they once thought he threatened. Not only is there a steady flow of scholarly articles and dissertations – for which Brecht with his many drafts, adaptations and alterations provides almost inexhaustible material – but less specialised students too are now very commonly taught Brecht, usually in their own language. Having myself started as an amateur in this field (amateur in the sense of a lover of the work, with no intention to profess it), I have before now felt slightly appalled as I stood before the notice-board in a British university looking at the names of some 250 first-year students opting to join a course on Brecht. But clearly there *is* a lot in him for them, just as there has been for me, and the chapters that follow are intended to show how even more widely relevant he still is than is generally supposed.

If my earliest writings on the subject were intended to map out some of the ground that he seemed to cover, more recently I have been trying to work out just how he fits into it: what does he have to say to the lover of English literature (and particularly poetry), to the visual artist, the musician, the film-maker, the modern historian and the student of the German avant-garde, not least in the theatre? He was not exactly a 'universal man', because whatever he touched he was treating as material for his own particular concerns: his poetry, his theatre, his Communist view of the world. But he was extremely curious, looked at everything with a fresh eye and never let accepted priorities and hierarchies inhibit his often highly original judgements. These we can find concentrated in his work, even packed, however implicitly, into a single poem. By showing some of their contexts I hope to suggest how rewardingly they can be folded out.

In 1994 a book called *The Life and Lies of Bertolt Brecht*[1] appeared in England and the US, arguing that many of his plays had been written for him by mistresses who provided 'text for sex'. This titillating thesis was generously publicised in both countries, though without convincing knowledgeable readers. One way of setting the record straight was through the International Brecht Society yearbook, whose 1995 issue devoted some 130 pages to a detailed analysis of the author's evidence. Another was the publication by Methuen of a cross-section of Brecht's songs and poems whose qualities even in translation showed him to be a major poet. A third might have been to discuss the actual achievements and experiences of his chief woman collaborator, Elisabeth Hauptmann, who had been presented as the real author of eighty per cent of *The Threepenny Opera*, his great success. I regret that my own essay on her substantial (but rather different) contribution was not written in time for the first appearance of the present book fourteen years ago; and because it was available only to members of the Brecht Society, its evidence could be ignored or distorted. However, it belongs in the context referred to in the present book, and it can now be found after the chapters on Kipling and W.H. Auden.

Am I still interested in Brecht? Yes, and I know it each time I find myself making contact with the writer himself – as opposed to his cloud of interpreters on stage, platform or paper – or meeting those who are genuinely looking for him. I don't mean anything mystical by this, nor do I think of Brecht as lying in a deep freeze somewhere like the late Walt Disney, who used to appear in spirit (so colleagues told me) to governors of the California Institute of the Arts when I was teaching there. What I mean in the first place is any meeting with the immediate, undiluted evidence of his artistry, maybe in a theatrical performance or a song, maybe in an unfamiliar piece of writing or else in his always revealing original typescripts with their changes and corrections – evidence of a man at work – maybe again in the kick which he gives me (in more than one sense) when I try to match my language to his. In the second place I'm thinking of the questions which he stimulates in the young. It is those simple questions which are a challenge to answer, because they don't depend on expert or technical knowledge: such questions for instance as Why do you like Brecht? Why are so many theatre directors interested in him? Is he out of date and if so what should directors do about it? How far do his plays need to be adapted for an English, American, Australian, Indian audience today? So long as people ask these things I am compelled to think. And so long as Brecht makes us think, he is doing what he set out to do and his work is still charged with life.

2

Anglo–American forays

During the Second World War Brecht wrote a work in dialogue form which he called *Flüchtlingsgespräche*, or Refugee Conversations, Dialogues Between Exiles. He wrote it in Finland in the autumn of 1940, while England was still under the threat of a German invasion; he revised and finished it in Los Angeles at the end of 1944, when the war was nearly won. In 1960, four years after his death, it was published in West Germany and I wrote a review of it for the *TLS*. It is a splendid work, dating from the period of *Mother Courage* and *Puntila*: comic, acute, reflective and highly individual in outlook, it is based on Diderot's *Jacques le fataliste*. But what puzzled me was the epigraph: two short lines of English verse, presumably bearing on the refugee existence which Brecht himself led –

> He knew that he was still alive.
> More he could not say.

Underneath stood the name 'WOODHOUSE'.

I commented on this in my review and asked 'Was this really P.G. Wodehouse? And could Brecht really turn anything he touched into poetry?' The answer came from Geneva, from an old friend of Claude Cockburn's named Frank Jellinek, who had written a history of the Paris Commune, been with Trotsky in Mexico City immediately before his assassination, and was now living close to Voltaire's old house. Yes: it was taken from *Something Fresh*, the first book in the Blandings Castle saga, and refers to the Efficient Baxter's feelings after a struggle with an intruder in the middle of the night, as he gropes around and comes into contact with a tongue in aspic which he takes for a dead body. The words were pure Wodehouse. The spelling, the setting as verse, the relevance to the life of the anti-Nazi exiles were all supplied by Brecht.

I think this was the first thing that suggested to me that there might be more in Brecht's involvement with English literature than met the eye. For *Something Fresh* is one of those books like *The Wrong Box* or

The Good Soldier Švejk which act as a bond between those who know and like them; and I must say I was delighted to find that Brecht, who so appreciated Švejk, could apparently enjoy the Earl of Emsworth too. I knew of course the outward symptoms of Brecht's unusual penchant for English and American writing. *The Threepenny Opera* derives from John Gay; *Edward II* is adapted from Marlowe; the 'school opera' *He Said Yes* is virtually a translation from Arthur Waley; *Señora Carrar's Rifles* an adaptation of J.M. Synge's *Riders to the Sea*; *Round Heads and Pointed Heads* of *Measure for Measure*. The whole image of America that one finds in *Mahagonny* and *Saint Joan of the Stockyards* and other works derives partly from the novels of Frank Norris and Upton Sinclair, while the concept of the Three Soldiers (as it occurs in *Man equals Man*, the 'Cannon Song' of *The Threepenny Opera* and the 'Three Soldiers' poem) comes plainly from Kipling, and back beyond him from Thomas Ravenscroft and the early seventeenth century:

> We be soldiers three –
> Pardonnez-moi, je vous en prie –
> Lately come forth of the low country,
> With never a penny of money.

Where Brecht's picture of London originated I'm not so sure, though I think the influence of Edgar Wallace's dockland thrillers is visible in *The Threepenny Novel*; while of course the Salvation Army bulked large in his mythology. He was still occupied with *Coriolanus* when he died, and his last fully realised work was the adaptation of Farquhar's *The Recruiting Officer* which the Berliner Ensemble brought to London in 1956.

That, as I said, is what met the eye. And Brecht, on this showing, appeared to have turned to the English-speaking world and to English writing for five main things. First of all, for a low-level and unheroic view of the army, such as he also found in Švejk and in Büchner's *Woyzeck*. Secondly, for a way into an exotic world of adventure which embraced India and the South Seas but came to centre on the Middle West of the United States. Thirdly, for crime stories, the gangster mythology and the unvarnished biographies of the great business buccaneers. Fourthly, and specifically through the work of Arthur Waley, it provided a means of access to the literature, thought and drama of the Far East. And finally the Elizabethan playwrights gave him the example of a form of 'chronicle play' which became a model for his own 'epic theatre'. The affinities which all this represented were evidently more than skin deep. For one thing it is immediately apparent that Brecht has a sense of humour of the kind congenial to Anglo-Saxon audiences and readers. For another, there is a linguistic, stylistic closeness such as exists with very few other foreign writers, so that there are whole areas of Brecht's work – particularly his prose and his unrhymed verse – which go very effectively into English: much better, certainly, than into any other non-German language. But there must be quite a lot more than that.

Admittedly Brecht has even now not really broken through to the English-speaking audience. He has too often bored them, he has inhibited actors and directors from approaching him naturally, he has repeatedly been a box-office disaster. There are all sorts of reasons for this, ranging from uncertainties over copyright to misunderstanding of Brecht's theoretical writings. But at least it shows that the surface of Brecht's relationship with the English-speaking world is not as strong as all that. You certainly don't need to know very much about Brecht to realise that in some respects he was extremely un-English. He may have written, for instance, that his favourite saying was 'the proof of the pudding lies in the eating', but nobody is all that much of an Anglo-Saxon empiricist whose theoretical writings can occupy six or seven volumes. Similarly he may have stressed the element of entertainment in his plays, but the pedagogue was always there lurking in the wings. He was a Marxist preoccupied with dialectics, which is on the whole not a very English or American thing to be, even though Marx himself was much more the Victorian Londoner (and the Victorian father) than most people would think, while Engels of course was a Manchester business man. Above all he had a wholly German attitude to the concept of compromise on which so much in English life and English politics is founded; he saw it not as a dialectical resolution or synthesis but as a flabby and almost decadent damping-down of necessary conflict. This, I think, is why anybody brought up in Brecht's school complains that Brecht performances here are not 'sharp' enough, while to an English eye 'sharpness' so often seems a gratuitous mixture of aggressiveness and caricature.

Yet a signpost like the Wodehouse quotation is extremely intriguing, and I propose to devote these four chapters to trying to establish its really quite deep significance. The next two will deal with Brecht's relationships with a pair of great twentieth-century poets who, like him, could be light, serious or bitterly satirical, though supposedly from very different viewpoints: Rudyard Kipling and W.H. Auden. That on Elisabeth Hauptmann will follow. The rest of this one will discuss the more general process of give-and-take between a middle-class South

German provincial and the theatre and literature of the English-speaking world.

* * *

Until he had passed his mid-thirties Brecht had visited neither England nor the United States, and his knowledge of our language was rudimentary. He had however grown up as a writer in that particular climate of Germany in the 1920s where everything Anglo-Saxon was fashionable, both superficially (as with pipes and hats and dogs' names) and in a more fruitful way as a corrective to what had been heavy and pompous in the now discarded Hohenzollern empire. So besides the American settings which one finds in several of his works starting with *In the Jungle* in 1923, his whole conception of the theatre quite early began reflecting English influences and models. What England had to offer, in that context, was a more direct syntax, a tradition of understatment, a certain wit and logic (as seen respectively in Bernard Shaw and the 1920s detective story) along with the bald no-nonsense technique of presentation used at sporting events. Charlie Chaplin, whose figure dominates the 1920s as did no other single individual's, showed him how a situation could be conveyed by external gestures, with a minimum of 'psychology'. Shakespeare was the proof that complex situations could be narrated in a linear way, without the simplification and artificial consistency demanded by a 'plot'. Even the *songs* which Brecht used to break up the action had to be called by the English word. It is true that he took virtually nothing from the contemporary English theatre. But without the English *heritage* there would have been no 'epic theatre'.

When he got his first job at the Munich Kammerspiele as a dramaturg in 1922, following the nationwide success of *Drums in the Night* in that theatre, Brecht already had some acquaintance with the German translations of Upton Sinclair, Chesterton's Father Brown stories and Kipling's *Jungle Book*, *Barrack-Room Ballads* and *The Light that Failed*. He also knew *Hamlet*, *Antony and Cleopatra* and probably others of Shakespeare's plays. Almost at once these foreign influences bore fruit in two works that symbolise the two main directions of his reading. *In the Jungle*, which he had begun in Berlin the previous winter as an attempt to do for the city what Kipling had done for the jungles of India, was the first of his dramas to be inspired by what he termed 'cold Chicago', the cruel megalopolis of Sinclair's *The Jungle* and J.V. Jensen's *The Wheel*. *Edward II*, which he directed himself at the Kammerspiele in 1924, was an adaptation of Marlowe (by Brecht and Feuchtwanger) which trimmed down the cast, tightened the narrative of the original, hardened its characters and broke the regular rhythms of its language. Perhaps this would have been less easy to achieve with impunity in *Macbeth*, the play which he had originally been scheduled to direct instead. But Marlowe was not so revered in Germany as Shakespeare, and so the production, with its sets by Caspar Neher and its use of scene titles and interpolated songs (set in this case to Brecht's own tunes) could become something of a landmark in the German theatre's treatment of the classics.

Once Brecht had moved to Berlin in the autumn of that year he acquired an English-speaking collaborator in the shape of Elisabeth Hauptmann. From then till the end of 1932 she became a key member of what was known as the 'Brecht collective', that fluctuating body that worked with, for and through him during the eight remaining years of the Weimar Republic. Both the English and the American orientations of his work benefited. Thus *Man equals Man*, which had previously been an embryonic play about a Bavarian butter merchant and his loss of identity, now took on a fresh setting and a fresh impetus as a tale of the British army in Kipling's India. Indeed its 'soldiers three' went well beyond Kipling in the ironic realism of their dialogue, many of whose most vivid passages were cut before the première in 1926 and subsequently left unpublished. For instance the sergeant addressing his men thus:

> the queen had brought you together from all the corners of india   in two days' time you'll be crossing the afghan frontier under the roar of the guns   i knew we'd be getting the scum of every regiment but now i come to look at you it's far worse than i thought   it's my considered opinion that you're the most plague-ridden bunch of throwouts that ever wore its boots out in the queen's service   today i observed some individuals among the huts laughing in such a carefree way that it chilled me to the marrow   i know who they are and let me tell you there will be one or two hairs in *their* christmas pudding[1]

Hauptmann's translations of two poems by Kipling (see p. 44) figured in the first script of *The Threepenny Opera* in 1928 but were dropped before the performance, leaving Kipling's name rather mystifyingly in the programme credits. This most successful of all Brecht's works began life as a translation which she had made, apparently on her own initiative, of Gay's *The Beggar's Opera* following its great London success in Nigel Playfair's revival of 1920. By the time Brecht had made his adaptation and replaced all but one of the songs not much of the original was left: instead the collective had created a new world of more topically relevant crime, whose nineteenth-century setting was dictated simply by the available costumes. Their joint version in turn was elaborated to make first the Pabst film, then in 1934 the *Threepenny Novel* where it came together with further elements from Brecht's English and American reading.

It was the 'American' plays of the same years that most notably developed the Shakespearean or 'epic' strain in his work, though they also connected less directly with *The Threepenny Opera*. And here too Hauptmann did much of the spadework. The plan in 1924 was to make a trilogy of plays on the theme of 'Mankind's Occupation of the Great Cities', starting with the revised version (now the standard one) of *In the Jungle of Cities*, and centring on a similar image of Chicago. Arising out of this there was the preoccupation with the great entrepreneurs, starting with the project of 1925 for a play about Dan Drew and the Erie Railway and leading to the study of Gustavus Myers's *History of the Great American Fortunes*. There was the idea of a play about *The Flood* which drove Hauptmann to collect material about hurricanes in Florida and eventually merged in the writing of the opera libretto *Rise and Fall of the City of Mahagonny*, Mahagonny being an imaginary American city somewhere near Miami; two of its songs were in Hauptmann's home-made English. There was a vast unfinished play called *Wheat* or *Joe P. Fleischhacker from Chicago* which was based on Frank Norris's Chicago novel *The Pit* and in 1926 sent Brecht for the first time to the study of Karl Marx. There were books like Louis Adamic's *Dynamite* and Sherwood Anderson's *Poor White* which inspired such poems as 'How the ship "Oskawa" was broken up by her own crew' and 'Coal for Mike'. There was *Happy End*, the Chicago gangster and Salvationist play which Hauptmann wrote as a successor to *The Threepenny Opera* in 1929, but which flopped largely because Brecht only provided the songs (including the Kipling-based 'Surabaya-Johnny') and otherwise failed to collaborate.[1] All these projects moved in a world of American crime, religion, business and urban living which Brecht saw as analogous not only to Shakespearean tragedy but to the situation in contemporary Germany too. All except *Mahagonny* (which Brecht felt was swallowed by the opera 'apparatus') either fizzled out or failed. Then at the end of 1929, still in collaboration with Hauptmann, he took such elements as seemed most usable from this whole complex – the Chicago setting, the Shakespearean form, the New York millionaire, the Salvationist and the 'Hosanna Rockefeller' finale from *Happy End* – and made them into a new play which borrowed its industrial background from Sinclair's *The Jungle* and its title from Shaw's *Saint Joan*. This, the culmination of five years' effort, was *Saint Joan of the Stockyards*, a classical tragedy written largely in verse. It was not staged in Brecht's lifetime, but was broadcast by Berlin Radio in 1932.

Meanwhile his direct concern with Shakespeare continued. Unlike the German classics, he argued in 1927,

> Shakespeare doesn't have to think. Nor does he have to construct. He leaves construction to the spectator. Shakespeare would never twist the course of a man's fate in Act 2 in order to prepare for Act 5. With him everything takes its natural course. The lack of connection between his Acts reminds us of the lack of connection in a man's fate as reported by someone who has no reason to want to tidy it up so as to strengthen an idea which can only be a prejudice by an argument which is not derived from life.[1]

This came from a broadcast talk introducing the adaptation of *Macbeth* which he made for Berlin Radio with the director Alfred Braun. At the beginning of 1931 a radio adaptation of *Hamlet* followed, giving Brecht's interpretation of the young prince as a man who rightly and prudently hesitates, then is so overcome by the sight of Fortinbras and his soldiers (in Act IV, sc. 4) as to conclude that a bloody massacre can be launched with less logical justification than he has himself. In the process he translated Ophelia's songs[2] with the same kind of free, sensitive simplicity as Auden later showed in translating 'Ging er in goldenen Schuhen' from *The Caucasian Chalk Circle*. No other writer is so often mentioned in Brecht's theoretical notes as Shakespeare and besides these two plays and *Coriolanus* (which he saw soon after arriving in Berlin in an impressive production by Erich Engel) he refers repeatedly to *Lear*, *Richard III*, *Antony and Cleopatra*, *Othello* and *Julius Caesar*, interpreting all these as plays about great passionate individuals whom Shakespeare shows as breaking all earlier restrictions. The only play on which Brecht seriously worked in this period however was *Measure for Measure*, which he was commissioned to adapt at the end of 1931 for Ludwig Berger to direct with the left-wing Gruppe junger Schauspieler formed after the breakup of Piscator's company. The rise of Hitler led him to update and rework this continually until it finished up as *Round Heads and Pointed Heads*, a quasi-Shakespearean play set in an imaginary South American country and describing a racial policy such as the Communists thought Hitler was pursuing for logical class ends. Not much survives of the original except the figures of Angelo and Isabella, and the main strength of the new version lies in its (subsequently added) songs.

Much more than any other of his models of whatever nationality,

Shakespeare interested Brecht as a practical man of the theatre, dealing shrewdly with his actors and readily amending his texts. That theatre moreover was itself part of an age which Brecht especially admired, an age of exploration, release and unbounded curiosity as exemplified in men like Francis Bacon, Descartes and Galileo. At the same time Hauptmann introduced him to an important new strand in his theatrical thinking when she came on Arthur Waley's *The Nō Plays of Japan*, two or three of which she translated, also making a radio feature about their principal author Seami and his approach to acting. It may well be that Brecht already had some inkling of this exceptionally austere and elegant theatre in 1929 when he wrote his first *Lehrstücke*, or didactic plays, for Hindemith's summer festival at Baden-Baden. Certainly a year later he openly adopted its methods in the text of the school opera *Der Jasager* (*He Said Yes*) with Kurt Weill, which was almost word for word Hauptmann's translation of *Taniko or the Valley-hurling* from Waley's collection. Henceforward the verbal simplicity and concise concrete imagery of the Waley translations acted as a lifelong stimulus, along with the oriental modes of thought which they expressed. Later he came to notice Waley's class-conditioned limitations – we might see them more as the limitations of 1920s Bloomsbury perhaps – describing that 'excellent sinologist' as an 'ass' for not seeing how Po Chü-I (and for that matter Brecht himself) could treat instruction and entertainment as indistinguishable, and criticising him for calling Confucius a 'gentleman' rather than a sage.[1] All the same, Waley remained Brecht's bedside reading.

What seems refreshing in Brecht's attitude to our literature, even at this early stage before he could read it very fluently, is his refusal to be overawed by the accepted distinctions between high and low art. Some of his verdicts of the 1920s are those of a reviewer or else of a man called to give an opinion on something he knows mainly from hearsay: in this spirit he writes approvingly of Samuel Butler and Stevenson (who he imagines is an American), of Frank Harris, Theodore Dreiser and James Joyce. Others, however, clearly reflect his spontaneous choice of reading, and it is interesting that these should relate to two more or less non-'literary' areas where English writing unpretentiously excels. So we find him a little later in his letters recommending Slatan Dudow to study the writings of Eddington and Russell on the grounds that

> these people, operating in a field where everything is continually labile, have a wonderfully careful manner, the cautious approach of research itself. They

contradict their opponent [. . .] as they contradict themselves in the course of a piece of research.[1]

Similarly with the crime story, which he first discussed in the 1920s, seeing its strength as lying in its acceptance of specific needs on the reader's part and a 'healthy pattern' like that of the revue or operetta: a set framework within which the author's skill could be admired as is the virtuosity of a variety artist. There was a legend around that time that Brecht had been caught with the dustjacket of *Das Kapital* wrapped round an Edgar Wallace; and certainly he did read Wallace, who was much translated into German, while a Wallace play – probably *The Ringer* – was staged at the Deutsches Theater during Brecht's year there, with his friend Homolka in the leading role (Homolka being the actor who played Baal in 1926 and for whom Brecht later conceived the role of Azdak). 'What do you consider to be kitsch?' a newspaper asked him, to which he replied that he couldn't condemn kitsch without denouncing 'a whole series of phenomena which I personally have no intention of giving up'.

> If I say Werfel is kitsch, then I have to admit that Edgar Wallace too is kitsch. (But all this can do is to stop me reading Werfel. No-one is going to deprive me of the great Wallace.)[2]

Later, when Brecht was reading more in the original, he wrote an essay bringing such stories within the general orbit of his aesthetic. They were founded on logic, he said, and demanded a logical approach by the reader; they dealt with deeds rather than psychology; their essence was 'the establishment of the causality of human actions' particularly as seen after a catastrophe. These qualities, attributed by him to Dorothy Sayers, Austin Freeman and John Rhode, made the crime story, for all its primitive aspects, 'better suited to the requirements of people of a scientific age' than any avant-garde novel (a view which recalls to me my first sight of Bertrand Russell, sitting in the train to Oxford in the 1930s, reading a yellow-bound Edgar Wallace). Moreover the rules and conventions conditioning this form were specifically English.

> The good English crime novel is above all *fair*. It displays moral strength. *To play the game* is a point of honour. The reader is never tricked; all the material is presented to him before the detective solves the problem. He is put in a position to tackle it for himself.
> It is extraordinary how closely the basic pattern of a good crime novel resembles the way a modern physicist goes to work.[3]

*   *   *

Brecht left Germany in 1933 immediately after the Reichstag Fire. Hauptmann remained for some months, then emigrated to the US. By the end of that year Brecht, his wife Helene Weigel and their children Stefan and Barbara had moved into the house at Skovsbostrand near Svendborg in Denmark where they were to live till 1939. Here he continued working on *Round Heads and Pointed Heads* and in 1934 wrote the *Threepenny Novel* as a final spinoff from Gay's musical play. Once that novel had been handed in to its Dutch publishers at the end of the summer he embarked on a series of major travels: to London the same autumn, to Moscow the following spring, thereafter to Paris for the International Writers' Congress for the Defence of Culture (against the Nazis, needless to say); to New York from October till the new year, and again to London in summer 1936. These trips not only showed Brecht for the first time what London and New York were actually like outside the pages of a book; they also gave him some kind of role in the international movement against Fascism and war which in those days linked writers of many countries ranging from Wells and E.M. Forster to Ehrenburg and Mikhail Koltsov. So on his first London visit (which produced the 'Caledonian Market' poem and the sonnet on 'Buying Oranges' near Covent Garden) he saw the Group Theatre production of *Sweeney Agonistes* and met Rupert Doone, its director; while in Moscow he met John Lehmann and Herbert Marshall; and Harold Clurman and Lee Strasberg were there at the same time. Thereafter he was one of the writers published by *New Writing*, the Paris *Commune*, *Left Review* and other journals supporting the Popular Front; and though always less well known than Ernst Toller by 1936 he was no longer wholly unfamiliar to the British Left. Nor was he unknown in the US, though there the effect of his first visit was somewhat different. For the Theatre Union production of his play *Mother*, for which he came, was something of a disaster, and his intransigent attitude to it alienated him in due course from the greater part of the American left theatre movement and its associated writers. Admittedly it seems that Strasberg may have begun rehearsing the even more didactic and non-naturalistic *Measures Taken* (*Die Massnahme* or *The Decision*) though evidently he had 'for political reasons' to break off, leaving this play to be first performed in English by a left-wing chorus under Alan Bush in London a year later.[1] But generally the impression remained in the United States – as it did not in England – that Brecht was an impossible man with whom to deal.[2]

The first work of Brecht's to be seen in London was one of the least substantial, the ballet *The Seven Deadly Sins* which he wrote in the form of a series of songs to Weill's music for a short-lived ballet company financed by Edward James, husband of its principal dancer Tilly Losch. After opening in Paris this came to the Savoy Theatre at the end of July 1933 and was described by Constant Lambert the same year in his book *Music Ho!* as a work of 'considerable strength' and a great advance on either *Mahagonny* or the 'early and crude' *Threepenny Opera*.[1] The latter had indeed a bad name in England in the 1930s, though *The Times* Berlin correspondent reviewed its première in 1928 with surprising insight. For its BBC broadcast in 1935 was sweepingly damned by the leading critic Ernest Newman, who considered text and music alike to be feeble by comparison with Gay, while Percy Scholes's *Oxford Companion to Music* even as late as 1950 was still misdating it and terming it 'a gross travesty of the original' on the reputed authority of 'Britons who have seen it'. This being so, it seems surprising that the English translation of *The Threepenny Novel* (published in 1937 under the title *A Penny for the Poor*) got such good reviews, notably in *The Times Literary Supplement*. Of course Brecht's novel had profited much more than the play from his and Hauptmann's reading, for not only are some of its more disgraceful business details seemingly derived from *The History of the Great American Fortunes* but the new character of Lord Bloomsbury (originally spelt Blumsbury) is pure Wodehouse and there are stylistic as well as topographical echoes of such Edgar Wallace works as the J.G. Reeder stories. But the book didn't sell, nor did Brecht expect it to. For, so he told Feuchtwanger,

> the reviews said the book was pretty unpleasant, and it seems that the English are not so especially fond of unpleasantness as are the Germans.[2]

It was during the second half of the 1930s that Brecht began to see the rise of Stanislavsky's 'Method' in USA and USSR alike as a threat to the kind of anti-illusionistic theatre practised by himself and Erwin Piscator. Whether or not he was at all aware of the impending role of this naturalist revival in the new Soviet orthodoxy, it looks as if he first came to dislike it through his experience of the 'left' theatre in New York (where he was already aware of Odets's decline since *Waiting for Lefty*) and the theoretical articles in that movement's journal *Theatre Workshop* which began coming out in October 1936. For a time it seemed that Piscator might be able to oppose this with a Moscow-financed international journal to be published from Switzerland, and that summer Brecht had written to him urging that it was

quite wrong that we are making no propaganda for our way of approaching
theatre and film[1]

to halt the Method's growing influence in Paris and New York. Within
weeks however Piscator's position in Moscow had crumbled, so that
early the following year Brecht took the initiative into his own hands and
proposed forming a small 'Diderot Society' which would act as an
international pressure group and exchange theoretical ideas. Among
those whom he tried (with virtually no success) to recruit for this scheme
were Auden, Isherwood and Rupert Doone of the (London) Group
Theatre, and Max (Mordecai) Gorelik and Archibald MacLeish in the
United States. Gorelik appears to have been his only positive ally among
the English-speaking five, for he was an advocate of the 'epic theatre' and
his sets had been the one aspect of the disastrous *Mother* production that
satisfied Brecht. Being on the board of *Theatre Workshop* he now (in the
April 1937 issue) condensed the Notes to *The Threepenny Opera* as an
antidote to what he termed 'the fusion of theatrical elements into one
emotional system', calculated to smother 'any genuine interest in
understanding the world'.

With the new wave of criticism in Moscow now rejecting all such
forms of avant-garde thinking not only in the theatre but in literature
too, Brecht found himself turning to English art and writing for
examples of a realism that was not naturalistic: the satires of Swift, the
prints of Hogarth which he had studied in relation to *The Beggar's
Opera*, the cartoons of Low (Antipodean originator of Colonel Blimp),
Bleak House by Dickens and, quoted at length in his own line-for-line
translation, *The Mask of Anarchy* which Shelley wrote after Peterloo – a
prototype which Brecht later followed in his own telling satire of 1947,
'The anachronistic procession, or Freedom and Democracy'. Yet his
London experiences of 1934 and 1936 do not seem to have tempted him
to settle in England, and for all his dislike of the Method and its hold on
the American theatre, by 1938 Brecht was beginning to see the United
States as the best place for him to go. Hanns Eisler had emigrated that
January, Piscator was to follow by the end of the year; and when Brecht's
first American friend, the scriptwriter Ferdinand Reyher, arrived to see
him in Denmark just after the Munich Agreement he had already made
up his mind. So *Galileo* was planned, in consultation with Reyher, as a
film script for the American market, and when it turned out instead to be
the first of a whole batch of major plays Brecht still talked of making a
film treatment of it later.[2]

By March 1939 the whole Brecht household were on the immigration quota and Piscator had got a promise of $1000 for them from Dorothy Thompson – Sinclair Lewis's journalist wife – along with an invitation for Brecht to teach at the New School in New York. This is where Piscator was setting up his Dramatic Workshop under the aegis of another good friend of the émigrés, the school's president Alvin Johnson. The main problem then was to get some kind of visa for Margarete Steffin, she being the Berlin working-class girl who had succeeded Hauptmann as Brecht's principal collaborator and secretarial aide. But already he thought it worth getting to grips with 'the newer "realistic" American literature' of James M. Cain, Hemingway, Steinbeck and others and introducing English phrases into his comments on it. Thus his diary for 5 March, with the interpolated phrases in italics:

> it all starts with the film experience (and will end with hollywood). the cinema, particularly in the silent era, needed unforeseen quantities of plot (consumption of expression). the psychologists of the day discovered behaviourism, psychology as seen by the camera-eye. today literature is catching up. but what these *hard-boiled men* are doing is turning out *hot stuff*; their job is to generate emotions, they are members of the great emotion racket. so they take the easy way out and fall back on the emotions as motive forces. they fit out the *man in the street*, roosevelt's *new deal* man, garage mechanic, agricultural worker, reporter, with a 10 hp motor apiece complete with all essential brakes. the result is that romantic character the souped-up petty bourgeois.[1]

Books like *Of Mice and Men*, *The Postman Always Rings Twice*, *Serenade* and *No Pockets*, which helped him to such conclusions, were, he said, 'Hollywood run riot', examples not of realism, but of a 'hectic verism' that ignored class structures and dispensed with any moral or political point of view.[2] Later he listed under the heading of 'Opinions I don't share' the hypothesis 'That Hemingway has a brain'.

If the United States struck Brecht as a country with possibilities but no worthwhile literary tradition, England appeared to be the exact opposite. Unhappy over the Soviet-German pact and the dual invasion of Poland, he was surprised by the British declaration of war, and perhaps as a result came thereafter to develop a concern with England's literature and even England's survival that was new, but at the same time short-lived, diminishing perceptibly once Hitler had turned against Russia and the Brechts had reached the United States. During this period of waiting however, which saw the completion of *Puntila*, the *Flüchtlingsgespräche* (Dialogues Between Exiles) and most of the unfinished *Messingkauf Dialogues*, he was also taking *Picture Post*, listening to the BBC and reading Macaulay, Boswell, Waley on Confucius, Arnold and Newman on the translation of Homer, and Lytton Strachey and Racine, while when in his diary he comments on Wordsworth's 'She was a phantom of delight' he contrasts this with the image of the English countryside in August 1940 being defended by the Home Guard against invasion. A list of the English-language books on his seventeen-year-old son's table in Finland at the beginning of 1941 includes Swift's poems, Thackeray's *Book of Snobs* and *Miscellaneous Contributions to Punch*, *Lady Chatterley's Lover*, three plays by Shakespeare, the J.L. Martin constructivist anthology *Circle*, the Webbs' *Soviet Communism: A New Civilisation?* (the edition with the question mark), Edgar Wallace's *Again the Three Just Men*, and from across the Atlantic F.M. Ford's *New York is not America*, Granville Hicks's *The Great Tradition*, and H. Rugg's *Introduction to Problems of American Culture* and *Changing Governments and Changing Cultures.*[1] Meanwhile the German armies were rolling victoriously forward, a continual threat to the family's lives. 'As I listen to the news in the morning,' wrote Brecht shortly before starting work on *Puntila*,

> simultaneously reading boswell's life of johnson and glancing out through the birch trees and the mist of the lake, the unnatural day begins not so much on a discordant note as on no note at all.[2]

* * *

When Brecht reached California in July 1941 those of his plays which he most wanted to see performed in America were in the first place *Galileo*, *The Good Person of Szechwan*, and *The Resistible Rise of Arturo Ui*, the last of which had been rapidly written only two months before leaving and was intended specifically for the American theatre. After these in priority came *Mother Courage*, which had just had its première in neutral Switzerland, and the two dozen anti-Nazi scenes of *Fear and Misery of the Third Reich*. The earlier plays were not seen as likely candidates, nor for some reason (possibly connected with the shared copyright) was *Puntila*, which virtually vanished from Brecht's horizon for the next seven years. Of the five best prospects all had gone in the original German to Piscator; furthermore *Galileo* had been translated by Desmond Vesey and was being worked on by Reyher, while *Courage* had been sent for translation to one of Brecht's US guarantors, the poet H.R. Hays. Scarcely any of them however came anywhere near an actual production. Elisabeth Bergner turned down *The Good Person of Szechwan*, as did the film actress Anna May Wong; Piscator, who had begun discussing this play with the Theatre Guild, lost interest; Weill toyed with the idea of making an opera of it, but was still toying eight years later. *Ui* briefly interested the CIO unions, leading Piscator and Eisler to urge Hays to make a rapid translation; however, he seems to have ceased work on learning that Brecht had tacitly condemned his *Fear and Misery* translation, and in any case the CIO felt the Hitler theme to be inappropriate while the US was not yet at war. *Courage* appeared in print in *New Directions* in 1941 but was never to my knowledge even considered for a professional production, while *Fear and Misery*, reworked in a wartime framework as *The Private Life of the Master Race* and translated afresh by Eric Bentley, had a short and poorly received run in New York a few weeks after the war ended. Only *Galileo* reached the Broadway stage in a major production, and this only happened once Brecht himself was on his way home.

The fact is that although Brecht had felt confident enough of his ability to earn his way with film stories and plays to jettison his prospective job with Piscator in New York, he could never adapt his talents to the requirements of the market. In so far as he managed to sell himself to Hollywood at all (with the story of *Hangmen Also Die* and the still unexploited film rights to his new play *Simone Machard*) it was thanks to the generosity of Fritz Lang and Lion Feuchtwanger, old German friends who had successfully established themselves there. Never reconciled to the naturalism of the American Left theatre even in its least corrupted form, he found it impossible to accept those of its members who, like Clifford Odets, had compromised with Hollywood's standards; and they in turn treated him at best with condescension (as did Orson Welles). This influential group of 'progressives' had, it seemed, no use for his work in either medium, and as a result the only professionals who gave him employment were with one exception émigrés who had known him from Munich or Berlin. *Schweik in the Second World War* was written for Weill and Ernst Josef Aufricht, the original producer of *The Threepenny Opera*, with Peter Lorre briefly taking a hand; *The Caucasian Chalk Circle* for Luise Rainer (though it also included a fat part for Homolka); the new framework for *Fear and Misery* originally for Max Reinhardt. Elisabeth Bergner too tried to interest Brecht in writing a film story of the kind that would best meet local demands: he described her idea as being on some such lines as

a girl is hypnotised, runs off in a trance, does something in a trance, isn't really in a trance after all, just pretending to be in a trance, and on top of that there's supposed to be a message. difficult.[1]

More reasonably, they discussed a stage production of Thomas Heywood's *A Woman Killed With Kindness*, and finally settled on a new Brecht adaptation of *The Duchess of Malfi* in which Bergner would appear on Broadway. There was only one comparable non-German to become seriously interested in Brecht and his work, and that was the English actor Charles Laughton. Interestingly enough, their joint adaptation of *Galileo* was the only one of all these enterprises to be fully carried through and, in Brecht's own view, to succeed.

The that 'gigantic baby' as he termed it, certainly nerican myth, which Brecht expressed for Chicago gangster setting of *Arturo Ui*. two indigenous projects like a play *on River Anthology* or a black version ill turned down), generally his view rrowed and sharpened, as in the which he wrote for Hanns Eisler to set language itself rather that moved into his mind, re after three years in California he actually found his erman becoming affected:

n [he wrote in late 1944] i forget a german word – i who only now gain recall an english one. when i try to find it what comes to mind is not the high german words but dialect expressions like dohdle for godfather.[1]

This was not so much because of the demands of his social life, since the German-speaking community in that part of the world is a large one and relatively few of his acquaintances came from outside it. But even within his own émigré circle it had become normal to use the kind of hybrid vocabulary anticipated in his earlier note on the 'hard-boiled' verists of the Hemingway school and now nourished by the jargon of the studios and the language of wartime regulations. So Fritz Lang is described sitting behind a *Bossschreibtisch*, the images *verblurren* (or 'go fuzzy'), Alfred Döblin has to leave his $60-a-month house in 1941 when he, like other refugees who 'picturewriterkontrakte bekamen', 'fired ist'. Once America has entered the war Brecht finds Theodor Adorno 'wegen des curfews sehr jumpy'; later in his *Duchess of Malfi* adaptation, he tells Bergner, 'Bosola wird Librarian, ein frustrated Scholar'. It is not surprising then that something of the same linguistic cocktail began to seep into his work wherever the two languages met. This was the case first with *The Duchess of Malfi* itself, where the plan was for Brecht to make the dramaturgical changes which H.R. Hays would then put into

passably Websterian English and work into the text – a process which
led Brecht into such intermediate pieces of patchwork as this:

> DUCHESS: My mind is full of shadows, there are questions
> by now forgotten because never answered
> aber jetzt riesig aufsteigend out of childhood's innocence
> All of them entangled around my brother Fernando
> Even now nicht erlaubend eine nackte antwort.

Subsequently W.H. Auden was brought into this collaboration in place
of Hays; the fairly disastrous eventual results will be described when we
come to consider his contribution in more detail. But already it seems
that Brecht was able to think in a kind of half-English, which in turn was
not without its effect on his German. 'Als wir kamen vor Milano' for
instance, the first line of the song which he wrote for the soldiers to sing
in Act 2, scene 1, is not in correct German word order, but English.

Much the same can be seen in the case of *Galileo*, which went through
an even more complicated process. After setting aside all previous
translations, including one specially made for him by two young
American writers who had previously worked with Döblin, Laughton
got Brecht himself to give the meaning sentence by sentence in English,
then wrote the result down literally, and began acting back and rewording until both men were satisfied. This initially led to some odd
phrasing – 'blind placed faith deposed by healthy doubt', for instance,
was their first rendering of 'wo der glaube 1000 jahr gesessen hat, ebenda
sitzt jetzt der zweifel' in Galileo's first long speech in scene 1 – and in
Brecht's copious typescripts (of which there is a bigger pile than for any
of his other plays) there are rough sketches like:

> Rede des Mathematikers
> Das Universum des göttlichen Aristoteles mit seinen
> mystisch musizierenden Sphären und Kristallnen Gewöl-
> 　　　　circles　　　　　　　　heavenly bodies
> ben sowie den Kreisläufen seiner Himmelskörper,
> 　　　obliquity of the ecliptic
> seinem Schiefenwinkel der Sonnenbahn/den Geheimnissen
> 　　　　Sternen
> der Table of Cords, dem/Reichtum des Catalogue
> 　　　　inspirierten
> for the southern hemisphere/der/construction of a
> celestial globe in ein Gebäude von grosser Ordnung
> und Schönheit.
> The Universe of divine Classics.[1]

On top of this there were later additions by other hands such as the ex-Hungarian George Tabori who knew better than either Brecht or Laughton what would be found acceptable on Broadway. Perhaps the most interesting aspect of the collaboration however was that Brecht found himself able to use the English actor's experience and talent to reorganise and compress his own great play, at the same time making it more apposite to an era which was about to perfect and use the most devastating weapon in the history of the world. Often the result conflicted with Brecht's own wish to establish a definitive version, for in Laughton he saw the heir of that marvellous Elizabethan age where works of genius had gone up like fireworks, consumed by its theatre as so many 'texts'. This presented him with problems when it came to preparing a new German text around the time of his return to Europe in 1947; and in his eventual compromise between Laughton's dramaturgically tightened story, and those great poetic 'arias' which he now wished to restore, future generations may perhaps be able to identify – along with obvious Anglicisms like 'die Zunge in der Backe' for Laughton's 'tongue in cheek' – just how much he retained of an un-German sense of theatre and an English habit of thought. To Laughton he put it mock-apologetically (in the English which they always used):

> in order to keep me busy now I am translating back 'Galileo' into German, a 'helluva job'! It is especially difficult to remember that sort of twilight (lack of clarity) which my poor country is so fond of.[1]

Not long before he and Laughton first met, Brecht had once again been reading about the Elizabethan theatre, which he found 'in many ways resembles the Hollywood business' in its penchant for collective work, re-use of old stories and dependence on the box office. But it was Laughton who brought Shakespeare's original texts to life for him, perhaps for the first time, in private readings of *Measure for Measure*, *The Tempest*, *King Lear* and parts of *Hamlet*, *As You Like It* and *Antony and Cleopatra*; he likewise read extracts from Dickens and the Bible. Brecht's own reading at the time is indicated by a diary entry giving his 'plan for the day' in 1944, soon after finishing work on *The Caucasian Chalk Circle*:

> get up at 7. radio. make coffee in the little copper pot. morning: work. light lunch about twelve. rest with crime novel. afternoon: work or pay visits. evening meal at 7. guests after. at night half a page of shakespeare or waley's collection of chinese poems. radio. crime novel.[2]

There is also some evidence that he was taking steps to extend his knowledge of the English poets. Thus Shelley for instance served him as a starting-point for the poem 'On thinking about Hell'[1] with its highly unflattering picture of Los Angeles, while he also read recent poetry by Eliot and Auden, and wrote a poem 'Young Man on the Escalator'[2] described as 'In the style of T.S. Eliot' (though the connection is hard to see). There is even what appears to have been a 'counter-poem' to Pound's 'E.P. Ode pour l'élection de son sépulcre'.[3] Meanwhile he was characteristically gumming into his diary verses of a somewhat lower order, including current soldiers' songs such as 'Dirty Gertie from Bizerte', the bowdlerised 'Bless 'em all' and a parody of Kipling's 'Mandalay' ending:

> Pack a load to Grizo Bay
> Where the float-plane Zeros play
> And the bombs come down like thunder
> On the natives 'cross the way.[4]

With Eisler he made a version of 'The Old Gray Goose', a traditional American song which they turned into 'The Durable Grey Goose', who flies off eastwards honking loudly.

Thus equipped and acclimatised he made some first tentative efforts to write or translate into English, though it is difficult to say just how far he was helped in this by his family, or by the younger Viertels and poets like Albert Brush and Naomi Replansky from among their friends. Those short verses, for instance, which introduce the various scenes of *Galileo* (and were beautifully set by Eisler for boys' voices), were not in the earlier German version and their simple directness is surely due in the first place to Brecht. A translation of the 'Song of Chaos' from *The Caucasian Chalk Circle* uses the same typing conventions as we know from his German working scripts:

> why must our sons bleed like cattle on st. johns day?
> why must our daughters weep like the willows at dawn by the shores of lake urmi?
>
> the shah of shahs has to have a new province, oh woe!
> the peasant has to sell his milch cow . . .

with the refrain:

> is that so? is that so?
> yea, yea, yea, yea, yea, that is so.[5]

Among the *Duchess of Malfi* papers too in 1956 was his handwritten
English version of the first scene of *Man equals Man*, which was
evidently made in the middle 1940s and goes thus:

Kilkoa

Galy Gay sits one morning upon his chair and tells his wife:

GALY GAY: Dear wife, I believe that it is within our means to buy a fish today.
That should be alright for a porter, who drinks not at all, smokes very
little and has almost no vices. Do you think, I should buy a big fish or do
you need only a small one?

WIFE: A small one.

GALY GAY: That small fish, what kind shall it be?

WIFE: I would say, a good flounder. But please look out for the fish wifes. They
are loose and you have a soft heart, Galy Gay.

GALY GAY: That's true but I hope they would not bother with a porter of such
small means.

WIFE: You are like an elefant which is the most clumsy animal of the animal
kingdom, but he runs like a freight train once he gets started. And there are
those soldiers who are the most awful people in the world and who are said
to be swarming at the station like bees. Sure they stand around at the
market and you're lucky if they don't rob and kill you. You are only one
and they are always four.

The small errors here are unimportant by comparison with the accuracy
of the tone, which is remarkably close to that of the unforgettable
deadpan German of the original. It is a great pity that he did not
complete it, but even so I thought it worth incorporating in the Methuen
edition of the play, and made some adjustments in the other scenes to
conform. (Anyone interested may like to compare the result with the
same scene in the earlier Random House edition.)

*   *   *

This was the nearest Brecht ever came to becoming an English-language
writer, and although it is not unusual for commentators to speculate on
the likelihood of his settling for good in the United States if he had only
been more successful, the argument is a futile one, for he never had it in
him to succeed either in Hollywood or on the conventional Broadway
stage. This limitation, needless to say, reflects more on the conventions
in question, than on those laws which Brecht laboriously made for
himself; nor does the fact that he would have liked to be able to conquer
the new world and bend it to his own theatrical rules affect the point.

The fact is that, following the Hollywood première of *Galileo*, he returned to the German-language theatres of Europe and the tradition from which he had so largely broken away. There the task, as he saw it, was to rebuild a whole German culture that had been shattered by twelve years of Nazi dictatorship and devastating war, and he chose with whatever reservations to do so through that Soviet-occupied part of his country which still held his political allegiance. To this end he had to re-establish a repertoire and a standard of acting; moreover he wished authoritatively to stage his many unperformed plays; and it was with a view to both aims that he and Helene Weigel set themselves to create their own company, the Berliner Ensemble. One result of this was to direct Brecht to those German classics which had previously not much concerned him (or in some cases attracted him), but on which any future repertoire must draw: Kleist, Gerhart Hauptmann, and the early Goethe. A second, in regrettable conformity with East German cultural policy, was to make him rather play down his debt to the Anglo-Saxon world; thus Kipling (as James Lyon has pointed out) does not figure in the account which he gave of the poetic sources 'Where I have learnt',[1] while all allusions to the BBC's wartime broadcasts in *Schweik in the Second World War* were changed to refer to Radio Moscow. The third and most important was to reduce the time available to him for fresh creative work. As a result the kind of stimulus he had drawn from outside Germany was no longer so excitingly and entertainingly absorbed into his writing.

All the same, habits die hard, and even in Berlin in the seven last years of his life Brecht was still making use of English and American models. So he could write off to America for copies of the musicals *Of Thee I Sing* and *Pins and Needles* for possible production; he could also write songs for a production of *Volpone* at the Communist-run Scala Theatre in Vienna; read *Waiting for Godot* and start devising a 'counterplay' which would bring out the characters' class origins; try to set up a *Hamlet* production with Peter Lorre as the prince; and talk to his young assistants about tackling a play by O'Casey. Once again it becomes difficult to disentangle his activities in such directions from those of Elisabeth Hauptmann, who had returned from America to join the board of the new Ensemble. Thus it was she who was mainly responsible for the adaptation of Farquhar's *The Recruiting Officer* as *Trumpets and Drums*, moving it forward some seventy years to embrace the war against the American colonies, though once more as with *The Threepenny Opera* Brecht himself wrote the songs. Synge too surfaced again in a production of *The Playboy of the Western World* translated by the young dramatist

Peter Hacks and interpreted (with Brecht's approval) as showing the 'Western' world's appreciation of murderers – which was hardly the Irishman's point. And finally there was the preparatory work for *Coriolanus*, which Brecht himself translated, starting in 1951, but thereafter adapted much less radically than he and his assistants had at first envisaged. Essentially his version differed from Shakespeare's original in having Brutus arm the people to defend Rome and accordingly stripping Volumnia of her role in saving the city. It was not produced by the Ensemble till eight years after Brecht's death, when it was seen as one of the company's most brilliant achievements. Thereafter the directors effectively restaged it in London with the National Theatre, returning to Shakespeare's unchanged text.

In 1960 Reinhold Grimm published a list of some five dozen books that were in Brecht's bedroom at the time of his death.[1] These included a fair number of old editions of German and Latin classics, the latter sometimes in German translations, as well as copies of Brecht's own works and new books evidently sent by his publisher or given by friends. Among the rest were Pope's translation of the *Iliad*, Karl Kraus's of the Shakespeare Sonnets, the 1927 German edition of *Schweik*, a 1947 German translation of Waley's *Three Ways of Thought in Ancient China*, Miller's *Tropic of Cancer*, Kenneth Rexroth's *One Hundred Poems from the Japanese*, a 1907 German translation of Wilde's *The Ballad of Reading Gaol* and what are described as 'four English-language crime stories and spine-chillers'. Perhaps this slightly job-lot dismissal of an important element of Brecht's reading – not to mention his 'means of production', as he termed such books – is symptomatic of the barrier which literary scholars still put between proper literature and 'Trivialliteratur' or more or less improper reading material. In the study of Brecht at all events such distinctions are quite wrong. Which side would 'Woodhouse' fall, for a start? And Edgar Wallace, and soldiers' songs, and James M. Cain? To Brecht the whole of our literature from *Hamlet* to Hammett was one unbroken, if too often bloodstained web.

America stood for him – for better or worse – as the land of the future. 'O Aasland, Kümmernisloch!' says the conclusion of the first of his five 'Germany' poems, written in 1920,

> Oh carrion land, misery hole!
> Shame strangles the remembrance of you
> And in the young men whom
> You have not ruined
> America awakens.[2]

Eckart too, in the revised version of his first play *Baal*, sees the ruined industrialised landscape of Germany and points to photographs of Manhattan whose tall buildings indicate 'a great power in the human race'. The important thing, he says, 'is to *be there*!' So America was not so much the land of the free, in any political sense, as the land of possibilities, of free development such as England had known four centuries ago. England by contrast was in decline – thus the phrase 'that empire is finished' in the poem 'The Son'[1] originally referred to Britain, not France. At the same time its writing, its syntax, and its modes of thought provided models of clarity in a variety of respects. Unacceptable as was its class structure, its self-interested imperialism and its political compromises in face of Hitler, it still had an unbelievably rich and coherent past literature, giving the impression to Brecht of many generations of notable writers living and interacting in a single city – something that Germany, ravaged by the Thirty Years War and split into small states till 1870, could never achieve. Of course he could have derived the same impression from France, where Paris has long been an even more all-absorbing centre than London. But whether for linguistic or for temperamental reasons, or perhaps again because it is also at the root of America's, the English tradition was more congenial to him than was the French.

In the end the benefit is ours. It is not only that the use which Brecht made of his English and American reading must make him accessible to our own readers, and ultimately to our theatre-goers, in a way that more purely German writers often are not. For at that point something else begins. Here also is a highly perceptive and original outsider, a genius, who runs his eye over us, our whole culture from major branches of the entertainment industry down to popular jingles, and judges it all from a consistent, non-discriminatory (unsnobbish), largely practical, independent point of view. In this way Brecht does that seemingly simple thing which his often mystifying theory of alienation is intended to make possible. He takes a new look at a familiar area. And by so doing he suggests to others how they too can look at it afresh.

3

The case of Kipling

During the early 1970s two accidents drove me to go rather more systematically into the relation between Brecht's writing and that of Rudyard Kipling. First of all I was asked by John Cox the opera director and Alexander Goehr the composer to put together a stage show about the two writers for performance by their Music Theatre Ensemble. Then Adrian Henri sent me Charles Carrington's biography of Kipling and asked me to review it along with the new *Penguin Book of Socialist Verse* for an issue of the *Poetry Review* which he was editing. The fact that there was some connection between the two poets had of course long been known. Kurt Tucholsky in 1930 had written mockingly of a figure he called 'Rudyard Brecht' who exclaimed exotic nonsense phrases like 'Remington to larboard!', while it must have been Brecht or Elisabeth Hauptmann who inserted the credit 'additional ballads by Villon and Kipling' in the original programme of *The Threepenny Opera* in 1928. I had myself probed a little further in my first Brecht book, where I made some brief suggestion about Kipling's contribution to specific Brecht works. Since then however Michael Morley in Auckland had written an illuminating article on the earliest of all Brecht's borrowings from Kipling,[1] followed in 1975 by the American James K. Lyon's book-length study of the whole business.[2] Of such stuff is *Literaturwissenschaft* made – or at any rate the brief review of the Kipling-Brecht relationship which follows.

*   *   *

Now what would you put in a book of 'socialist verse'? The most obvious way to compile such an anthology, to my mind, would be simply to put together the poems and songs best known in the (international) socialist movement, so that interested or merely nostalgic parties could look up anything that has played a political role, from *Jerusalem* and the *Carmagnole* via the IWW songbooks to the Aldermaston songs and beyond. Alternatively, a more complex and much more instructive book could be made by separating out the various categories of verse that seem to come under the 'socialist' heading: utopian, pacifist, humanitarian, Marxist, poems of national liberation, poems by workers (which most socialist poems aren't), poems by men primarily interesting for their political activities (like Mao or Ho Chi Minh, or indeed the young Marx), and so on. This would make clear the difference between woolly rhetoric and the much rarer poetry of clear political recognition; between conscious demonstration of right feeling and true personal involvement; between bad and good writing. The commentary then would need to be modelled on Brecht's note on an impeccably 'correct' communist poem by one Fritz Bruegel, which he tore constructively to pieces. And the basic questions would be those which ought to concern us all: can bad art further good politics? can evil politics stimulate good art? should we be trying to relate ethics to aesthetics at all?

Few of the poets in the anthology which Henri had sent me really stood out as contemporaries of ours, facing the kind of problems that have perplexed us since, say, 1950: Brecht obviously, Holub, Rożewicz, Yevtushenko, Cavafy (though the 'socialism' of his poetry seems questionable), Auden too in his individual way. On the other hand as soon as you turn to Kipling, who was anything but a socialist, you feel just the freshness, relevance and force that the great majority of those in that anthology lacked. And this is what unites him, across all barriers of age, language and ideology, with Brecht. Not only was there the direct relationship resulting from Brecht's translations and imitations of Kipling, whom he first read in a German version before 1918, and his later, more critical comments on him; but there were also a number of less evident parallels which Carrington's biography incidentally brings out, even though it never refers to Brecht, who was scarcely known in the United Kingdom when the book first appeared in 1955. Thus Kipling too was steeped in the language of the Bible and the hymn-book; he was acquainted with General Booth of the Salvation Army, an institution which Brecht (and Hauptmann) referred to again and again; like Brecht, he was influenced by Horace and other Latin poets but knew little Greek. Both men were basically un-'literary', in a way that Aragon, Becher, Neruda and other 'socialist poets' were not; that is to say they respected men for the direction of their actions rather than the quality of their feelings – 'What a man does, that he is!' is Carrington's phrase for it – and wrote as if they regarded their own extraordinary talents less as a mark of superiority than as an obligation. Though they cared little for any abstract concept of 'labour' – the tasteful Lady Bountiful figure of late nineteenth-century socialist imagery – each of them sought to gear his aesthetic to *work*: Kipling by his concern with the detailed 'shop' of the new technology, and the men who talked it; Brecht by his love of the outward signs, performed on the stage or imprinted on an object, of a job well done.

It is these deep preferences that determined their attitude to their medium. 'For Kipling', said T.S. Eliot, 'the poem is something which is intended to act'; and we all know that the same was true of Brecht, leading him in the direction of popular forms, clear language, rough rhythms and 'gestic' or syncopated line breaks. Though Kipling showed his ear for dialogue in the scenes called 'The Gadsbys' he had little truck with the theatre – 'actors are rummy folk' was his reservation when Irving in 1897 wanted him to write a play. But the influence of the music-hall on his verse is self-evident, and whether or not his song 'At the Back of the Knightsbridge Barracks' was really written for a music-hall as he claimed (I tried to track it down, but without success) a few lines from it had a decisive effect on Brecht. That whole 'plebeian' tradition which Hans Mayer has linked with Brecht is in fact strongly stamped on Kipling, with his penchant for dialect and slang, his remarkable knowledge of Indian low life and his retailing, in short story form, of what Carrington calls 'the current coin of the barrack-room', which no English writer had so exploited before. 'Search English literature', says Carrington, 'and you will find no treatment of the English soldier on any adequate scale between Shakespeare and Kipling'.

True enough, private soldiers, indeed 'other ranks' generally from the Sergeant-Major down, are a rarity in any literature before our time – which is one reason why *The Red Badge of Courage* is such a remarkable book. As for Germany and Austria, search their literatures (Brecht might in turn have said), and you will not find the soldier treated on any adequate scale between Büchner and Hašek. Shakespeare, Büchner, Kipling, Hašek – the four main pillars of Brecht's work. . . .

Brecht's way into this aspect of Kipling's writing was almost certainly via the Hanns Sachs translations of *Soldaten-Lieder und andere Gedichte von Rudyard Kipling* which first appeared in 1910. His Augsburg friend Hans-Otto Münsterer recalls Brecht having this book, and he still owned a copy at his death (though it was one marked with the name of his collaborator Margarete Steffin). He also, as James Lyon has shown, knew a number of Kipling's prose works at an early stage – anyway before 1920 – including *Kim*, *The Jungle Book*, *The Light that Failed* and the selection of stories which Leopold Lindau translated around 1900 and published in 1913 under the title *Mylord der Elefant*. From this reading

Brecht derived his central image of an exotic military-imperial world somewhere between Suez, Hong Kong and the South Pacific (which he knew from Gauguin's *Noa-Noa*), peopled by Malays, Chinese and elephants and dominated by brutal and licentious British soldiers, the boozing, looting but still penniless descendants of Ravenscroft's 'soldiers three'. This image linked quite satisfactorily with the much commoner mid-European nostalgia for a wild America of cowboys and Indians derived largely from the popular but wholly imaginary stories of Karl May, a retiring Saxon bourgeois who called his strong blond hero Old Shatterhand. It helped to dictate Brecht's slightly amazing geography in the early 1920s; it nourished (if it did not actually inspire) his penchant for amoral adventurers like those in his early 'Ballad of the Pirates', in Baal's last song and in the Villonesque ballads of that time. It wholly permeated the version of *Man equals Man* which he and Hauptmann started making in 1924, where the brutal trio were at first called Polly Baker, Jesse Cakewater and Uriah Heep, and their adventures in the Indian-cum-Chinese pagoda derived from Kipling's story 'Krishna Mulvaney'. It provided John, Jim and George, the three soldiers of the 'Cannon Song' in *The Threepenny Opera* and (in the first script) various details of Macheath's and Tiger Brown's shared military past. 'Remember Peshawar!' the latter sentimentally exclaims, when the former asks him for a small loan.

In 1932 the same image once again gave birth to the three soldiers who figure in Kipling's long 'children's poem' of that name, and if they are now located very much in Germany and are called 'Hunger', 'Accident' and 'Cough', George Grosz's original illustrations show them with the British tin hats, moustaches and snarling teeth of *Man equals Man*. The Elephant too moved with remarkable agility from Kipling's world into that of Brecht. 'Mr. Keuner's favourite animal', as he became, with his amiability, his size, his capacity (also according to Kipling) to dance and drink, and his plain grey colour so beloved of Brecht, was at the same time the central four-legged figure of *Man equals Man* and even more prominently of the farcical scene *The Elephant Calf* which later became detached from the main play for separate performance 'in the foyer'. 'Seven Rajahs stood round my cradle' says the alleged military elephant Jackie Pall. Small carved elephants, too, took on a private significance in the love affair between Brecht and Margarete Steffin; there were six of them when he wrote 'The Nineteenth Sonnet' to her from Paris in 1937, and when she died in Moscow in 1941 he asked the Soviet Writers' Union to keep her 'small figures and elephants' for him along with her papers and photographs and travelling chess set. Steffin, once again, was his collaborator when he wrote *The Good Person of Szechwan* with its 'Song of the Eighth Elephant', where the image of the great beasts clearing a wood seems to echo the 'Elephants a-piling teak/In the sludgy, squidgy creek' of Kipling's 'Mandalay', one of Brecht's beloved exotic names.

Brecht, Elisabeth Hauptmann once said to me with absolute accuracy, was 'ein Namensfetischist'; he 'had a thing about names', whether human or topographical. 'Stimmt ihn an, den Song von Mandelay', sing the Men of Mahagonny as they queue impatiently outside the brothel in scene 14 of Weill's opera, which also has a 'Bar von Mandelay' in scene 8 whose failure to open impels the hero to want to go to Georgia (USA): a good example of carefree Brechtian geography. That 'Song of Mandelay' comes more fully, again to Weill's music, in *Happy End*, where the name has no relevance except as a place where seaside brothels once flourished. Burma too is the location of 'Surabaya-Johnny' in the same play, which of course is itself set in Chicago. 'What a bit of all right in Uganda!' says the final quartet of the *Elephant Calf*, and goes on to speak of a poker game (doubtless played in the Boer War) with Kruger the South African leader; it is sung by the soldiers three and the unmasked elephant Jackie Pall. The Benares Song ('Let's go to Benares/Where there's money plenty') and the Alabama Song, located on opposite sides of the globe and both of them actually written in Hauptmann's English, are again placed in *Mahagonny*. Right through the 1920s East and West can be found jumbled up in Brecht's work in such ways, whatever Kipling may have said about their not meeting; and even much later the old imagery briefly reappears. Thus the indecently suggestive 'favourite song of our glorious company' sung in Shrewsbury gaol by the recruiting officer of *Trumpets and Drums* (1955) is not only Kiplingesque in style; the 'Gaa' of its amatory triumphs can hardly be anywhere but Goa on the Indian subcontinent.

In one sense this is just local colour, of a jazzy, superficial Art Déco kind. But as soon as one looks at a specific Kipling model and sees what use Brecht made of it the relationship begins to seem much deeper. Thus in 1890 Kipling published a story in *The Civil and Military Gazette* called 'My Great and Only'.[1] It describes him on a visit to London wondering whether to write for the stage, being put off by the falsities and affectations of the straight theatre, then finding the music-hall much truer to life and eventually meeting a 'Great and Only' – i.e. some performer like Joseph Vance, say – for whom he writes a song. It is about a girl and a soldier, and the only completely quoted verse goes:

At the back of the Knightsbridge Barricks,
When the fog's a-gatherin' dim,
The Lifeguard waits for the Undercook,
But she won't wait for 'im.
She's married a man in the poultry line
That lives at 'Ighgate 'ill,
An' the Lifeguard walks with the 'ousemaid now,
An' (*awful pause*) she can't foot the bill!

Oh, think o' my song when you're gowing it strong
An' your boots is too little to 'old yer;
And don't try for things that is out of your reach,
An' that's what the girl told the soldier, soldier, so-holdier!

Now Brecht can hardly have known this story, which was only published
in book form in the United States and not in the standard Macmillan
edition. But the refrain was made into an epigraph to the short story
'Love o' Women', which was among those included in Lindau's
translation:

O do not despise the advice of the wise,
Learn wisdom from those that are older,
And don't try for things that are out of your reach –
An' that's what the Girl told the Soldier!
  Soldier! Soldier!
Oh, that's what the Girl told the Soldier!

In turning this quatrain into a full-length 'Ballade von dem Soldaten' for
his first book of poems (i.e. by 1922) Brecht followed the translator in
rendering its last line '[Sagte] das Weib zum Soldaten', so that his poem
is now known as 'Ballad of the Woman and the Soldier', which implies
an older speaker, herself presumably wise and very possibly a mother.
He thought of including his ballad in the 1923 production of *In the
Jungle* (but settled instead for the more nautical 'Fifteen Men on a Dead
Man's Chest'); then put it in his *Pocket Devotions* (or *Taschenpostille*)
with the note 'After an English Soldiers' Ballad'. In 1939 he gave it to
the 'Finnish' son Eilif to sing in scene 2 of *Mother Courage*, initially in a
setting by Paul Burkhard, and changed the line

The Monge river gleamed in the light of the moon

(which sounds exotic, though the only Monge known to me is the
Napoleonic mathematician after whom the Paris Métro station is
named), to the more Scandinavian

The shingle roof gleamed in the light of the moon.

Translating the refrain back for Cox and Goehr in the 'Music Theatre' show which we called *Never the Twain*, I kept those lines as Kipling had written them and translated the rest of the poem in a similar style. The result can be heard on Robyn Archer's first Brecht record, where it once again figures as the 'Ballad of the Girl and the Soldier'.

But there is more to it than that. For Kipling's story, after having shown his affinity with Brecht where the music-hall was concerned, goes off in two other equally relevant directions. Having described his song and the way the 'Great and Only' simply annexed it without benefit of copyright, Kipling suddenly lifts it all into another realm thus:

> for the girl (which, as you have seen, of course, is wisdom) will tell that soldier (which is Hercules bowed under his labours) all that she knows of Life and Death and Love.

Prophetically too he reflects:

> But it will take a more mighty intellect to write the Songs of the People. Some day a man will rise up from Bermondsey, Battersea or Bow and he will be coarse but clear-sighted, hard but infinitely and tenderly humorous, speaking the people's tongue, steeped in their lives and telling them in swinging, urging, dinging verse what it is that their inarticulate lips would express. He will make them songs. Such songs! And all the little poets who pretend to sing to the people will scuttle away like rabbits. . . .

The really interesting thing about this passage is not that Kipling would necessarily have admired Brecht's work if he had known it, nor even that his three alliterative place-names almost demand to be carried on 'Bavaria or Berlin', but that a prescription so close to Brecht's later aims could have been written without his knowledge some thirty years before he was in a position to make it come true.

Let us take a second example of Kipling's direct influence and its ramifications. Around 1925 Brecht and Hauptmann hatched a plan to publish a selection of new translations of Kipling's poems, and approached the former's then publisher Gustav Kiepenheuer about it. Kiepenheuer, who had sent Hauptmann to get Brecht's own promised book of poems out of him, was not interested, and anyway one of his new backers proved unacceptable to Brecht. Hans Reisiger, however, who had translated *Kim* in 1921, was about to embark on a collected edition for the Paul List Verlag, and it was agreed that Brecht and Hauptmann should prepare their book and meantime could freely publish their versions in magazines. So Hauptmann translated half a dozen poems, including 'The Song of the Banjo' whose particular meaning for Brecht will be referred to later, 'The Ladies' and 'Mary, Pity Women!' (All the information in this paragraph I owe to Lyon.)

She did this work on Brecht's behalf and for Brecht to put his name on after first making his own improvements. It was exactly the same spirit as that in which she worked on the dialogue of *The Threepenny Opera*, and she included both 'The Ladies' (which Macheath was to sing in a subsequently eliminated scene in the Cuttlefish Hotel, while waiting for ladies to arrive) and 'Mary, Pity Women!' in the first version of that play. The latter poem was to have been sung by Lucy to Macheath in gaol, after the refrain of the first verse had already been cited in an earlier score:

> Nice while it lasted, an' now it is over –
> Tear out your 'eart an' good-bye to your lover!
> What's the use o' grievin' when the mother that bore you
> (Mary, pity women!) knew it all before you?

It is a very beautiful poem, based on a story which a barmaid told Kipling when he was back in London on leave in the 1880s and staying opposite Gatti's-under-the-Arches next to the present Villiers Street wine bar; moreover Weill set its refrain to a very beautiful tune. Revising the script, Brecht decided to throw the whole thing out (which is one of the reasons why Lucy's part is now so thin) and to convert it instead into a new song called 'Surabaya-Johnny' which uses much the same theme and metre and one or two of the same lines and was almost immediately put into *Kalkutta 4 Mai*, a play by Lion Feuchtwanger which Brecht had likewise been revising and which was staged – appallingly badly in Brecht's view – in July 1928. Hauptmann meanwhile fought for the refrain of 'Mary, Pity Women!' to be kept in, and was effectively backed in this by Weill. So they secured its retention as 'Polly's Song', though most English versions of *The Threepenny Opera* don't recognise its origin and retranslate it more or less ineptly. It is the one justification for the reference to Kipling in the programme credits – the 'Cannon Song' (in my view, and *pace* Lyon) being a pastiche without origins in any specific Kipling work.

The Kipling-based 'Surabaya-Johnny' was originally to have been sung by the Berlin cabaret artist Kate Kühl, then in 1929 Brecht and Hauptmann put it into *Happy End*, their would-be successor to *The Threepenny Opera*. The new play quickly failed, but in Kurt Weill's setting the song, which is less authentic and unsophisticated than Kipling's original – itself a simple tale of pregnancy and abandonment, without any exotic trappings – was a lasting success; it too is moving, but at a distance and with a touch of irony. It continued to be sung by such artists in various countries and languages (there was a good French recording by Marianne Oswald) until in 1939 Brecht put it too into the first script of *Mother Courage*. Here in the third scene he has Courage talking to the camp whore (who started out as Jessie Potter from Batavia – another place in Java – and was then changed to Jeannette Poittier from Flanders before ending up as Yvette). 'Just don't you go on again about your Johnny', she says, thereby giving Jeannette an excuse to sing the song. This, according to James Lyon, is what actually happened in the Zurich production of 1941, when Kurt Weill's tune was used. Then in the next version Jeannette's mythical man becomes Henny, a ship's cook from Holland (perhaps so that he could have known Surabaya, a port in a Dutch colony), and the song is slightly tinkered with to make 'The Song of Pfeif-und-Trommel-Henny', fife-and-drum Henny, which fits the same tune, with Burma now changed to Utrecht. Finally, in the stage script of 1946, this is deleted in favour of the Fraternisation Song, later set by Dessau, which retains just one quatrain from its predecessor and ultimately from 'Surabaya-Johnny', even though the metre of the refrain is changed; it also keeps the start 'Ich war erst siebzehn Jahre', like the earlier 'Ich war jung, Gott, erst sechzehn Jahre', or Nanna's 'Meine Herren, mit siebzehn Jahren' from *Round Heads and Pointed Heads*, a Villonesque variation on much the same theme. In the Berliner Ensemble's production of this version Henny too went, and the Dutchman became Pieter, an army cook from Utrecht, while the 'Pfeife' ceased to be a musical instrument and became simply a tobacco pipe – leading Ernst Busch, who played the part in the second production in a thick Dutch accent, to introduce a Dutch song about pipes.

A third example of Kipling's far-reaching effects on Brecht: as early as 1894 (so Morley tells us) Leopold Rosenzweig translated his novel *The Light that Failed*, which in 1917 became the model for Brecht's Psalm-like poem 'About a Painter'.[1] This describes Caspar Neher (later to be Brecht's principal stage designer) painting dead 'brown men' in a desert war, then sailing from Ceylon to Port Said and creating his masterpiece on one of the ship's bulkheads: two episodes that are taken from the adventures of Kipling's hero Dick Heldar.

Also in this novel is a short poem which serves as an epigraph to one of its chapters.

There were three friends that buried the fourth,
The mould in his mouth and the dust in his eyes,
And they went south and east and north –
The strong man fights but the sick man dies.

There were three friends that spoke of the dead –
The strong man fights but the sick man dies –
'And would he were here with us now', they said,
'The sun in our face and the wind in our eyes'.

Once again, these verses haunted Brecht, whom Carl Zuckmayer recalls singing them – though he doesn't say to what tune. He introduced them into the 1923 version of *In the Jungle*, almost word for word in Rosenzweig's language, to be sung by John Garga and Manky towards the end of what eventually became scene 7, following Shlink's exit. Some six or seven years later its key line became inverted as

The sick man dies but the strong man fights

and incorporated in two songs sung by the Merchant in the 'Lehrstück' *The Exception and the Rule*, as he makes his way across the desert towards the Inner Mongolian town of Urga. Finally in 1934 the same line came to provide titles for two of the chapters in *The Threepenny Novel*. Parallel with these direct borrowings, there was a much freer development of the poem's imagery in Brecht's long poem 'Death in the Woods', where the friends – now several of them – gather round the dying man, cursing him as he presses into the earth, then bury him under a tree and 'ride off quickly over the plain'. In the *Devotions* this version of the theme is set in the 'Hatoury Forest', with the Mississippi roaring in the background, but in *Baal* when Baal recites it to Eckart as his latest work there are no geographical allusions. Kurt Weill was attracted to Brecht's poem, perhaps simply because it deals with death, and set it as one of the sections of the *Berlin Requiem* which he composed for Frankfurt Radio in 1928 during the run of *The Threepenny Opera*. It was later taken out of that work and treated as a separate composition.

There are a great many minor quotations or echoes from Kipling's works in Brecht's, particularly in those written before about 1930 when the Englishman's imperialism and sense of racial superiority had not yet come to jar on the international Left. 'Oh East is East and West is West/ Their hireling minstrel cried' says one of Brecht's first critical references, in a poem written during his visit to London in 1934.

But I've observed with interest
Bridges across that great divide

> And huge guns rolling East I've seen
> With cheerful troops keeping them clean.
> Meanwhile, from East to West, back rolled
> Tea soaked in blood, war wounded, gold . . .[1]

Yet even then there were instances like the prose translation of 'If' (made by Margarete Steffin, according to Lyon) which he unacknowledgedly incorporated among his *Me-ti* aphorisms in the later 1930s under the title 'Ideals of a Man in Former Times'. Likewise after his return to East Germany he thought (says Lyon) of basing something for children on 'The Elephant's Child' from *The Just So Stories* and recommended the young soldiers of the People's Army to read *The Light that Failed* and *The Jungle Book*.

At the same time the most serious signs of a real affinity between the two writers lie in other works of Kipling's which had no such direct literary repercussions but seem to enshrine attitudes which Brecht quite simply shared. He actually marked two of these, so Lyon tells us, in the 1936 Inclusive Edition of the poems which a new acquaintance, Gerda Singer, gave him in London that year. They were 'The Craftsman', written in Horatian metre and describing Shakespeare's discovery of his characters from everyday experience – which is clearly something that Brecht liked to believe – and 'When 'Omer smote 'is bloomin' Lyre' with its picture of Homer singing to the people and stealing his material wherever he could – the appealing point here being Kipling's parenthetic comment 'the same as me'. 'He writeth best who cribbeth best' said Kipling on another occasion, and this unblushing acknowledgement of just the sort of offence Brecht was so often accused of, and indeed practised in Kipling's own case, could not but seem endearing to him. For such poems undercut all claim to that high poetic status which sets the great writer on a peak with his Muse, well apart from ordinary grubby people.

And so in its way does 'The Song of the Banjo', one of the group which Hauptmann chose to translate. For this instrument, seen by Kipling as a bastard descendant of the Greek lyre, travels 'with the cooking pots and pans' and goes where no piano or violin can penetrate, through wars, deserts, work camps, precipitous railway lines, round the world and down the centuries 'from Delos up to Limerick [Kipling's one poetic allusion] and back', fulfilling its mission to 'jeer the fatted Soul of Things'.

> And the tunes that mean so much to you alone –
> Common tunes that make you choke and blow your nose –

> Vulgar tunes that bring the laugh that brings the groan –
> I can rip your very heartstrings out with those.

Even here there is a link with one of Brecht's own allusions, since the 'Johnny Bowlegs, pack your kit and trek' which Kipling cites is the song referred to as 'Johnny' in *Man equals Man*, which can thus be identified as the Boer War Afrikaans song 'Jannie mit dem hoppelbeen'.

Brecht never met Kipling and there was a great deal of his work which he simply did not know. In the German editions of the poems which Brecht at first used there were only 29 poems all told, by Lyon's count, and these mostly dated from before 1896 (which was when Kipling finally returned from the East and became to a great extent an establishment poet). Even the 'Definitive Edition' of the English texts moreover contains unexplained omissions. (It is in fact an unbelievably confused, unannotated and haphazardly, if at all, edited book – a disgrace to a great poet.) But what once again is interesting aside from the direct connections between the two writers is the number of similarities or half-echoes which surely cannot have been based on any kind of knowledge. Anyone reading Brecht's later poem 'The little rose, o how should it be listed?' for instance,[1] might well posit some link with Kipling's formally similar poem of 1897 that starts 'The rose that glimmers by the garden wall' and ends up 'Suffice it she was born and now is red.' Similarly with 'If we only understood' published in the Jerusalem paper *The Truth* in 1913, which can be sung to the same Eisler setting as Brecht's East German 'Children's Anthem'.[2] Yet these two Kipling works, like others even more remarkable, are only to be found in the Kipling Society's privately printed *Readers' Guide to Rudyard Kipling's Work*, and would almost certainly not have been accessible to Brecht. The conclusion then is that many of the less clear-cut resemblances between works by Kipling and works by Brecht have nothing to do with any direct borrowing or imitation. Under the apparent political incompatibility, in other words, they had many opinions, tastes and prejudices in common and shared some important joint background reading (Villon, Horace, hymnbooks and the Bible, for a start); and this in itself was enough to make their pens converge. Even Edgar Wallace forms a humble part of their kinship, for Kipling, who knew Wallace in Africa, once sent a batch of his thrillers to King George V as an aid to convalescence.

*   *   *

But as soon as one begins to grasp the reasons that made Kipling so congenial to a German communist poet a third of a century later, the plot really thickens. Were the two men ideologically closer than their most loyal readers would care to imagine, or is there an approach to the writing of such committed, communicative, extrovert poetry whose effects are so alive and powerful as to make even serious political differences seem relatively superficial? Either possibility would have some quite startling implications, and this makes Carrington's Kipling biography a very interesting book indeed. For Kipling really was a puzzle, even more than that strange (and still largely undisclosed) man Brecht. Even today the commonly accepted picture of Kipling hardly allows for the uniqueness of his family background, though the facts are well enough known; he was born at a point of intersection between the Pre-Raphaelites – Burne-Jones being an uncle and Morris one by adoption – and the political world represented by his cousin Stanley Baldwin; so that he could reject aestheticism, become a practical journalist and, later, get the ear of the men in power without in any sense being a philistine. He was indeed a natural highbrow,[1] exceedingly widely read, who took great pains to conceal his background and everything else to do with his personal life. For all his public stance as the voice of a certain collective unconscious he consistently refused honours, positions and any suggestions of writing to order – the Laureateship, knighthood, the O.M., membership of the British Academy: it makes an impressive list, not least when compared with Brecht's acceptance in 1954 of the Stalin Peace Prize. Yet somehow Kipling slipped quite early into the corridors of power, so that on being elected to the Athenaeum at 32 he could celebrate by dining with Rhodes, Milner and the Editor of *The Times*.

It was an extraordinary transition for a man who had arrived in London eight years earlier as a clever satirist and storyteller with a vein of new material to work: an admirably direct writer, as *The Times* termed him in a leader on his Indian books, but 'comparatively wanting in style'. Judged by those early writings he was a populist, a literary innovator, a social critic who would qualify for any book of Radical Verse with his belief that 'it will be the common people – the 3rd-class carriages – that'll save us'. He might even have become a socialist, like his 'Uncle Topsy' Morris (who died just as Kipling came finally to settle in England). But as it turned out he became something very different: not, as Carrington makes clear, 'the poet of orthodox conservatism' which he has sometimes been taken for, but 'the very opposite of that, his admiration was always for the irregulars' – in other words an unwitting fascist of a potentially quite sinister kind. Of course the potential in question was damped by the very English practices and conventions in which Kipling also believed, as well as by his own natural humanity; thus the drill hall and volunteer company which he established near his home, like the Boy Scout movement which embodied certain of his ideas, were fortunately very different from their subsequent equivalents in Germany and Italy. None the less it gives one a twinge today to find Kipling saying around 1907 that 'our ploy must be to develop Rhodesia as well as we can. It's the last loyal white colony', or telling Rider Haggard in 1925 about a meeting with 'a female Checko-Slovak':

> My dear old man, we made some new nations after the war that might well not have been created. A Checko-Slovak is what came up and fermented after Austria putrefied . . .

As for that unhappy concept, the White Man's Burden, the secondary meaning (of moral 'whiteness') posited by his biographer has never meant much to those who are not (physically) white themselves, and the gaff was anyway blown long before by Theodore Roosevelt, for whom the poem in question was particularly intended. It was, he said, 'rather poor poetry, but good sense from the expansionist standpoint'.

There is a problem here, and much of the interest of the Carrington biography relates to it. Just what made Kipling veer right rather than left in the course of the 1890s precisely when writers like Verhaeren and Romain Rolland were going the other way? It is easy enough to pick out certain milestones: his marriage in 1892 (after which he never visited India again), his first characteristic public poem the previous year, his discovery of a platform for such verses in *The Times* (from 1895), his final return from expatriate life in 1896, above all perhaps the South African War and the annual visit which he made from 1901 to 1908 to the house built for him by Cecil Rhodes in the grounds of Groote Schuur. But which, if any, of these was decisive and just what they all really marked is something that Carrington's biography never tries to establish, possibly because at the date when the book was written few people in this country took Brecht seriously and his debt to Kipling was virtually unknown. Once take the links with Brecht into account, and this failure becomes in every sense critical, since it is exactly in the contrast between the pre-1896 Kipling, with whom Brecht had these affinities, and the subsequent ally of the *Morning Post* and Max Aitken that a fresh understanding of political art ought to be found. To put it at its crudest, Brecht and the early Kipling had something of a common approach to writing. In Kipling's case, with his absorption into the British Establishment this became directed rightward till he came to express ideas that would have been frightening in any less civilised hands. What pushed Brecht to the left some thirty years later was what those less civilised hands in fact made of them: in other words the Nazi versions of white supremacy, expansionism, a disciplined youth movement, gentlemen rankers, legions that never were listed, and all the rest. Somewhere, though we cannot yet put our fingers on it, the possibility of these abrupt switches of direction is built into Kipling's work and personality – one need only think what the name *Kim* has come to stand for since H.R. Philby was found to be in 'the Game' as Kipling termed it – and might also by analogy be latent in Brecht's, already strongly marked by paradox and love of dialectical oppositions.

How does this bring us round again to Socialist Verse? First of all, by showing that the essence of the matter lies not in outward demonstrations of ideological stance but in the kind of down-to-earth social- and political-mindedness which determines the style, level and intelligibility of a man's poetry rather than its particular emotional veneering. There would indeed be more to be learnt, both technically and politically, from an anthology of committed verse of all denominations, including at one end Claudel, say, who lies in many ways close to Aragon and Senghor and was much admired (with political reservations) by Brecht, and at the other end the ribald anonymous song and the advertising jingle. Then there is the whole question of performance: Brecht's verses grip where Mayakovsky merely hectors and Eluard incants and Neruda thumps over the reader like a breaking sea. 'Mandalay' and 'Gunga Din', oddly enough, can effectively grip a modern audience, even though Carrington treats the second of them as nowadays discredited. Once again, there is more in Kipling than you think, and its example makes a lot of more politically palatable verse seem flatulent and unreal. For there is surely something slightly wrong when a political poet is accepted by his contemporaries as a poet with a capital P even when they hate what he is trying to say, since this suggests that the 'poetic' attitude (as, I think, with Mayakovsky) dominates and possibly even nullifies the political one. It is better then to earn the intense dislike which is often felt for Brecht and still persists in the case of Kipling. 'To this day,' says Carrington, 'he makes men lose their tempers, a sure proof of his importance'. How many writers is this now true of? Pound, Evelyn Waugh, yes, and perhaps Yevtushenko; certainly not the established socialist/communist rhetoricians, who seem the more acceptably harmless the more words they use. Perhaps there is a comparable tribute to be seen in the dislike, on stylistic grounds, of Italian critics for Svevo and Silone, or of Slavists for Hašek, or indeed in our own Establishment's hostility to pop poetry and the Liverpool poets. Of course this is not a proof of importance so much as simply of vitality. All the same it would be nice to think that socialism too was alive.

4

The case of Auden

In 1957, when I was writing my book *The Theatre of Bertolt Brecht*, I wrote to W.H. Auden to know if he was at all influenced by Brecht's work. I had heard about their collaboration on a version of *The Duchess of Malfi* in the United States, and I had been impressed by a translation by Auden and James Stern of Act 5 of *The Caucasian Chalk Circle*, which had appeared in *The Kenyon Review* in the spring of 1946, about a year and a half before Brecht left America. I wasn't quite sure who Stern was, though I seemed to recall a story by him appearing in the late 1930s in John Lehmann's *New Writing*, which had also printed a poem and a short scene by Brecht. But I had seen various parallels between Auden and Brecht – for instance in the former's balladesque poem 'Victor', which recalled Brecht's 'Apfelböck', if in a more facetious and condescending manner – and wanted, as an admirer of both poets, to find out more.

Auden, then staying on Ischia, told me that he had met Brecht a number of times, particularly when working on the *Malfi* adaptation, which he called 'an appalling flop'. He had lost the script of the *Caucasian Chalk Circle* translation, and wrote that

> The early Brecht, like *Hauptpostille*, *Mahagonny Stadt* and the *Drei Groschen Oper*, have certainly influenced me.[1]

Sic, *sic* and *sic*: what he was referring to was *Die Hauspostille*, Brecht's first book of poems; *Aufstieg und Fall der Stadt Mahagonny*, his opera with Weill; and the *Dreigroschenoper* or *Threepenny Opera*.

Eighteen months later I wrote to him again, because I had been told via Eric Bentley and Brecht's son Stefan that Auden had once made a translation of *The Threepenny Opera* too. I had also then been talking to John Cullen of Methuen about the publication of some kind of English Brecht edition, and wanted to know if Auden had ever translated any of the poems and whether he could tackle any further plays. He answered:

No, I never did a translation of the *Dreigroschenoper*, though I should have liked to very much.[1]

He had translated none of the poems apart from the *Caucasian Chalk Circle* songs, but said that he had 'toyed and still toy with the thought of some day translating *Baal* [by which I think he meant the introductory Chorale or hymn from that play] and *Das ertrunkenes Mädschen*' (i.e. 'Die Ballade vom ertrunkenen Mädchen', another song from *Baal*).[2] As for plays, he had just completed his version of *The Seven Deadly Sins* with Chester Kallman for performance that November, but 'I don't really want to spend much time translating Brecht or anyone else'. At best he and Kallman might be interested in doing *Aufstieg und Fall der Stadt Mahagonny* because it was 'all sung, and the problem is making an English version rather than a translation in the strict sense'.[3] This they were in fact to do some two years later, though their version remained long unperformed and was only published in the United States in 1976. It and *The Seven Deadly Sins* are now in the Methuen *Collected Plays*.

Then in 1971 Auden published his commonplace book under the title *A Certain World*. Here he includes a section called 'Unfavourites and Favourites', with a list of what he terms 'my pets': a select team of fourteen of those 'elder modern poets . . . from whom I have learned most'.[4] At their head is 'Berthold Brecht (the lyric poet)'. *Sic*.

That is where I started to become curious again, and began seriously trying to find out what the relationship between the two writers really was. What I have managed to put together is still full of gaps and unsolved puzzles, but here it is in its present incomplete state.

*   *   *

Auden was at Oxford from 1925 to 1928, going down that summer. Breon Mitchell, who wrote a paper in *Oxford German Studies*[5] on the subject, quotes him as saying that 'he knew no German and no German literature' at that time. More recently Gabriel Carritt, who was one of Auden's closest Oxford friends, told me that Auden had lent him books by Toller and Brecht, and was already talking about the latter before leaving for Germany in August 1928. This seems surprising, as Brecht at that time was still virtually unknown outside his own country, and his first book of poems *Die Hauspostille* had only been published in German the previous year. Toller by contrast had had some of his plays produced in London and elsewhere in Britain, and translations had appeared not only of the main plays but of his *Swallow Book* of prison poems. If

Auden knew of Toller – which is likelier, since there had by then been a number of translations (and London productions) of his plays – it could perhaps have been from a student performance: there is no record of any Toller production at the Oxford Playhouse in his time.

But in the autumn of 1928, when Auden arrived in Berlin for a year's stay, *The Threepenny Opera* opened in Berlin, and he did see this – apparently very soon after arriving. I think he must also have got hold of the *Hauspostille*, and it is possible that he came to know *Mahagonny* from records. He himself did subsequently write some more or less frivolous poems in German (which have not been published). As for his friend and collaborator Christopher Isherwood, who followed Auden to Berlin about six months later, he neither met Brecht at that time nor came into contact with his work, though he had some rather nebulous dealings with Willi Muenzenberg's organisation International Workers' Aid (or IAH, or Mezhrabpom, a body directly responsible to the Comintern), where Brecht's name would have been, sometimes approvingly, sometimes censoriously, a household word. Gerald Hamilton, the slippery original of Isherwood's Mr Norris, did, rather amazingly, speak on Muenzenberg's platforms; he must have been somebody's spy.

Hitler came to power, Isherwood left Berlin, Brecht went into exile. At the end of 1933 the Brechts moved into the Danish cottage where they were to spend the next five and a half years. From October to December 1934 Brecht was in London, staying with the composer Hanns Eisler in lodgings in Calthorpe Street off the Gray's Inn Road, working on film projects and Communist songs. Auden by then had written the very Expressionist *The Dance of Death* and become involved with the new (London) Group Theatre, for whom he drew up a list of recommended plays. Among these were unspecified 'plays by Brecht with music by Weill', which he thought Isherwood might be asked to translate.[1] Evidently the two men themselves did not meet at that time, nor were there yet any performances of *The Dance of Death* that Brecht could have seen. What he did however see on 16 December was one of the five private performances of T.S. Eliot's *Sweeney Agonistes* which Rupert Doone staged in the Group's rooms off the Charing Cross Road; for Doone wrote two days later to report that 'Bert Brecht, the writer of the German "Beggar's Opera" ' had been in the audience, as also had Yeats. Yeats's interest seems to have been due to his hope that the Group might perform his own Noh-style plays, which Dr Michael Sidnell acutely suggests may have been the models for the Eliot piece. Whether or not Brecht too sensed this link with the Noh, he was delighted with Eliot's short, stylised play and told Doone that 'it was the best thing he had seen for a long time and by far the best thing in London. He is going to send us a play of his with Hindemith he was so impressed'.[1]

Brecht's later writings however contain no reference to the plays of Eliot (or for that matter of Yeats), nor does he ever seem to have sent the promised play, which can only have been the Baden-Baden *Lehrstück*. The London theatres otherwise he found 'antediluvian', while London itself was a 'nasty tough little city' whose inhabitants were 'among the most devious in Europe'.[2] No doubt this impression was only reinforced when he was refused admission to the Savoy Hotel, where Herbert Asquith's daughter Elizabeth Bibesco had invited him to discuss ways of helping the Nazis' opponents. By his own account a flunkey 'of ministerial rank' took exception to his clothes and turned him away.

Some eighteen months later, in July 1936, he nonetheless paid a second visit, primarily to work on a film involving his friend Fritz Kornter; this was a now forgotten adaptation of *I Pagliacci*, with the stout tenor Richard Tauber in the leading part. By then he had not only been to the United States (for the first time) but had also met John Lehmann in Moscow, and now he saw a number of further people connected one way or another with Auden. Thus William Coldstream, at whose house in Upper Park Road, Hampstead, Auden stayed when working for the GPO Film Unit in 1935–36 – the time of *Coal Face* and *Night Mail* – vaguely recalls seeing Brecht at the unit's offices in Soho Square; Basil Wright likewise half remembers having lunch with Brecht, Cavalcanti, Lotte Reiniger of silhouette film fame and her husband Carl Koch, at a Soho restaurant. Eric Walter White, Benjamin Britten's biographer,[3] visited Brecht in Abbey Road, where he was staying with the Van Gyseghems of Unity Theatre, and recalls discussing the *Pagliacci* film. A.J. Ayer, then on the point of becoming my philosophy tutor, once told me that he too had met Brecht in London, but now remembers nothing about the occasion. And it must have been around the same time that Brecht visited Rupert Doone and Robert Medley again, who had by now presented *The Dance of Death* and the Auden–Isherwood *The Dog Beneath the Skin* – the latter in February 1936. I talked to Medley, who was not entirely clear about dates but recalled Brecht inviting them both to Denmark if there was a second world war.

Though Auden later said[4] that they first met when Brecht was in Hollywood, the two men must have made some kind of contact during 1936, if only on the telephone, because when Brecht got back to Denmark that August he wrote saying:

dear comrade auden,

before i left london i made a small arrangement with an american literary agent by which he would pay you an advance of £25 for an english version [*nachdichtung*] of one of my plays. it's not a large advance, but it's something. one of them, die rundköpfe und die spitzköpfe [*Round Heads and Pointed Heads*], is probably going to be produced in copenhagen this autumn. if you came to see me you could see one or two of the rehearsals. i hope you haven't forgotten your promise to come? i would be very glad if you did.

yours cordially,
bertolt brecht[1]

It is my guess that Auden had considered visiting Copenhagen on the way either to or from the *Letters from Iceland* trip; however, he never did so, and Brecht's letter must have reached England some weeks after he and Louis MacNeice had set off. MacNeice himself incidentally never met Brecht and, according to his wife Hedli Anderson the singer (for whom Auden and Britten wrote their cabaret songs, including one called 'Johnny'), did not like what he knew of Brecht's work. The term 'comrade' in the letter – the only time in their slender correspondence that Brecht so addressed him – suggests Auden's political position a few months before he decided to volunteer for the International Brigade: if he wasn't actually in the Communist Party he must have been very close.

Another thing that Brecht must have done at some time during his second London visit was to arrange for the English publication of his *Dreigroschenroman* – the *Threepenny Novel* first issued in 1937 by Robert Hale as *A Penny for the Poor*. Isherwood translated the verses for this, most of them being taken from the songs in the play. But he still had no direct contact with Brecht, his participation having been arranged by the main translator Desmond I. Vesey, then a newly-appointed director of Robert Hale's publishing firm but previously in Berlin, where Brecht's right-hand woman Elisabeth Hauptmann had known him. Vesey, who is now dead, was the son of an Indian Army general and was rumoured to be working for the British Secret Service in Germany just before the Reichstag Fire. When I met him in the 1960s he struck me as a plausible enough candidate for such a role, and he was certainly in MI5 in the Second World War.

That more or less concludes the story of the Brecht–Auden relationship as it began in England in the 1930s. It was appreciative enough on Brecht's side for him to include Auden and Isherwood, as well as Rupert Doone the dancer-director, in the proposed Diderot Society, or society for *Theaterwissenschaft*, which he tried inconclusively to set up the next year: this would have been a group of about a dozen like-minded persons in different countries including Eisenstein, Piscator, Jean Renoir and Archibald MacLeish. He may also have read the Auden–Isherwood plays since he referred to those plays approvingly in his 'Notes on the Folk Play' of 1940, written in Finland while waiting to leave for the United States.[1] What he didn't care for, he said, was their use of symbolism – something that comes across most strongly, of course, in *The Ascent of F6*. The Group Theatre probably had the script of this work by the time of Brecht's 1936 visit, prior to its publication on 24 September and its première on 26 February 1937 (both these dates being after Brecht had returned to Denmark).

*   *   *

The Second World War broke out, Auden and Isherwood settled in the United States, and in 1941 the Brechts followed. Like Auden, Brecht had been asked to teach at the New School in New York, but instead he settled in Santa Monica, an attractive seaside suburb of Los Angeles where he finally met Isherwood through their joint friend Berthold Viertel, the Austrian film and theatre director and excellent poet, who was the prototype of the unforgettable Bergmann in Isherwood's novel about the movies *Prater Violet*. 'This I wrote this morning', says Bergmann in a scene that is clearly taken from life, 'after reading your book [i.e. Isherwood's second novel *The Memorial*] . . . My first poem in English. To an English poet.' 'I took it and read', says Isherwood, and quotes:

> When I am a boy, my mother tells to me
> It is lucky to wake up when the morning is bright
> And first of all hear a lark sing.
> Now I am no longer a boy, and I wake. The morning is dark.
> I hear a bird singing with unknown name
> In a strange country language, but it is luck, I think.
> Who is he, this singer, who does not fear the gray city?
> Will they drown him soon, the poor Shelley?
> Will Byron's hangmen teach him how one limps?
> I hope they will not, because he makes me happy.

After being introduced by Viertel on 19 August 1943, Brecht asked Isherwood to dinner on 20 September, and according to both men's accounts it seems that they got on well, though Brecht by then was aware of the new religious preoccupations of the two English writers, describing Isherwood in his journal as 'ein kleiner mönchersatz' – a little imitation monk in his Buddhist garb. Admittedly Isherwood got up and left that particular party when Brecht said that Aldous Huxley was 'gekauft', had sold out. But Brecht later gave him *The Good Person of Szechwan* to read in the hope that he might translate it. Isherwood politely refused – unfortunately he cannot remember whether it was the new, shortened version of the play or the standard 1940 version – but offered to lend Brecht one or two hundred dollars to tide him over till he could get a production set up. This struck Brecht as 'a lot', he noted in his journal, 'as I know he's got nothing'.[1]

Isherwood's own account of their meetings in Santa Monica can be found in his *Diaries*, Volume One. 'I liked Brecht immediately,' he notes on 20 August. 'He's very lively, alert and nervous, with a high-pitched voice, not unlike Forster's'.[2] A month later, after seriously discussing the *Duchess of Malfi*, they get on to the subject of Vedanta, and Brecht 'fairly blew his top. To him it's all fascism and superstitious nonsense'. What angered Isherwood here was Brecht's

> claim to be more *honest* than a man like Aldous, and his conviction that everyone who disagrees with him is getting a paycheck from the capitalist bosses.

To Viertel, who tried to bring his two friends together, he wrote that he 'genuinely and truly liked' the Brechts and their son Stefan.[3] However, he sharply changed his view a few months later when Brecht tried to get him to translate the still unfinished *The Caucasian Chalk Circle*. Tempted at first to agree to this, Isherwood wrote Brecht off as 'utterly ruthless, opportunistic and selfish' as soon as he felt that Brecht was asking him to cut down on his 'non-Brecht obligations' (which would have included the Hollywood Vedanta shrine and its devotees).[4] This was not long before he became involved in the writing of his last European book, *Prater Violet*, whose completion in autumn 1944 seems to have coincided with a loosening of his intimacy with Viertel too.

The Duchess of Malfi and *The Good Person of Szechwan* were among various projects which Brecht had been discussing with the actress Elisabeth Bergner, whom he knew from Munich and Berlin, and who was then hoping that her prewar London successes would help her to get recognised as a star in the American theatre and cinema, something she never in fact managed to do. In New York they had settled on an adaptation of Webster's play which Brecht was to make for her, simplifying and redrafting the story himself (in a mixture of English and German) but leaving any new writing to be done by the American poet

Hoffman R. Hays. Hays, who came from one of the earliest New York families, had worked with Hanns Eisler on a satire called *The Medicine Show* for the Federal Theatre in 1939, and also scripted a rejected Davy Crockett musical for Kurt Weill. An underrated writer, he was one of the only two English-language poets since Kipling whom Brecht himself translated, the other being not Auden but the Santa Monica writer Albert Brush.

Hays completed two or three scripts on the basis of Brecht's polyglot draft scenes, then in the winter of 1943 he was surprised to learn from Bergner's producer husband Paul Czinner that Auden too was to be brought in. This followed a letter from Brecht to Auden at Swarthmore College asking him to take part and saying 'As you can imagine I would get great satisfaction from being able to work with you'.[1] Bringing in Auden must in my view have been Brecht's decision rather than Czinner's, for apparently he was already waiting for Auden to make a translation of his long poem 'The Children's Crusade' (which never materialised, though Britten set the poem as an oratorio some twenty-five years later). In any case Hays promptly left in a rage, and ever afterwards he refused to let the adaptation be performed or published with both his and Auden's names on it.

Auden and Brecht saw each other in New York early in 1944, but in fact their subsequent versions still contained a lot of Hays's work. You can see Auden's hand in some of the later scripts, most clearly in the Echo scene, the Epilogue (which is half Auden, half Webster, and very beautiful) and also – in my opinion – in the shortened rendering of Brecht's soldiers' song 'Als wir kamen vor Milano':

> I wrote my love a letter
> When we entered fair Milan:
> Oh the war will soon be over
> For the cook has lost his coppers
> And the captain's lost his head
> And we've shot away our lead.
>
> But when we left the city
> Then a second war began
> Though the first was scarcely over
> And I'll drink a thousand beakers
> With a whore upon my knee
> Till my love again I see.[2]

This occurs in Act 2, scene 1 of the last script copyrighted under

Brecht's and Hays's names only, and thirty years later Hays insisted to me that it must be his work. But it sounds to my ear much more like Auden, and both Isherwood and Stephen Spender agree.

While the *Duchess* was getting under way, and within a few weeks of his first approach to Auden, Brecht had got involved with another German émigrée actress who wanted a Broadway play from him. This time it was Luise Rainer, who had made a great hit in the film of Pearl Buck's Chinese novel *The Good Earth* and now during winter 1943/44 got Brecht commissioned by a would-be New York impresario called Jules Leventhal to write her *The Caucasian Chalk Circle*. When Isherwood turned down the job of making the English translation, Brecht, on completing the first version of the script in June 1944, proposed that Auden be commissioned instead. Auden however only got the script some two months later, after a preliminary translation had been made (for $250) by James and Tania Stern, close friends of his who had been sharing a shack with him on Fire Island. James Stern, I later discovered, was an Irish-born writer descended from a Frankfurt banking family; his father was an officer in the 13th Hussars and his brother became champion jockey of Ireland. His wife, a gymnastics teacher, was German, being the sister of the former Soviet art administrator Alfred Kurella, sometime secretary to Henri Barbusse and later chief cultural pundit of the SED.

Auden's first reaction, even before seeing their rough version, was that the play would probably 'have to be completely remodelled'.[1] Then a few days later he suggested that he and the Sterns might collaborate, but only if and when the producers 'got serious'.[2] How serious they might have got is hard to make out, since Luise Rainer abandoned the whole project once she came back from entertaining the armed forces and saw the script. But it was still on in December, when Brecht had read the rough translation and was looking forward to the finished '*Nachdichtung*' which Auden had just contracted to make. 'This matters enormously to me', Brecht wrote (in German) to Stern. 'I mind more about having an English version by him than about getting a Broadway production'.[3] In the end however Auden only translated the verses – which Brecht was at that stage expecting Eisler to set – and made adjustments to the Sterns' dialogue. Two finished scripts were then typed by Stern, who later destroyed one of them, perhaps because Brecht decided it was 'wholly unusable'.[4] The other was sent in November 1945 to John Crowe Ransom, who in due course printed the last act in *The Kenyon Review*.

By that time the war was over, but *The Duchess of Malfi*, like Mother Courage and her cart, dragged wearily on. Work on both plays had been interrupted shortly after the German surrender by Auden's departure for some four months as a member of the Morale Division of the US Strategic Bombing Survey, to report on the effects of the war on the civil population; Stern, who was part of the same team, has given a vivid account of their findings in his book *The Hidden Damage*. Meantime his wife Tania stayed in Vermont where she had the company not only of the Czinners but of Viertel, the Zuckmayers and the Budzislawskis – Hermann Budzislawski being a communist journalist who worked for Dorothy Thompson. Brecht too was there in July.

On his return that autumn Auden was summoned to Chicago by the Czinners to do what he called some rehashing of the *Malfi* script: 'scholars', he told a friend, 'will be *appalled*'.[1] As things eventually turned out, they were not, because rather than let Brecht direct it Bergner brought over George Rylands, who decided to go back to Webster's original text. All Brecht's and Hays's work was thrown out of the window; Brecht asked to have his name removed from the whole undertaking, leaving only Auden in the end to figure as author of a song or two; these, along with Webster's lovely dirge, being set by Britten, who however was out of sympathy with the whole production (so that according to Eric White none of his music has survived). The play opened in Providence in September 1946, was seen in Boston by an appalled Brecht, moved to the Ethel Barrymore Theatre in New York and folded after a month. Two years later Auden had still not been fully paid. 'God forbid that anyone should get hold of that Duchess of Malfi', he wrote to me in 1958. 'I cannot recall the incident without a shudder.'[2]

To round off the story of Brecht and Auden in America: it was in 1945 that Reynal and Hitchcock, who were Hays's publishers, decided to bring out an edition of Brecht's poems in Hays's versions. Hays told me that Brecht had wished Auden to take part in this too, but the publishers had 'stood by' him and not allowed it. The following year this developed into a more ambitious scheme for an American Brecht edition, again with Reynal and Hitchcock, for which Eric Bentley was to select and edit some plays. Bentley told Stern that he wanted to include *The Caucasian Circle of Chalk*, as it was then called, and after the publication of the *Kenyon Review*'s extract he got the script from Ransom. However, only the fifty *Selected Poems* translated by Hays ever appeared; Reynal and Hitchcock were swallowed up in another firm, and the edition never came about.

Brecht appears to have understood from Bentley that Auden would have no objection if Bentley and Maya Apelman made a new translation of the play – though according to Stern Auden subsequently said he

would mind. Anyhow the three earlier translators lost track of their one
surviving script, and very soon they had lost interest in it too. This
script has never been traced. Thus when the play was finally staged in
May 1948 in a mid-Western college production by Henry Goodman, it
was in Eric and Maya Bentley's translation. This was copyrighted in
1947 and published along with *The Good Woman of Sezwan*.

* * *

I myself only came into the story in 1956, by which time Auden was
spending much of his time in Europe and Brecht, of course, seemed
ensconced in his theatre in East Berlin. I went there to see him that
summer – it was not long before his death – and was told by his young
daughter Barbara that the one suitable translator for his work was
someone she called Arden; it took me a moment to realise which writer
she meant. Later I was to find this view borne out by her brother and her
mother, though none of the family seemed very clear as to what Auden
translations there might already be. So I wrote to him, and in due course
set about finding a copy of the Auden–Stern *Caucasian Chalk Circle*
script. Bentley put me on the track of a microfilm which Brecht's Danish
mistress Ruth Berlau had made and deposited in the New York Public
Library, and after some false alarms Robert Macgregor of New
Directions eventually located it and had it copied for Methuen, to whom
I had proposed it.

As the translation was still in rather a rough state and did not tally
with the final German text, Auden and the Sterns undertook to revise it.
In October 1959 Auden wrote to Stern from the Austrian village of
Kirchstetten where he had now settled:

> Methuens sent me pages from Chalky Caucasus, which I have revised as best I
> could. It's terrifying when a fifteen-year old corpse which one has completely
> forgotten suddenly comes out of its grave. The only places where I have been
> deaf to your question-marks are the Azdak lyrics and the Mrs Plushbottom
> limerick. When the words are to be sung, the translator has either to do a
> version which will correspond exactly to the music (I have never seen the
> music for this play. I suppose it exists)[1] or assume that new music will be
> written for the English version: in either case the suitability of words to setting
> is much more important than being literal, I believe: my practice is to read the
> original first for its meaning (my German is much better now) and then put
> the original out of my head and re-create.[2]

At the end he added a PPS: 'There is one line, I have left to you since I

am very uncertain what it means. *Schrecklich ist die Verführung zur Güte.*'
This sentence – 'terrible is the temptation to goodness' – is, interestingly
enough, the key line of the play.

The revised translation is now in volume seven of the Methuen
edition of the Collected Plays, along with the final Hays version of the
Duchess of Malfi script, which includes the song which I think is by
Auden. The Auden–Kallman *Seven Deadly Sins* and *Mahagonny* have
likewise appeared as part of volume two. Hannah Arendt wrote of these
in *The New Yorker* that she knew of 'no other adequate rendering of
Brecht into English'. Though they are very good, I don't agree. Auden's
translations of the *Mother Courage* songs, which he did for William
Gaskill's National Theatre production of May 1965, are in his *City
Without Walls*; Spender thinks them among his best work, but they don't
fit Paul Dessau's settings, and they diverge too much from the originals
for my taste, in both meaning and gist. Nor did they really tell in the
production, where they had (so I later gathered from Chuck Mallet the
voice coach) to be laboriously adapted so as to fit the notes, and were in
my view very badly sung. But not long after that Spender told me that
Auden would like to translate the whole play, so I wrote again to him in
August 1971 to ask if he was still prepared to do this. He answered from
Kirchstetten on 6 September:

> On thinking it over, I have decided I cannot do *Mother Courage*. The truth is
> that I think Brecht was a great lyric poet, but a second-rate dramatist. His
> natural poetic sensibility was pessimistic, even Christian, and he tried to
> harness this to an optimistic philosophy, e.g. he apparently wants us to take
> *M.C.* as a picture of what life is like under capitalism, but I can only interpret
> the play as 'That is what, since Adam fell, life is like – period'.[1]

At that time I was beginning to get together the English-language edition
of Brecht's *Poems*, which eventually saw the light after various
cumulative idiocies, being finally published in London in 1976 and in
New York in 1980. I had already asked Auden in 1969 if he could
translate some of these, and he answered that at present he had no time
and it would not be fair to say that he might do some at a later date.
Little did he know how long it would all take. So two years later I asked
him again and discovered, a bit to my surprise, that he had never seen
the collected German *Poems* which had appeared between 1960 and
1967, full of previously unpublished stuff and revolutionising many
people's ideas about Brecht's work.

I got the publisher to send him the posh leather-bound edition, and
also organised an unrelated but agreeably coincidental *bonne bouche* in the

shape of a small and very good lunch party to celebrate the fiftieth anniversary of the St Edmund's School Literary Society – this being the preparatory school on the borders of Surrey and Hampshire where Auden ii and C. Bradshaw Isherwood both went and I later followed – the society's founders having been himself, Harold Llewellyn-Smith and the headmaster's daughter, my dear godmother Winnie Morgan-Brown. Encouraged by his geniality on this occasion (which he attended in his bedroom slippers), I wrote afterwards to send him an unpublished Brecht poem whch I had found in Berlin, called 'Begegnung mit dem Dichter Auden'. It goes:

> lunchend mich wie sichs gehört
> in a bräuhaus (unzerstört)
> sass er gleichend einer wolke
> über dem bebierten volke
>
> und erwies die referenz
> auch der nackten existenz
> ihrer theorie zumindest
> wie du sie in frankreich findest

and can be found on page 418 of the *Poems* fairly freely translated as

> ENCOUNTER WITH THE POET AUDEN
>
> Lunching me, a kindly act
> In an alehouse (still intact)
> He sat looming like a cloud
> Over the beer-sodden crowd
>
> And kept harping with persistence
> On the bare fact of existence
> I.e., a theory built around it
> Recently in France propounded.

I thought that this might amuse him, and asked if he could tell me anything about the occasion referred to. He answered, after thanking me for getting up the lunch,

> I'm afraid I must cry off the Brecht translations because I cannot do anything for some time, and, evidently, time presses. So sorry.
> I was amused [or it could be 'amazed'] by the verses you sent me. I recognise neither the locality nor the opinions I am supposed to have expressed. The last time I saw BB was, I think, in East Berlin in 1952.[1]

I have never managed to find out any more about their meeting, and it is possible that Auden disliked the allusion to the French brand of existentialism, which (says his executor-cum-editor Edward Mendelson) he despised. So I couldn't help wondering if paragraph 2 of the letter might not have helped inspire paragraph 1. Had I put my foot in it? Anyway Auden never translated any of the Brecht poems he so admired – or if he did he kept it to himself. And this was my last contact with him. Alas.

*　*　*

Now what were Auden's real feelings about Brecht? Why, after admiring his writings and collaborating apparently painlessly with him, did he switch to an attitude of evident distaste for Brecht after the Second World War? In 1975 I got a letter from Charles Monteith of Faber's saying, among other things:

> Auden said to me – not once but many times since it was one of his favourite conversation-stoppers – that of the literary men he had known only three struck him as positively evil: Robert Frost, Yeats and Brecht! When I asked him to expand a little he said, about Brecht, 'He was simply a crook. Never gave up either his Austrian nationality or his Swiss bank account'.[1]

I don't think myself that these are the kind of actions which make a man a crook, let alone positively evil, and I am sure that Auden felt this revulsion from Brecht long before anyone became all that interested in the details of Brecht's civic and financial status. So I asked another of his close friends what he thought the real reason was. His answer (as I understood it at the time, though he later denied it) was that Auden had simply been afraid: to have aligned himself with Brecht in the McCarthy era, following Brecht's own hearing by the Un-American Activities Committee, could have done him serious harm. I asked Edward Mendelson; he had no idea. I asked Isherwood. He said 'No comment'.

Mendelson's private speculation was that Brecht and Auden were at bottom very much alike. Both started as romantic anarchists, then converted to an orthodoxy around the age of thirty. Auden, he suggested, 'may have felt that *he* converted to the true orthodoxy while B converted to a false one, and that while he, Auden, believed in his, B (Auden may have felt) did not believe in *his*'[2] – to which I would add that the opposite feeling, or any twinge of it, could have been even more alienating. Similarly Hannah Arendt, who had an immense regard for Auden but an untenably ambiguous attitude to Brecht, wrote of Auden as reflecting 'the obvious influence of Brecht, with whom I think he had more in common than he was ever ready to admit'. Whether or no they explain Auden's apparent postwar dislike – which Brecht and his family, so far as I know, never shared – I think these remarks are largely true. For as writers the two men did indeed have many common characteristics, while always being very opposite in their private lives and, after Auden's visit to Spain in 1937, increasingly so in their political and philosophical convictions.

They liked hymns, the Bible, the poems of Kipling, old and new popular ballads, scientific thought and technical gadgets. They were naturally musical; they could laugh. They had wonderful imaginations, which, like Kipling, they could harness to simple colloquial language and quite rigid and traditional verse forms. They wrote clearly. They had a subversive, plebeian angle on things. They didn't try to bullshit you. I look at Auden and John Garrett's anthology *The Poet's Tongue*, which to me is the best anthology ever made, and I find anonymous ballads like 'Lord Randal', Webster's Dirge from the *Duchess*, 'Casey Jones', one or two Hymns Ancient and Modern (including 'Hail Thee, Festival Day', which we used at St Edmund's to sing before the annual Ascension Day picnic), not to mention pop songs, W.S. Gilbert, and Jean Ingelow's marvellous long poem about the tidal wave on the Lincolnshire coast. I read Brecht's remarks about 'Das Seemannslos', the nineteenth-century song he quotes in two or three of his plays, and turn to the corresponding English ballad by Arthur C. Lamb with its opening quatrain:

> Stormy the night and the waves roll high,
> Bravely the ship doth ride;
> Hark! while the light-house bell's solemn cry
> Rings o'er the sullen tide.[1]

And I *know* that if Auden had known it he would have put it in.

I read Brecht's song of the cranes in *Mahagonny*. I read Auden's 'O lurcher-loving collier, black as night', written for the film *Coal Face* in 1935. I'm glad to have lived when these things were written, and I just can't take such writers' personal hatreds very seriously. In heaven, in the historical dialectic or, more surely, in the verdict of posterity, these two unique poets will be reconciled.

5

The role of Elisabeth Hauptmann

All this absorption of English literary echoes in Brecht's work came sooner or later to involve Elisabeth Hauptmann, whose responsibilities, from being mainly secretarial at the outset, ultimately proved much more creative (even though they never extended to the principal authorship of *The Threepenny Opera* as the allegations in *Life and Lies*[1] assert). Towards the end of her life she was the subject of an East German television programme entitled *Die Mitarbeiterin*, the Collaboratrix or Fellow-Worker, and this is what for about half a century she was, except for those years when exile forced her and Brecht apart. The term comes from the preliminaries to his plays, where she figures as one of his collaborators, as distinct from her ongoing role as his editor, in thirteen of the twenty-six best-known plays to have been written after she joined him (that is, leaving aside the special case of *Happy End*, which is dealt with below). Unfortunately, when the East German Academy issued the posthumous compilation of her 'Stories Plays Essays Recollections', somebody had the bright idea of calling it after the first of the stories included *Julia ohne Romeo* (Juliet Without Romeo).[2] This vulgar decision, which she would surely have detested, had the effect of sliding her over, from her acknowledged place in the 'Brecht Collective' of the 1920s, into the new category of 'Brecht's Women'. Even today, some twelve years later, when Sabine Kebir has just given us a careful study of 'Elisabeth Hauptmann's work with Bertolt Brecht',[3] based on such previously neglected material as Hauptmann's correspondence with Walter Benjamin, her independent archive of exchanges with the Brechts, her thirty pages of 1926 diary entries, and the wide-ranging answers to the makers of *Die Mitarbeiterin* in 1972, there is still a lot to be explained. The *Life and Lies* case is left in tatters, the collective nature of Brecht's working methods made clear. But we still await a scholarly analysis of the exact division of responsibility for the collective's output when Hauptmann was central to it. This remains the largest unsolved question in Brecht's life and works.

Long before I met Hauptmann those collaborators' names used to fascinate me: in her case doubly so when she also emerged as Brecht's editor in 1950. Even when I had come to know her quite well and to love her dearly, she seemed a continual mystery. Just what had she done? Whatever it was she was playing it down. She neither gossiped nor was the subject of gossip; she still claimed that *Happy End* was the work of one Dorothy Lane and that she herself had merely translated it; she seemed never to have been the occasion of any of Brecht's erotic poems; indeed the one poem which she hinted to me had been addressed to her was that positively anaphrodisiac 'Song about the Good People' (*Poems 1913–1956*, pp. 337–9) which he is thought to have written around the beginning of the Second World War. Against that, she had clearly not only done a lot of spadework for those plays, finished or unfinished, to which he put his name between 1924 and 1933; she had actually written parts of them – the Alabama and Benares songs in *Mahagonny*, the original translation of Gay's text for *The Threepenny Opera*, the bulk of *He Said Yes*, the 'Urbild Baals' ('Model for Baal'). Admittedly Brecht's rather condescending poem may have been right when it commented that such 'good people'

> . . . don't seem to be able to finish anything by themselves
> All their solutions still contain problems.

But if she could so collaborate with him without seeming to want credit for it, might she not in the same retiring way have done rather more?

Some seven months older than Brecht, Hauptmann was the daughter of a Westphalian country doctor and his American-born wife, living near Paderborn. At school and college she studied English, then went to work as a teacher and private tutor close to the recently drawn Polish frontier, in an area of large landed estates and intense right-wing political activity. In 1922 she moved to Berlin, where she did some freelance writing and translating and became an occasional reader for Gustav Kiepenheuer, who that year brought out Brecht's *Baal* and announced his forthcoming publication of Brecht's first book of poems, the *Hauspostille*. A couple of years later, when Brecht himself came to settle in Berlin in the wake of his theatrical associates Engel and Neher, Kiepenheuer was awaiting no less than three books from him; for the *Hauspostille* had still not been handed in, while he had subsequently promised to follow up with *In the Jungle* and the still unperformed *Man equals Man*. Hauptmann having been introduced to this dilatory writer by a friend in November 1924, Kiepenheuer deputed her to go and work with him from the beginning of the new year and get all three books out. From then till the fall of the Republic she remained his closest collaborator, working for the first two years on her salary from Kiepenheuer and thereafter (it seems) on her own freelance earnings and an

uncertain share of Brecht's. Later their views might vary as to the intensity
of this work, but by her accounts in *Julia ohne Romeo* it commonly lasted
from six or seven in the morning until late at night. Starting as secretary
and editor, she never seems actually to have directed a play; but outside the
theatre itself she came to take part in every aspect of his working life.

Once the first, monster version of *Man equals Man* was finished Brecht
had it bound in red leather and gave it to her with a handwritten
introduction:

> these are the main manuscripts of the comedy *man = man* or *galy gay*, along with
> the beginnings of an *urgalgei* written many years earlier. at the end of 1925 i gave
> this to bess hauptmann, who had worked with me unpaid the entire year. it was a
> troublesome play and even piecing together the manuscript from 20 lb. of paper
> was heavy work; it took me 2 days, ½ bottle of brandy, 4 bottles of soda water, 8 to
> 10 cigars and a lot of patience, and it was the only bit i did on my own.
>
> > brecht

During the constant writing and rewriting to which they subjected this
play, Hauptmann had what she called 'a minor inspiration' which in her
view marked the beginning of her real usefulness to Brecht. A note of hers
on the typescript situates this in scene 8 – the one which starts with Galy
Gay asleep on his chair – and the relevant passage proves to be Polly Baker's
exclamation 'What an utter elephant!' which leads Galy Gay to say
'Elephant? Elephants are a goldmine of course' and so on (as on p. 33 of
Manheim's and my *Brecht Collected Plays: Two*, 1994). It is not hard then
to infer the problem, which must surely have been how to introduce the
elephant topic at all. Far more important, however, than Hauptmann's
rather laboured solution was her insight into the world of Kipling, which
Brecht had decided to make the setting for what had started as a thoroughly
Bavarian play. For thereby she helped to generate a small poetic ferment
which we see at work not only in *Man equals Man* and the *Hauspostille* but
also in the music-theatrical works with Kurt Weill. Having got to know
Kipling first in translation, Brecht could now explore him further through
her.

Along with the consequent extension of Brecht's range went their joint
exploration of certain aspects of America (for instance, Hauptmann's
research into hurricanes and millionaires), of the world of sport and of the
activities of the Salvation Army, whose meetings and hostels she and her
friend Margaret Mynatt were deputed by Brecht to visit. The new
interests, ideas and approaches which ensued can be seen today as a whole
small complex which became common to her and Brecht and keeps
surfacing in one after another of the works which they left us. So

Hauptmann supplied the Alabama and Benares songs (marked by her respectively 'English by Hauptmann' and 'By Hauptmann. Brecht's handwriting' on the Brecht Archive photocopies) in the batch of 'Mahagonny Songs' that were now added to the *Hauspostille*, variously used in the little and big *Mahagonny* operas, and briefly echoed by Galy Gay at the end of scene 8 of *Man equals Man*. Did she also contribute to the 'Chewinggum Song' (*Poems and Songs from the Plays*, no. 23) and the 'Poem on a Dead Man' (*PSP*, no. 27) which concluded both *Mahagonny*s and figured in the *Berlin Requiem* too? Both hands are detectable on the typescript of the former, whose protagonist recalls the 'Chewinggumjohn' of the title story in *Julia ohne Romeo* (published under the pseudonym Catherine Ux in the magazine *Das Leben* in August 1926), while Hauptmann's alone is to be seen on the latter, which the Brecht Archive dates c. 1925. In 1928 her Salvation Army story 'Bessie Soandso' – Brecht incidentally always called Hauptmann Bess – appeared in *Uhu*, a magazine for which Peter Suhrkamp worked, along with a charming picture of her in the appropriate uniform, borrowed from a production of Kaiser's *From Morn to Midnight*. Moreover there is another English-language song by her, starting 'As long as you're sane' (Brecht Archive 451/39), which has a fourth stanza written in German by Brecht.

The hurricane-millionaire nexus which they thus established floated through various projects like 'The Man From Manhattan' and 'The Flood' before coming to rest in the big *Mahagonny* and *Saint Joan of the Stockyards*. Sport too recurs in a variety of ways, not only as a theme ('Life Story of the Boxer Samson-Körner', the story 'Hook to the Chin' and the rather scrappy 'Boxerroman' (Boxer Novel) in the Brecht Archive 424) but as an influence on staging, a model for audiences and a source of imagery; thus in the 1925 *Man equals Man* script when the soldiers give Galy Gay his first taste of chewing gum they explain that 'once you've got its innermost taste on your lips you'll find your tongue can't do without this sport any more than a boxer without his punchball'. With all this went a new deadpan style of narration as seen in the two opening passages which Hauptmann considered 'classic': those of the story 'Four Men and a Poker Game' and the first scene of *Man equals Man*. As for the Kipling influence, it runs through a number of works from *Man equals Man* on, starting with the 'Man equals Man Song' (later dropped from that work), the 'Song of Widow Begbick's Drinking Truck' and the 'Uganda' song (in the subsequently detached *Elephant Calf*), also inspiring the pastiche 'Song of the Three Soldiers' in allusion to *Soldiers Three*, which at first appeared as one of the additions to the *Hauspostille*, though without its refrain. The refrain itself, with its familiar words 'The troops live under/The cannon's thunder', etc., figured under the title 'Cannon Song' in the programme of the first Berlin production of *Man equals Man* in 1928.

We cannot say that the works in question were significantly attributable to Hauptmann, merely that she had some share in them and that this particular complex of interests and influences was common to Brecht, Hauptmann and Emil Hesse-Burri who went to make up the initial 'Brecht collective' (later to be augmented by Eisler, Reich, Dudow and Borchardt). But it should be possible to go rather further in establishing her responsibility for those that follow. These comprised above all the main works with Kurt Weill, who had been drawn in by his spontaneous enthusiasm for *Man equals Man* and the *Hauspostille* early in 1927. Here Hauptmann played a central part, providing the original 'book' for both *The Threepenny Opera* and *Happy End* – the one a translation from the eighteenth-century *Beggar's Opera*, whose radical adaptation once Brecht took it up will be described at the end of this chapter, the other following an outline by him – then going on to translate virtually the whole text of *He Said Yes*, this time from the English of Arthur Waley. She was involved in the first two *Lehrstücke*, which in the *Versuche* edition are signed respectively 'Brecht. Dudow. Hauptmann' (*The Baden-Baden Lesson on Consent*) and 'Brecht. Hauptmann. Weill' (*Lindbergh's Flight*); while *The Exception and the Rule* derived from a translation which she made of a French version of the old Chinese play *Ho-Han-Chan* and called *Die zwei Mantelhälften* (The Divided Coat). In fact, if Hindemith was one generally unacknowledged originator of the *Lehrstück* form, Hauptmann was the other, for it was she who read Waley's *The Nō Plays of Japan*, translated some of them and wrote the radio play about Seami which is included in *Julia ohne Romeo* along with an important interview on the subject which she gave in 1966. It was Weill, she says there, not Brecht, who read her translation of Waley's version of *Taniko* and suggested making it into an opera for children. So if Brecht was undoubtedly drawn to this didactic form and put it to masterly use, there is no good evidence that it was ever, as so often assumed, his particular invention.

The literary influences which she communicated to Brecht at this time went far beyond Kipling, for besides introducing him to Waley as an accessible guide to the Far East she helped widen his view of English and American literature in general, not least with reference to the Elizabethans (a role that seems to accord with Brecht's nickname for her). It should also perhaps be noted that the 'City' poems of the mid-1920s involved her collaboration, if only as copyist, and that they reflect some of the collective's common themes – hurricanes, Rockefeller, Standard Oil – besides clearly voicing for the first time a woman's point of view. These splendidly severe poems, as we know, spilt over into *Mahagonny* and, with the 'Song of the Flow of Things', into the 1931 version of *Man equals Man*. Nonetheless Kipling and his influence also belong in the collaboration with Weill, not only in the *Berlin Requiem* and *Mahagonny* but in the twin musicals for the Theater am Schiffbauerdamm: the great success of 1928 and the great flop of 1929. For originally *The Threepenny Opera* was to include translations of Kipling's 'The Ladies' and 'Mary, Pity Women!' as well as the full 'Cannon Song' which marries the new refrain with the old *Hauspostille* verse. Meanwhile into *Happy End* went 'Surabaya-Johnny', a variant on the second of these which Brecht had intended for Feuchtwanger's *Kalkutta 4 Mai*, then given to Franz Bruinier to set in 1927, apparently as an independent cabaret song. 'The Song of Mandelay', which overlaps the men's chorus in the brothel scene of *Mahagonny*, is once again a pastiche whose typescript bears snatches of a tune noted in Hauptmann's hand. The 'Bilbao Song' may relate to a lost 'Song of the Bilbao Men' which was to have been sung by the soldiers in the 1925 *Man equals Man*.

Happy End has long been one of the great Brechtian problems, since Brecht's anxiety to wash his hands of it (following its failure) started a long process of mystification that became compounded by Hauptmann's insistence that the 'book' really had been adapted by her from a story called 'Under the Mistletoe' by one Dorothy Lane in the St Louis magazine *J.L.'s Weekly* – St Louis being where Hauptmann's sister had gone to live. To make matters worse, the story with its cast of Salvationists and Chicago gangsters bears an uncertain, and in 1997 still unexamined, relationship to the Runyon-based *Guys and Dolls*. Even in the interview of 1964 which is now printed (for some reason) among the 'Bibliographical Pointers' at the back of *Julia ohne Romeo* she never came entirely clean, though she dates the operation from the story 'Bessie Soandso' of 1928 and says that Weill was a prime mover, wishing 'once again to write a score like that for *The Threepenny Opera*'. At the same time however we have an incomplete and undated letter from Brecht to her (*Letters*, no. 146) which seems to suggest that Massary (meaning the film star?) was at first involved (perhaps as a backer?) and goes on to outline the story of Ecclesia Dick ('worst crook in Chicago') and Mimosa Bess of the Salvation Army ('You can't undress Mimosa Bess') which Hauptmann was to write and take the credit for. On top of this we can assume Aufricht's natural wish as producer to repeat the successful recipe which had launched and established his theatre.

At the outset the recipe was as before: 'book' by Hauptmann, songs by Brecht, music by Weill, directed by Engel, set by Caspar Neher, with Theo Mackeben and the Lewis Ruth band. On the earliest typescript, for instance (Brecht Archive 994), there is no mention of 'Dorothy Lane', just

Happy End
by Elisabeth Hauptmann
Songs by Bert Brecht and Kurt Weill.

However in this case Brecht, for whatever reason, undertook a much less radical reworking of the first script than he had done with her translation of *The Beggar's Opera*, where, as the editorial notes to the Manheim/Willett translation show, virtually nothing of the original text was left finally intact. For only a handful of amendments in his writing are to be found on the *Happy End* scripts (though the issue is confused for the student by the fact that the Brecht Archive catalogue classifies these under the same heading as another, untitled *Heilsarmeestück*, 'Salvation Army play'). What is generally regarded as being his is the songs, but even here there are considerable uncertainties. Thus five songs are included in the *Gedichte* section of the 1967 *GW*, but several more are not: for instance not only the shortened version of the 'Branntweinhändler' ('Brandy-peddler') poem from the *Hauspostille* (which is natural enough) and the final 'Hosanna Rockefeller' (which for some reason is excluded from the scripts) but also 'Obacht, gebt Obacht' ('Watchful, Be Watchful'), the 'Song of the Tough Nut', the prologue (omitted also from volume 2 of the catalogue) and all the Salvation Army songs (which I have tried unsuccesfully to trace in various hymnbooks). Does this then indicate that Hauptmann may have had some hand in the writing of the songs? Cursory inspection of the Archive photocopies suggests that this is not impossible, and it is notable that the 'The Sailors' Song' too is amended by her in an almost proprietorial way.

My own feeling then is that *Happy End*, like *The Threepenny Opera*, was a product of the collective even though the degree of involvement of its members altered while it was being written. At the time, as commonly now, it was regarded as Brecht's show; for instance it was he to whom Aufricht and Engel turned when the end of the last act was found to be unsatisfactory. How the earnings were divided I am not sure. In 1974 John Fuegi considered that Hauptmann, Brecht and Weill took equal shares. The agent as before was Bloch-Erben of Berlin, to whom Brecht later wrote that the advance for *Happy End* had gone entirely to Hauptmann; she also seems to have had a share of his regular payments from them. For *The Threepenny Opera* she originally had 15 per cent (as against Brecht's 60 and Weill's 25) but 2.5 per cent got knocked off this when the original translator of the Villon passages used in some of the songs demanded payment). So the two cases were at the outset not dissimilar, and the major differentiation, by which *Happy End* became excluded from the canon of Brecht's plays and disowned even by Hauptmann, only took place after that work's failure in September 1929. Subsequently the waters became further muddied by the re-functioning of some of the same material to make first the unnamed 'Salvation Army play' on which Burri also worked, then the unfinished *Breadshop* and finally *Saint Joan of the Stockyards* where the gangsters vanished and the millionaires and the Chicago Salvationists came together under a quasi-Elizabethan dramaturgy. Signed 'Brecht. Borchardt. Burri. Hauptmann' in the *Versuche*, and handled once again by Bloch-Erben, this was prefaced by a note saying that it was 'developed from the play *Happy End* by Elisabeth Hauptmann'. In modified form it re-used 'Watchful, Be Watchful' (also known as 'Kampflied der Schwarzen Strohhüte', 'Battle Hymn of the Black Straw Hats', or 'Der kleine Leutnant des lieben Gottes', 'God's Little Lieutenant') as well as 'Hosanna Rockefeller' and one or two of the Salvation Army songs.

During 1929 Hauptmann joined the KPD, a step that matches the beginning of Brecht's close association with that party. Nevertheless, she was not among the principal collaborators on his three most openly Communist works: *The Decision* by 'Brecht. Dudow. Eisler'; *The Mother* by 'Brecht. Eisler. Weisenborn', and the film *Kuhle Wampe* on which he worked with Ottwalt, Eisler and Dudow. She was back in the team again however for the first version of *Pointed Heads and Round Heads* by 'Brecht. Burri. Hauptmann' and throughout the whole pre-Hitler period she played a special part in the production of those short stories which tended to appear whenever his theatrical prospects were in the doldrums. Here the seven short stories of her own included in *Julia ohne Romeo* are of particular interest, since in theme and style they seem indistinguishable from what Manheim and I, in our edition, termed 'Brecht's Berlin Stories'; or more precisely the eleven stories that start with 'Conversation about the South Seas' and end with 'The Job'. Add the evidence of these works to that of the corresponding Berlin typescripts in the Brecht Archive – which, in contrast to the scripts of such clearly Brechtian products as *Me-ti* and the Keuner stories, seldom bear any mark in Brecht's hand – and it looks as if Hauptmann's contribution in this area may have been considerably greater than has been allowed.

For example there are no marks of Brecht's hand on the scripts of 'Conversation about the South Seas', 'A Little Tale of Insurance', 'Four Men and a Poker Game', 'Life Story of the Boxer Samson-Körner', and only a few on 'North Sea Shrimps', 'Barbara' and 'The Monster'. The extraordinary 'Letter About a Mastiff' on the other hand was entirely typed by him, and it looks as if he must have been mainly or wholly responsible also for 'Safety First' and 'Bad Water'. Hauptmann's marks by contrast are frequent, though the fact that they are also found on the

Bavarian stories suggests that Brecht to some extent left her in charge of this whole department, including the submission of stories to magazines or theatre programmes, and the preparation of a selection which Bloch-Erben were to circulate. But the stylistic resemblances imply a lot more than secretarial responsibilities. Admittedly it is not easy to convey such things, since style is a matter either of general *Gestalt* (which has to be judged subjectively) or of detailed verbal analysis such as no one (to my knowledge) has yet practised on Brecht's prose. But a few samples from *Julia ohne Romeo* may serve to give some indication. There James G. Luck, the young American banker who comes up against 'Chewinggumjohn' in the title story,

> filled the post, that is to say a rickety green writing table with a telephone through which he could issue orders to people without a telephone who could have been his fathers.

The story of 'Dishy Edgar' and the motorcycle begins:

> One of the few phrases in the Bible that really influence the conduct of so many men is the sentence 'And he shall be thy Lord'. This sentence is indeed followed by a lot of stupid men – and by practically all clever women.

Similarly the two closing sentences of 'In Search of Extra Income', which was published by *Uhu* in January 1931, and describes a young married woman's drift towards prostitution:

> If a man cannot sell his fellow man, then he may be driven to sell himself. Tens of thousands of faceless men and women in tens of thousands of situations are hourly ransacking their selves to find anything about them that is saleable, their head or their legs, their youth or their age, their night hours or their summer. In this way they keep seeking ever new tricks and trying to exploit ever new disappointments to improve their position, which is beyond improvement.

The most powerful of Hauptmann's stories (and the one that stood out for me from Wieland Herzfelde's important *30 neue Erzähler des neuen Deutschland* where it appeared in 1932) is 'Gastfeindschaft' (Inhospitality) when an unemployed man is invited to spend Christmas with a bourgeois family. This seems closely akin to Brecht's 'The Job', whose final cadences the passage just quoted also recalls. The likenesses indeed are such that one might be tempted to think that the Brecht story too must have been written by her. However, there is a letter from her to Brecht, sent after she had reached St Louis in 1934, which makes clear that both of them had written versions based apparently on notes of the same real-life incident. Faced with this final evidence of overlap perhaps we can go no further than simply to suggest that the work on the eleven Berlin stories must have been shared, and that because they were only a secondary aspect of Brecht's work the major responsibility was quite likely to be Hauptmann's. As for their function, it was first to back up and help publicise the plays; secondly, of course, to increase Brecht's earnings (out of which Hauptmann too got paid) – never more successfully than during the run of *The Threepenny Opera* when 'The Monster' won the *Berliner Illustrierte Zeitung*'s short story prize. Both parts of the dual operation depended on the use of Brecht's name; so it may in effect only have been the leftovers that got published under Hauptmann's. But we cannot say definitely, only point to this quite large area of uncertainty and indicate the spots where detailed research and clarification are most needed. What is sure is that *no* imaginative prose work published under Brecht's name makes any reference to collaborators, nor is there any sign that Hauptmann wished this otherwise. In fact she gave the impression of positively wanting to remain in the back room.

*　　*　　*

Such is my somewhat tentative reading of Hauptmann's literary role up to 1933. Then with the advent of the Nazis everything changed. Not only the Brecht collective but the whole of Weimar culture broke apart, leaving her to spend the rest of that year working illegally for the KPD and doing what she could to salvage Brecht's affairs. More than once her flat was searched, says Fritz Hofmann's short biographical postscript to her book, though she was lucky in that part of it was sublet to Lili Brik and her then husband, a Red Army general on attachment to the Reichswehr under the secret agreements of 1922, while Margaret Mynatt as a British subject could help to get Brecht's papers safely away. According to Sabine Kebir she made a brief visit to the Brechts in Denmark, but decided she must come back to Berlin to rescue his remaining papers. There she was arrested and put in solitary confinement, only to be released on the insistence of foreign friends and their lawyer, who maintained that she was on the way to join her sister in America and was guaranteed by another relative who was a senator.

From Paris, where she immediately went, she might have joined the Brechts in Svendborg; indeed she had already sent some of her clothes and effects there. Brecht however had reacted furiously to the news that a suitcase full of his precious papers had been left and probably lost in Berlin. Kebir's evidence here is fragmentary, but it seems clear that he spoke of breaking off all relations so sharply that the old mutual confidence and commitment could never be completely restored.[1] With Margarete Steffin now taking over much of her role in the Brecht set-up, Hauptmann left Paris around the end of 1933 to join her sister in the middle West of the land where their mother had grown up. This was at the beginning of Franklin Roosevelt's New Deal, when the European Left had started looking hopefully to the United States not only for political support but also for further progress in theatre, literature and the other arts. Exactly what Hauptmann did in her fifteen-odd years there is by no means clear, though Hofmann says she at first did housework and she herself describes (in the essay 'As a Teacher in the States') teaching in various schools, including a spell at a college for blacks in the South and five years in a big progressive school which she termed 'comparable with the very best of the schools I saw in Germany in the late 1920s'. Though never uncritical she evidently felt at home in her maternal country, developing a considerable affection for it and identifying with its liberal traditions.

Evidently some of her ensuing correspondence with Brecht has been lost, while at least one of his letters was never given to the Brecht Archive. But as matters stand, his *Letters 1913–1956* includes just one letter addressed to her between 1933 and 1946, and any collaboration on the writing of short stories seems to have stopped. Only 'As a Teacher' and the descriptive 'En Route by Greyhound' in *Julia ohne Romeo* suggest that she ever tried to keep her hand in as a writer. She came to New York in 1935 to help mediate in his dealings with Theatre Union over their production of *Mother*, after which she was hoping to visit Hans Borchardt in the USSR, possibily in the hope of working there; he however was about to be deported, and it sounds as if the trip fell through. A little later Brecht was trying to get her to write on American theatre for the Moscow German-language magazine *Das Wort*; but apart from this there is no more evidence of her playing any part in his affairs until he had made up his mind to leave Scandinavia for good. Then in 1940/41 she swung into action, getting William Dieterle and other Hollywood friends to subscribe to the family's maintenance till Brecht could get a footing in California. At that time she was herself at 1626 North Martel Avenue, Hollywood, but then moved to Greenwich, Connecticut, where Brecht was to find her on his first visit to New York in spring 1943.

By then she had given up teaching and was living with Horst Bärensprung, a socialist lawyer who had been police president of Magdeburg before Hitler came to power. Arrested by the Nazis, he had (says Sabine Kebir)[1] escaped and gone to China, where he helped organise Chiang Kai-shek's army and its intelligence service. He was however no writer, and it was Hauptmann who helped him with radio talks, schemes for a play and a film script and eventually, at Carl Zuckmayer's instigation, his memoirs. He would return to Germany in 1946, as a police president once more, but already Brecht had noted in his *Journals* that Hauptmann 'would be glad to work again' despite her other commitments, notably as executive secretary of the Council for a Democratic Germany. Work, that is, at the only work that counted – his own. Soon she was once again harnessed up, collaborating marginally on *The Duchess of Malfi*, supervising the translation of *Fear and Misery of the Third Reich* by Eric Bentley, who was taken aback to see how much authority Brecht gave her (e.g. to rework the 'Peat-bog soldiers' scene), then in 1947 co-writing the film treatment for 'The Coat' after Gogol, in which Brecht hoped to interest Peter Lorre. By then she was married to Paul Dessau, who had established himself in Santa Monica in order to collaborate with Brecht. He was her second husband, her first brief marriage to one Friedrich Hacke having ended in divorce before 1933.

Her return to Germany in 1949 was virtually organised for her, for Brecht not only wanted her on the board of the newly-formed Berliner Ensemble but also arranged with Peter Suhrkamp, apparently without consulting her, that she should be engaged as editor of the resumed *Versuche* series which he started publishing that year, and thereafter of all his works. With this she acquired a different, rather remoter role in the expanding circle around Brecht, which was already turning into something far less tight-knit than the pre-Hitler collective: a mixture of middle-aged matriarchy on the one hand and an apprenticeship system on the other. So where once the *Versuche* used to follow the text of a play with the names of the team who wrote it (starting with Brecht's), from number 9 on they would ascribe it to Brecht and prefix it with a note giving his collaborators, a not insignificant distinction. Among these Hauptmann herself figured only twice, each time together with the young Swiss director Benno Besson: as working on *Dom Juan* and the Farquhar-based *Trumpets and Drums*, which were the two last Berliner Ensemble adaptations to appear under Brecht's name. The second in particular appears to have been conceived very much on *Threepenny Opera* lines, starting with Hauptmann's translation of another English eighteenth-century comedy which she transported forward – this time so as to celebrate the American colonies' independence – while Brecht supplied a number of songs to be set in Weill-like style by Rudolf Wagner-Regeny. Among these was the 'Army Song' with its Kiplingesque references to military pursuits in 'Gaa'.

In the winter of 1955/56, which was when I first met her in London, Hauptmann was one of the three exceptional women who seemed for better or worse most influential in Brecht's work and life – a life which had not much longer to run. Helene Weigel was the mother of his children, the head of his company and the actress associated with his greatest roles. Ruth Berlau was the woman whom he had loved, very much under the irrational conditions of what his ballad called 'sexual obsession', from the mid-1930s till around the time of his return to Europe, and who since then had become perhaps his outstanding personal problem. Hauptmann was the *Mitarbeiterin* or collaboratrix whose inspiration and judgement lay closest to his own and had dovetailed with it most productively. Besides this trio there had also been Margarete Steffin, the only woman whose contribution could compare with Hauptmann's, and at the same time a beloved mistress and a representative of that Communist working class in whose political instincts he believed. That all four had loved and been loved by Brecht – within the varying frameworks imposed by their own temperaments and his – is clear, and now that he was having affairs with younger members of the company each of the three survivors was left with something different. Weigel with the titular position, the prestige and the material advantages; Berlau with a driving sense that he should still be loving her, a long history of psychological instability and, alas, a drink habit to which to be driven. But Hauptmann? For Brecht she was still what he had termed in a testimonial of 1934 'one of the most reliable and hard-working people I know'; moreover the problems created by Berlau had brought her and Weigel (it was said) closer to one another than they had ever been before. But how far was she now being taken for granted, and how far did she mind?

I've never assumed that any woman who came into Brecht's orbit was instantly to be categorised as one of his 'mistresses', and am well aware that the two great love affairs of his maturity – with Berlau and with Steffin – started circumspectly. Whether or not it was true, as Hanns Eisler claimed, that in time he cut his preliminaries down to the two words 'Say "ja!"' ', in neither case, it seems, was a full sexual relationship established right away. I did however believe from various hints and indications that the charming and reticent fifty-nine-year-old whom I got to know well in Berlin in 1956, and after Brecht's death, must have been in every sense his principal partner between the start of their work together and his marriage to Weigel in April 1929. I never asked her about this, nor until Klaus Völker reported it in his book did I learn about her alleged suicide attempt at the time of that marriage, though neither is that without relevance to the story of *Happy End*. But I was able to see her briefly with Brecht at Buckow and to register the endearing mixture of solicitude and decisiveness, of detachment and long familiarity with which she approached this shy, considerate yet relentlessly purposeful man. And she did on one occasion – some years later, I think – volunteer to me that Brecht should not be thought of as an unjust and egotistical lover: you knew exactly where you were with him, she said; he would make no false promises or exaggerated professions of love; when it was all over no bad feeling remained. In this she may have been prompted by her awareness of the sympathy which many of us felt for Ruth Berlau, whom Brecht's death had left high and dry on the scrapheap (and she herself treated with great consideration). Berlau had expected a lot and lost not only Brecht but herself. Yet despite what Hauptmann said it is difficult to read some of Brecht's writings to or about Berlau (e.g. the Lai-tu stories) without feeling that they have a spurious ring.

Critics tend to be exceptionally censorious about Brecht, either because they resent the power of his writing or because they feel he is a god who has somehow failed them. Part of the all too familiar [even a dozen years ago, let alone in 1997] non-literary 'case' against him is that he allowed himself to be politically manipulated by severe, more or less fanatical Communist women: Weigel, Hauptmann and Steffin. Another, more recently developed indictment which could be equally demolishing is that he was the male pig *par excellence*, carelessly exploiting these same women in bed and at the typewriter. Such arguments not only rest on a wilfully selective attitude to the evidence but seem on the face of it to contradict one another, while Hauptmann's role in his life in particular is difficult to reconcile with either. For she really did choose to sink herself in the collective and merge her literary identity with his, and she continued to love the work long after she had, to all appearances, ceased in any erotic sense to love the man. But what about his role in hers? Was she really as relativistic in her attitude to 'personality' as the soldiers in *Man equals Man*, or to literary property as Brecht himself in his more polemical mood? Was she as coldly and detachedly *neusachlich* (or matter-of-fact) as all that? It is a great pity that she never found the time or the concentration – or maybe the necessary self-assertiveness – to sit down and write her reminiscences, which might have given us a careful, critical account of the whole poetic, theatrical and politico-artistic complex we call 'Brecht'; of the contribution made to it by herself and other almost faceless collaborators; of the human cost or sense of fulfilment which this facelessness involved. The signs are that she became slightly less satisfied with her anonymity following the establishment of the new, enlarged, state-subsidised Brecht complex centring on the Berliner Ensemble; then still less so after Brecht's death in August 1956. This was when she let it be known, for instance, that she had written such minor items as the English-language Mahagonny Songs and the biographical note on 'The Model for Baal'; later, as I have noted elsewhere, she told Rosemarie Hill (who had come to help with her editorial work) that her own share of the work on the plays ought to have been made more clear, and now be more fairly rewarded – something that Brecht himself had apparently intended, though without clear provisions. Feeling ignored (so she told me) by the East German theatre historians and even, once Palitzsch and Weber had left, by Brecht's younger followers at the Ensemble, she welcomed foreign visitors like Bernard Sobel and myself, once saying that we were the only two people who were really interested in her experience of the theatre of the 1920s; she also spent some time helping Keith Hack over his adaptations of *The Breadshop* and *Man equals Man*. After Brecht's death she had hoped to resume her own writing – with Guy Fawkes as one promising subject. A few sparse fragments of reminiscence, record and comment also began to appear, starting with the extracts from her 1926 diary in the Brecht memorial number of the Academy journal *Sinn und Form*. These too are included in *Julia ohne Romeo*: that is to say three pages 'On Brecht' on his methods of collaboration, written for his sixtieth birthday but not previously published; her important interview about the background to *He Said Yes*, published in 1966; five illuminating pages on Brecht's attitude to music, of the same year; an obituary tribute to Erich Engel; and part of a so-called 'Telephone Interview with Dorothy Lane' which traced the history of *Happy End* back to her own short story, describing that play somewhat deceptively as 'a kind of trial run for a play about the Salvation Army'. It is on the face of it surprising that more could not have been reproduced of the various earlier notes listed in volume 4 of the Brecht Archive catalogue, which include quite a bit more of the 1926 diary (starting with an entry 'With Busoni and a friend of his. That evening at Brecht's').[1]

Much the most interesting and impressive of her later writings however are two autobiographical pieces attributed to the early 1950s which are in the last section of *Julia ohne Romeo*. These describe opposite ends of her more personal experiences and are titled by the publishers 'Thoughts on Sunday Morning' – about a lonely weekend in East Berlin in autumn 1951 – and 'What It Was Like to Read at My Parents', three movingly written pages which would have made a perfect start to the reminiscences that she never wrote. As a child it appears that she hated having illustrations to the books she read, and tore them out, though she herself would draw copiously in the margins. She taught herself to read, sitting for preference near a window on the attic stairs. Up in the boxroom she and her sister found and read their parents' letters – passionate love-letters, letters about their mother's adoption in America, letters home from their father when he was a student, which they would cite in defence of their student brother – thereby gaining insights which few children are able to get. But the clear, vivid prose soon peters out, as it does too in the slightly longer account of her feelings of solitude on one of those many Sundays on which 'sometimes she thought she couldn't stand it any longer'. This piece touches on her need to earn money by uncongenial translation work, and on an unspecified attempt at suicide in the past.

> In the past she used to be invited out on Sundays, but that was a long time ago. Nor was she a particularly amusing guest.

So she turns to the newspapers, where an article on Brecht reminds her of the long hours she spent working with him – longer and later than he was nowadays prepared to admit.

> Things like the gluttony scene in *Mahagonny*, the Bible scene in *The Mother*, a lot of the poems – all of them were written late in the evening, or sometimes even later.

Now she has taken to smoking again. As a rule she cooks skilfully, reading a recipe 'like a musician reading a score'; but eating on her own 'was not . . . any fun for her'. Nonetheless she goes into the cold kitchen when the bell rings and a poor drop-out theology student appears who has been writing a play. And there it breaks off.

At least those two unfinished pieces tell us more about her than, being prejudiced like Brecht against anything 'psychological', she was normally prepared to say. And for those of us who, despite occasional argument and exasperation, had become very fond of her they are painful to read. Painful not only because they communicate her own pains which she so serenely covered up, but also because they bear out what Brecht had said in his 'Song about the Good People' whose patronising tone she appeared not to resent: that she could never complete so independent and personal a piece of writing or, in effect, write her own book. Whether this inability was an act of chronic self-denial unwittingly imposed on her by his demands and his assumptions, or the result of some already latent incapacity to value and maintain her own initiatives is at present impossible to say. It may well remain so. But because it too is relevant to our understanding of Brecht's collective methods, and of the sacrifices involved in them, the uncertainty has to be stated here.

I hope that readers will condone my motives for writing so largely speculative an account of a still controversial area. I wish I had known the right questions to ask Hauptmann during her lifetime, or even known someone else who had actually asked them. 'Whereof one cannot speak, thereof should one remain silent' is a principle which I would normally accept, not least when addressing an informed audience, who may well be contemptuous of guesswork. This applies particularly in the case of so charming and diffident a woman, whose personal dealings were marked by a dry wit and an extreme delicacy of feeling: she would have found our sort of inquisitiveness painfully intrusive. All the same, as we come to learn more and more about the still expanding nebula called 'Brecht', we see what a vital part of it Hauptmann was in one way and another, and how easy it is to get him wrong if we fail to allow for her role as writer, communicator and person. What I have done then is to state what I know about that role and its implications, filling this out with informed speculation based, if need be, on intangibles and subjective impressions. My feeling was that even so makeshift an attempt to treat her achievement as a whole might serve as a challenge to scholars to find out more and do the job better. The East German collection of her original writing may have been an inadequate start, but at least it was a suggestive one, and I thought it must surely inspire further research.

* * *

John Fuegi, as principal editor of the 1983 *Brecht Yearbook* in which this chapter originally appeared, appended a useful Note on the collaborators' respective responsibility for the writing of *Happy End*. On 16 April 1929, four and a half months before the première, Hauptmann wrote formally to Brecht to say that she had written a play under the pseudonym 'Dorothy Lane' for production at the Theater am Schiffbauerdamm, for which Brecht had undertaken to write the song texts. Brecht confirmed this on 2 May, specifying that he would have the right to use those texts separately for 'cabaret etc'. There was thus from the outset an apparent separation of effort, which was aggravated by Brecht's engagement in the new didactic musical theatre launched at the Neue Musik festival of that summer, followed only months later by the refunctioning of Hauptmann's play to make a large-scale social drama in the shape of *Saint Joan of the Stockyards*.

The much more complex division of labour in the writing of *The Threepenny Opera* during the previous summer is set out in my notes to the Manheim–Willett Methuen edition in 1979; but for the sake of completeness it needs to be summarised here. As has already been suggested, Hauptmann's initial translation seems not to have figured in Brecht's plans until the spring of 1928 and the earliest discussions with the producer Aufricht and his team. If they had a script before them at that point it has not been preserved; the title is still *The Beggar's Opera*, and there is nothing to suggest that Brecht had started to work on it. His first recorded involvement appears to have been the production of the stage script duplicated by Brecht's and Hauptmann's agents, Felix Bloch Erben. Who contributed exactly what to this we do not know, but it still contains a good deal of material from Gay's original, including the characters of Suky

Tawdry and Mrs Coaxer; Jenny was Jenny Diver, while there were two of Gay's original songs as well as two from Kipling. The stable wedding was new, as was the second prison scene, while Gay's Lockit was replaced by the martial figure of Police President Tiger Brown.

All this probably reflected the collective ideas of Brecht, Hauptmann, Helene Weigel, Weill and Lotte Lenya, who worked on the project in the south of France during that May and June. Its title is given as

The Beggar's Opera
die Luden-Oper
Translated by Elisabeth Hauptmann
German adaptation: Bert Brecht
Music: Kurt Weill

To it had been added titles of eight new songs – two of them deriving from Villon – and the final chorus, after which came further radical changes, comprising further songs, more Villon, new speeches and many cuts made either by the same group of collaborators or during the Berlin rehearsals that took up the whole of August – the new title and the 'Mack the Knife' song being last-minute inspirations. No one with any experience of show business can be surprised to learn that at the end of that month the only remnants of the original were Peachum's opening song and a few lines in scene 6 (the first prison scene). Likewise the Kipling songs disappeared apart from four lines.

It should perhaps be noted that Hauptmann, whose editorial responsibilities included the publication of the final text, was present throughout, but never claimed a prime role in the adaptation.

6

Brecht and Expressionism

There are still parts of the world – the Soviet Union being till recently one of them – where Brecht is treated as an Expressionist and the term 'Expressionist' is used to some extent in a pejorative sense. Whatever one may think about the pejorative, there is an immediate and obvious difference between Brecht and the Expressionists properly speaking. He was younger. Thus Franz Werfel and Johannes R. Becher were some seven years older than him, and even Toller was four. In other words, throughout the heyday of the movement he was an Augsburg schoolboy, though admittedly a very gifted one who wrote poems. Perhaps this Bavarian provincial background put him somewhat outside the Expressionist orbit, for he never seems to have discussed the movement with Münsterer, our most vivid authority on that period of his life, who was a close friend of his towards the end of the First World War. Unlike the Expressionists, too, he never seriously took part in that war; indeed the myth-makers have made much too much of his army service, which in fact was performed locally and only lasted four or five months, half of this period falling after the war. So by the time he came on the literary scene in Munich the Expressionists were running out of steam. And Brecht, who had never really shared their revolutionary hopes, was not so traumatically disillusioned when the new republic left these unfulfilled.

Even if he had been of the same generation his temperament would surely have shielded him from the worst Expressionist excesses. For despite all his extraordinary vitality he had deep reserves of scepticism, detachment and humour. 'Humor ist Distanzgefühl', 'Humour is a sense of distance', he noted in 1920, some fifteen years before he began formulating his eventual concept of *Verfremdung* or 'Alienation'. Nor did he have much use for Nietzsche, who had been the real prophet of the movement. He himself was far too conscious of his own individuality and his own genius to stand being grouped with any artistic or literary movement whatever, even disclaiming *Die neue Sachlichkeit*, the new sobriety of the mid-1920s with which he was much more closely linked. He never belonged to the League of Proletarian-Revolutionary Writers, founded in 1928, and resented its criticisms of him, notably those put forward by Georg Lukács around 1930, though by that time he at least shared its political views. Among his own entourage indeed the same highly developed sense of Brecht's uniqueness has even lived on since his death, making it seem almost blasphemous to mention his name in connection with any other writer unless with the very great. To speak of him as an Expressionist was, and is, to court instant contradiction.

However, that is to admit that he gets spoken of as such. Not only are his early plays often treated as part of the Expressionist theatre, but when the Berliner Ensemble visited Moscow in 1957 one of the reproaches against their productions was that they were too 'expressionistic', meaning apparently too remote from Socialist Realism as defined and long enforced by Stalin's lieutenant A.A. Zhdanov. For generally speaking non-Germans (and/or non-Germanists) tend to use this concept in a very broad sense, not just in relation to the Expressionist movement of 1910–1922 but as a way of describing what they feel to be common to the great majority of twentieth-century German artists and writers, from Wedekind to Günter Grass. They see such originators of *Neue Sachlichkeit* as Grosz and Beckmann, for instance, as being expressionists much like the people they were reacting against; and true enough, these artists are closer to Expressionism than to any of the Latin, Slav or Anglo-Saxon movements. It is in this sense that we most often hear Brecht talked of as an expressionist: a sense which, it seems to me, can be distinguished from the other by the use of a small-letter 'e'.

It is certainly true that his literary ancestry was very much akin to those of the Expressionists proper. There is a page in Brecht's *Schriften* (GKA, vol. 22, 1993, p. 317) which defines the 'historic line of the epic theatre' as passing from the Elizabethans 'through Lenz, Schiller (early works), Goethe (*Götz* and both parts of *Faust*), Grabbe, Büchner. The line is strongly marked and easy to follow'. To this can be added Wedekind and, so far as the poetry of *Baal* and the *Hauspostille* is concerned, the German translations of Rimbaud. Of course what Brecht derived from such examples was something rather special: for him Rimbaud for instance was not so much the mystical searcher as the exotic adventurer, while in Wedekind he saw the cabaret singer as well as the demonic exponent of the sexual urge. But much of what he saw in the theatre in his early days was more or less Expressionist; he too was strongly affected by his first encounters with the big cities; and he might

well have been expected to end up as an Expressionist in the strict sense
of the term.

Anybody familiar with his work knows that on the contrary his first
theatrical ventures were something of a demonstration against that
movement. At Munich university in 1918 he wrote the first version of
Baal as a kind of 'counter-play' to Hanns Johst's Expressionist play *Der
Einsame* (The Lonely One), which he had sharply attacked at the seminar
directed by Artur Kutscher, a friend and admirer of Johst's and no great
admirer of the student Brecht. For the Augsburg *Volkswille* two years
later he criticised six new plays which Gustav Kiepenheuer – subsequently his own principal publishers – had brought out under the
general title *Der dramatische Wille*. Among these he much preferred Iwan
Goll's surrealistic farce *Methuselah* to Toller's first play *Die Wandlung*,
and labelled the whole series 'Dramatic Will, minus the drama'. Then in
Berlin in 1922 his attempt to direct Arnolt Bronnen's violently distorted
play *Vatermord* was cut short by flaming rows with such Expressionistic
actors as Heinrich George: 'Brecht', said Bronnen, 'ruthlessly chopped
any word ejaculated to purely expressive effect'. Not long after, he
violently if privately accused 'all that crowd of Werfels, Unruhs,
Zuckmayers' (in the collected edition the names are tactfully omitted) of
being not merely untalented but feeble and corrupt – this of course being
in Carl Zuckmayer's early Expressionist period. Repeatedly over the
years he ridiculed what he termed 'O-Mensch Dramatik', the drama of
'O Man!', a favourite cry of many Expressionist poets. He attacked the
editor of *Der Sturm*, the pioneering Expressionist journal, who had
complained of his unacknowledged borrowings from Rimbaud in *In the
Jungle of Cities*. All this in the most aggressive language.

And yet there were aspects of Expressionism which were congenial to
him. He had, for instance, a high regard for the plays of Georg Kaiser,
which he respected not only for their structural technique but also for
their appeal to the spectator's intelligence rather than his emotions. He
became a personal friend of Alfred Döblin, though this was after
Döblin's Expressionist period and before his conversion to Catholicism,
following which his relations with Brecht became more distant. From
1921 to 1923 he formed a working alliance with Arnolt Bronnen,
maintaining throughout his life the Bertolt with a 't' and the writing
without capital letters which he had then adopted. Though he normally
treated any kind of mysticism, or even mystery as suspect, he more than
once put Kafka in a special category, calling him 'a truly serious
phenomenon', a genuine epic writer to be compared with no other
contemporary apart from Wedekind, even in due course a practitioner of

'Alienation'. He actually seems to have read Kafka (which was not always the case with his more sweeping judgements) and the experience surely underlies that extraordinary short story 'Gaumer and Irk'. This is thought to date from the later 1930s, the very time when Brecht as a good communist should have been adhering most closely to Realism.

Moreover all three of Brecht's first plays are in some measure touched with Expressionism. In *Baal*, for all its consciously anti-Expressionist features, the theme owes something to the story of Rimbaud and Verlaine, the episodic structure recalls that of *Woyzeck* and late Strindberg, while the title echoes 'Der schwarze Baal', a short story by the Expressionist Paul Zech, who was later to write a not dissimilar Rimbaud play which was staged by Erwin Piscator. Likewise Baal's song 'The Drowned Girl' strikingly resembles not only Rimbaud but Georg Heym's Ophelia poem 'Die Tote im Wasser' (The Dead Girl in the Water) – Heym being, of all German poets, the most comparable with the early Brecht, even though Münsterer says that Brecht had yet to read him. *Drums in the Night* derived its Expressionist aspects from the hero's great ranting speeches, along with the quasi-symbolic use of the moon in the background and the 'Ride of the Valkyries', as Brecht termed the wild pursuit in Act 3, itself somewhat reminiscent of Kaiser's *Hölle Weg Erde* (Hell Road Earth) – another of the plays in *Der dramatische Wille*. All this was underlined by Otto Falckenberg's Munich production, with its angular sets by Otto Reigbert, one of the best-known Expressionist designers; also by the grotesque attitudes of the actors and, in the Berlin version, Alexander Granach's declamatory delivery. Thereafter the first version of *In the Jungle* (1923) was not only larded with quotations from Rimbaud but bore colour indications for each scene such as 'Wood, low trees with faded brown foliage. Whiteish mist' or again 'Garga's attic: yellow wallpaper, colour wash. The evening flowing down the panes like dishwater'. Or an even more Expressionist description: 'Night. Fleeting cry from down below. The wood partition, as it were, shaking. A ship'. Thirty years later Brecht wrote that he was really thinking of something he had himself seen in Jessner's Berlin Staatstheater in the winter of 1921/22 while working on this play. For *Othello*, with Fritz Kortner as the Moor, Leopold Jessner had 'created a peculiar dusty light on the stage by means of criss-crossing spotlights'. This explains the 'ivory faces' and the comment by Garga 'At last I'm beginning to see something when I half close my eyes in the chalky light'. Such a use of light is very different from the brilliant uniform lighting on which Brecht was to insist later, but to me it belongs to the atmosphere of the play.

All this is somewhat hidden from the modern audience, because it sees Brecht's three first plays in their definitive form. In *Baal* for instance the opening scene as we have it in the Collected Works – and, necessarily following this, in the Random House/Methuen editions – was actually written in the 1950s. As for the rest of the play, it was greatly shortened between 1918 and its first production in 1923, then transformed again for the version directed by Brecht himself for one of Moritz Seeler's 'Junge Bühne' Sunday productions in Berlin in 1926. Here the ambience became more technological – Baal lives in a garage, not in the classic poet's garret, and the dialogue is shorter, drier and with more reference to the industrialisation of the landscape. This text had however not been used since that time till we made it the basis for the BBC's 1982 television production with David Bowie in the lead; the standard text is basically that of 1922. *Drums in the Night* in due course became politically and artistically unacceptable to Brecht, who for a time in the later 1920s hoped to overhaul it for a production by Piscator with the sociologist Fritz Sternberg as his adviser. But nothing was finally done till it appeared in the first collected edition of the 1950s, when Kragler's great tirades were largely trimmed and the two acts (to my mind most unconvincingly) reworked so as to introduce a counterweight to what Brecht saw as his own negative and cynical dismissal of the working class. *In the Jungle*, like *Baal*, was rewritten in the days of *Die neue Sachlichkeit*, but this time the new version at once supplanted the old. The Rimbaud quotations were cut down and the directions about colour and light disappeared for good, to be replaced by a spuriously matter-of-fact chronological exactness: 'Private office of C. Shlink. On 20 October 1915, one o'clock in the afternoon', and so on throughout.

All this can be seen as a further reaction against Expressionism. And that is how critics judged Brecht's contribution at the time. Julius Bab, for instance, welcomed the realism of the first two acts of *Drums in the Night*, while even Alfred Kerr, normally Brecht's severest critic (though one who like Brecht was driven into exile by the Nazis in 1933), found it 'undoubtedly not so bad as most Expressionist dramas, though undoubtedly not so good as the best of the genre (what's more, not "Expressionist-Expressionist" but school of Georg Kaiser)'. Like his chief rival Herbert Jhering, Kerr drew comparisons between Brecht and Ernst Toller, a writer 'ten times further advanced in Expressionism'. To him the latter was vastly to be preferred, while to Jhering Toller, along with Werfel, wore this mode 'like a fashionable garment to cloak their outdated sensibilities'. Brecht in short made his appearance on the German stage at the very moment when everything in the arts was changing, with the financial stabilisation of 1923 as an additional inducement for it to do so. Alert critics, who were already looking for something new, harder and more realistic, saw signs of this not only in such now neglected playwrights as Bronnen, Hans Henny Jahn and the Austrian Czokor but in the 24-year-old Brecht and his two chosen collaborators, the director Erich Engel and the designer Caspar Neher. Jhering clearly judged these to be the successors to Expressionism, and in this conviction he gave Brecht the Kleist Prize for new writing in 1922. He saw the actual turning point as being in 1924, with Brecht's own production in Munich of Marlowe's *Edward II* as adapted by Lion Feuchtwanger and himself. But at the same time something had gone, and it is interesting to read the same critic's view of the revised *In the Jungle of the Cities*. For there he laments the loss of colour and atmosphere due to its transposition into what he calls 'die kühlere Luft des sachlichen Kampfes', 'the cooler air of the objective struggle', that was to be fought out between 1925 and the next great social crisis in 1929.

* * *

Brecht has become so classic an example of a committed writer – known as such to thousands of young people who have never heard of Toller or Becher or Friedrich Wolf – that it is easy to forget quite how unpolitical he was in those early years. True enough he was full of fighting spirit, but he fought mainly in the literary ring and on behalf of his own works. That distinctive aggressivity which we have already seen persists recognisably enough into 1928; yet even in *The Threepenny Opera* the hatred of the bourgeoisie which he so pungently expresses is the hatred felt by an artist, an intellectual, ultimately by somebody from a bourgeois background. However hard his interpreters have tried to argue the contrary, it remains difficult to believe that his critique in that work is based on any serious political or economic analysis. And certainly that is what the Communist Party critics found at the time.

In February 1919, which is when Toller returned to Munich in order to join up with Kurt Eisner, the republican leader there, Brecht served on a Soldiers' Council in Augsburg, his home town. He is supposed to have sheltered one of the local revolutionaries, Lily Prien; he worked for Wendelin Thomas on the Augsburg Socialist paper, the *Volkswille* – Thomas later became a Communist Deputy – and certainly he differed from his friend Müllereisert and (it is said) some of his own family, who at the time of the Soviet Republic supported the Whites. But we should be careful not to take his political involvement at that time too seriously. 'We all suffered from a lack of political convictions', he wrote of the Soldiers' Council later, 'and I in particular from my lack of any capacity for enthusiasm ... soon afterwards I was discharged'. Clearly he was none too proud of the experience. It was in the first months of that year that he wrote the now vanished original version of *Drums in the Night* under the title *Spartakus*. And nobody, least of all himself, has any great respect for the political significance of that work. At least in the versions which we now have, the revolution taking place in the streets is little more than a suitably topical background for the *Heimkehrerdrama* – the then almost hackneyed dramatic theme of the returned soldier – which is the real essence of the play. There is even some difficulty in telling whether it is really the Spartacus Rising or the revolution of November 1918, for until the appearance of the twenty-volume Collected Works in 1967 there was some inconsistency between the attack on the newspaper offices, which is a historic incident of *January* 1919, and the stage direction (now cut) specifying an '*autumn* night'.

A similar uncertainty applies to 'The Legend of the Dead Soldier' which the publican sings in the same play, where Brecht originally appeared to think that the First World War had gone on till the spring of 1919: 'And when the war had reached its fifth spring ...' – something that again was amended in 1967 to read 'And when the war had reached its fourth spring ...' Not only the critics but Brecht himself (when discussing it with Piscator) came to treat this play as being concerned exclusively with the Revolution of 1918, and the historical ambiguity thus implied has survived the changes made to the last two acts. Notably by their references to an unseen revolutionary nephew of the landlord's – a worker at the Siemens factory – these are meant to introduce a 'proletarian' element to offset the soldier's 'contemptible' decision to turn his back on the revolution and finally go off to bed with his rediscovered fiancée. In my view they harm the play, and it is worth noting that Brecht himself never saw them tested in a production.

Partly on account of his stint with the Soldiers' Council – the German revolution's form of Soviet – and partly because of his contributions to the Independent (or Left) Socialist Party's local paper a number of commentators have assumed that Brecht was one of that party's active, even revolutionary members. I must say I doubt this. For surely no true revolutionary comrade of Toller's in 1920 could have criticised him as harshly as did Brecht in writing of *Die Wandlung* without referring to the playwright's actual situation as a political prisoner in a Bavarian gaol. As for the 'Song of the soldier of the red army' (*Poems*, pp. 22–23), long suppressed by Brecht's own choice, I just don't believe that its subject was only the red forces in Bavaria (which Toller at one time commanded), as Elisabeth Hauptmann used to claim. The question on which this argument hangs – was it red with a large or a small R? – strikes me as beside the point: I simply cannot see Brecht romanticising his fellow-Germans in this way. I think it deals rather with a Red Army of Brecht's imagination, made up of adventurers somewhat like Baal and springing from the poet's extremely hazy ideas about what was then taking place in Russia and possibly Hungary too – an army just as mythical as the 'big red bear' of his 'Lied vom Hauch', the Song of Breath. I don't mean this as a criticism of the poem itself, which is marvellous.

Mythology alleges too that Brecht was put on a Nazi black list at the time of Hitler's Beer-cellar Putsch in 1923. This would suggest that he must have been a serious opponent of that movement, but I have never seen it substantiated. Both of our first-hand sources as to his attitude at the time agree that he then took the Nazis rather lightly. Thus Bronnen tells us that he and Brecht went to hear Hitler make a speech at the Zirkus Krone; after which they spent the evening imagining alternative ways of staging such an event. As for Bernhard Reich, he says that Brecht's chief worry during the putsch was that it would interfere with the rehearsals of *Edward II*. To Brecht, Hitler seemed a much less serious threat than he did to Feuchtwanger, who is said to have concluded then and there that he would have to leave Bavaria. It is certainly worth noting that up to about 1927–28 nobody spoke of Brecht as a man of the left, let alone a revolutionary. He may have had revolutionary principles, but his early diaries show him adopting a very sceptical attitude to a lecture on the new Russia by Alfons Goldschmidt, subsequently one of Piscator's regular political consultants, while a note of 1926 suggests that 'the mob on the left is all right as long as it fights; but once it has won it will have to be replaced'.

'Unlike many of my comrades in the present struggle', says a fragmentary essay from his Scandinavian years, 'I arrived at my Marxist point of view as it were by a cold route'. There is a lot of truth in this. Elisabeth Hauptmann has told us how he started reading Marx in 1926 after finding it necessary to study a bit of economics in order to write his (eventually abandoned) play *Joe P. Fleischhacker from Chicago*, whose story is set in the speculative wheat market of that city. His work with Piscator, his involvement with the latter's documentary plays and his friendship with Fritz Sternberg all stimulated him to take his researches considerably further, finding that they offered him a key to the kind of social dramaturgy that governs the production of contemporary events. But it was not till 1929, in other words after *The Threepenny Opera*, that he became genuinely committed on an emotional plane. Sternberg in his small book on Brecht thinks it was the reaction of the Berlin (Socialist-directed) police to the May Day demonstrations of that year that finally swung Brecht's sympathies in the direction of the Communist Party, and this could well be right. He himself said in the fragment quoted at the beginning of this paragraph: 'Right, I thought (I'm crudely lumping a number of different thoughts together), in that case I can open my heart to pity. You see, I had to have some kind of reinsurance to vouch for my pity, I may have been afraid that pity without prospects can destroy a man without reason'.

At all events it was 1929, the year of the Wall Street crash and of Stresemann's death, that marked this pivotal point for Brecht, and with it he became not just a political writer, but a deviser of new forms of committed art and an exceptionally consistent believer in the primacy of politics. This led him to adopt a much more extreme position than Hasenclever, Rubiner, Toller or the great majority of the most activist Expressionists; and he reached it by a route almost diametrically opposed to theirs. For in their case it was the logic (or illogicality) of Expressionism that impelled them towards an all-inclusive emotional absorption in politics or pacifism: towards *Der politische Dichter* (The Political Poet) or *Tag des Proletariats* (Day of the Proletariat), to cite characteristic titles respectively by Hasenclever and by Toller. But Brecht's was the opposite: as he moved away from Expressionism he began learning about the social mechanism in a quite cold and *sachlich*, objective way. And at the same time as he did this some other equally genuine Expressionists like Johst and Gottfried Benn were directing their metaphysical, Nietzschean, aristocratic or *völkisch*, earthily racist convictions towards National Socialism. That Johst, the author of *Der Einsame*, should have gone on to write *Schlageter* – the play that contains the famous phrase so often misattributed to Goering: 'When I hear culture I take the safety catch off my Browning' – becoming first the leading Nazi dramatist then the president of the Reichsschrifttums-kammer, or Reich Writers' Chamber, while his critic Brecht became one of their principal enemies: that, in the most literal sense, is what we can call poetic justice.

* * *

It was developments like these that forced many anti-Nazi intellectuals to reconsider Expressionism after 1933. The question was whether the Nazi views of such former Expressionists as Benn and Johst, Kurt Heynicke and Emil Nolde were not ultimately due to the Expressionist ideology itself. A debate ensued which rested on some doubtful enough assumptions: above all on the supposition that the Nazis were likely to welcome Expressionism as a valid part of the national cultural heritage, their *Kulturerbe*; but also on the solidly traditionalist aesthetic preferences of Lukács. It was Lukács who launched the operation in 1934, following an open letter attacking Benn by Klaus Mann, to which Benn publicly replied. The main debate however took place in 1937–38 in *Das Wort*, with Alfred Kurella taking the lead against Expressionism and the philosopher Ernst Bloch prominent in its defence. A dozen other writers took part on one side or the other, and finally the honours were about even, with the supporters of Expressionism winning the intellectual argument while its detractors gained the political decision. In other words they refused to withdraw, and this determined the attitude of all those who followed the Moscow line in cultural affairs. The result was that Expressionism was effectively banished from the area covered by official Socialist Realism. Its counterpart Revolutionary Romanticism had been allowed gradually to slide from official favour since the two formulae were jointly sanctioned at the Soviet Writers' Congress of 1934.

Brecht's position in these debates was peculiar. Without being a Communist Party member, he nominally edited *Das Wort* with Feuchtwanger and the novelist Willi Bredel, a former political prisoner of the Nazis who had escaped to Moscow, then fought in Spain. None of the three in fact seems to have had much influence on the paper's policy, which was decided from day to day by the former actor Fritz Erpenbeck virtually without their being consulted, as Brecht's correspondence was in due course (see p. 204f.) to make plain. To anyone like Brecht the brand of Socialist Realism proclaimed under Zhdanov's auspices in 1934 must have been unbearable: though he never overtly rejected it, his remarks on the theatre of Stanislavsky denied it by implication, while in 1936 his own announcement of the 'alienation effect' represents a degree of heresy that can hardly have been unconscious. Meanwhile those of the German exiles who followed the Moscow reviews – and this included many non-Communists in both hemispheres – were being given the doctrine according to Lukács, which was put across concertedly by Becher as editor of *Internationale Literatur* and by Erpenbeck in the office of *Das Wort*.

It was a situation which certainly moved Brecht to write a number of essays, of which 'The Popular and the Realistic' and 'Breadth and Multiplicity of Realism' (see pp. 107 and 114 respectively of *Brecht on Theatre*) are probably the best known. Altogether they occupy no fewer than ninety pages in the second volume of *Schriften zur Kunst und Literatur* in the 1967 German Collected Works, where they are grouped under the general heading 'Formalism and Realism'; to say nothing of the numerous references to the same theme in the *Journals*. The main aim was to criticise Lukács's narrow insistence on particular models derived from (mainly nineteenth-century) bourgeois realism, for instance Balzac, Gorki and Thomas Mann. But they make it clear at the same time that Brecht had grown much more tolerant towards Expressionism, so that he could stand up not only for Kaiser and Sternheim and for Franz Marc's blue horses but also for the plays of Toller, in which he found important elements of realism, and of Reinhard Goering. He admitted that they had been among his sources: 'Quite honestly I find it easier to learn in places where similar tasks have been confronted. To put it bluntly, eyeball to eyeball with death, it's harder for me to learn from Tolstoy and Balzac'.

So he could say that although he himself was against the excesses of Expressionism he now looked back at that movement as a kind of liberation. 'Today many of us view the wholesale cutting-down of Expressionism with misgiving, being afraid this means that acts of liberation are to be suppressed as such'.[1] Such a change of attitude demands to be explained, and I am not sure that Brecht's mistrust of Socialist Realism in general and the role of Lukács in particular as *Kunstrichter*, or arbiter of the arts, constitutes an adequate motive. An even more interesting problem arises from the fact that *none* of these writings appeared at the time either in *Das Wort* or anywhere else. Just one was ultimately published in the *Versuche* booklets not long before Brecht died. All the rest, including presumably the typescript which I saw him remove from a chest of his papers forwarded from Stockholm, were published for the first time in 1967. 'Eyeball to eyeball with death . . .': there is a contradiction here that would repay detailed investigation.

In the 1950s, following Brecht's return to settle in the Soviet sector of Berlin, the relationship of Expressionism to Socialist Realism became more complicated. Formalism of course was frowned on quite as severely as in Moscow; but the effects of Expressionism in its native country were too profound to be easily got rid of, whether by the Nazis or by the Stalinists. Much the same thing as occurred in Federal Germany took place in a slightly different form in the Democratic Republic, not least because the Asso or Association of Revolutionary Artists, founded in 1928 as a counterpart to the Proletarian-Revolutionary Writers, was rooted in the work of Otto Dix, George Grosz and Käthe Kollwitz – all of whom were more or less connected with Expressionism at some point. As a result the paintings of Otto Nagel and the Grundigs and the critical writings of Wolfgang Hütt (like those of Ernst Fischer in Austria) stood against any attempts to impose cast-iron one-hundred-per-cent Soviet Socialist Realism; and the same thing is true of Brecht's committed theatre. Moreover Lukács's fall from grace in the later 1950s made it easier to get away from that nineteenth-century Realist tradition which had become so associated with his views. Other types of *Kulturpolitiker*, or culture politicos, came along like Kurella, who were prepared to support forms arising out of *Neue Sachlichkeit* and agit-prop, such as the montage and reportage that Lukács had so disliked. The reputation of the 1920s once again rose, and it is by no means irrelevant that from 1954 to 1958 the new Ministry of Culture had a former Expressionist at its head.

Becher is a fascinating figure, and it is difficult not to sense a strong contrast between him and Brecht, the two great East German poets of the 1950s. Personally I find the rhapsodic poems of Becher's Expressionist period quite ridiculous, and I think I share enough of Brecht's critical views to be sure that left to himself he would have judged them much the same way. He never discussed them in print, but he can hardly have overlooked all those ejaculations of 'O Man!!!', often with several exclamation marks, like that. Thereafter Becher evolved towards Communism along lines which were more like those followed by Louis Aragon than Brecht's increasing austerity of style. Becher was romantic, sport-loving, vain, lacking irony and all sense of the ridiculous. He joined the Proletarian-Revolutionary Writers, Brecht not; he edited *Internationale Literatur*, Brecht never really edited *Das Wort*; he worked for the Soviet authorities in the Second World War, Brecht for no authority but what he imposed on himself; he returned with the occupying army, Brecht slowly followed on. Both men were communists, but up to that point their roads had been pretty far apart even though in Munich they may have known one another well: indeed until 1951 there is no mention at all of Becher in Brecht's critical writings. Becher for his part thought of himself more in relation to Gottfried Benn: they were the two Expressionist poets whose political divergence had been the most extreme, and they were also the two who had survived. For him there were only two B's; the third was another kettle of fish.

Here too is a subject that needs to be explored. For in the German Democratic Republic of the 1950s Brecht and Becher found themselves cooperating in a worthwhile cause, the re-establishment of German culture. Thus Becher had rescued the novelist Hans Fallada and encouraged him to write his fine novel *Jeder stirbt für sich allein* on the basis of some Gestapo records, while Brecht took issue with the idea of Wilhelm Girnus who wished to reject Barlach's sculptures as being too formalist and 'negative', i.e. not optimistic. Again, he sharply attacked the officials of those 'Cultural Commissions' which preceded the establishment of the Ministry of Culture, hoping to check their incompetences by means of the Academy of Arts of which both Becher and he were members. All the same I doubt if the two men were often wholly of one mind. Becher adopted the role of poet laureate: national anthem, biography of Walter Ulbricht, songs for the Communist youth movement, ghastly sentimental poems about the Soviet Union and the Red Army: 'Stars of unending glowing', 'Sterne unendlichen Glühens' – how strange that he should have had to turn back to the old Expressionist vocabulary for that kind of thing. And still the use of the word *Mensch*, 'Man!' There were fewer compromises on Brecht's side: the tedious poem 'Erziehung der Hirse' (literally: 'The Training of Millet'), supporting Lysenko's views of agriculture and including that reference to Stalin which seems (as we shall see later) to have unhinged Hannah Arendt; a fairly non-committal reaction to Stalin's death; the anti-West German cantata called the *Herrnburger Bericht* (*Report from Herrnburg*) which was effectively concealed in the Collected Works; also a splendidly ambiguous message for some celebration or other in connection with President Pieck:

> If Wilhelm Pieck were not the president of the most progressive part of Germany he would have to become it forthwith.

Even then he was not straying far from his true convictions. I only wonder just how far he defied them in 1955 when E.F. Burian, having originally been nominated as director, dropped out and Brecht found himself having to direct the Berliner Ensemble in an indifferent play by his Minister called *Winterschlacht*.

'The Poet avoids shining harmonies . . .' so starts one of Becher's most frequently cited Expressionist poems. Around 1954 Brecht insinuated it in the new version of scene 1 of *Baal* which is now part of the standard text of the play. This is the episode where Baal attends a reception given by some very bourgeois, indeed Augsbourgeois patrons of the arts, which he breaks up in scandalous fashion. In the first, 1918 version a young man tries to counter Baal's taste in poetry by reading unspecified verses by the Expressionist (August) Stramm, Novotny (?) and A. Skram, the last being either a misreading of the manuscript or an early twentieth-century Scandinavian writer. In the 1922 published version these rather baffling references are cut. But somewhere between its republication by Suhrkamp in 1953 and the East German edition of 1955 Brecht, abetted by Elisabeth Hauptmann and his early friend H.F.S. Bachmair, substituted this 1916 composition of Becher's along with Heym's 'Der Baum', though without naming the two poets; which implies these to have been allusions for the initiated only. But allusions to what? Heym, whose poem is far from being what Kerr called 'Expressionist-Expressionist', is the Expressionist most frequently compared with the young Brecht. And Becher? Bachmair, so Elisabeth Hauptmann told me, was not sorry to have a dig at him; and if she connived at this, then so certainly did Brecht.

If so it raises all sorts of questions, even quite mundane ones. How were the rights agreed? What method did Brecht use to explain his cannibalisation of the poem to Becher, and how did the latter react? It is clear that the Minister must have had some difficulty in understanding the mentality of his fellow-Academician, since in his diary Becher explains the famous image of the cloud in the poem 'Recollecting Marie A.' by speaking of 'a cloud formation, in whose wispy evanescence the loved visage too remains unforgettable', thereby wholly missing the point. Was Brecht relying on the same solemn naivety in order to take the piss? Or was there some intention, conscious or not, to turn *Baal* into a counter-play not merely to the Expressionism of Johst but also in some degree to that of Becher: to that of the Right *and* that of the Left? It is fascinating to read Becher's reminiscences of the 1950s about his Expressionist days: he laments his excesses of language; he criticises his novel *Erde* and other follies of the Expressionist period; yet 'There is also a lesson to be learned from us, that Man needs to be wholly gripped by something'. This is exactly what was lacking in Brecht's case, though not in Johst's: the old 'lack of any capacity for enthusiasm' which he may have been emphasising once more by contrasting his own early poetry with an early poem by the Minister on whom his theatre depended.

In any case here we have two very different sorts of communist poet. And that difference is one which could be followed further. What about Neruda for example: is he to be classed with Brecht or with Becher? And Aragon: why did he always seem so reserved about Brecht's work while greatly admiring that of Becher, who had much the same attitude as himself not only to words but to his country and to his wife? Which side are future generations going to come down on? My own view is that an enthusiastic poet is very likely to be a feeble one, and indeed this, despite the cases of Blake and Shelley, is a very English opinion. Hence the fact that such American neo-Whitmanites as Ginsberg and Corso have had so little success with our critics and with most of our poets aside from the very young: for however much we may have sympathised with their stance their rhetoric has never been convincing. This is where Brecht's example could be so useful to us. It is all very well for the best English poetry today to be ironical, precise, intelligent and craftsmanlike; so long as it lacks vitality and doesn't say much it will ultimately bore people as it already bores the non-English. Undoubtedly Brecht should not be followed in everything he did. But his example could reinforce those of Kipling and Auden and the Australian ballad-writers and give strength rather than emotional verbiage to such stricter and less self-assertive forms.

7

Brecht and Piscator

At first glance you could hardly have two more contrasting types. On the one hand there stands the actor turned director, would-be impresario, elegant, distinguished, even lordly; on the other the poet turned playwright, would-be philosopher, awkward, unkempt, deflating even himself. Look at their photographs, or their handwriting for that matter, and you would hardly expect them to coincide at a single point, let alone become friends and allies. Yet they both attended the same theatre seminar at Munich University, they both became Other Ranks in the imperial army, they both turned to Communism in postwar Berlin, they both followed a Marxist approach to the theatre, they both put the collective above the individual artistic personality, they both fell foul of official party aesthetics and distrusted the Stanislavsky method, they both were in the United States during the Second World War and returned to work in Berlin, whose theatre still reflects the impact of their ideas. You can even identify a sizeable core of actors and a repertoire of plays which met both men's demands and tastes, from *Troilus and Cressida* to *The Good Soldier Švejk*. Musically and visually they were conditioned by a common group of friends: Kurt Weill, Hanns Eisler, John Heartfield, George Grosz. It is not just a matter of establishing how far they learnt from one another, though Brecht (the younger man) always acknowledged Piscator's influence; more that they shared areas of common ground which most other theatre people avoided. And so their paths inevitably crossed and recrossed, time and again.

In all kinds of ways they interlock. For instance, Piscator stages *Saint Joan* with Luise Rainer in Washington in 1940, then chooses *The Chalk Circle* by Brecht's old friend Klabund for the second production of his New York Studio Theatre in March 1941. Brecht (who had written his own first St Joan play in 1930–31) is simultaneously preoccupied with these same two themes, which lead him on arrival in America to write a second St Joan play *The Visions of Simone Machard*, then in 1944 to make his own new version of *The Chalk Circle* which he writes for – Luise

Rainer. The relationship is almost incestuous, in a way that largely excludes other leading directors and dramatists of the German Left: Friedrich Wolf, for instance, or Gustav von Wangenheim or the Hungarian Julius Hay. Over a sector of the globe from the Volga to Los Angeles, Brecht's and Piscator's plans overlap; their movements intersect; their desire to join forces flickers up; from time to time a working alliance is apparently proclaimed. And yet in fact they scarcely ever worked together after 1928, and when they did, it went wrong.

Brecht would send Piscator his new plays, but he became increasingly chary of letting his friend have any hand in their direction. Piscator in turn never showed any real enthusiasm either for the plays themselves or for the theoretical principles on which they were supposedly based; indeed it was not till after Brecht's death that he first directed a Brecht play. Similarly with their physical movements: you find Brecht in 1935 paying his first visit to the United States and telling Piscator that he really ought to come over; then Piscator in 1939 doing exactly the same to Brecht; but once they are both in America they remain 2000 miles apart. The same after Brecht's return to Europe in 1947: he does all he can to get Piscator to follow, but in the end the one goes to East Germany and the other to West. They are bound together almost like the two little figures in a weather-house: stuck to the same footing and reacting equally sensitively to the climate. And each withdraws into his box as the other comes out.

*   *   *

Once again there was a crucial age difference. Piscator, unlike Brecht, went right through the First World War, much of which he spent as a front-line signaller in Flanders while Brecht remained at home. This experience determined Piscator's political allegiance: he detested militarism and welcomed the Russian Revolution which closed down one end of the war, then on leaving the army became a founder member of the German Communist Party. Brecht meanwhile was embarking on his 'cold route', which had not yet reached even as far as the first burgeonings of Marxism by the time of his move to Berlin in 1924. In that year he was just a very junior assistant at the Deutsches Theater, whereas Piscator was a recognised director with a new-style production at the Volksbühne to his credit, as well as a pioneering Communist pageant that for the first time made dramatic use of film. Admittedly Herbert Jhering, the critic who was most aware of the younger man's promise, could class them together as part of a single new trend, the overcoming of theatrical Expressionism, notably by their respective treatments of Marlowe's *Edward II* and Schiller's *Die Räuber*. But whether either of them yet felt any affinity with the other is doubtful. What we do know is that around 1925 Brecht wrote a satirical poem called 'The Theatre Communist' which ended with the lines

> For 3000 marks a month
> He is prepared
> To put on the misery of the masses
> For 100 marks a day
> He displays
> The injustice of the world.[1]

It seems not impossible that this was in fact directed against Oskar Kanehl, the Communist dramaturg of the Lessing-Theater in Berlin, who was then publicly campaigning against the plays of Brecht's friend Arnolt Bronnen (soon to become a Nazi). According to Elisabeth Hauptmann it was not meant to apply to Piscator, though Piscator himself thought it was.

In any case within a few years of this piece of tactlessness the two men were allies, and in 1927 Brecht, while still some way from any commitment to Communism, became part of the first Piscator company's 'dramaturgical collective'. This was a group of about a dozen writers who in accordance with Piscator's concept of teamwork were to overhaul and adapt all the new company's plays. At that time Piscator felt that every existing playwright was more or less inadequate to the tasks of the new epic, political, confrontational, documentary theatre which he was leading, so that a firm hand was needed to get its texts into shape. Among a variegated team that included the Expressionist Alfred Wolfenstein and the anarchist Erich Mühsam, Brecht alone truly agreed with Piscator's aims and the principle of collective work; indeed his statement in the opening programme bore on just this point. As a result he was one of the only members of the collective who got on with that work without chafing, the others being Piscator's chief dramaturg Felix Gasbarra, who had been found for him by the Communist Party, and the Viennese journalist Leo Lania – known later to Anglophones as editor of an American news magazine called *United Nations World*.

What Brecht actually did in that epoch-making first season at the Theater am Nollendorfplatz was a certain amount of revision of Alexei Tolstoy's *Rasputin* and Lania's own *Konjunktur*, supposedly coping with the last-minute objections of the Russians and the party officials to the latter; but his main work was on the dramatisation of Hašek's *Švejk*.

Here unfortunately accounts differ as to the division of responsibility. Brecht refers more than once to it as if all the writing had been done by him; however, he also talks as if he and Piscator ran the Piscator companies as equal partners, which was certainly not the case. Piscator on the other hand treats the adaptation exclusively as his own. The only surviving scripts (unless Piscator's pre-1936 papers turn up in Moscow) seem to be those in the Brecht Archive, which bear the names 'Brecht, Piscator, Gasbarra, George Grosz' on the cover, in that order and in Brecht's hand, though the typing of the text is not his and bears no mark of his revisions. Meanwhile of course the official adaptors of Hašek's novel remained Max Brod and Hans Reimann, who had the sole rights and apparently got their percentage through thick and thin.

Like *Something Fresh* (the Wodehouse novel to which allusion was made earlier) *Švejk* is a book that forms a bond between those who know and love it, and it was to run like a leitmotiv through the Brecht–Piscator relationship for the rest of its life. From the outset Piscator's production of the stage version in the first quarter of 1928 was not only influential for Brecht's ideas of staging and design, and incidentally for his high opinion of George Grosz as an artist, but also taught him how radically the development of stage machinery and projections could transform the structural possibilities open to the 'epic' playwright. He got positive benefits from Lania's *Konjunktur* too, that rather disastrous play about the foreign exploitation of Albania's oil resources which at least tried to tackle the same problem as had bedevilled his own *Joe Fleischhacker* project: that of establishing a dramatic form for the discussion of complex economic relationships. Not only did he work on its script, but later in London he and Lania tried to develop it into a more Brechtian, didactic work to be called *The Oilfield*, of which a splendid final chorus and other fragments remain. And yet for all the similarity of his concerns he never had any play performed by the Piscator companies, whether in his own time as a dramaturg or in their later, less fashionable phase. *Joe Fleischhacker*, or *Weizen* as it was also called after its theme, the Chicago 'wheat pit', was on the first company's list of possibles, but it was never finished; nor were *The Breadshop* or *Aus Nichts wird Nichts* (*Nothing Comes from Nothing*), both of which Piscator might have considered too. There were merely some inconclusive discussions about a revamped version of *Drums in the Night* and a possible adaptation of *Julius Caesar*. For though Brecht at this time seems to have found it easy enough to finish his operas with Weill and to write the first of the didactic *Lehrstücke* which followed, he never achieved that epic analysis of modern capitalism for which he was striving till he wrote *Saint Joan of the Stockyards*, a play which was completed too late for Piscator to perform – or, as it turned out, for anyone else.

In the crisis year of 1929, when his first company had gone bankrupt, Piscator made a speech summing up his achievements to date. Instead of private lives, he said, he had dealt with general issues, instead of luck with causes. 'Reason was put on a par with Emotion, while sensuality was replaced by didacticism and fantasy by documentary reality'.[1] Anyone who knows Brecht's *Mahagonny* notes will see how close these antitheses come to the table which he drew up there to show contrasting aspects of the 'epic' and 'Aristotelian' theatres. On fundamentals the two men agreed, and if Piscator still saw no reason to stage Brecht's plays, while Brecht in turn was critical of the extravagances which had ruined the first company, Brecht was still prepared to accept its political line (which he would allow Gasbarra to dictate to him, even while rejecting Gasbarra's literary judgements). What stopped him from sticking with Piscator at this juncture – that is to say, following him into limbo for a year, then on to the second and third companies – was the improbable success of *The Threepenny Opera*, which effectively tied him to the rival regime at the Theater am Schiffbauerdamm. Brecht treated this as 'my' theatre, at least in his later writings, and in the course of his work there was able to build up what amounted to a loosely organised company of his own choice, partly overlapping with Piscator's. Thus Erich Engel, Caspar Neher, Peter Lorre, Oskar Homolka, Lotte Lenya, Carola Neher and Helene Weigel worked for Brecht; Hanns Eisler, Ernst Busch, Alexander Granach and Wolfgang Roth for both; Traugott Müller, Edmund Meisel, Lotte Loebinger, Erwin Kalser, Heinz Greif, Albert Venohr – and of course Lania and Gasbarra – purely for Piscator. Between them these people, a lot of whom later emigrated, were the cream of the German left-wing theatre, and after many vicissitudes their survivors were to play a crucial part in its revival after the Second World War.

With Brecht now risen well above dramaturg status, Piscator had meantime launched – and simultaneously torpedoed – his second company with a yet more extravagant production of a not very good play, Walter Mehring's *Der Kaufmann von Berlin* (The Merchant of Berlin) whose failure coincided almost exactly with that of Brecht's *Happy End*. After that Piscator was reduced to working as an employee of his own 'actors' collective' (from which the third company emerged) with very restricted means. Though the productions which followed got far less publicity than those of the first company – not least because they came too late to be illustrated and discussed in Piscator's classic book

The Political Theatre – Brecht held two of them to be among Piscator's best. These were Carl Credé's pro-abortion play *§218* – a travelling production which was a cross between a play and a public meeting, and included a gramophone recording of Brecht's and Eisler's 'Ballad of §218' – and Friedrich Wolf's *Tai Yang erwacht* (Tai Yang Wakes Up), a kind of *Gegenstück* or counter-play to Klabund's *The Chalk Circle*, which probably helped in the genesis of *The Good Person of Szechwan* and was given a highly original production, involving further elements of informality and audience participation which turned into something like a *Lehrstück*. At the same time Brecht saw that Piscator himself was no longer all that interested in the third company's work, after which (as Brecht put it to a Danish interviewer) 'he went gloomily off to Moscow to make films'. The Nazi takeover was then still nearly two years away.

* * *

Piscator's only film, on a Soviet script derived from Anna Seghers's *The Revolt of the Fishermen of Santa Barbara*, contains some fine shots and scenes, but it misses the simple, almost mythical grandeur of Seghers's Communist novella; moreover it abandons all Piscator's own principles of documentary precision in favour of a vague revolutionary romanticism such as he himself had criticised in *The Battleship Potemkin*. Released in 1934, it took the best part of three years to make, and its relevance to events in Germany, never very great at the best of times, became increasingly remote. It was thus a great contrast to Brecht's collaborative film *Kuhle Wampe*, which was made in 1931–32 and finished up as a truly original work, the only film ever properly to reflect his structural, dramatic and political ideas. Whether or not Piscator appreciated this, when Brecht came to Moscow for its première in 1932 he evidently saw him as a worthwhile ally, perhaps almost an equal. There they came to an agreement not to let their new plays – *Saint Joan of the Stockyards* and the *American Tragedy* adaptation which Piscator called *The Case of Clyde Griffiths* – be performed anywhere without consultation. Piscator prepared to supervise the translation of three of Brecht's plays by their mutual friend Sergei Tretiakov; and from now on they maintained touch.

Two things in particular seem to have brought them together at this point. First of all Piscator no longer had a monopoly of the political theatre, which Aufricht at the Theater am Schiffbauerdamm, Gustav von Wangenheim with his Truppe 1932 and such offshoots of the former Piscator companies as the Gruppe junger Schauspieler and the

Junge Volksbühne had now carved up between them, not to mention the spreading agitprop movement. Secondly the new arbiters of German Communist culture, led by Georg Lukács in the magazine *Die Linkskurve* (Left Wheel), had started to find fault with them both. The one, so the argument went, had depended too much on appealing to a bourgeois audience, and his documentary approach was too objective; while the other (whom the party had anyway only recently begun to take seriously) was criticised for making use of montage and non-Western techniques and for veering towards agitprop. By their formal innovations, it was felt, they had become truants from Europe's central realist tradition.

When Hitler came to power some months later, Piscator made Moscow his base, though he could no longer work in the theatre there (not having mastered the language). Instead he became head of MORT, the International League of Revolutionary Theatres, with the task of coordinating and encouraging the work of left-wing theatre groups throughout the world. In this capacity he commissioned Brecht and Eisler to write one or two songs, including their 'United Front Song' of 1934, then called a meeting of theatre directors in Moscow for the following spring to which he invited Brecht. Whether any formal conference ever took place is not yet clear, but beside Strasberg and Clurman, Cheryl Crawford, Joseph Losey and Edward Gordon Craig were all in Moscow around that time; Mei Lan-fang gave his now famous demonstration of Pekin opera acting; while Brecht learned of the Russian Formalist concept of the 'device of estrangement' or, in German terms, *Verfremdungseffekt*. As well as Tretiakov (whom he knew from Berlin) Brecht again met Eisenstein on this occasion and saw a number of productions including Okhlopkhov's versions of *The Start* and *Aristocrats* in the round and Michoels's *King Lear* at the Jewish Theatre (which Piscator had been lobbying to put on *Round Heads and Pointed Heads* with himself as director). There was a Moscow Brecht evening attended not only by Wilhelm Pieck and all the leading émigré literary and theatrical figures but also by Tretiakov and Semyon Kirsanov. According to Bernhard Reich, a lifelong friend of the Brechts who was then Piscator's deputy at MORT, there were two non-German members of the Comintern Executive there, the Latvian Vilis Knorin and the Hungarian Béla Kun.

Reich reports that his wife Asya Lacis (Walter Benjamin's great love, and herself a Latvian) took Brecht to see Knorin in his official flat, where the conversation lasted for two hours. Knorin, whose field was international affairs:

considered that the most important task for an anti-Fascist writer at that time
was to show how Fascism meant the threat of another world war ... It is
extremely likely that this conversation with Knorin convinced Brecht that he
must concentrate on portraying the impending war of conquest, so as to alert
us to it and condemn it.[1]

What ground Brecht covered with Piscator during the two months of his
visit is not exactly known, though there had been a *Švejk* film project for
which Piscator wanted him to write the script, while some fragmentary
notes in the Brecht Archive relate to a discussion about the various
Moscow productions which Brecht saw. Clearly they also talked about
setting up a German-language theatre in the USSR, though Brecht
wrote home to Helene Weigel to say that the chances of this were
'slender'. At the same time however Piscator was considering all kinds of
comprehensive plans for MORT, including the setting up of centres in
Prague, Paris and New York, the publication of a theoretical journal of
high quality from Zurich and the broadening of the organisation's appeal
to conform with the new Comintern policy of the Popular Front, as
announced by Dimitrov at the Seventh Congress that July. Among these
projects was one for the making of short anti-Nazi films, starting with
the story of a civil servant who had been murdered by the Nazis and the
ashes of his body delivered to his widow along with a bill for its
cremation. There seems every possibility that he discussed this notion
with Brecht, and if we connect up his plan with Knorin's reported views
we may well have found the origins not only of the 1936 'German War
Primer' poems (*Poems 1913–1956*, pp. 286–9) and the *Lenin Cantata*
composed by Eisler, but also of the short anti-Nazi sketches which
Brecht began writing when he came back from his American trip at the
end of the year. These were independent playlets calling for no elaborate
staging, which could be used in various selections and combinations by
the exiled theatre groups. In 1938 they were given the collective title
Fear and Misery of the Third Reich. (For their subsequent filming by
Pudovkin see p. 139.)

Five months after leaving Moscow Brecht was in New York to help
prepare the English-language production of *Mother* by Theatre Union,
one of the companies under the wing of MORT. The following March
the Group Theatre staged *The Case of Clyde Griffiths* there under
Strasberg's direction. Both plays fell flat, being regarded by the
American critics (and seemingly by the actors too) as hopelessly
schoolmasterly and schematic in their approach. Unlike Brecht, who
made himself much disliked by Theatre Union and got a bad name

throughout the American Left theatre as a result, Piscator stayed away. He was fully occupied in the USSR with his scheme for a German-language theatre, which he was now trying to realise at Engels in the German-speaking Volga Republic, a city of 60,000 inhabitants and two houses with drains, a high incidence of malaria and a German dialect dating back to the eighteenth century. He had begun planning a film to be made there with Julius Hay as scriptwriter, though he would apparently have preferred Brecht.[1] But optimistically he still hoped to get Brecht as the theatre's dramaturg, or at least as his house playwright along with Friedrich Wolf, while Reich would come as deputy to himself, going ahead to set the company up. Invitations and proposed terms of employment were sent to many of the left actors already referred to, including Carola Neher, Ernst Busch and Helene Weigel. Brecht turned down the dramaturg's job on financial grounds, but suggested that he and Weigel might come to inspect the living conditions.

By autumn 1936 all such plans were having to be reconsidered as the great Soviet purge got under way. Foreigners now were suspect; MORT was being closed down; the Engels scheme was soon abandoned; a whole succession of arrests began; and it seemed that the USSR was no longer a safe place for German Communists to work in. Piscator himself had left in July in connection with new plans to shift MORT's offices either to Prague or to Paris, where a big conference was to be organised during the 1937 International Exhibition. To Brecht, who wanted him to come and stay in Denmark, he wrote a depressed letter saying that 'a lot of people' were now advising him to stay in the West, and finishing up 'Write me, *old fellow* [these two words in English], what you think. There aren't that many friends'. On 3 October Reich wired him not to leave Paris, and a few days later he got an unsigned letter from Wilhelm Pieck the party secretary advising him not to come back. While many German Communists certainly condemned him for leaving (and for the rather grand style of life which he was thereafter to adopt), Brecht was more understanding. 'You know you can count on me, I think', he replied, 'and I'm counting on you. God knows there aren't all that many people'.[2] In practical terms this meant that Brecht now floated his own 'Diderot Society' scheme for the exchange of views that might otherwise have been published by MORT. Piscator for his part once again launched out on film projects, starting with a fresh version of *Švejk*, for whose rights he began negotiating with the Prague lawyer Dr Löwenbach that same November. He seems to have consulted a great many people about the possible implications of this, ranging from the Austrian embassy to Arthur Koestler, who was himself engaged on writing an updated *Švejk* novel which never saw the light. His main collaborator on the initial treatment was Lania. Henri Jeanson was engaged as the French scriptwriter. Brecht was only to be brought in once the backers and exhibitors had been convinced.

On being told of his plan in April 1937 Brecht briefly welcomed it and said that he would cooperate at any time. A fortnight later Piscator sent him an essay (about 'film length') for the proposed 'Diderot' correspondence and Brecht replied that 'Whatever happens you really must not do *Švejk* without me'. Then the treatment arrived, and struck Brecht as 'not bad', though in particular the opening 'needs to be more serious, not like an operetta. The staging of the war shouldn't be ridiculed, it has to be a terrible business which comes down suddenly on that calm and peaceable creature Švejk'. As for the latter, he must not just be 'an idiot, as in some barrack-square farce', but

> is really nothing less than the nightmare of all dictators, this 'common' man with his 'base' thoughts, his deaf ear for Higher Things, his inadequacy that subverts their marvellous schemes – a sacrificial victim with flaws.

Like all Piscator's Paris projects this one came to nothing, but at least it kept the lines of communication open. Thereupon Brecht sent him a First World War film story (presumably the one called *Die Judith von Saint Denis*) and proposed a film on the Spanish War character Potato Jones. Helene Weigel wrote to him about the possibility of her going to Spain, feeling that her 'hibernation has been going on too long'. Brecht himself visited Paris for the Anti-Fascist Writers' Congress, then for a production of *The Threepenny Opera* at the Théâtre de l'Etoile; which must have been galling for Piscator, since once again it was put on by Aufricht, who unlike him had managed to take over a Paris theatre; at any rate he was critical enough of the production to draft some long and interesting notes about it. As for Slatan Dudow's Paris productions of *Señora Carrar's Rifles* in 1937 and eight scenes from *Fear and Misery of the Third Reich* in 1938, we have no record of Piscator's reactions, if any. It is fairly clear however that Brecht had not offered him the chance of staging these new works, though he did send him the script of the second in the hope that he might take it to America with the German travelling company which he was (vainly) negotiating with Gilbert Miller to set up.

* * *

Once settled in New York, Piscator thought of the Brechts. 'Do you remember', asks a letter of 15 June 1939,

> how you cabled me in Moscow to come here at all costs, on account of the vast opportunities? And I didn't. Why are you imitating me?

Hanns Eisler had applied for a refugee's visa a year earlier, after spending six months in the US as a visitor. Brecht applied some time early in 1939, but must already have decided to do so by the previous November when he wrote *Galileo* specifically for American consumption. Piscator himself had arrived on the first day of the year, still hoping that Miller would stage the ambitious adaptation of *War and Peace* on which he had been working. When within a matter of weeks this was finally rejected, Piscator realised that his only chance of getting a visa was by having a teaching job. This was arranged in May when Alvin Johnson of the New School commissioned him to set up a Dramatic Workshop which would in effect act as its theatre department. From that point it was Piscator who was primarily instrumental in getting Brecht into the country, though there were also friends in California, led by Fritz Lang, who had independently started organising a fund to support the family once they arrived. For in addition to hiring Carl Zuckmayer to run a playwrights' course and Eisler to teach theatre music, Piscator now persuaded Johnson to engage Brecht as a 'Lecturer in Literature' as from May 1940, and this is what ultimately allowed the family to get their visas in Helsinki and escape via Russia in the spring of the following year. It all entailed a good deal of correspondence, in the course of which Brecht on his side showed both gratitude to his sponsors and optimism about his chances in the US. Thus, having already sent Piscator a copy of *Galileo*, he told him on 27 May that he would

> be bringing new plays, but above all an intense desire to work. i believe the u.s.a. to be among the few remaining countries where one can freely do literary work and submit plays like fear and misery of the third reich.[1]

Repeatedly he spoke of looking forward to their collaboration.

Only once he had landed in California in the summer of 1941 did he begin to discuss what he might teach:

> purely theoretical lectures would be much harder for me than seminar work, what's more i doubt if they would be of any immediate use to the students. i would far sooner work in the no-man's-land between dramatic construction and performance style, and try to establish one or two points of difference between playwright and director, director and actor, actor and thinking human

being etc. for instance we have the author being helpless in the theatre, the actor being helpless where dramaturgy is concerned, and both being helpless in the sphere of social effects.[1]

It was then the summer vacation, and his offer from the New School ran only up to the beginning of the next term. Whether or not it could be prolonged, Brecht was doubtful if he could afford life in New York (the proposed salary not being high), and Feuchtwanger for one was advising him to stay put in the Los Angeles area. There is no evidence that Piscator pressed him on this point, and thereafter the prospect of his visiting the East Coast became conditional on the production of his plays. Of these, Piscator had not thought *Galileo* suitable for an American audience; *Puntila* he may not even have read; he liked H.R. Hays's translation of *Mother Courage* when it was published, but we have no record of his reaction to the play itself. But *Fear and Misery of the Third Reich* (which Brecht suggested they might work on at the New School), *Arturo Ui* (written with a view to America) and *The Good Person of Szechwan* all now came under discussion.

The first of these had dropped out by the following spring, when it appeared that Max Reinhardt might stage it. The second was rapidly translated by Hays when Piscator and Eisler thought that they might get trade union backing for a production, presumably at the New School; however, the unions' verdict was that 'it is not advisable to produce it'.[2] The only serious proposition therefore was the third, which Piscator hoped to get produced by the Theatre Guild but planned to direct himself, if necessary with his own Dramatic Workshop. John Latouche, he reported, the writer of the patriotic progressive 'Ballad for Americans' and an admirer of Brecht's, was keen to translate it. About this prospect Brecht was cagey, thanks no doubt to a letter from Hays which warned him of the bad reception of the Dramatic Workshop's first productions and suggested that Piscator's misjudgements might wreck Brecht's chances with the Guild. In November therefore he started trying to interest Elisabeth Bergner in the play, and thereafter let Piscator wholly drop out of his plans for the next two years.[3]

Whether any of these projects had ever seemed all that important to Brecht is doubtful, for he mentions none of them in his *Journals*, while his last letter to Piscator about them is thought to date from September 1941. He was at best a fitful correspondent, and on top of that (as he explained apologetically to Hays) he felt 'crippled' by 'the unaccustomed windlessness and isolation from world affairs that i have fallen into here' and also by the death of his collaborator Margarete Steffin. 'i don't', he said, 'even get around to thanking those who helped to get me here, which lies heavily upon my conscience'.[1] Piscator however became extremely angry, partly about Brecht's failure to make a translation agreement with Hays, and his duplicity over *The Good Person of Szechwan*, but above all about his failure to keep in touch. 'Brecht hasn't written for $1\frac{1}{2}$ years', he told their mutual friend Mordecai Gorelik in a letter written in English and dated 21 January 1943:

> I have never in my life witnessed such unfriendly behaviour – nearly hostile – as Mr Brecht's. I am a very bad subject for insults. He is quick to write even phone or send telegrams or friends to me when he needs me. At other times he's behaved like the worse word I can find a 'Hitlerite'. [Then about Hays and Bergner.] A man who can be so callous to personal relationships must not wonder when his artistic qualifications suffer too. Brecht behaves like a man without any sensitivity or imagination; a man who cannot think of another person's point of view, and the necessity for all of us – in this time – is to hold together. A bad comrade. There can be no excuse for this. Indeed if I showed the same behaviour, Mr. Brecht would perhaps today be sitting in Helsingfors. If that's friendship, to hell with it.[2]

At the same time, in response to a request via Ruth Berlau, he sent Brecht an official invitation to visit the New School. Brecht accepted, and when, only three weeks after the Gorelik letter, Brecht arrived in person for a long stay in New York, everything appeared to have been patched up. There was a Brecht evening at the New School; Brecht took Piscator to see the Fritz Lang film *Hangmen Also Die* on which he had worked for the equivalent of nearly seven years of what the New School had proposed as a salary in 1940; the two men sent a joint telegram of congratulation to Granach on his performance. And once again they began discussing *Švejk*.

This time there seem to have been two plans which got fatally tangled. Piscator, as he now told Brecht, had been talking to the Theatre Guild about the possibility of updating the 1928 *Švejk* version, on which he suggested that Brecht should collaborate. More or less simultaneously however Brecht was approached by Piscator's old rival Aufricht, who wanted him to make a musical version for Broadway which would be set by Kurt Weill. Brecht clearly told Piscator nothing about this, but spent a week with Weill outside New York in New City, drafted a story; and on returning to California quickly got down to the script. Actually this *Schweik in the Second World War*, as it became, was much more what he had discussed with Piscator – even incorporating his conception of the Švejk figure after reading the latter's film treatment of 1937 – than a text for any conceivable musical; and he not only wished Piscator to direct it (so long as Weill agreed) but asked Aufricht to commission a translation from Alfred Kreymborg, who had been Piscator's nominee. Meanwhile he seems to have sent Piscator a copy of the script, which was finished by the end of June; there is an undated list of criticisms of this by Piscator, who commented that Schweik's mastery of the Nazis was too easily achieved, that there were too many indecencies for 'American puritanism' and, finally (and accurately), that 'It is neither Brecht nor Hašek'. Piscator at this point was still counting on a Theatre Guild production of the 1928 version and assuming that his title to the stage rights remained valid. Whether or not he had been told of Aufricht's involvement, he certainly failed to realise that the latter had not only raised the money for a production but had been in touch with the Hašek lawyer, who was now in New York, and had got the rights from him. Not yet realising that Weill saw no practical chance of success for Brecht's text unless it was radically Americanised, he was furious when Kreymborg wrote 'in the frankest and friendliest spirit' to say that he was now translating Brecht's version rather than Piscator's, and being paid 'a real advance as against no offer from the Guild', adding by the way that the backers were insisting on an American director. Piscator first reacted by starting a diatribe to Brecht which accused him of 'Brecht'sche Schweinerei' and threatened physically to 'knock the "poet" off his amoral Olympus'; but then abandoned this in favour of a cold letter addressed 'Dear Mr Brecht', with copies to Aufricht, Kreymborg and Weill, asking them to discuss their plans with him unless they wished to hear from his attorneys. By the beginning of 1944 Aufricht had returned the backers their money, and Weill had abandoned the project, of which nothing more seems to have been heard from either side.

For some eighteen months there was, not surprisingly, no recorded contact between Brecht and Piscator, though the former had once again been in New York for four months that winter. Then came a further joint fiasco, this time in connection with the wartime adaptation of *Fear and Misery of the Third Reich* which Brecht had made for Reinhardt to stage in New York under the title *The Private Life of the Master Race*. These scenes, of course, had been known to Piscator for many years, and once the Reinhardt plan had fallen through he planned to stage the new adaptation at the New School in a translation to be made by Hays. According to Hays, Piscator abandoned this task on finding that Brecht was allowing a rival version to be prepared. This was Eric Bentley's, which he made that same winter in consultation with Elisabeth Hauptmann (then living in New York) and also with Brecht. Apparently it was Brecht's understanding that Berthold Viertel should stage the play, and when a year later he was approached to let Piscator direct it for a new group called 'The Theatre of All Nations' he at first did not reply. However, writes James Lyon,

> After repeated letters to Brecht drew no response, Bentley forced the issue and authorized a production on his own.

Though Brecht denied the translator's right to do this, at the end of April 1945 he agreed to let the production go ahead. Extensive notes and sketches show how Piscator now proposed to set about staging the play: it would begin informally with the actors and stagehands preparing the stage; the pianist would then play 'The Star Spangled Banner', after which a giant SS man with a revolver would force him to switch to the Horst-Wessel song; then there would be a discussion about dictatorship and democracy, taking in some remarks about the epic theatre and leading to the start of the play itself, or more precisely its new wartime framework. Piscator also did the casting, which included the extremely old and eminent but far from Anglophone German actor Albert Bassermann and his wife, as well as a number of other émigrés and some students from the New School.

Brecht arrived from California on 23 May 1945, just three weeks before the opening, by which time the relevance of the play had been largely destroyed by the Nazi surrender. At first (so Eric Bentley says) he wanted to cancel the performance. When this proved impossible he tried to have the critics excluded, and thereafter was 'very destructive'. At the end of the first week Piscator walked out, writing to 'Dear Mr Brecht' (in English) that he had been hesitant about the whole thing:

> You came late, not to say too late, and your presence didn't help ... Unfortunately I can't permit myself the luxury of an artistic failure. On the other hand, when I direct I need the time for myself without you co-directing – and when you direct you need the time without me. For my part, I have conceived a different physical performance from yours, and I have greater difficulties in following your version – enough so that I suggest you take over the directing, and I withdraw.[1]

Instead Brecht brought in Viertel, whose wife Elisabeth Neumann was in the cast, and wrote tactfully to Piscator saying:

> Dear Pis,
> The ghastly thing is that time is too short to allow one to think out theoretical disagreements ...[2]

and going on to thank him for none the less 'preventing anybody from getting the . . . impression that we have become bitter enemies.' None of this could stop the opening on 12 June from being a disaster. The nine scenes took about three hours; Bassermann got unintended laughs; his wig kept slipping; the 'Jewish Wife' scene, already heavily cut, had to be dropped after the first night. 'Dear Bert', wrote Piscator quite genially three days later,

> At different moments the other evening I wanted to jump over the footlights, come backstage, and beat you. Not because I personally felt insulted when I saw the results of this work, but at the more objective harm you have done to yourself.[1]

More significantly, he complained about Brecht's intellectualism and his way of constructing the play:

> you had not the idea of an epic play as you put the scenes together, but in your mind it was nothing but un-epic, disconnected, disunified – a series of coincidental scenes written one after another and laid side by side.

For of course Brecht's concept of 'epic' involved the principle of montage, of 'one thing after another' and 'each scene for itself', as Piscator must surely have known. 'Our ideas on epic theatre are so different that I preferred to leave him alone', he wrote to Leon Askin on 3 July. To Egon Erwin Kisch he wrote on 18 June: 'I left . . . to avoid endangering our whole lifelong friendship'.[2]

*　　*　　*

They never worked together again, and in due course (according to Eric Bentley) Brecht gave instructions that the Dramatic Workshop was not to perform his works. Yet now that the war was over they once more discussed combining forces somehow when they returned home. 'I'd like to know what you think about theatre work in Berlin,' wrote Brecht in February 1947, suggesting that if Piscator was favourable they 'ought to work out a plan and send it over'. The positions of the two men at that time of course differed greatly. Piscator's capital lay in the Dramatic Workshop and his home in New York; Brecht's in his scripts, which however had proved to be not to the American taste. Piscator had applied for American citizenship; Brecht was stateless and likely to remain so. Piscator, the former Communist Party member, had kept quiet about his views (which he had seemingly modified); Brecht, the non-member, was shortly to be examined by the Un-American Activities

Committee. None the less they now exchanged letters reasserting their closeness to one another, though it seems that Piscator envisaged their working within one and the same theatre whereas Brecht more realistically argued that they must make a two-pronged attack, since

> there is a part of my works for the theatre for which I need to evolve a specific style of performance that differs from yours . . . You yourself are the last man to believe in drawing a hard-and-fast line between the writer of plays and the person who stages them.

It is clear that Brecht already had in mind a reconstruction of that core of left-wing actors and others whom they had been able to draw on before 1933 and whom Piscator had later tried to attract to the Volga Republic; and since 1945 some of these had indeed begun gathering around the East Berlin theatres. Friedrich Wolf too wrote from Berlin pressing Piscator to come and direct a production for the Volksbühne, and very soon after Brecht himself had arrived there for his triumphant production of *Mother Courage* at the beginning of 1949 he, Wolf and Jhering had virtually mapped it all out. The idea was that while Brecht himself would take over Aufricht's former Theater am Schiffbauerdamm and form his own company there, Piscator would become Intendant of the Volksbühne once its bombed-out theatre was rebuilt, supposedly in 1950. The party, so Wolf assured Piscator, had nothing against him, while Brecht proposed getting him a production in Zurich on the way, asked him to direct *The Days of the Commune* for the new Berliner Ensemble and assured him that he could perfectly well avoid committing himself to any political stance outside his work. Piscator still hesitated, for as late as February 1950 Brecht was writing to his friend Reyher to say 'We're all very interested in Piscator's intentions. He must at least pay a visit to the scene of his former triumphs. . . . He is so needed!'

Though both Wolf and Jhering were now on the Volksbühne's board, and Piscator's old protector Wilhelm Pieck was about to become the first president of the new East German state, no official invitation ever came. The reason is still not clear, but in Piscator's own view there were other prominent East German theatre people who were opposed to his appointment, and evidently he suspected that they had blocked it. At the same time the Volksbühne building was certainly taking much longer to restore than had been predicted, only reopening in 1954, the same year when Brecht at last moved into the Theater am Schiffbauerdamm. And no doubt Piscator himself finally decided the matter in October 1951 when, with the Dramatic Workshop collapsing under him, he returned not to Berlin but to West Germany, noting that 'Nobody had asked me to come, neither the lot in the West nor those in the East'. There he took directing jobs wherever he could get them, using the Hamburg theatres with his old friends Hans Rehfisch and Günter Weisenborn initially as a kind of artistic base. Weisenborn had worked with Brecht on *The Mother* in 1932, and now collaborated with him on one or two further projects, including that for an *Eulenspiegel* film. Brecht and Piscator however, it seems, had finally stopped corresponding, nor did they see each other again. In 1955 Jhering took Piscator for his first trip into East Berlin, where he saw Brecht's productions of *Mother Courage* and *The Caucasian Chalk Circle*, met some of his collaborators including such mutual friends as Eisler and Heartfield, and appeared surprised at the warmth of his reception. He did not publicly meet Brecht; nor did he start to become officially accepted in East Germany till after Brecht's death the following year, when there were once again moves to attract him to the East Berlin theatre. This was when the East German Academy (to whom we now owe the only proper edition of his writings) made him one of their few outside members. Thereafter, with Willy Brandt now becoming mayor of West Berlin, Piscator eventually became Intendant of the separate (Freie) Volksbühne in that half of the divided city, and brought it in some respects notably closer to the Berliner Ensemble. For among the new documentary plays which he put on, *The Case of J. Robert Oppenheimer* was also produced by the Ensemble (for whom its author Heinar Kipphardt had worked as a young dramaturg), while in 1965 Peter Weiss's *The Investigation* had simultaneous premières at both theatres.

*　　*　　*

In 1947, during the last moment of mutual support before Brecht left America, Piscator told him that 'I have always regretted the accident that prevented our ever having a single full and authentic collaboration'. Was it quite such an accident, we may ask. Looking back now over those thirty years that followed Brecht's first tactless poem, the ambiguities of their relationship seem fairly plain. To start with, as a young man in Berlin Brecht found in Piscator's productions the dramaturgical approach and the technical devices which he came to associate with epic theatre: that is the narration, the step-by-step construction and the breaking of illusion, along with the use of visual aids for documentary back-up and chorus-like comment. It was he who theorised about these things in print – Piscator scarcely did so – but it was Piscator who worked them out in practice. Back in those days Brecht, lagging a little as befits somebody six years younger, was only just feeling his way towards full acceptance of Piscator's concept of a politically engaged theatre and, more generally, of the need for the theatre to teach and instruct; something in which he later came to believe even more uncompromisingly than Piscator himself. But at least from the 1930s on Brecht gave the older man generous credit: in the Danish interview reprinted in *Brecht on Theatre*, for instance, in his Swedish lecture on Experimental Theatre and in the *Messingkauf Dialogues*, where he rated him 'one of the greatest theatre men of all time'. The trouble was that Piscator could not follow all Brecht's scattered theatre writings, a lot of which remained unpublished; and, because Brecht was apt to speak of 'epic theatre' without any references to priorities and credit, Piscator got it into his head that Brecht, who professed the greatest contempt for bourgeois ideas of intellectual property, was stealing his ideas.

This might not have mattered if Piscator had remained as famously successful as he had been (in all but the material sense) between 1924 and 1931. But the fact is that from then on, while he may have cut a distinguished figure, he was going downhill artistically while Brecht went up. This is not to say that everything that Brecht wrote got better and better – though indeed Piscator's most unproductive years were those of many of Brecht's finest poems and plays. But a writer's reputation is more or less cumulative, since you can always still read his early works, whereas a theatre director gets judged by what he does here and now: whatever his past achievements they have vanished in smoke, and practical men like backers and producers are ruthlessly realistic about this, as Piscator found to his cost in Paris and New York. Of course the two men found themselves in alliance time and again: with their contrasting characters and common convictions they were unique but complementary people. But even this useful relationship became less easy once Piscator had abandoned the political theatre, as he did in the United States; moreover, as he detached himself further from Communism (though never to the point of becoming an anti-Communist), there were kind friends to help put him against Brecht. This can be seen for instance in the long correspondence of the 1950s (in the West Berlin Academy) where Gasbarra re-establishes contact with Piscator after working for the Italian Fascist radio in the war; it contains some malicious little prods and sneers to that effect.

So despite Piscator's final table of pros and cons with its conclusion that Brecht 'was the greater one after all',[1] there was in his later years this nagging sense that Brecht, dead or alive, had to be put in his place. Thus to a French interviewer in 1956:

Brecht is my brother, but our views of totality differ: Brecht unveils significant details of human life while I attempt to give a conspectus of political matters as a whole. In a sense you can say that his Mother Courage is a timeless figure. I'd have tried to portray her more historically by showing the Thirty Years War.[1]

Certainly Piscator wanted to define his position with regard to Brecht: for he rejected (or, more precisely, misunderstood) Brecht's notion of Alienation, he never really liked Brecht's plays (as Reich pointed out with particular regard to the 1930s), and he made notes for a sequel to his book *The Political Theatre* which would trace these differences out. Sometimes his criticisms were well founded: thus he saw the weaknesses of *The Caucasian Chalk Circle*, commenting on the quasi-operatic music and the oversimplification due to the use of masks: poor good, rich bad. But it would hardly have helped the two men to come to a constructive understanding if they had indeed been able to join forces in Berlin; the gap between their respective temperaments was too serious for that. Indeed Piscator himself was too serious, and this was part of the trouble: if he had had more sense of the ridiculous there would have been less to quarrel about.

'Brother in spirit', wrote Piscator in his 'pro' column, then on the other side, 'not always a good one'. Back to Pro: 'gave help none the less'. Con: 'when I was unsuccessful. When I had success he was far away'. Yet wasn't this perhaps true of both of them? Once the difference in seniority was no longer felt by either, what repeatedly brought them together was not so much their 'successes' as their difficulties, or at least their shared problems: the advent of the Nazis, the realities of Socialist Realism, the great purge, the need to get a footing in the United States, finally the return to a ruined and demoralised Germany where everything would have to be rebuilt. Each time their instinct made them seek one another out with a view to making a joint stand. Then as soon as the danger was over, off they went on their own concerns once more. What they had in common, perhaps, only bulked so large because it was unique to them, in other words when they felt like a threatened minority. At other times it was not enough to outweigh their actual and potential differences. Looking back at their exchanges now it seems that it was Brecht, for all his frequent lack of consideration, who saw this the more clearly. What kept them linked was the fact that they remained apart.

8

Brecht
and the motion pictures

One of my earliest introductions to Brecht was through my teacher Joseph Gregor's little book *Das Zeitalter des Films*, which related cinema to the theatre and literature of the first third of the twentieth century. There he quoted irresistibly from the 'Ride of the Valkyries' episode in the 1922 *Drums in the Night*, which is set in Berlin with two bowler-hatted businessmen apprehensively pissing against the red-brick barrack wall, and followed by the stage directions:

> *Exeunt both. Wind.*
> *From the left now the entire Ride of the Valkyries: Anna, as if fleeing. Next to her, wearing an evening coat but no hat, Manke, the waiter from the Piccadilly Bar, who behaves as if intoxicated. After them comes Babusch, dragging Murk, who is drunk, pale and bloated.*[1]

This scene, so much in the Expressionist tradition – and it was the Expressionists who were the first writers to see the imaginative possibilities of film, when Kurt Pinthus edited *Das Kinobuch* for Kurt Wolff in 1913 – seems naturally cinematic, with its vivid visual images and its combination of fluidity and abruptness:

> MANKE: She is vanishing already as she hastens to the slums. Like a white sail she can be seen still, like an idea, like a final cadence, like an intoxicated swan flying across the waters . . .
> BABUSCH: What are we to do with this sodden clod?

Any dramatist who can write like this at the age of twenty-two seems made for the movies, and conversely the cinema soon became one of Brecht's favourite forms of entertainment, helping to shape his plays. Chaplin, Eisenstein, Pudovkin were among those whom he regarded as formative influences, while, if he himself made little or no use of film in his productions, many of his ideas about epic theatre were developed in conjunction with Piscator, perhaps the greatest of all exponents of the theatrical use of film. This interest of Brecht's was closely related to his love of crime stories, that other rapidly developing 'low' art which dealt with 'men in action' and events that had tangible consequences; the appeal of the two media to him was similar. 'Been to the cinema a lot', he noted in his diary for 6 July 1920. 'Specially detective dramas'. So in New York too, when he and Eisler were there for the somewhat disastrous production of *The Mother* in late 1935, they used to pursue what they termed their 'social studies' along those lines: thus Eisler's account two decades later:

> Then we drove off to 42nd Street and had a look at the gangster films featuring that splendid man Jack Cagney, *Public Enemy Number One* and so on. Those were our social studies.[1]

No play more obviously reflects these interests than *The Resistible Rise of Arturo Ui*, which was written hurriedly in 1941 with a view to the American market – 'the gangster play we know' as Brecht termed it in English – and is like a marriage between the Elizabethan theatre and the classic black-and-white movies of Warner and First National. Careful and appreciative study of such lurid films by both actors and directors underlay the play's eventual production by the Berliner Ensemble.

If Brecht, then, learnt from the cinema from quite an early stage in his career, it is only more recently that the cinema has wished to learn from Brecht. Starting in the late 1960s, when Wolfgang Gersch and Werner Hecht edited the playwright's previously unpublished film treatments and stories and devoted an extremely interesting small volume to *Kuhle Wampe* (the one film that seems really to have fulfilled his aims), there has been a wave of cinematic interest in his work and ideas. Little-known films of, by or relating to Brecht have been shown both in Germany and elsewhere, while the theorists of cinema have devoted enough attention to his writings and their contemporary implications to make him seem more of a figure in the cinema today than he ever was in his lifetime. 'I am convinced,' said a writer in *Screen* a few years ago, 'that in terms of what kind of fiction films *should* be made, Brecht is the theorist to contend with'.[2] Likewise Ben Brewster and Colin MacCabe, who organised the Edinburgh Festival discussion on 'Brecht and the Cinema' in 1975, felt that his was 'the framework within which it is possible to begin to think of a revolutionary cinema'.[3] Yet Brecht's actual ventures into the film medium were never all that satisfactory, and as time progressed they fell further and further below the standard set by his other work. Of course they were mainly motivated by the wish to make money, first in Munich in 1921, then in California twenty years later; but then so were *Drums in the Night* and *The Threepenny Opera*, to name only two outstanding cases, so it can hardly be said that this was bound to be harmful. The trouble, I think, lay deeper, in an area where Brecht was only briefly able to exercise much control. It was the question of the 'apparatus'.

*   *   *

'Why aren't there any pirate films?' Brecht asked himself in 1920. 'One day I'll write some . . . One must try to establish oneself in Germany somehow.' Soon afterwards he was working at a film project called *The Pirates* with Caspar Neher:

> Life of a woman. Grows up on the savannahs and is lugged across every conceivable ocean.[1]

This lost work is probably the same as the 'Hannah Cash' film about the heroine of the ballad which he wrote around then (in *Poems 1913–1956*, p. 69); a film which was to end with the woman alone on the poop of a ship whose crew is drunk, sitting by the helm as it rises and falls in the grey sea.

> You see it indistinctly, you see everything indistinctly, – it's swimming in something rainy, grey, alarming, the water is all around now. You can hardly see at all, just something grey, lost, shadowy; it goes up and down, and down and up . . .[2]

So he described the scheme in his diary. By then his ambition has become tangible; it is to 'dig for gold', and it certainly seems to relate to his love affair with Marianne Zoff who, as he says, 'Is prepared to be given fur coats, rings, dresses'. In those days the Bavaria Studios were in Munich, and Brecht, through an agent called Klette, had his eye in particular on a series being made there about an English detective called 'Stuart Webbs', which came out between 1920 and 1924. This had been launched before the First World War by the well-known producer Joe May, with Ernst Reicher as director and principal actor; and Klette waved large sums of money – or at any rate, large figures – under Brecht's nose. The latter's three early scripts[3] were written with this stuff in view. 'Film plans looming up', says his diary for 25 February 1921.

> New theory of money: comfortable, elegantly cut, broad grey trousers, well

hitched up; soft squashy hat, out-thrust face, rather sharp; relaxed to the point of recklessness.

The self-image here sounds like The Saint, and one trembles to think what might have come of Brecht if he had succeeded. But *The Mystery of the Jamaica Bar*, which would have been the liveliest of these silent crime fantasies, was turned down by Reicher that spring; and neither *The Diamond Eater*, for which Brecht envisaged a cast including Kortner and Sybille Binder as well as his Marianne, nor *Three in the Tower* which he and Neher wrote specially for her, ever came near production. Yet all three films can be conceived as good German silent mysteries of that time, complete with officers, criminals, detectives and Wedekindish members of high society. At the same time too he was noting down ideas for advertising shorts for Zambesi cigarettes, Sunlight Soap and other products. There were discussions in Berlin with Olga Tchekhova the newly arrived Russian actress, and with Richard Oswald and Terra Films. There is the story which Brecht wrote with Arnolt Bronnen for a competition run by Oswald, about an exotic struggle like those in *In the Jungle* or 'Bargan gives up', with a dash of Professor Challenger thrown in. Though it won no prize Bronnen claimed that this further adventure fantasy eventually served as the basis for a film called *Insel der Tränen*.

What turned Brecht away from the film industry after that year was not so much his initial failures, perhaps, as the resounding success which he scored in the theatre with *Drums in the Night* in the autumn of 1922. How far this success was financial as well as artistic is not exactly known, but it is worth noting that already in 1921 he was reckoning to get five times as much for *Drums* as for *The Diamond Eater*, which he expected to be his most lucrative film. But if his hopes of the main film companies went into cold storage at this point he did have one brief involvement in the movies soon after the première of *Drums* when he joined the Munich clown Karl Valentin, the director Erich Engel and others in making the farcical short *Mysteries of a Hairdressing Saloon* featuring Valentin and his partner Liesl Karlstadt. What Brecht's contribution was cannot now be identified, though there is another Valentin short whose titles read as though Brecht wrote them. These are marvellously comic films, which measure up to those of the great Hollywood silent clowns (though differing interestingly in their use of the close-up).

Already we can see some of the film ideas which Brecht took over into the theatre: the use of titles themselves, to start with, whether narrative as in the story with Bronnen –

Starving, he works to establish communication with the world.

– descriptive, as at the start of *The Diamond Eater*, where characters like the PUBLICAN, the FAT MAN etc. are introduced with 'Their names hanging over them like signs', or comprehensive like the titles to the 'Acts' in *Three in the Tower* –

'THE YEAR OF MOURNING' or 'THE AMAZING LIFE' or 'THE MADONNA AMONG THE BEASTS'

These categories anticipate, respectively, the projected inter-scene titles of plays like *Puntila*, the presentation of the characters at the start of *Arturo Ui* or the Five Types of Human Misery in scene 2 of *The Threepenny Opera*, and the headline-like titles proclaimed by Kragler at the end of *Drums in the Night*. The actual writing of the scripts too, shot by shot and in short narrative sentences, sets the style for Brecht's lifelong practice of writing out the *Fabel* or story of a play. There are small details which recur in the plays: for instance, Paduk – a name from the one-acter *Lux in Tenebris* – having tried to kidnap six society ladies by means of the mysteriously rotating Jamaica Bar – says, like Mother Courage twenty years later, that 'I'd sooner look after a bag of fleas'. The real significance, however, of the three early scripts lies in their establishment of the linear cinematic narrative punctuated by titles, the insistence on narrative rather than plot, and the avoidance of any 'psychological' indications.

There is a clear difference between Brecht's first two plays and *In the Jungle*, with its exotic story and more detached characterisation, the first of a planned trilogy about the great cities which occupied him on and off until *The Threepenny Opera* in 1928; and it could well be that the influence of the cinema has something to do with this. For Brecht wrote the original version of *In the Jungle* during the winter that followed his concentrated assault on the Munich studios, and in the meantime he had also encountered Chaplin's work. Visiting Marianne in Wiesbaden, he saw *The Face on the Bar-Room Floor* (also sometimes called *The Ham Artist*), which made so strong an impression on him that he wrote a poem about it more than twenty years later, recalling how Chaplin as a painter told of his lost love in a Paris bistro and tried to draw her face in billiard chalk on the floor. At the time he found it

profoundly moving, it's unadulterated art. Children and grown-ups laugh at the poor man, and he knows it: this nonstop laughter in the auditorium is an integral part of the film, which is itself deadly earnest and of a quite alarming objectivity and sadness.[1]

This 'objectivity' of Chaplin's is something that Brecht thought about, in conjunction not only with his admired friend Karl Valentin, who he found shared the same 'virtually complete rejection of mimicry and cheap psychology',[1] but also with the problems of the modern playwright. As he put it some ten years later in his easay on 'The Threepenny Lawsuit', 'What the film really demands is external action and not introspective psychology' and this is what it got from Chaplin. Hence his delight on first seeing *The Gold Rush* in 1926, which led him to sit down and applaud the youthfulness of an art which 'didn't dispel one's enjoyment of certain personal experiences by means of a dramaturgy that has all the experience of a sagging whore'.

> Film has no responsibilities. It doesn't have to over-strain itself. Its dramaturgy has remained so simple because a film is a matter of a few miles of celluloid in a tin box. When a man bends a saw between his knees you don't expect a fugue.[2]

The same simple principle of 'one thing after another' is among the bases of the epic theatre.

The same year as *The Gold Rush*, *The Battleship Potemkin* was shown in Germany, where its enthusiastic reception helped to determine its success not only in other Western countries but also within Russia, where it had not at first gone down well. In Brecht's mind the Soviet silent cinema, with its great revolutionary films, was linked with Chaplin, and Walter Benjamin later provided the explanation when he said that the American comics too showed bourgeois society being subverted and overthrown; indeed Wolfgang Gersch quotes a very interesting study of the Cologne cinemas in 1926 showing that, while the middle-class houses liked German films, the great successes among the working class were Chaplin's and Eisenstein's, with Fairbanks, Tom Mix and the Western in general as runners-up. Chaplin's influence on Eisenstein, Kuleshov and the rest of the Soviet avant-garde is of course well known. What Brecht however liked least about Eisenstein's work at this time was its assault on the audience's emotions; indeed even Piscator thought it not factual, historical and expository enough. Yet in its use of montage – and particularly of abrupt contrasts, switches and appositions – it clearly relates to the epic theatre as understood by Brecht, with its dissection of the story and visible stitching-together of the pieces. Not that Brecht in any way learnt this form of construction from Eisenstein, for it was already in the air; indeed Eisenstein himself seems to have been at least partly inspired by the photomontage techniques of George Grosz and John Heartfield at the beginning of the decade, which in turn derived from cubist collage. But, as Gersch rightly says, Eisenstein's subsequent intellectual rationalising of his procedures was congenial to Brecht, and he quotes Sergei Yutkevitch in the 1960s as seeing a 'profound inner correspondence' between the theories of the two men. In due course it extended also to their common interest in the theatre and art of the Far East, another of the offences which Georg Lukács, the principal enemy of montage as a structural method, was to hold against them both.[1]

It is one of the small ironies of progress that although Brecht derived his ideas of externalised, behaviouristic acting, of 'literarisation' and punctuation by means of titles, and of linear, objective-sounding story-telling so largely from the silent film, from then on all the films with which he was actively concerned were talkies. It is true, as Gersch has established, that there were still one or two silent projects occupying Brecht around 1926, particularly as a result of his friendship in Berlin with Lotte Reiniger and Carl Koch, two lifelong partners of whom the former became known for her clever but (to my mind) hopelessly ingratiating silhouette films, while the latter became an assistant to Jean Renoir, worked on *La Grande Illusion* and also privately filmed parts of *The Threepenny Opera* in 1928 and *Man equals Man* in Brecht's remarkable production of 1931 (some frames are reproduced in *The Theatre of Bertolt Brecht*). Among those projects (of which little, if any, record remains, and they were clearly tentative) was one for filming Kafka's *Metamorphosis*; but it seems to have been Elisabeth Hauptmann who mainly handled them, and it cannot be said how far they personally involved Brecht. He should none the less have been prepared for the radical changes threatening most of his favourite aspects of cinema as a result of the introduction of sound following Al Jolson's *The Jazz Singer* in 1927, for not only was he alert generally to new technologies but he had attended the Baden-Baden festivals at which Hindemith, Eisler and Dessau – all in some degree classifiable as 'his' composers – had tried out their film music. This had been written for the first primitive attempts at synchronisation, using shorts by Richter, Ruttmann and others: experiments which in due course were to lead to Eisler's specialisation in film music between 1940 and 1947, itself a substantial factor in Brecht's American experience. However, the simple fact is that by the time Brecht's silent-film methods in the theatre became known outside Germany the silent film itself was a thing of the past. The new medium had new rules, and it was this contradiction which led Brecht to have to rewrite the rules his own way if he was to succeed in it at all.

* * *

Pabst's film of *The Threepenny Opera* is an awkward problem for faithful
followers of Brecht, because he himself dismissed it as 'a pathetic botch-
up', 'a barefaced distortion' and had no good word to say for it, though
generations of us have thought it a brilliant film none the less and one
that gets closer to being an authentic performance of that work than
anything one can now see in the theatre. The root of this paradox – or
contradiction – lies in the nature of film-making, which even more than
the theatre demands an extensive 'apparatus' ranging from the raising of
bank loans to the provision of hot coffee in distant locations for the
camera crew, and accordingly cannot function if the members of that
apparatus are unable to make the occasional compromise. Brecht would
certainly have been more prepared to do so himself if the apparatus in
question had been publicly or cooperatively owned; but as it was he
wished to make the film on his own terms and felt that he was in a strong
position to do so. For here he had an immensely successful hit which
might make a mint of money for its producers; the sound film was still a
very new medium, whose rules had not yet been established; and he had
written into his contract with Messrs Nebenzahl and Robinson of the
production firm Nero provisions by which he would have a say
(*Mitbestimmungsrecht*) in the script, though specifically no right of veto
over the film. Also he had secured the engagement of Piscator's former
dramaturg Leo Lania to write it with him. This contract was signed on
21 May 1930, soon after Brecht's definitive (as it now seems)
commitment to the Communist Party.

Irrespective of the political question, which was not quite so much of a
factor as he later claimed, Brecht always wanted to change his works once
written, and in the case of *The Threepenny Opera* (perhaps in order to
continue to exploit its world-wide stage success) he did so via a change of
medium: the film treatment 'The Bruise' leading in 1934 to the story's
final transformation in the *Threepenny Novel*. Whether or not Nero were
prepared to be a party to this, they were faced with a double problem, for
first of all 'The Bruise', as Brecht began hurriedly dictating it to Lania
over the telephone that August, very radically altered (and to some
extent politicised) the story to such a degree that they did not look like
getting anything like what they had thought they were buying; and
secondly the work was running behind time, for when Lania took the
first part of his script down to Brecht in Bavaria to complete it he saw
that this would need a further fortnight's work. Nero promptly told
Lania to come back, then, four days later, asked Brecht to stop further
collaboration. When he refused they formally denounced their agreement.

By then, says Gersch (whose account I am generally following, since it is based not only on Brecht's own version in 'The Threepenny Lawsuit' but on reports in the trade press at the time), cinemas had begun booking and the publicity campaign been set in motion, so they let Pabst go ahead and start making the film which – as an added complication – was being shot in two versions, the second with a French cast. Lania at this point dropped out and went to London – it is not clear whether he resigned or was sacked – and was replaced by the Hungarian communist film theoretician Béla Balázs (an old friend of Lukács). Brecht and Weill thereupon sued Nero for fulfilment of their rights, Weill in turn having been banished from the film when he protested against changes to his music in the wedding scene. Though the two collaborators formed a common front Weill, who had had a right of veto, won his case and Brecht did not, on the grounds that many of his basic ideas had been used and that his contractual 'say' gave him no right to block completion of the script. That was in November; then on 19 December an accommodation was reached between Nero and Brecht, by which Brecht retained the rights for further film versions and Nero promised to describe Pabst's as 'freely adapted from the Brecht–Weill stage play of the same name'.

Gersch, like other students of Brecht, on the whole takes Brecht's view and argues that Nero not only wanted to make money, which is clear enough, but also had political objections to the new material that Brecht was introducing and eventually damped down its political impact by botching the great beggars' demonstration and softening the photography. Personally I doubt whether this was due to anyone but Pabst, whose divergences from Brecht's views – notably about the 'human aspect', which he said he wanted brought out more – were surely predictable from the start. Nero themselves went a long way to forestall such accusations by taking on Lania and then Balázs (who later said that he was never asked to make any concessions), while even the third script writer, Laszlo Vajda, though his role has never been made clear, wrote *Kameradschaft* for Pabst and had played a leading part in film affairs under the Hungarian Soviet government of 1919. In fact, these people kept a great deal more of Brecht's new ideas from 'The Bruise' than his accounts ever gave them credit for, and in the event the German Right were strongly enough opposed to the finished film for Wilhelm Frick to ban it in the state of Thuringia, where he was Nazi Minister of Education from the beginning of 1930; and Baden and Braunschweig followed suit. Moreover thanks largely to the authenticity of the casting (with Carola Neher as Polly) and of the performance of the songs (under

Theo Mackeben) it still seems a far better result than might be expected
from the commercial cinema – a work to be compared with Fritz Lang's
M and René Clair's *À nous la liberté*, with both of which it has features in
common – and incomparably better, by all accounts including Gersch's,
than the version made thirty or so years later by Wolfgang Staudte with
Curt Jürgens, Hildegard Knef, Sammy Davis junior and the Brecht
family's agreement. Of course it is not a major political work, but even
the much further developed *Threepenny Novel* is some way from being
that, and Brecht in both cases was trying to make his play – of which for
mixed reasons he was very fond – bear a quasi-Marxist superstructure
for which it was just not suited. Perhaps the root of the trouble lay in his
willingness to embark on the operation at all.

The real value of Brecht's battle with Nero, which he rightly claimed
was not about money, was twofold. First, it led to the writing of the
essay on 'The Threepenny Lawsuit',[1] which was sub-titled 'A sociologi-
cal experiment' and is now seen as a classic early media study to set
alongside some of Benjamin's and subsequently Enzenberger's writings.
More importantly, it led him and his collaborators to approach the next
operation in a radically different, almost wholly successful and satisfactory way. This began early in 1931 when the young Bulgarian director
Slatan Dudow – a Berlin theatre student who had spent much of 1929 in
the Moscow theatres before joining the new Brecht–Eisler partnership as
director of *The Decision* and subsequently *The Mother* – had tried to get
production backing for a film project about a Berlin working-class weekend, seemingly a counterpart to the less class-conscious *People on Sunday*
made in 1929 with Nero's backing by a group including Siodmak,
Wilder and Zinnemann, all later eminent in Hollywood. At what point
Brecht came into this scheme is not quite clear, but it must have been
after Dudow's first short film on Berlin living conditions in 1930, *Wie
der Berliner Arbeiter wohnt*, which was made for the IAH (Mezhrabpom)
German firms Prometheus and Weltfilm. It looks as though the new film
was finally set up during the summer of 1931, following the première of
Pabst's *Threepenny Opera* on 19 February. By then Prometheus was on
its last legs – it actually closed down on 20 January 1932 – and so, wrote
Brecht not long after,

> With our experience of the Threepenny Lawsuit fresh in our minds we got a
> contract made – apparently for the first time in the history of the cinema – by
> which we, the actual makers of the film, were recognised in law as the
> producers. This meant sacrificing all claim to regular payment, but guaranteed
> us otherwise unobtainable liberties in our work. Our little company consisted

of two film writers, a director, a musician and last but not least a lawyer. Of course organising the work involved much more trouble than the (artistic) work itself; that is to say we came more and more to treat organisation as a significant part of the artistic work. This was only possible because the work as a whole was political.[1]

The members of the company, in the order here given by Brecht, were Brecht and Ernst Ottwalt, Dudow, Eisler, Robert Scharfenberg and Georg Hoellering. The slender backing came partly from one of the actors (so Brecht said) and partly from Lazar Wechsler of the German–Swiss production firm Praesens, which had recently produced the feminist film *Frauennot-Frauenglück* made by the Eisenstein group during their West European travels.

From *Weekend Kuhle Wampe* as the film was at one point called – Kuhle Wampe being a tented weekend camp on the outskirts of Berlin – it developed into *Kuhle Wampe – oder Wem gehört die Welt?*, posing the question 'Whom does the world belong to?'. Ottwalt, a former nationalist who had become a communist and (unlike Brecht) a member of the Proletarian-Revolutionary Writers' League, seems to have joined the group after Brecht, but the division of final responsibility between them is unclear; moreover it was Dudow who had had the basic idea, along with the notion of bringing in the (communist-led) workers' sports organisation and other major elements, while Brecht seems for much of the time to have been at the director's elbow and often to have rehearsed and directed the dialogue. At all events the finished film is as distinctively a Brecht work as are his other collective works of the time, starting perhaps with *The Threepenny Opera* and not excluding *Happy End* of which he chose to wash his hands; and so far as is now known he was satisfied with it. Among the aspects which still seem most characteristic of him is, first, the structure in three main sections formally titled ONE UNEMPLOYED MAN LESS, THE IDYLLIC LIFE OF A YOUNG PERSON, and WHOM DOES THE WORLD BELONG TO?, which refer to the film's three main 'gests'; respectively suicide, eviction and the mass singing of the 'Solidarity Song' with its final line 'And whose world is the world?'[2] Secondly there is the appalling engagement party in the crowded hut, which is like an intermediate stage between the early farce *A Respectable Wedding* (c. 1919) and the wedding scene in *The Caucasian Chalk Circle* (1944). Thirdly there is the non-naturalistic dialogue, and fourthly (though this is a principle shared with Eisler) the use of music as an independent element and not to create moods, the beautiful song 'The spring' or 'The walks' (*Poems 1913–1956*, p. 183), which was half-sung by an unseen Helene Weigel, being the most remarkable example. What must have been Dudow's however – and is also very striking, as well as historically relevant – is the use made of Maxim Vallentin's agitprop group 'The Red Megaphone' and the thousands of 'worker sportsmen' who take part in the energetic and optimistic final section. Most of the film was shot in real-life locations and using amateur extras, while the professionals, who included Ernst Busch, Herta Thiele, Gerhard Bienert and Fritz Erpenbeck, came largely from the ex-Piscator collective 'Gruppe der jungen Schauspieler'. It is a most original work, and a document of the time.

Kuhle Wampe was made, rather amazingly, in the period between August 1931 and March 1932, only months before Hitler's Chancellorship, when Brecht, Eisler and Dudow were rehearsing and (in Eisler's case) composing *The Mother*, and Brecht himself was also co-directing the Berlin *Mahagonny*. In January it ran into trouble when Tobis, who shared the Western Electric monopoly of sound recording, threatened to withdraw their equipment; then at the end of March it had to go before the censors. On the authority of General Groener, the Defence Minister, the film was considered by officials of the Labour and Interior Ministries and passed by them to the Berlin board of censors, who banned it against the dissentient voices of Rudolf Olden and Paul Otto. The national (top) board then confirmed the ban, despite the evidence of Count Harry Kessler, who came forward to testify[1] that censorship had actually been more liberal under the Kaiser and that any state which felt threatened by this film must be on its last legs (which indeed it was). The producers then made some cuts to meet the main objections, the only substantial one being the removal of 36.5 metres devoted to a naked bathing scene with worker-sportsmen and -women, and resubmitted it to the first board, who now let it through. Brecht, who had already shown himself amenable enough to the give-and-take of teamwork under high pressure (thereby suggesting that he might have been more able to work with Pabst on *The Threepenny Opera* had he not had an inbuilt resistance to the capitalist producers), now was surprisingly relaxed in his attitude to the censors, who he evidently felt had complimented *Kuhle Wampe* by detecting the hidden dangers which it presented to the social order. The world première in Moscow, held soon after this final clearance, fell rather flat, since the Russian audience (according to Reich) not only found the film's approach too cool but could not relate German standards of poverty and bad housing to their own.

Nevertheless it still seems an all but unique film, comparable only perhaps to Carl Junghanns's German–Czech production of the same time, *So ist das Leben*, which is structurally and thematically akin. And certainly it was a vindication of Brecht's insistence on capturing the 'apparatus' rather than trying to come to terms with it. He already proposed to follow it up with another film based on a scheme for a short play to be called *Santa Lucia* for which he and Hauptmann had been making notes. This 'play about the corruption of the proletariat by sheer poverty'[1] was to tell the story of a butcher's family and the various economic factors represented by a knackered carthorse, a broken-down second-hand car, a dying aunt and a legacy which, after serving to restore the family's fortunes, can be applied to pay for her tombstone. The plan got no further before 1933, and the surviving story, written very much in Brecht's and Hauptmann's deadpan short story style of that time, was possibly designed to be made instead by Mezhrabpom in Moscow.

* * *

From that point on, Brecht's hope of capturing the apparatus or by-passing it through alternative channels dwindled, then disappeared; and for the whole of his stay in Scandinavia, which was so productive in terms of plays, poems and theoretical writings, he remained practically out of reach of the cinema except as a consumer. As we have seen, he kept in touch with Piscator, particularly with reference to any possibility of filming Hašek's *Švejk*, and was marginally involved in some of his ex-employer's optimistic film plans, whether in Russia (where Piscator's plans for the Volga Republic incidentally included setting up a film industry there) or later in Paris and Switzerland. Via Hanns Eisler he made contact with the original *Švejk* adaptor Hans Reimann and is said to have exchanged ideas with him; he also had a contract with Mezhrabpom-Film for *Round Heads and Pointed Heads* which came to nothing, and tried vainly to get Helene Weigel a part in Wangenheim's Dimitrov film *Kämpfer* for the same studio. Probably through Eisler, too, he came to know and admire Joris Ivens, who had been making the Magnitogorsk documentary *Song of Heroes* (along with Eisler, Tretiakov and Herbert Marshall) back in 1932 when he first visited the USSR. All these connections however led nowhere, and his two forays into the British commercial cinema were not even financially very rewarding. The one, in 1934, failed when Korda turned down a story which Brecht and Lania had prepared about Semmelweis and the campaign against puerperal fever in mid-nineteenth-century Vienna; the other, in 1936, was undertaken purely for money and consisted in working on the dialogue of a preposterous *Pagliacci* film starring Richard Tauber, for which Eisler rather ignominiously directed the music while John Drinkwater wrote the script. It was on this visit that Brecht, through Koch and Reiniger, made contact with the GPO film unit and first became interested in Auden. He is said around the same time to have sold the story of *Happy End* (which has a still mysterious similarity to *Guys and Dolls*) to a French film firm, identity not known. But generally the relevance of the late 1930s to his work lay in the increasing convergence (and for his subsequent editors, confusion) of his film stories and his short stories proper, as in *Tales from the Calendar*; also in the echoes of Chaplin that can be observed in *Puntila* and *Arturo Ui*, where the twice-weekly programmes at the local Svendborg cinema (mainly devoted to American films, as he told Piscator) had had their effect.

In 1941 however he went to the source, when instead of going to the New School in New York as invited, he settled in California, where his ship had arrived. It was there that Elisabeth Hauptmann, who had been working as a teacher in St Louis, had organised promises of money for him from wealthy German friends in or around the film business, and these encouraged him to work on the West Coast, evidently making it clear that they would help him establish himself in the movies. Except that he never signed a long-term contract (and perhaps was never offered one), his experience was very similar to that of Carl Zuckmayer two years earlier who, after writing the *Rembrandt* script for Korda in London, arrived as a refugee in Hollywood, was entertained by Fritz Lang, William Dieterle, Max Reinhardt and Berthold and Salka Viertel (all of them friends too of the Brechts) and introduced by them to the great tycoons who

> at first showed themselves very kindly disposed to a newcomer rated in the old country as a 'successful author'; they reckoned on one's conforming, changing, fitting in with their company procedure and style of work, and I was given the notorious seven-year contract which ... binds the signer unconditionally to his firm while giving it the right at any time to dismiss him with a week's notice.

'Never have I heard the word "happy" so often as in that antechamber to hell, Hollywood', Zuckmayer writes, and when Arnold Zweig's *The Case of Sergeant Grischa*, on which he had started to work, was cancelled because of anti-Russian feeling due to the Finnish war, and he was given a Don Juan story starring Errol Flynn to write instead, he refused – to Fritz Lang's profound horror – was promptly sacked and went back to New York to teach for Piscator. Here the similarity stops. For Brecht, though expected in New York, stayed on in that 'mortuary of easy-going' Los Angeles, which he was soon to describe in even more damning terms.

During his six Californian years Brecht worked on one film for Lang, sold another through Feuchtwanger, and wrote some twelve or thirteen film stories that have been published, as well as others that have not (like the nine-page project for a film of 'The Children's Crusade') and a great quantity of shorter proposals or ideas. Some at least of these were written 'on spec.', some were collaborations with more experienced film people like Ferdinand Reyher, a German-American who had been a Hollywood writer and consultant since 1931, or Salka Viertel, who was scriptwriter for *Queen Christina* and other Garbo films. Generally however his advisers seem to have been friends in the industry who were mostly German and had a rigid and (ultimately) money-grubbing mid-European notion of what Hollywood wanted, based on a paternal contempt for the mass audience. These people wanted to do what they could for the Brechts short of actually accepting his ideas, and a number of their kindnesses were perhaps not too seriously meant. Elisabeth Bergner (whose stature in Hollywood was based entirely on her Berlin and London reputations) not only engaged Brecht in the *Duchess of Malfi* stage project but seems to have given him his first job collaborating on a film story – which was later abandoned, retailed to Billy Wilder and, in Brecht's view, exploited by another writer. Similarly Gottfried Reinhardt, the son of Max, describes in his memoirs how, as an assistant producer for MGM, he tried to persuade his colleagues to take the Brecht–Reyher story called 'The King's Bread' and how very flat this fell thanks to its ignoring of the two basic Hollywood rules: have a love interest, and avoid class clashes. This attempt was purely due to good will and a knowledge of Brecht's significance, and Reinhardt says he knew at the time that it was useless: the story 'had as much chance of being sold to MGM as *Gone With the Wind* had of being played at the Berliner Ensemble'.[1] Another indulgent, but in the end unproductive adviser in such matters was Brecht's early Berlin discovery Peter Lorre, who had made his film reputation in *M*, then gone on to establish himself in Hollywood with such films as *The Mask of Dimitrios*. Brecht's poetry apart, most, if not all of the work which he did in Hollywood involved such personal links.

The story Brecht sold through Feuchtwanger was *Simone Machard*, or more accurately (since MGM found the play difficult to understand) the novel which Feuchtwanger had based on it; and it was pure generosity that led the latter to pay over $20,000 to his younger and less secure friend. The film however was never made, partly because the chosen star was having a baby and partly because the fall of France was soon to be regarded as a stale topic. The one finished movie with which Brecht was practically connected was Fritz Lang's *Hangmen Also Die*, which earned him rather less ($8–10,000 by Lyon's estimate) and occupied him full-time for the greater part of 1942. This story of the Czech wartime resistance and the assassination of Reinhart Heydrich, the SS 'protector' of the non-Slovak (or western) half of Czechoslovakia, was originally hatched by the two men on the beach at Santa Monica on the very day when the event was reported in the papers, following which they began working together on the story, from nine to seven (so Brecht noted) each day. Lang, he found, judged their ideas repeatedly according to whether audiences would accept them:

> the master mind of the underground hiding behind a curtain as the gestapo searches the house: the audience will accept that. likewise policemen's corpses falling out of wardrobes. likewise 'secret' mass meetings in a time of nazi terror. lang 'buys' that kind of thing. interesting too that he's far more interested in surprise than in tension.

By the end of July another refugee, Arnold Pressburger, had agreed to produce the film, after which the established scriptwriter John Wexley was brought in to write the screenplay with Brecht. Wexley during the 1930s heyday of the American Left theatre had written a number of plays, including *They Shall Not Die* about the trial of the Scottsboro blacks and *Running Dogs* about the Chinese Red Army, and in 1939 he wrote the script of that remarkable quasi-documentary film *Confessions of a Nazi Spy*. But, like other left writers of that time (notably Odets, whom Brecht also knew), he was now much more in tune with the conventions of Hollywood than with Brecht's idiosyncratic views. As he told Wolfgang Gersch in 1965,

> Brecht could never get entirely used to American methods, American points of view, nor to the ideological approach that needed to be followed at that particular moment in history. Lang on the other hand was not exactly conservative, but he was not very far to the left and he was deliberately cautious . . . A lot of what Brecht wanted could not be fulfilled: either it was not practicable, or else it would have met with intense hostility.[1]

Wexley and Brecht seem to have worked on one or two outlines, then on two overlapping versions of the script, one which they handed to Lang and another, the version which they would ideally have liked to see made, which they wrote at Brecht's house privately, then abandoned after about seventy pages; this is now lost. By the time shooting began in November the first, official version was nearly twice as long as it should have been; Brecht then stopped work and Wexley, without telling him, cut it down to shooting length, restoring some previously cut material in the process, after which Lang made still further cuts and changes in the shooting, mostly without consulting Brecht and, in the latter's view, at his expense. This was one cause of Brecht's ensuing resentment, and another was the crediting of the screenplay to Wexley alone: something that Wexley said had been part of his initial agreement, though it certainly came as a shock to Brecht and a sharp lesson in Hollywood ethics. But much more important was the character of the finished film, which had music by Eisler and a cast including H. H. von Twardowski (as Heydrich), Alexander Granach and Reinhold Schünzel, all of whom had played Brecht roles in Berlin. Though connoisseurs of wartime anti-Nazi films claim that it is not bad of its kind, it remains an almost unrelievedly disappointing work, conveying a wholly unreal picture of wartime Europe – let alone wartime Czechoslovakia – of the Nazi occupation and the problems of any resistance movement. Brecht must bear part of the responsibility for this, for I do not believe the film would have been all that much better had the script been as he wished. It would still have seemed like stereotyped play-acting in a studio, among unconvincing exteriors and under theatrical lights.

'The more Brecht learned', says James Lyon, 'the more steadfastly he resolved to write film stories for Hollywood on his own terms or not at all'.[1] That is one way of putting it, and he certainly had some intriguing ideas; for instance the short project called 'Helene of West Point' which starts off: 'Cross between the *Iliad* and the Chinese story in which a father kills himself.'[2] But if one looks at the actual results they hardly bear this out: for instance the following (randomly picked) paragraph from a story written with Salka Viertel and Vladimir Pozner in 1945:

> People shout, people cheer, people sing the Marseillaise. Children wave the Tricolour, women jump on the running board of Jean's car, embrace and kiss him. He glances at them hopefully, looking for a familiar smiling face framed in blonde curls. There are many blondes, all of them smiling, all of them strange.[3]

This is not exactly the author of *Kuhle Wampe* writing, and in my view it would be more accurate to say that whatever good resolutions Brecht may or may not have made, he kept on trying to write what he thought would be acceptable. What is very true of him throughout his life is that he wrote better when in conflict with the conventions under which he was living and working than when trying to maintain harmony with them. Thus his sharpest criticisms of capitalism were made in the 1920s, his best East German poems were written after his 'positive' period was over, and similarly he could write marvellously *about* Hollywood (as in the 'Elegies' of that name) while writing very uncharacteristically and often rather badly for it. The fact is that one cannot join a system without making concessions, but one has to make none in order to attack it; and Brecht was most acutely himself when biting the hand that paid him. So there was something incongruous in his being lined up with his old antagonist John Howard Lawson[1] and the rest of the 'Hollywood Nineteen' unfriendly witnesses before the House Un-American Activities Committee when in 1947 it mounted its inquiry into the supposed communist penetration of the motion pictures. For except in the most superficial way Brecht had never aimed to 'penetrate' these; in everything he wrote for them he was trying to conform to their conventions. Fortunately he was not able to, and colleagues like Lang and Wexley soon found out that he was not naturally agreeable enough to make it worth their trying to help him; hence the growing lack of consultation. 'That kind of thing can be bad for one's handwriting', he noted on finding himself tempted to write slick transitions and 'smart' – he uses the English word – lines.[2] Even so he made some sad concessions, and Dieterle, a long-standing friend who had made some of Hollywood's most serious biographical films, was surely right when he told Lyon that 'success in Hollywood would have harmed Brecht immeasurably'.[3]

*   *   *

Though it cannot be said that Brecht's actual 'handwriting' suffered from his Hollywood experience, there was a seeming lack of political objective in all his major American works which is also felt in his plays. For they too were written neither for the desk drawer nor for any kind of alternative or fringe theatre but for the apparatus as he found it in that country, and with commercial acceptance in view. The difference lay in the scale and power of the apparatus – which in the case of the film companies was beyond all Brecht's previous experience – and in the fact that unlike films, plays are not always written with the apparatus leaning clumsily over the writer's shoulder and making its pressure felt. His return to Europe, then, in the autumn of 1947 might have been felt as a liberation in both areas, and where the theatre was concerned it soon proved to be so, not least because he and his wife were aiming to have an apparatus of their own; *Antigone*, for instance, and the adaptation of *The Tutor* are works which Brecht would hardly have considered writing with Broadway in mind. Perhaps however just because of this concentration on the establishment of a Berlin Ensemble, he never attempted to pick up the film where *Kuhle Wampe* had left off. For a while he still pursued one or two projects that had been originated in Hollywood, including a scheme for filming *Galileo* with Laughton in Italy under Joseph Losey's direction, which never got off the ground. Meanwhile the administration in the Soviet Zone had set up its own film industry in the shape of the German Film Company (DEFA), in relation to which Brecht was once more to be an outsider, whether as film writer or as voluntary adviser on policy. So the *Eulenspiegel* story which he and Günter Weisenborn began planning in 1948 was conceived, somewhat amazingly, for one of the Nazis' great box-office draws, the jovially masculine Hans Albers; and for two years DEFA were hoping to make this. Though Dudow had now returned to Germany and was one of the leading DEFA directors the old understanding between the two former collaborators seemed, according to Gersch, to have gone; and Brecht proved more anxious to see DEFA using great Hollywood directors like Stroheim or even Lang for prestige films and Erich Engel for projects where he himself was involved. Once he too was back in Germany and the Ensemble had been set up, these were confined to the filming of his own stage plays.

His plays, however, were not made for filming in the modern medium, and the two which he could see before his death – if one excepts straight film records of Ensemble productions – both disappointed him, though both were by famous directors. The one was a curiosity which had been filmed thirteen years before he saw it in Moscow in 1955, but never released; this was Pudovkin's film of five scenes from *Fear and Misery of the Third Reich*, under the title of *The Murderers are on their Way*. The other was the Austrian (Wien-Film) film of *Puntila*, directed by Alberto Cavalcanti, which was first shown at the end of May that same year. Brecht had had a good deal of say in the script of this, which was initially written by Vladimir Pozner, his Franco-Russo-Hollywood friend; the music was by Eisler; and although Brecht had originally wished the director to be Ivens (who had made the World Federation of Trade Unions film *Song of the Rivers* for which Pozner had written the script and Brecht the theme song) he accepted Ivens's nomination of Cavalcanti instead and subsequently wanted the latter also to film *The Caucasian Chalk Circle* and *The Visions of Simone Machard*. Nevertheless *Puntila* was hopelessly vulgarised, with a robust good-looking Matti quite lacking in irony; colourful costumes and settings; and a performance by Curt Bois as Puntila in no way comparable with his elegant clowning as recorded by H. J. Syberberg in his (unauthorised) 8mm footage of Brecht's stage production; the same gifted interloper also filmed much of the Ensemble's *Urfaust* production and parts of *The Mother*. Bois incidentally had also been in Hollywood with Brecht and was in a preposterous film of 1944 called *Gipsy Wildcat* whose licentious baronial soldiery look very like those in *The Caucasian Chalk Circle* as Brecht staged it later.

For nearly all of Brecht's time in East Berlin his relations with DEFA were dominated by the ups and downs of the *Mother Courage* film. These are far too complex to follow in detail, as one scriptwriter or team of writers followed another, sometimes in collaboration with Brecht, sometimes not, until the original director Erich Engel gave up. Then in 1952–53 the project stagnated – according to Gersch, because the producers were nervous of the accusations of 'formalism' currently being directed at Brecht's theatre work – only to be resumed in 1954. There was a question of making the film in Italy, but Luchino Visconti, to whom Emil Burri's 1952 script was sent, turned it down. In the end therefore it was settled that the film would be made by Wolfgang Staudte, with Helene Weigel as Courage, and in 1955 he, Brecht and Burri hammered out a final script. The best things about this perhaps were the parallel established with the post-World War II occupation of Germany, with its 'babylonian confusion of languages', and the cold douche offered to the prevalent self-pity when, following Eilif's death, Courage is referred to as 'one of the little people' and the First Peasant comments: 'Nerts to that. The little people are the worst of the lot. Why? The big shots plan it, and the little people carry it out'.[1] At the same time Kattrin's character is interestingly developed, and she is given a very plausible lover. It seems a great pity then that the film, which was now a German–French co-production, with Simone Signoret playing Yvette and Bernard Blier the Cook, was broken off after only ten days of shooting. The trouble seems partly to have been a personal incompatibility between Brecht and Staudte, who considered quite mistakenly that the writer had 'an utterly hostile attitude to the cinema'.[2] More important, however, were Brecht's objections on the visual side, for he was against shooting in colour and wanted a drab, daguerreotype-like effect; he dismissed the costumes as too operatic; and he objected alike to the sandy exteriors (which look good in the surviving stills) and to the massive and ornate interiors (which look like Hollywood clichés). In the end all that DEFA could come up with was a wide-screen film of the stage production transferred to a huge studio floor, which Palitzsch and Wekwerth made after Brecht's death.

There is no sign that Brecht in his later years thought again about the problem of the apparatus, which had got so much more complex, more entrenched and more rigid in its practices since the early sound days. He undoubtedly complained about it and insulted it, but only after first taking it as he found it; and since those more fluid and hopeful (if not actually revolutionary) early times it had become much the same everywhere. For the laws and conventions of these great apparatuses nowadays transcend differences of political system: an opera house or a ballet company imposes similar demands in terms of material, artistic conventions and acceptability by the audience whether it is in Moscow, Paris or New York; in fact the main difference between the Soviet film industry and others is merely that it seems to operate without Hungarians. Perhaps this was too big a problem for Brecht to tackle when he got back, and all the evidence is that he accepted the changed situation and chose rather to get on with the main task of realising, circulating and accurately fixing his pile of wholly or locally unperformed plays. Despite the considerable potential merits of the *Mother Courage* script this was in cinematic terms a regression: where once Brecht had introduced some of the silent cinema's methods into the theatre he was now (as most clearly in *Puntila*) theatricalising the sound film. The question then is whether his misconceived attempt to establish himself in Hollywood accelerated this decline, and whether he might not have been better engaged theorising about cinema at the New School, where Eisler's film music project led to the composition of *Fourteen Ways of Describing the Rain* (to Ivens's documentary *Rain*) and to his book *Composing for the Film*, whereas his ensuing Hollywood hack-work led to one Oscar nomination and a lot of money. What it did do, however, was to infect Brecht from then on with a Hollywood-like view of star values and big names that was difficult to reconcile with the basic principles and attitudes of his writing. Nor did he make any systematic attack on the roots of such values, brilliant as his private criticisms of their surface manifestations often were. 'You don't go unpunished in Hollywood', the more cynical Eisler told him; and this may well have been right.

Yet, in spite of the apparatus, the cinema – and the television for that matter, which Brecht never had time to get to grips with – has some encouragingly open minds, and, like Brecht, it takes its ideas and influences as much from other domains as from its own. So Losey, for instance, claims to have been influenced by such aspects of Brecht's theatre as its precision of gesture, words, music and sound, its economy of movement and the combination of fluidity and contrast, contradiction etc. in its structure. Godard for his part has a character in *Tout va bien* quote from the *Mahagonny* notes, while in *Le Mépris* Fritz Lang (a nice piece of irony) speaks Brecht's self-abasing poem 'Hollywood' about the trade in lies; altogether Godard's 'literarisation' of the screen and his exposure of the mechanics of the medium recall Brecht. Other cinematographers have picked more on such aspects of Berliner Ensemble staging as the worn brown or grey costumes, the concentration on set elements that have a dramatic function and the otherwise uncluttered space. Some have shown a Brechtian preference for plebeian characters and stories or filmed Brecht's own, as in Helmut Nitschke's DEFA film of *The Two Sons* (1969) from *Tales from the Calendar*, René Allio's of *La Vieille Dame indigne* (1964) or the Italo-German co-production of episodes from the unfinished Caesar novel under the title *History Lessons* (1972) by Straub and Danièle Huillet. More recently Stewart Mackinnon's episodic *Because I am King* (1980) centres on a riveting performance of the Brecht–Hindemith *lehrstück* in a disused factory, while Fassbinder, Kluge, Michael Verhöven and Volker Schlöndorff are among the West German directors in whose work Brecht's influence has been seen. The unfortunate thing, perhaps, is that Brecht was never able to turn again to the problem of how to organise the apparatus so as to take account of its development since 1932 and transform it into a 'significant part of the artistic work' in a good sense rather than a bad. True as it is that he 'provided the framework', he only did so over a very short period and when many of the conditions of film-making were very different from now. To have gone further he would have had to work out how like-minded teams with worthwhile aims, as in the making of *Kuhle Wampe*, could acquire enough independence, financial responsibility and exemption from restrictive practices, under the aegis of the great film corporations and television hierarchies that now control the art.

9
Brecht and the visual arts

Viewed as it mostly is today (and as Auden apparently viewed it) *The Rise and Fall of the City of Mahagonny* is among the least understood of Brecht's works. Its present reputation has little to do with the author's original intentions; it is seen partly as the super-decadent golden-twenties Son of Threepenny Opera, partly as evidence that opera can move with the times, yet remain within the grand old operatic framework. Brecht himself never disputed this, since he lost interest once it became clear that his libretto had escaped from his own kind of theatre into the traditional opera house and therefore would never be staged as he wished. Nevertheless it is a key work, being the extreme example of a structural principle that Brecht shared with several of his contemporaries (Grosz, Heartfield, Eisenstein, Hašek, Dos Passos, Joyce) yet applied more widely than any. This was montage, a method which can perhaps be regarded as the most radical and fruitful contribution of the 1920s to the portrayal of an increasingly complex reality. For *Mahagonny* was a montage in more than one sense: its text was glued together from previously-written poems of several periods, its structure was designed to avoid any kind of illusion (including that of being an opera), and finally its three creators – writer, composer and designer – were each meant to contribute independently in such a way that the audience would get three distinct impressions in their three media rather than a Wagnerian *Gesamtkunstwerk* where these media fused in a new totality. This last kind of montage was what Brecht called the principle of 'separation of the elements': an extension of that 'exercise in complex seeing' which is demanded in his *Threepenny Opera* notes.

From this apparent act of abdication, which henceforward became a part of his theatrical theory, it might be assumed that Brecht was a purely literary gent with a wall eye and a tin ear, who unlike the omnicultural Wagner felt forced to leave the visual and musical aspects of his theatre to others. And indeed where the former was concerned Brecht's own disposition might be thought to bear this out. For there was seldom a painting and even more rarely any colour on his bare white walls, nor was he a visual thinker who used graphic elements to plot his ideas on paper: his aids were scissors and paste. Yet anybody who saw a Brecht (or Brecht-dominated) production will know that these were at once identifiable from their look, a look that has since been copied by theatres that otherwise have little in common with his. For with respect to all the visual aspects of the theatre – set, projections, costumes, lighting, props, movement and grouping of the actors – he had quite definite ideas and decided judgements, and time and again the results were stunning to the eye, as a glance through the volume *Theaterarbeit* will show. The problem then is not unlike that which we shall encounter with the music: was he simply lucky in his collaborators, and wise to leave those 'elements' to them, or did he influence the direction of their work and ensure that it met his own standards none the less? My own conclusion is that he not only himself had a highly skilled eye but could also analyse what he saw in such a way as to offer a permanent contribution to the visual arts. And this could be for the very reason that he bothered so little with art except as an aid and guide to matters where his judgement was sure.

*　　*　　*

About the luck there is no doubt, in that he was able to work out his ideas and practice in a society that produced some brilliantly congenial artists. In particular he was blessed with a lifelong friend and collaborator whose talent measured up to and interacted with his own. This was his Augsburg schoolfellow Rudolf Caspar Neher, a teacher's son with whom he shared virtually all his early formative experiences. Whether Neher would anyway have abandoned painting and illustration for the theatre is uncertain, for his teachers at the Munich Academy (from which he graduated in 1922) told him that stage design was part of 'applied art' or *Kunstgewerbe* and consequently to be looked down on. But correspondence and diaries show Brecht constantly prompting and advising Neher and consulting him about his own plays: telling him (at the age of sixteen) that 'a modern painter must read Zola', recommending him to make political drawings like Goya, offering to submit his work to the Munich paper *Simplicissimus*, then in 1920 persuading Lion Feuchtwanger to recommend to the Kammerspiele in that city some of his designs. Those early theatre drawings of Neher's – indeed right up to the end of the 1920s – are very beautiful, using a delicate, slightly splintery, washy pen and watercolour technique not unlike that of Klee (who was in fact stationed on an Augsburg airfield at the end of the First World War, though there is no evidence that the two men met). Though the examples shown by Brecht were not, it seems, enough to convince the Kammerspiele to let Neher design *Drums in the Night* there – which instead was given a typically Expressionist setting by Otto Reigbert, a more established figure – he did design *In the Jungle* for Erich Engel some six months later, then worked with Brecht on a *Macbeth* project for the Kammerspiele, followed by that production of *Edward II* which established many of Brecht's methods as a director. At the same time he was making illustrations for *Baal*, *Drums in the Night* and *Edward II*, though only the last of these appeared in published form.

By 1923 Neher was working in Berlin, and from then on he was increasingly in demand in that city, notably at the Deutsches Theater (for whom he did six productions in 1925, including *Coriolanus* with Engel and *The Chalk Circle* with Reinhardt himself) and subsequently at the Staatstheater (including Jessner's *Hamlet* with Kortner in 1927). Thereafter he also worked freelance for the theatres at Essen and began a short but fruitful collaboration with Klemperer's Berlin Kroll-Oper, for which he designed not only *Carmen* but also Milhaud's *Le Pauvre Matelot* and Janáček's *From the House of the Dead*. At the same time he seems always to have been available to work with Brecht, providing drawings (again unpublished) for what he called *The Four Soldiers from Kankerdan* – i.e. the first version of *Man equals Man* – and the *Taschenpostille* or *Pocket Devotions*, and designing virtually every important Brecht production, whoever the director, right up to the advent of the Nazis in 1933. About the only significant Brecht première for which he was not responsible was the concert performance of *The Decision* at the end of 1930, which was looked after by his friends and colleagues from the Kroll-Oper, Teo Otto and Wolfgang Roth. All three men were to be known as Brechtian designers after the Second World War.

Whether Neher ever really shared Brecht's political views is uncertain, but unlike him he did not go into exile after the Reichstag Fire of February 1933. Thanks perhaps to his involvement with *Mahagonny* – and particularly to his co-direction with Brecht of the 1931 Berlin production – he had begun to branch out into direction and libretto-writing, starting with the text of Weill's next opera *Die Bürgschaft* (staged by Carl Ebert in 1932). Thereafter, while still continuing to design for the Deutsches Theater after the Nazi takeover, he wrote the text for four operas by Rudolf Wagner-Regeny and worked on some of Ebert's opera productions at Glyndebourne and the Vienna Opera:

activities that encouraged a certain traditionalism in approach. He did not collaborate any further with Brecht after the Paris première of *The Seven Deadly Sins* in the spring of 1933, nor is there any record of subsequent correspondence or contact between the two friends (though they may well have been in touch indirectly). Yet in 1946, a year after the German surrender, Brecht could simply pick up the threads again in the most matter-of-fact way: 'Dear Cas', he wrote,

> I got your address from Kasack after spending months trying to find it out. Clearly our primary job at the moment is to survive. The best thing would be to resume our theatrical collaboration as soon as possible. I've been asked for plays by Berlin (Deutsches Theater) and Heidelberg (Hartung), and in each case will insist that you do the sets . . .[1]

Agreeing to meet in Switzerland in the autumn of 1947, they instantly started work on a number of new projects of which the first and (ultimately) most important was the staging of *Antigone* in the small theatre at Chur a few months later. Though one major plan fell through – for a new-style Salzburg Festival in which the two men would join forces with the Austrian composer Gottfried von Einem, a scheme frustrated when the former Nazi Herbert von Karajan was brought in as overall director – the other led to the establishment of the Berliner Ensemble, for which Neher designed *Puntila* and *The Mother* and co-directed Lenz's *The Tutor* with Brecht. He should also, it seems,[2] have designed *Mother Courage*, but the promised visa never reached him in time. Though Brecht then hoped that he would spend at least part of each season with the Ensemble, the collaboration virtually came to an end with the public controversy in 1951 over the East Berlin State Opera's production of Brecht's and Paul Dessau's *Lucullus* opera, for which Neher again did the sets. The friendship however did not, and its meaning is indelibly recorded in the short poem called simply 'The Friends':

> The war separated
> Me, the writer of plays, from my friend the stage builder.
> The cities where we worked are no longer there.
> When I walk through the cities that still are
> At times I say: that blue piece of washing
> My friend would have placed it better.[3]

This concept of *Bühnenbau* – stage building or stage construction – was special to Brecht, who seems to have coined the word to describe Neher's particular approach to the staging of Brecht's plays as it developed in the 1920s. The method can be called one of Selective Realism, aiming to provide only what was directly needed by the play and the actors – a door, a chair, some indication of a wall, a cyclorama or a screen for projections etc. as the case might be, all brought together once again in a kind of montage. Starting perhaps with the use of a half-height curtain in the Darmstadt production of *Man equals Man* (1926) the boundary between the two men's visual ideas became increasingly blurred as Neher came to provide projected drawings and a boxing ring stage for the *Little Mahagonny*, a band on the stage and screened inscriptions for *The Threepenny Opera*, a portable set made of gas-piping and simple canvas screens for *The Mother* and a skimpy, flimsy wooden set for Brecht's own Berlin production of *Man equals Man* with huge projected drawings and grotesque costumes for the soldiers, two of them mounted on stilts. Along with these disparate elements, which in the full *Mahagonny* were meant to function as an independent interpretation of the play's story, went his practice of making small sketches which were not so much illustrations as visualisations of the action and groupings for each episode, on which Brecht came to base the blocking of the scenes. Admittedly his approach to the post-World War II productions was less fragmented, and hence less striking, but he still seemed to work with Brecht as with nobody else, acting less as a designer in the conventional sense than as a co-director, almost a co-author, working through a visual medium to attain something more than a purely visual result. *Antigone* in particular still looks marvellous: a semicircle of long benches for the actors backed by screens of dull red rush matting; undyed sackcloth costumes; a stand to hold the few props; four wooden posts topped by horses' skulls defining the acting area. It was never seen outside Chur, where it only had a few performances. Fortunately Ruth Berlau's photographs remain.

* * *

We don't know exactly when Brecht first met George Grosz, but it must have been within a year or two of his move to Berlin in 1924. He might already have known Grosz's bitter political and anti-militarist satires; indeed there is some evidence that his 'Legend of the Dead Soldier' was consciously derived from the former's drawing of a skeleton being passed fit by army doctors.[1] By then, however, Grosz was drawing regularly for the Communist *Der Knüppel* (The Truncheon), to which Brecht too made the odd contribution in 1926–27, while he was also doing occasional theatre work such as the painted settings for Georg Kaiser's

Nebeneinander and the more complex sets and projections for Piscator's
Volksbühne production of *Das trunkene Schiff* in 1926. This was an epic
play about Rimbaud by Paul Zech which could well have interested
Brecht, though there is nothing to show that he even saw it; for his own
involvement with Piscator only began some eighteen months later,
reaching its peak in the dramatisation of Hašek's *The Good Soldier Švejk*.
Here Grosz and Piscator worked out a scenic conception based on new
technology – combining drawings by the former with the use of a
treadmill stage – which made possible a radical form of play construction, more 'epic' than Brecht's wildest dreams. For the surviving script
(for which Brecht wanted Grosz to share the credit) shows how the
three-act structure of the first adaptation became loosened up and
allowed to flow scenically through time and space much as does Hašek's
great rambling novel. Moreover, though there is now no trace of Grosz's
cartoon film which accompanied the 'Anabasis' section, the many
drawings and notes for it show his draughtsmanship reaching new
imaginative heights, mixing the symbolic, the atmospheric and the
bitterly realistic as never before. With this as a flickering background the
Good Soldier trudged on against the motion of the invisible (though by
no means inaudible) treadmill, which sometimes would carry cut-out
Groszian figures towards him, sometimes bring on an item of solid
scenery (e.g. a real-life rustic latrine), then come to a halt while the next
absurd military incident was played out.

During this time Grosz and Brecht became good friends, with the
result that Brecht not only devoted a verse of the 'Ballad on Approving
the World' to him in 1933 –

> My friend George Grosz's men with heads like bullets
> (You know them from his drawings) are, it seems
> About to slit the human race's gullets.
> I give my full approval to their schemes.

– but also got him to illustrate the 'children's poem' *The Three Soldiers*
when it was included in the *Versuche* series in 1931. Like his work for
Švejk, these illustrations represent a quite visible reversal of the decline
in Grosz's work which had begun with his growing disillusionment well
before he left for the United States in 1932. However, they remained
exceptions and from then on it was Brecht who appeared to be the party-
line Communist while Grosz fell into a deep apolitical cynicism with
largely paralysing effects. Brecht himself had no wish to break their

alliance; indeed he hoped that Grosz would illustrate Wieland Herzfelde's proposed Malik-Verlag edition of his plays, which was to be published in Czechoslovakia; and during 1935 Grosz actually visited him to discuss details. But he never appreciated how impossible it was for Grosz to recapture the conviction, spirit and style of his earlier work. Grosz did a few drawings, so he told Herzfelde;

> Brecht himself had seen some of them (and thought they were good, but BB has no idea of art) . . . I live in a totally different country, and would have to cast my mind back several decades.[1]

Nothing materialised. Personal relations continued good, though with some fluctuations whenever Grosz became too obsessed with Brecht's refusal to criticise Stalin; and soon before leaving America in 1947 Brecht again asked for drawings, this time to accompany his Shelleyesque anti-West German ballad 'The Anachronistic Procession' which he wanted to send ahead to Europe as a herald of his own return. Grosz refused on the ground that he could no longer cope with political slogans. And once Brecht had gone back to Europe the connection broke.

Unlike Neher, Grosz in the 1920s was part of a movement of politically conscious artists, most of them drawn from Dada and/or the Novembergruppe, who came together with Piscator in 1924 to form a short-lived Red Group. Backed by Herzfelde and his Malik-Verlag, this included the former Dadaists Rudolf Schlichter and John Heartfield, both of whom contributed to *Der Knüppel* – Heartfield indeed was one of the editors – and were acquainted with Brecht. Schlichter, who like Grosz was at that time an excellent realistic draughtsman with a socially critical eye, may first have come into contact with the playwright through his own brother, who ran a Berlin restaurant frequented by theatre people; he drew Brecht and in 1927 painted the well-known portrait of him in a leather jacket (now in the Munich Lenbach-Haus) as well as others of Helene Weigel and their increasingly embarrassing right-wing friend Arnolt Bronnen. Heartfield on the other hand had trained in Munich as a commercial artist, but rivalled Grosz in his blazing hatred of the First World War and combined with him in a number of Dada montages. Throughout the Weimar period he worked intermittently in the Berlin theatre: first for Piscator's early Proletarian Theatre, then for Reinhardt's Deutsches Theater, then for Piscator again in the Communist Party's 1925 Berlin pageant (notably for its pioneering use of newsreel material), in the studio production of Franz Jung's *Heimweh* and finally, in 1931, in Friedrich Wolf's Chinese play *Tai Yang erwacht*. Though Brecht never actually worked with Heartfield till after the Second World War he was greatly impressed by the staging of the Wolf play, with its use of portable banners with political slogans on one side which could be turned around and held together to make a projection screen. Moreover he was well aware of Heartfield's development of a new artistic genre in the shape of political photomontage – the cutting and combining of photographs to make a propagandist point. Like his own epic theatre this too was a form of selective realism, for 'The camera can lie just as can the typewriter' (as he wrote in an approving message to the *Arbeiter-Illustrierte-Zeitung*, the genre's main vehicle, in 1931). This made it justifiable to take scissors and paste to its photographs so as to 'restore the reality of the actual events'.[1]

This Red Group of ex-Dadaists formed the nucleus of the more socially-critical element in *Neue Sachlichkeit* – New Objectivity as it is sometimes called, or New Sobriety, New Matter-of-factness – the trend which became established by a painting exhibition held at Mannheim under that title in 1925 and thereafter was held to have supplanted Expressionism as mid-Europe's guiding principle in the contemporary arts. Like Expressionism it extended far beyond the artists originally exhibited under its banner (who also included Dix and, for a short while, Beckmann, as well as a group of so-called Magic Realists centring on Munich), and came to embrace the music of Weill and Hindemith, the satirical verse of Tucholsky and Erich Kästner and the new functional architecture associated with the Dessau Bauhaus. Inevitably then the Brecht of the mid-1920s – that is, of *Man equals Man* and the collaborations with Weill – tended to be classed under the same heading, though it was not long before his position began to seem ambiguous. Thus there is a polemical note which Brecht wrote around 1927–28 to the address of the Essen dramaturg Hannes Küpper (whose colleague Hein Heckroth had recently drawn Brecht's portrait in pure *Neue Sachlichkeit* style) treating Küpper as a protagonist of that movement, which he certainly was. From this it seems that, while admitting that he himself was against 'that dreadful helpless lack of *Sachlichkeit* which is all that keeps the present-day bourgeois theatre going', Brecht didn't have much faith in the new movement:

> it will have to come in the theatre . . . *sachlichkeit* will come and it'll be a good thing when it does* till then nothing more can be done but this quite necessary and inevitable step forward will be a reactionary affair that's what i'm getting at *neue sachlichkeit* is reactionary[2]
>
> *i hope so by lenin

– a verdict which today fits the argument of those younger German sociologists who blindly and arbitrarily dismiss the whole movement as a bourgeois manifestation not all that far removed from the Nazi culture that followed. Nevertheless Brecht unashamedly awarded Küpper *Die literarische Welt*'s poetry prize in 1927 for a utilitarian poem about a champion cyclist: and in this utilitarianism, as in many other respects (clarity of expression, use of montage, participation in Hindemith's musical experiments, preoccupation with the city and with technology, use of documentary material, addiction to sport and the Anglo-Saxon myth, not to mention aversion to capital letters), Brecht remains a product of the movement and the time, however unassimilable an individual genius he may also have been.

While the Red Group and its friends were certainly Communists they were not proletarians, and they always remained distinct from the 'proletarian' movements that developed after 1928, let alone the Socialist Realism which subsequently emanated from the USSR and had many formal similarities with Nazi art. If these friends of Brecht's, then, can be separated from *Neue Sachlichkeit*, it is on political grounds; for in other respects their work conflicted only with the movement's more reactionary and Italian-orientated Magic Realist wing. As early as 1925 the Red Group itself and the magazine *Der Knüppel* were losing their political momentum, and shortly after Brecht had begun writing for the latter they were supplanted by artistically inferior substitutes in the shape of the Association of Revolutionary Artists – or ARBKD – and the satirical magazine *Rote Pfeffer* (Red Pepper). Neither Grosz nor Brecht contributed to this new magazine, it seems, while the 'Asso' or Association included none of the artists previously linked with Brecht, not even Heartfield (who unlike Grosz and Schlichter retained his Communist convictions throughout his life). This is not to say that the Asso was not of importance in itself, both as a focus of opposition to the Nazis and in due course as a significant factor in the visual tradition of the German Democratic Republic, helping to differentiate this from Socialist Realism in the Soviet sense. But it, together with the Soviet cultural manoeuvres which gave it its initial status, had no direct influence on any visual aspect of Brecht's theatre before the advent of Karl von Appen as his main designer after 1951. And just as the leaders of the Red Group remained outside it, so did Brecht himself remain outside its sister body the BPRS or German Proletarian-Revolutionary Writers' League. Indeed it was in the pages of the latter's journal *Die Linkskurve* that Lukács's influential criticisms of Brecht, Piscator and Ernst Ottwalt were first expressed.

* * *

It was in 1930 that Brecht first began trying to systematise his ideas about the visual aspects of his theatre, and he continued to elaborate them during his exile in Scandinavia and subsequently in the United States. They were based primarily on his work with Neher, though they also reflected the staging of *Švejk* and in due course came to touch on Heartfield's setting of *Tai Yang erwacht*. Clearly they were not preconceived or thought up in isolation (as they might have been had he really remained unaffected by *Neue Sachlichkeit*) and from the first they posit a montage-like approach by which the theatre 'has a tension which governs its component parts and "loads" them against one another'.[1] Though the 'separation of the elements' is already implied in *The Threepenny Opera* with its use of projected texts and its interruption of the action by songs, the first full consideration of the new methods derives from what was perhaps the most austere of all his conceptions. 'In the first production of *Die Mutter*', he wrote,

> the stage (Caspar Neher) wasn't supposed to represent any real locality: it as it were took up an attitude to the incidents shown; it quoted, narrated, prepared and recalled. Its sparse indication of furniture, doors etc, was limited to objects that had a part in the play, i.e. those without which the action would have been changed or halted. A firm arrangement of iron piping slightly higher than a man was erected at varying intervals perpendicularly to the stage; other movable horizontal pipes carrying canvases would be slotted into it, and this allowed of quick changes. There were doors in frames hanging inside this, which could be opened or shut. A big canvas at the back of the stage was used for the projection of texts and pictorial documents which remained all through the scene, so that this screen was also in effect part of the setting. Thus the stage not only used allusions to show actual rooms but also texts and pictures to show the great movement of ideas in which the events were taking place . . . [These] don't set out to help the spectator but to block him; they prevent his complete empathy, interrupt his being automatically carried away.[2]

Thereafter Brecht began writing an extensive work on what he already termed the *Bühnenbau* (or stage construction, rather than the normal term *Bühnenbild* or stage picture) of his epic theatre, though it never got beyond a wide-ranging collection of fragments. The principle here was that for the designer 'the right starting-point is zero': in other words his initial contribution must not be a fully prepared scheme but a sober consideration of the bare theatrical space and the use which the actors would make of it. 'A wall and a chair are already a great deal', he noted.

'What's more, putting up a wall properly and placing a chair properly are very far from easy'.[1] The actors and even the musicians, then, were to be situated according to similar principles, for 'the grouping is an extension of the stage construction, and is one of the constructor's [i.e. the designer's] principal tasks'.[2] This was to be achieved by means of the kind of sketches which Neher used to provide. The designer would have to work with the actors, modifying his provision and placing of the various scenic elements to meet whatever might emerge from the rehearsals. This meant that the set was best built up as a series of independent movable elements which ideally – a solution perhaps only hinted at in the Piscator–Grosz *Švejk* and otherwise not even approached – would manifest themselves as and when called for by the actions of the actors. 'Wherever they conduct business, counting-houses spring up; wherever they drink together, bars.'[3] These essential elements – and nothing more – needed to be realistically made, with a sense of the social usage which they are supposed to have undergone: for 'the art of abstraction has to be applied by *realists*',[4] though by realists allergic to any creation of illusion. Thus projections were never to be used to amplify an image but as a separate thread in the texture of the production. Add the brilliant stage lighting which Brecht specified should have visible sources as at a sporting event, plus the projected scene titles whose object was to stamp each episode as part of a historical record; and it only remained for the audience to put it all together for themselves. 'The spectator must be in a position to shift the component parts around in his mind's eye, in other words to make a montage.'[5]

In this whole economical, functional approach, with its balance of constructivism and realism, which in the hands of a great artist could achieve images of extraordinary originality and beauty, a special part came to be played by materials and workmanship. Thus for *Antigone* in 1948

> Particular care was taken over the props; good craftsmen worked on them. This wasn't so that the audience or actors should imagine that they were real, but simply so as to provide audience and actors with beautiful objects.[6]

What Brecht meant by beauty in this context was something not exclusively visual but social and historical too, the cumulative imprint of human skills and labour over many years. Memorably expressed in a poem which he wrote about 1932, starting

> Of all the works of man I like best
> Those which have been used.

> The copper pots with their dents and flattened edges
> The knives and forks whose wooden handles
> Have been worn away by many hands: such forms
> Seemed to me the noblest.[1]

– this 'labour theory of beauty', as it might be termed, was one that he evidently shared with Neher, of whose sets he later wrote that

> They display a lovely mixture of his own handwriting and that of the playwright. And there is no building of his, no yard or workshop or garden, that does not also bear the fingerprints, as it were, of the people who built it or who lived there. He makes visible the manual skills and knowledge of the builders and the ways of living of the inhabitants.

A similar low-level interest in anonymous humanity seems to underlie yet another aesthetic principle, which derived from his search for examples of the 'alienation effect'. This was the naïvety first propounded by Courbet's friend Champfleury some eighty years earlier when the latter began his pioneering studies of popular imagery in France. Such a naïve eye, for Brecht, is capable of looking at the most familiar sights with a certain critical wonder, as in that fairground painting of *The Flight of Charles the Bold after the Battle of Murten* of which he wrote (in relation to Chinese acting) that

> The fleeing commander, his horse, his retinue and the landscape are all quite consciously painted in such a way as to create the impression of an abnormal event, an astonishing disaster. In spite of his inadequacy the painter succeeds brilliantly in bringing out the unexpected. Amazement guides his brush.[2]

It was characteristic of Brecht's persistent homogeneity, under all his seeming inconsistencies and contradictions, that his visual and theatrical concept alike should be so shaped by the lives and work of obscure ordinary people.

* * *

With the Second World War imminent, this new concern with art's more plebeian aspects brought Brecht into contact with two widely different yet remotely related artists who helped to influence his vision from then on. The first of these was the elder Brueghel,[3] whose works seem to have begun seriously intriguing him when Helene Weigel gave him the two classic books of reproductions compiled by the Viennese art historian Gustav Glück (soon to be his neighbour in Santa Monica).

Ostensibly Brecht's interpretation of some of the best-known paintings in Glück's selection centred on the artist's gift for balancing conflicting elements in such a way as to 'set off the oddness' of them all: the desperate servant's attitude of the *Fury of War* for instance, or the tiny scale of Icarus's hopeless disaster compared with the indifferent rustic world in the foreground. Often what sticks in the reader's mind is the perceptive vividness of Brecht's descriptions: thus the Tower of Babel

> has been put up askew. It includes portions of cliff, between which one can see the artificiality of the stonework . . . Powerful oppression prevails, the attitude of the men bringing up the building materials is extremely servile, the builder is guarded by armed men.[1]

Such words suggest an unusual alertness to visual implications.

Then just before the German invasion of Poland he met a strange self-taught artist called Hans Tombrock, a Westphalian miner's son who had had his citizenship annulled by the Nazis after joining one of the more eccentric 1920s movements: the Communist league of tramps organised by the ex-sailor Gregor Gog. Intrigued by Tombrock and anxious to help him, Brecht got him to make some drawings based on the playwright's own life – notably one crowded, vivid scene in the Brechts' temporary Swedish home, with a band of friends discussing the fall of the Spanish Republic – and on some of his works, including a number of short poems which Brecht wrote to raise money for him, thus:

> Glancing up from reading about some world event
> I find my milk bill is overdue
> So don't just buy weapons, please, but pictures too.
> The fact is: the Last Trump is imminent.
> Anno domini 1940.[2]

Gog meanwhile wrote from the USSR (where he was shortly to be banished to Siberia) to commission Tombrock to make an illustrated edition of *Galileo* for the Kiev State Publishing House. Though this plan fell through, it drew Brecht to think about the visual aspects of the play, and Tombrock's drawing of the carnival, for all its clumsiness, significantly catches something of Brueghel's crowded popular scenes.

Mother Courage had its world première in Zurich that year, followed during 1943 by those of *The Good Person of Szechwan* and *Galileo*, all three being designed by the politically sympathetic Teo Otto. There is no evidence that Brecht himself was in a position to influence any of these wartime productions, and only Mother Courage's wagon, with its authentic workmanship and central role in the staging, became part of

his own vision when he came to direct the play with Erich Engel on his
return to Berlin. For him the most significant experience of those years
was, rather, the Hollywood production of *Galileo* on which he began
working with Charles Laughton some six months before the end of the
war. Though Robert Davison was the eventual designer (Brecht having
tried in vain to get Neher over from Europe) it seems that this was only
decided in 1947 once the two collaborators had finally settled on Joseph
Losey as the director; and they did most of the preliminary work
themselves.

> For a while this embraced everything we could lay hands on. If we discussed
> gardening, it was only as a diversion from one of the scenes in *Galileo*; if we
> combed a New York museum for technical drawings by Leonardo to use as
> background pictures in the performance, we would get diverted to Hokusai's
> graphic work . . .[1]

They got John Hubley, who was then one of Disney's draughtsmen and
later with Stephen Bosustow at UPA, to suggest groupings as Neher
used to do; but for some reason this was not a great success. Then they
worked out an elaborate scheme of costumes and colour, going largely to
Brueghel for inspiration, particularly in the carnival scene.

> Each scene had to have its basic tone: the first, e.g., a delicate morning one of
> white, yellow and grey. But the entire sequence of scenes had to have its
> development in terms of colour. In the first scene a deep and distinguished
> blue made its appearance with Ludovico Marsili, and this deep blue remained,
> set apart, in the second scene with the upper bourgeoisie in their grey-green
> coats made of felt and leather. Galileo's social ascent could be followed by
> means of colour. The silver and grey of the fourth (court) scene led into a
> nocturne in brown and black . . . then on to the eighth, the cardinal's ball, with
> delicate and fantastic masks . . . moving among the cardinal's crimson figures.
> This was a burst of colour, but it still had to be fully unleashed, and this took
> place in the ninth scene, the carnival. After the nobility and the cardinals the
> poor people too had their masked ball. Then came the descent into dull and
> sombre colours. The difficulty of such a scheme of course lies in the fact that
> the costumes and their wearers wander through several scenes; they have
> always to fit in and to help build up the colour scheme of the scenes that
> follow.[2]

This was the experience uppermost in Brecht's mind when he
returned to the collaboration with Neher and the eventual setting-up of
the Berliner Ensemble. However, the formal simplicity of the *Galileo*
setting, like that of the Chur *Antigone* which followed, might well have

proved too austere for a Berlin audience to whom his methods were by now so entirely strange. For the *Mother Courage* production therefore he took over Teo Otto's wagon and its positioning, but combined this with a use of the revolve not dissimilar to that of the treadmill in *Švejk*, making it rotate against the wagon's movement. For *Puntila* he had a relatively elaborate set by Neher with a big screen for drawings at the back. For *The Tutor* Neher provided stylised eighteenth-century settings and costumes, using the revolve at one point to show the main characters successively miming their actions as time passed in their different environments. Generally there was a half-height curtain on which the scene titles were projected, and the stage was brilliantly and evenly lit. At first the colours tended to be subdued, most notoriously so in *Mother Courage*, whose deliberate greyness (grey being Brecht's favourite colour) led the Soviet occupation authorities in 1949 to suggest helping him out with supplies of paint. In fact as late as 1953 Strittmatter's East German play *Katzgraben* was given a memorably dingy appearance, this time in an effort to capture the effect of old photographs, which also had a certain appeal for Brecht. With this exception however the austerity steadily dwindled, and the distance travelled since 1932 can be graphically seen by comparing Neher's beautiful but quite detailed sets for the Ensemble *The Mother* (which used projections by Heartfield to fill out the picture) with those which Brecht's earlier notes (quoted above) had described.

For the last two years of Brecht's life, starting in 1954, Karl von Appen was the chief designer for the Ensemble. Belonging to the same generation as Brecht and Neher, he had given up an early career as a stage designer in Frankfurt in order to work as a painter in Berlin and Dresden, where in 1932 he joined the Asso. Underground work for the Communist Party had led to his arrest by the Nazis, so that he spent most of the war years in a concentration camp before returning to become director general of the Dresden opera and theatres between 1947 and 1949. For all his political and administrative experience von Appen remained primarily a painter, no longer a 'stage builder' like Neher but a 'stage picturer' or *Bühnenbildner* in a more traditional sense. Following the almost monochrome *Katzgraben* he now provided Brecht's company with settings as varied as those for *Trumpets and Drums* (stylised black-and-white flats, back-drops and cut-outs recalling eighteenth-century engravings) and the deliberately more colourful and ingratiating *The Caucasian Chalk Circle* (a fluttering silk backcloth with a Georgian mountain village shown as if in a Chinese painting, accompanied by solid Neher-like elements on stage and a *Courage*-like use of the revolve). He

too took to imagining groups of the play's characters, whom he painted
in gouache in some detail, giving them rounded figures along with
humorous faces not unlike those of the actors portraying them. Always
more static than the groupings habitually sketched for Brecht by Neher,
these pictures had something in common with the work both of
Tombrock and of Brueghel. They may not have related so closely to
Brecht's blocking of the action, but they surely helped to underline the
plebeian element in his plays. And never was Brueghel's influence on
Brecht's stage so practically evident as in the crazy wedding scene of *The
Caucasian Chalk Circle*.

* * *

Following his seventeen years' absence from the Berlin theatre the
change in Brecht's visual concepts seems a marked one, and nowhere
more so perhaps than as instanced in the picture included, apparently
without irony, in *Theaterarbeit* to illustrate 'the old masters' concept of
beauty': a massive grinning Tyrolese peasant woman by Dürer, such as
the Nazis themselves might have admired. Such shifts of taste cannot be
ascribed purely to Brecht's new formulations of the 1930s and 40s, nor to
his own evolution alone. For while none reacted quite so sharply as did
the American Grosz, not one of the artists closest to Brecht worked as
interestingly or radically after those seventeen years as he had done
before. Up to a point this reflected not only their own ageing but also the
age in which they lived, for a similar return to convention can be seen in
the work of Dix, Kokoschka and other members of the old mid-
European avant-garde, most of whom no longer attempted the former
shock effects, let alone managed to achieve them. Moreover for those
who followed the Communist line there was an additional dampener in
the doctrine of Socialist Realism which the party had continued to
preach ever since 1934 and was once again trying to enforce. Extensively
as he might argue with its official proponents in his unpublished papers,
Brecht could be seen to have conformed with its principles in a number
of important respects: for instance by his development away from
austerity and 'drabness', his new concern with popular elements, his
partial reconciliation with the emotions and his tacit abandonment of
some aspects of his own theories. The theories themselves in any case
were neither discussed within the Berliner Ensemble nor even known to
many of its members.

Rather more alarmingly, during the 1930s and 50s – the two high-
water marks of the official dogma – he could write some quite retrograde

things about the visual arts, speaking crudely against non-figurative art
and in favour of a simple proletarian approach. Thus his somewhat self-
righteous homespun philosopher Mr Keuner is made to say with
reference to a painting 'which gave one or two objects a particularly
arbitrary form'[1] that the artist can be like a gardener clipping a shrub: in
his anxiety to achieve form he chops away the substance. Similarly his
pseudo-Chinese sage Me-Ti meets a barge-hauler's son who is a
communist but paints in order to 'develop the forms of painting', to
which Me-Ti replies that this is playing into the exploiters' hands and he
should instead be painting barge-haulers.[2] (Wittingly or not, this would
surely have gratified admirers of that forerunner of Socialist Realism Ilya
Repin, who painted more than one highly dramatised picture of barge-
haulers on the Volga.) There is, moreover, a long poem[3] celebrating the
completion of the Moscow Metro which seems to praise the ornateness
of the stations – one of the high points of Stalinist architecture – while in
East Berlin in the 1950s Brecht took an approving interest in the
building of the dreadful Stalin-Allee (since renamed Karl Marx-Allee)
and was on good terms with its chief architect Hermann Henselmann.
Two pages of notes from that period show him setting up 'proletarian'
architecture against 'bourgeois' (i.e. the modern movement) and 'beauty'
against functionalism in a way that the Russians themselves subsequently
discarded. What was wanted, he said, was 'palaces for living in', and the
architects must recognise

> That socialism has led in Russia to the stressing of what is most Russian . . .
> and in Poland of what is most Polish; and that in Germany socialism will lead
> to the application of German tradition as seen in its most splendid periods[4]

– tradition which clearly is no longer to include the great radical German
architecture of the 1920s.

All the same Brecht was an exceedingly contradictory man, and the
apparent conformism of his new opinion never stopped him opposing
the official aesthetic whenever he objected to its implications, or, more
personally, to its spokesmen. So during the so-called 'Expressionism
controversy' of the mid-1930s he could note that (unlike the arbiters of
taste in Moscow) he liked Franz Marc's *Tower of the Blue Horses* and felt

> irritated when painters are told they are not to paint horses blue; I don't see
> any crime in that, society can surely stomach such minor rearrangements of
> reality.[5]

Curiously enough he came out more strongly at the beginning of 1952
when Wilhelm Girnus, one of the arts editors of the party paper *Neues*

Deutschland, chose to attack the sculpture of Ernst Barlach on the grounds that it 'contains no element that points towards the future' and 'has a lack of orientation towards that class to which the future belongs'. Admittedly Brecht was prepared to take such objections more seriously than they deserved, agreeing that it was 'perhaps a pity' that the *Beggarwoman* of 1906 didn't display the militant spirit of Gorky's *Mother* and stating that young artists should not be encouraged to imitate those works like *The Avenger* and *The Doubter* whose 'formal qualities strike me as a deformation of reality'. Nevertheless he disliked the 'impatient and fanatical tone' of Barlach's critics and flatly ranked him as 'one of the greatest sculptors we Germans have had'.

> The conception, the significance of statement, technical mastery, beauty without prettification, greatness without exaggeration, harmony without smoothness, power without brutality, all make Barlach's sculptures into masterpieces. At the same time I don't like absolutely all his work.[1]

It seems that Brecht was now uncertain how far public taste could move to meet the modern aesthetic. Thus whereas in architecture he supported the official line, according to which the 'new leading class' needed traditional ornamentation as evidence of palatial housing, so far as painting went he took a rather different view, holding that the workers might well learn to appreciate not only Van Gogh but *Guernica* too.[2] What is more he accused (if only in private) the pundits who argued otherwise of underrating the People and setting themselves snobbishly above it. Here, as in his notes on literary and theatrical 'formalism', he plainly mistrusted the official anti-'formalists', not least because their terms of reference seemed to him not so much political as quasi-medical: what worried them, he felt, was that the workers might become contaminated by 'unhealthy' art.

> When they're not summoning the doctor to make healthy works of art, they are sending for the police to punish a crime against the People.[3]

At the root of this he detected an undue reverence for tradition coupled with a failure to see how closely form and content are bound together for any artist, so that new contents require new forms. Yet he never went so far as to say that the campaign against formalism and cosmopolitanism should be abandoned, let alone that the magic doctrine of Socialist Realism might be pernicious nonsense. Outwardly he paid lip-service to all the main tenets of the official line as restated after the Second World War by Stalin's lieutenant A.A. Zhdanov. He merely disputed their interpretation, particularly when they seemed to threaten the work of artists whom he admired.

This put him in the unfamiliar position of being a defender of what he termed 'die Kunst schlechthin', or Art with a capital A. And one of his bases for this was his new status as an Academician of the East German Academy of Arts. This body was set up, originally as a would-be all-German successor to the old Prussian Academy, in 1950, and because of its broad and generally distinguished membership Brecht saw that it could be used as a check to the follies of a cultural administration which in those days was largely staffed by the sort of official

> who may be well-trained politically and very conscious of his political responsibilities, yet ... badly trained aesthetically and unconscious of his responsibility to the artist.[1]

A number of other prominent figures felt the same way as Brecht and chafed against the literal-minded application of what amounted to Moscow criteria, whether purely Zhdanovian or as laid down there by Lukács for the German emigration, in defiance of Germany's own revolutionary tradition. Following Stalin's death in 1953, and Brecht's greatly enhanced position as a result of his rejection of the so-called Rising of 17 June, their objections came to a head. Among the various attacks which they launched against the prevalent policy (notably the article 'Cultural Policy and Academy of Arts' which is included in *Brecht on Theatre*) was Brecht's satirical poem about the Art Commission's intervention to exclude supposedly 'formalist' pictures from the Third German Art Exhibition in Dresden. Not long after, the whole structure of such 'commissions' was swept away in favour of a full-scale Ministry of Culture presided over by Johannes R. Becher.

Among the artists to be excluded at Dresden was John Heartfield, who had returned to East Berlin from London at about the same time as Brecht from Zurich. In 1951 Becher as president of the 'Kulturbund' had promised Heartfield a full-scale retrospective 'as soon as possible'[2], while Brecht for his part formally recommended him as a 'classic' satirist and 'one of the most significant European artists'. Nonetheless Heartfield had remained officially neglected, partly perhaps because of his position as a 'Western' emigrant but primarily because by Moscow's criteria any kind of montage must be formalist. Brecht, who in Hanns Eisler's words 'was crazy about' Heartfield,[3] accordingly gave him what work he could designing posters and projections for the Berliner Ensemble and jackets for the East German (Aufbau) edition of his collected works. One of the first such jobs was the designing of Brecht's *Hundred Poems* edited by

Wieland Herzfelde, for which Heartfield provided a jacket bearing a photograph of a small Chinese lion made from the root of a tea bush. This worried the publishers, who rejected the lion on the grounds of 'formalism' because they couldn't see its relevance to a book of poems. Brecht explained in the epigram which goes

ON A CHINESE TEA-ROOT LION

The bad fear your claws.
The good enjoy your elegance.
This
I would like to hear said
Of my verse.[1]

This was to appear on the back of the jacket, but still it did not satisfy the firm, who wanted a plain typographic jacket for the first printing, which would be seen by officials and critics. Brecht, they pointed out, was at that time himself a subject of controversy, so 'it would be unwise to provoke criticism by gratuitous formalism'.[2] The result was a compromise, with half the book appearing in plain jackets and half with the lion, the latter proving notably more popular with the book-buying public. Not that this was of any great help to the artist, who went on being ignored by the official arbiters. Only when the combined efforts of Brecht and other friends had at last got Heartfield admitted to the Academy was the way clear for his full recognition and a proper retrospective show of his work. By that time Brecht was dead.

There were other East German artists of whose work he had appeared to approve, though he never ranked them with Heartfield and Grosz. Among these were the eminent sculptor Fritz Cremer and the painter Bert Heller, both of whom made portraits of him, along with the caricaturists Herbert Sandberg and Elizabeth Shaw, the latter being a witty former contributor to the British Left press. Brecht also greatly liked the pen drawings which the Pole Tadeusz Kulisiewicz made as a set of illustrations to *The Caucasian Chalk Circle*, though these sensitive and competent designs have (to my mind) nothing like the power of the *To Those Born Later* sequence by the Dane Palle Nielsen – perhaps the best of the many graphic works inspired by Brecht's writings. Nevertheless there was not one of these people who could satisfy Brecht's own spontaneous tastes as exemplified in the few pictures which he actually had on his walls. Perhaps he might have hung a Grosz there if he had owned one; certainly he had photographs made for him of some of Grosz's work. But I only recall a big scroll by Neher showing a heavy, sullen Baal, brooding over a lute,[1] and apart from some very small pictures like an old engraving of Karl Marx everything else was Chinese.

There is an interesting note of Brecht's on Chinese painting written around 1935 which explains its particular appeal for him: an appeal that certainly flies in the face of any accepted definition of Socialist Realism. For Chinese pictures, in his view, involve the free arrangement of many different things and people alongside one another, without their forcible submission to any principle of composition or perspective – in other words a form of montage:

> The eye can go on a voyage of discovery. The things depicted are like elements capable of independent existence, yet as combined together on the paper they form a whole, though not an indivisible one. You can cut these pictures up without their becoming meaningless, though not without their changing. Moreover Chinese artists have plenty of room to spare on their paper . . . In these gaps the actual paper or canvas comes to take on a definite value . . . Which means among other things very properly renouncing the total subjugation of the observer, whose illusion remains only partial.[2]

Much of this applies to certain paintings by Brueghel.

* * *

It is perceptions like these that really constitute Brecht's particular contribution to the visual arts. That is to say that neither his obvious themes and characters nor his public and would-be public statements on the politics of painting offer anything like the potential stimulus to the artist that comes from his attempts to describe what he considers beautiful or visually satisfying, and to work out why he does so. Once he starts going into his own relationship with the work of art, whether it be a picture or a stage set, and relating it to his whole socio-aesthetic outlook, then he comes up with thoughts that can be vividly suggestive to artists even today. One such chain of ideas certainly arises from his concept of beauty in relation to usage, to human wear and tear and ultimately to the evidence of the labour and experience that created it in the first place. For this makes sense of a number of common artistic prejudices that the avant-garde in our century has been too easily inclined to dismiss; explaining for instance why a black square by Malevitch is a hundred times more vital than comparable work done by some more permissively brought-up painter in the 1970s: the effort, the struggle sinks into the picture and somehow brings its surface simplicity to life. Then there is another still fertile vein that develops from the practice of 'epic' structure or montage, by which the minimal essential elements of the work, each firmly realistic in itself, are put side by side before the spectator, whose task and pleasure it then is to establish the relevant links, not ignoring the intervening blank (but carefully calculated) spaces. Both these basic Brechtian principles are very visible in the actual appearance of his stage, where they were made convincing by the combination of three-dimensional artistry and sheer pig-headed perfectionism with which his collaborators were inspired to realise them. Over and above this, and antedating Brecht, there is the old concept of 'alienation' (see pp. 234 ff.) by which the artist must continually say something fresh and unfamiliar about the most familiar things.

Artists don't really need a man like Brecht to tell them what to create or what concessions to make to public understanding. Except for illustrations it is generally the mediocre artist who bases his own work directly on a writer's – giving us his visualisations of Mack the Knife, say, or Pirate Jenny – just as it is the mediocre poet who will base a poem on a picture by Klee: it is as if such people were trying to stamp their own work with a certificate of authenticity, by latching on to a greater name. Against that it can be really stimulating to encounter a creative genius from some other field who has so laboriously worked out the principles underlying his work – structural, social, ethical, political – and tried to apply them to his judgement of all forms of art. The result is a diversified single-mindedness whose manifestations may sometimes seem perverse but will always be interesting because of the dynamic that informs them. Of course the theatre, like the cinema, offers particular encouragement to such an approach, just because it involves contact with (and demands judgement of) so many related arts. This is where Brecht differed from Wagner, because he never tried to practise those arts himself but made space for them alongside his own so long as they observed the same underlying principles. So where Wagner's texts have to be set off against his music – because to say the least they don't match up to it – or Eisenstein's rather feeble drawings against his films, with Brecht the visual beauty and precision of a production like *Antigone* is likely to convince any artist that such a writer's view will be worth listening to.

In such matters it isn't the quality of the writing, or the depth of the underlying philosophy, or the nature of the political stance that really counts. If the proof of the pudding is in the eating, the test of a man's claim to write about art is the effectiveness of his eye.

10

Brecht and the musicians

Among the many fascinating early photographs relating to Brecht's life in Augsburg there is a memorable picture taken on 12 December 1912. This shows seven cheerful-looking gentlemen in shiny top hats. Three have beards like Poincaré or George V; three have neat horizontal moustaches. Six are smiling, particularly the clean-shaven exception, who is showing his teeth. All carry canes at varyingly rakish angles; all wear what appear to be chrysanthemums in their button-holes. The neatest-looking, wearing the highest and stiffest collar, with his cane hooked over his shoulder, is Brecht's father. In front is a framed sign with gothic letters saying 'Apollo Tenoria Das Komitee'. They are the committee of the Augsburg glee club, photographed when Brecht was fourteen.

Some ten years later he wrote a poem called 'Song of the Roses on the Shipka Pass', which starts:

> One Sunday comes back to me from my childhood
> With Father singing in his mellow bass
> Across the glasses and the empty bottles
> His song 'The Roses on the Shipka Pass' . . .[1]

It is difficult not to associate this with the Augsburg glee club on the one hand, and the Victorian ballad-writer George R. Sims, author of 'Christmas Day in the Workhouse', on the other. For Sims wrote a poem called 'In the Shipka Pass', and the Shipka Pass, which is in Bulgaria, is not a very common theme to sing about, anyway for those outside that country. Moreover in Brecht's case the poem has a tune, and the tune is written in his own peculiar plainchant notation. This suggests that he sang it himself, to his own accompaniment on the guitar, the one instrument he knew how to play.

Brecht's poetry-writing began, so he said, 'with songs to the guitar, sketching out the verses at the same time as the music'. There was thus a 'musical appendix' to his first collection of poems, the *Devotions*, containing fourteen tunes,[1] and there are also tunes to other early poems in the Brecht Archive (they are now surely transcribed). This was in accordance with a certain German tradition by which poets would sing their own verses in private or public: something that is much less common in France, England or the United States. Following Frank Wedekind's example, which was particularly strong in Munich during Brecht's student years there, there was for instance a half-improvised cabaret following the first two nights of *Drums in the Night* in the Kammerspiele, with songs from the poets Klabund (Alfred Henschke), Ringelnatz and Brecht himself – all of whom were accustomed to performing at pubs or parties – as well as a turn by the marvellous Bavarian clown Karl Valentin, who had a strong influence on Brecht and (to judge from old recordings) sang with the same sharp clarity and rolled 'r's. Among the numerous descriptions of the young Brecht singing, Carl Zuckmayer's is of particular interest, since he too was just such a poet and sang at the same after-theatre party where he and Brecht first met:

> He had command of his instrument and loved complicated chords that were hard to finger: C sharp minor or E flat major. His singing was raw and trenchant, sometimes crude as a ballad-singer's, with an unmistakable Augsburg accent, sometimes almost beautiful, soaring without any vibrato, each syllable, each semitone being quite clear and distinct. [. . .] That evening he sang his ballad of 'Jakob Apfelböck', then 'Remembering Marie A.' (a song which he set to a vulgar hit tune well known towards the end of the war, which his text and his expressive musicianship turned into a haunting folk melody), the 'Ballad of the Pirates', the song 'Of the drowned girl' and maybe others such as I heard from him again and again over many years.[2]

In arriving at such tunes Brecht had some help from his younger brother Walter (who followed their father into the paper business) and his Augsburg friends, and some of them were indeed borrowed. Thus 'Marie A.' went to a fin-de-siècle tune called 'Tu ne m'aimais pas' or 'Verlorenes Glück' by one Charles Malo; the 'Ballad of the Pirates' to a still untraced tune which he called 'L'étendard de la pitié'; the 'Benares Song' to a mixture of 'One fine day' from *Madam Butterfly* and 'There's a tavern in the town'. Though the originals were popular, they were not in the normal sense folk songs ('the people has no wish to be folk', said Brecht, who considered the real folk tradition to be dead), and he recalled the women workers in the paper mill 'singing individual verses or entire songs with a certain irony, putting quotation marks, as it were, round a lot that was cheap, exaggerated, unreal'. It was in just this way that he enjoyed 'The Maiden's Prayer' (which his friend Pfanzelt played on the piano, laughing 'till his teeth wobbled'), or Salvation Army hymns or the late nineteenth-century song 'Asleep on the Deep' ('Stürmisch die Nacht') which repeatedly came to his lips or his pen. The essence of such melodies was that they encouraged the singer to adopt an attitude, either for or against their sentimentality; almost to act. But more commonly he devised simple tunes of his own which had much more rhythmical elasticity, almost like recitatives. These he set down in a rough notation where there was no time signature or bar lines, but a cross meant a longer note and a dot a shorter. The fact that they were without regular beats, stresses or sometimes bars shows how the rhythm was meant to follow that of the words; the metrics lay in the verse, whose shape and sense were not to be distorted by being sung.

*　　*　　*

From the outset Brecht's songs became an essential component of his plays, only *Señora Carrar's Rifles*, *Antigone* and the individual scenes of *Fear and Misery of the Third Reich* being conceived without them. At first the tunes were his own: the 'Legend of the Dead Soldier' in *Drums in the Night*, the ballad-seller's song in scene 2 of *Edward II*, and the songs in *Baal* and the original productions of *Man equals Man*. Then after he had been in Berlin for about a year he began working with professional musicians, initially with a short-lived friend of Klabund's called F. S. Bruinier, a pupil of the pianist Egon Petri's who had gone into theatre music and accompanying. With Bruinier he collaborated on settings of the 'Song of the Girl and the Soldier', 'The Ballad of Hannah Cash', 'Pirate Jenny' and the 'Barbara Song' (both written some eighteen months before *The Threepenny Opera*); also 'Surabaya-Johnny', which he gave to the cabaret singer Kate Kühl. Next, for the radio production of *Man equals Man*, he seems to have handed his tunes over to Piscator's music director Edmund Meisel, another composer who died around the age of thirty and is now perhaps best known for his score to *The Battleship Potemkin*. That play had not yet found a theatre in Berlin, and for the broadcast of 18 March 1927 Brecht himself not only delivered the introductory speech now included in *Brecht on Theatre* but also sang Meisel's new arrangement of the 'Man equals Man Song'. There was a regular critic on the weekly radio magazine *Der deutsche Rundfunk* who wrote two articles about this production, came to the studio and subsequently sent a copy of the script to his own publisher, the formidable boss of Universal-Edition in Vienna. Though the publisher, it seems, was at a loss what to make of it, the critic, who happened also to be a composer, saw the possibility of a major collaboration.

This was the origin of Brecht's six-year partnership with Kurt Weill, who was then just twenty-seven. A student of Busoni's at the Berlin Academy, he was already seen as one of Germany's most promising composers after Hindemith; moreover he was the first German or Austrian musician of any consequence to show an interest in setting texts by postwar writers. Even before Brecht came along he was composing the cabaret-like *Der neue Orpheus* for voice and small orchestra to a poem by Iwan Goll, while for the one-act opera *Der Protagonist* and the quasi-surrealist, jazz-influenced farce *Der Zar lässt sich photographieren* (The Tsar Has His Picture Taken) he turned to the older playwright whom Brecht most respected, Georg Kaiser. It was incidentally while visiting Kaiser that he met the young Viennese actress and dancer Lotte Lenya whose untrained voice and unpretty face were to become lastingly associated with the Brecht–Weill songs. He also, it seems, knew the poet Johannes R. Becher, and was acquainted with Brecht's first collection of poems even before reading *Man equals Man*. Not only did he get instantly bitten with the imagination and language encountered in these works; but he also shared the socio-artistic attitudes that underlay them.

A year after the *Man equals Man* broadcast we find Weill writing to Schott's magazine *Melos* to expound the 'epic opera' in terms that more than once echo Brecht's speech, with its concepts of the 'new human type' and the surrender of the private ego to the collective.[1] Then in March 1929 (in other words during the run of *The Threepenny Opera*) he is actually the first of the two to formulate that idea of the 'gest' and its expression which was to become a cornerstone of Brecht's theoretical writings. Seen in the context of the songs, this is the principle according to which, instead of processing the text for his own musical ends, the composer studies how the words communicate the gest or attitude by rhythmic means, including pauses, and must then respect it while underlining and adding to it by means special to music.[2] Whether or not they yet used the term to one another, the new 'gestic' approach underlay the Brecht–Weill collaboration from the first, for Weill shows (in the same article) how he took the gestic rhythm of the refrain to the 'Alabama Song' as Brecht originally sang it (in his 'wholly personal and inimitable way of singing') and gave it a far broader melodic appeal. At the same time, though he does not say so, he left the melody of the verse practically untouched.

This occurred in the course of that work on *Mahagonny* which was at once the start of their extraordinarily productive partnership and its eventual downfall. For at or around the time of the *Man equals Man* broadcast, the two men agreed to collaborate on an opera, then settled on a theme which would combine various unrealised ideas of Brecht's concerning a Wild West interpretation of Bavaria, a morality play on *The Flood* and the *Collapse of Miami, the Paradise City* following a hurricane. Into this cocktail would go the 'Mahagonny Songs' which Weill had already read, including the 'Alabama Song'. Almost at once there were interruptions. Before the libretto could get far, Weill was asked to provide a 'short opera' as one of a number of such works to be performed at the 1927 Baden-Baden festival, and this he saw as a useful 'stylistic exercise' for the main job. The first product then was the 'songspiel' or *Little Mahagonny*, consisting of the five 'Mahagonny Songs' plus the unpublished 'Poem on a Dead Man', with orchestral interludes and a band of ten (2 violins, 2 clarinets, 2 trumpets, saxophone, trombone, piano and percussion, according to the programme). This impressed (and greatly entertained) some of the most knowledgeable visitors to the festival, including Klemperer and Heinrich Strobel, and once it was over the way should have been clear for concentrated work on the full opera, for which the 'songspiel' was really just a spinoff, an experimental prototype, a skeleton. However, in addition to lesser jobs like the writing of incidental music for *Man equals Man* and Piscator's production of *Konjunktur* (with its splendid song about Royal Dutch Shell), half of the year 1928 was disrupted by what Weill called a *Gelegenheitsarbeit*, a job on the side. This was *The Threepenny Opera*, a seemingly unforeseen commission by a new impresario with whom neither man had worked before.

The success of this hurriedly mounted project had all kinds of repercussions for both Brecht and Weill, not to mention Ernst-Josef Aufricht the impresario in question, whose natural if disastrous reaction was to arrange for the lucky formula to be repeated the following year. Brecht at least managed to get the *Mahagonny* libretto finished before rehearsals began, but the powerful effect of the *Threepenny Opera* led him to feel that songs should really be treated as a separate theatrical element; that singing must be quite distinct from speech; and that the musical setting could heighten the effect of the words by irony and self-parody. In *The Threepenny Opera*, he wrote later,

> the criminals showed, sometimes through the music itself, that their sensations, feelings and prejudices were the same as those of the average citizen and theatregoer ... The tenderest and most moving love-song in the

play described the eternal, indestructible mutual attachment of a procurer and his girl.[1]

In such ways the music helped to show up middle-class morality by functioning as what he called 'a muck-raker, an informer, a nark'. Meantime Weill told the musical world (via Universal-Edition's magazine *Anbruch*) that *The Threepenny Opera* was largely about opera itself, an outdated upper-class art form now hopelessly out of touch with the modern theatre and its public. Not only had the two collaborators gone back to a far more primitive form of opera but in the florid writing of the finale they were using 'the very concept of opera to resolve a conflict, in other words as a factor in the plot'. And this entailed 'writing music that could be sung by actors, i.e. musical amateurs' – something that had surprised Weill by proving to be no restriction but 'an immense enrichment'.[2]

The full version of *Mahagonny* was composed between the writing of *The Threepenny Opera* and the attempt to repeat its success with *Happy End*; and it went off to Weill's publishers in April 1929. The libretto, as has already been said, was a montage, and for Brecht the finished work was to be a still clearer example for the 'separation of the elements' – that is, of text, music and visuals. Weill however saw the combination slightly differently, with the text as a 'juxtaposition of situations' or of 'genre pictures' or 'moral tableaux'. 'The music therefore no longer furthers the plot but only starts up once a situation has been arrived at'. This means that the music can be continuous, without any need for theatrical dialogue to link one such situation to the next. The projections admittedly are to be 'an independent illustration of the events on stage', but those events are so gestically shown in the music that scarcely any acting is required. 'The actor . . . can limit himself to the simplest and most natural gests', while grouping and movement can be such as can 'allow something close to a concert performance'. All these remarks were set down between the completion of the work and its first performance, and the essay in which they occur was intended to be Weill's introduction to a *Regiebuch* or director's script which he, Brecht and Caspar Neher would jointly compile.[3]

In the event Brecht never contributed his bit, but instead wrote his own separate 'Notes to the opera' which appeared in 1930 some time after the Leipzig première on March 9th. These fail to take up Weill's views about the degree of acting and movement required – perhaps because the latter evidently were not followed in the Leipzig, or indeed in any other production – though they somewhat mock Weill's concept of conveying both the meaning and the formal shape of the whole montage through the music. Once again Brecht, like Weill earlier, treats traditional opera as hopelessly outmoded, even when it uses modish trappings, and once again he sees an element of self-parody as a means of provoking the audience. What cannot much have pleased his partner, quite apart from the lack of solidarity implied, was his view that even *Mahagonny* adopts the 'basic attitude' of traditional opera, and is accordingly what Brecht termed 'culinary', something prepared by skilled cooks from many ingredients to go smoothly down the gullet. At the same time

> it attacks the society that needs operas of such a sort; it still perches on the old bough, perhaps, but at least it has started (out of absent-mindedness or bad conscience) to saw it through . . .

* * *

Brecht and, more ambivalently, Weill were not alone at this time in considering the traditional opera 'apparatus' to be out of key with a democratic modern society, though Brecht may have had a particular insight into the shortcomings of provincial opera houses while his first wife Marianne was a singer there. Such doubts about the functions of the opera medium – as also about the prevailing concert structure with its élite audience – were central to the whole trend of *Neue Sachlichkeit*. For if the most rigorous musical thinking of the later 1920s was associated with Schönberg and his school, the most interesting and the widest-ranging was that which centred on Hindemith and Heinrich Burkard and the annual festivals which they organised at Donaueschingen (1921–26) and Baden-Baden (1927–29). This was a group that looked to the recognition of social and economic realities rather than the voluntary development of non-tonal structures to demolish all existing musical conventions. Starting with a relatively simple attempt to reduce the scale and cost of musical performance by exploring the possibilities of the chamber orchestra, its 'Neue Musik' festivals tried to anticipate the new tasks that might be found for music in a society undergoing all kinds of changes. There was *Gemeinschaftsmusik* or Community Music for the amateur music movement and for schools; there was *Gebrauchsmusik* or Applied Music for the new openings provided by the media. What linked the two areas, simultaneously relating them to the neo-classicism of the immediate postwar years and to the concerns of Stravinsky and the younger French composers around that time, was a common preoccupation with economy of forces, ease of execution and accessibility to the unsophisticated ear. Thanks to these considerations (which were on the whole not shared by the Vienna school or the International Society for Contemporary Music), grand opera was seen as an economically wasteful and artistically incongruous hangover from the nineteenth-century imperial or princely courts: anything that dragged it into the modern world would be of interest. At the same time there was a sense of kinship with the concertante forms, dynamic rhythms and unsnobbish popular appeal of jazz.

Every musical contemporary who was to be of significance to Brecht, right up to the 1950s, was associated with this specifically mid-European movement, not only Weill and Hindemith himself but also Eisler, Dessau, Wagner-Regeny among the composers, along with the conductors Klemperer and Scherchen and critics like Strobel and Stuckenschmidt. Its experiments with mini-operas sparked off *The Little Mahagonny*, its exploration of film music drew in Eisler and Dessau, its concern with the growing musical role of the radio inspired Weill and Hindemith to compose *Der Lindberghflug* (or *Ozeanflug*, as it was later renamed) and, outside the festival proper, *The Berlin Requiem* for which Weill set a choice of Brecht texts to be broadcast by the Frankfurt radio, soon after the opening of *The Threepenny Opera*. Although all these certainly helped to shape Brecht's ideas, what really implicated him in the movement was Hindemith's proposal in 1929 to devote that year's festival to a new musical-dramatic form. This was the *Lehrstück* or didactic piece/didactic play (the word *Stück* can mean either), a type of staged cantata recalling the Noh theatre as well as the Jesuit drama of the seventeenth century. Though this form is now commonly assumed to have been Brecht's personal invention its context was in the first place a musical one, and its initial impetus a logical development of *Gemeinschaftsmusik*, by which the communal performance would be widened to include non-musical elements whose rehearsal would promote community spirit among those taking part. So Hindemith thought, anyway, when he composed his original *lehrstück* for soloists, chorus, orchestra and (for the scene with three clowns) the Lichtental Fire Brigade Band. Brecht, however, who wrote the linked texts for this and for the radio play *Der Lindberghflug*, *Lindbergh's Flight* (for which Weill initially set the 'European' and Hindemith the 'America' numbers, though only the former's music was subsequently published), immediately elaborated it into a much more rigorous conception. Claiming to have furnished only an incomplete text for *lehrstück*, whose didactic purpose in the festival context could not be more than 'a formal musical one', he argued that the participants in the new development should go much further. Instead of a superficial sense of community based on music they should be creating a positive 'counterweight to those collective entities now tearing the people of our time apart with a quite different sort of force'.[1] And this could be done in the form of an exercise by rehearsing and performing the almost ritualistic didactic texts which he went on to write.

Both the new pieces were, and still are, works of considerable power and austerity, and their central message was that of *Einverständnis* or acceptance of the harsh fate imposed by community interests in extreme situations. Brecht accordingly abandoned Hindemith's bald title *lehrstück* and called their work the *Badener Lehrstück vom Einverständnis* (or *Baden-Baden Lesson on Consent*); however, from then on he and Hindemith were unable to agree about anything, and as a result its further performance was rendered impossible for nearly thirty years. Though this effectively seems to have alienated Brecht from the whole concept of *Gemeinschaftsmusik*, which he thenceforward ridiculed, the implications for his understanding with Weill were less simple. On the face of it the two men's growing incompatibility may now seem straightforward and easily explained so – Brecht becomes a communist in the spring of 1929 just before these two works are written, loses interest in *Happy End*, which consequently flops that September, then starts collaborating with the communist Hanns Eisler on political didactic pieces that break right away from Hindemith's movement; after which Weill the democratic socialist can no longer follow him. But it wasn't really quite like this, and although Lenya was no doubt right when she said that her brilliant husband had felt cramped by 'the restraints of writing for untrained singers, children and the special needs of Brecht'[2] neither man had anyway wanted to be exclusively tied to the other. Moreover they still presented a common front not only in the dispute over the *Threepenny Opera* film (where Brecht wanted to impose radical political changes on the story) but also in withdrawing from Hindemith's 1930 festival. And the work which they wrote on that occasion took the *Lehrstück* form a step further in Brecht's new direction.

For whereas the two earlier pieces with Weill and Hindemith had had a certain static, oriental quality reminiscent of Milhaud's work with Claudel, the new 'school opera' *He Said Yes* took its text virtually unchanged from one of Arthur Waley's *The Nō Plays of Japan* which once again centres on *Einverständnis*. Musically this work, whose text, says its translator Elisabeth Hauptmann, was Weill's choice, is even more clearly and simply conceived than was *Lindbergh's Flight*, which already seemed surprisingly remote from the *Mahagonny* and *Threepenny Opera* songs; and its orchestration was open-ended. Weill however also specifically associated himself with Brecht's objectives, writing in an essay of August 1930 that 'a school play should not simply offer the boys [*sic*] the pleasure of making music but also give them the opportunity to learn something' – this 'something' being clearly identified by him with 'our' amendment of Waley's closing passage so that the sickly boy is not just killed by his comrades and then miraculously brought back to life, as in the Noh original, but first formally expresses his *Einverständnis*. In this way, says Weill, he proves

> by declaring his acquiescence, that he has learnt to accept all the implications of joining a community or associating himself with an idea.

This was a terribly two-edged principle in the context of the growing political violence, as critics and school audiences alike were quick to spot. But it led directly to its next, openly political development in Eisler's *Die Massnahme*: *The Decision*.

He Said Yes marked the creative peak of the Brecht–Weill collaboration, and indeed perhaps of the whole 1920s musical movement from which it had sprung. For what was changing was not only individuals and their political interests, but also the politico-artistic context of the times. The failure of *Happy End*, for instance, was not just due to Brecht's new commitments but part of a general shift of taste as Germany moved to the Right: the same process that brought about the bankruptcy of Piscator's second company, the ending of the Baden-Baden festivals and the closure of the Dessau Bauhaus. Economies too, following the Wall Street crash of October 1929, now struck at the avant-garde arts; indeed much of Brecht's evident disillusionment with *Mahagonny* might have been avoided if Klemperer's Kroll Opera in Berlin, which had originally intended to première it, had not been closed on budgetary grounds by the Prussian (State) administration. Pressed no doubt by his publishers, who from *Wozzeck* on had worked to revolutionise the repertoire of the traditional opera houses without ever attacking the tradition itself, Weill abandoned his earlier concept of an almost cantata-like production and gave the première to the opera house in Leipzig. From then on virtually all performances of this work were given in opera houses and with opera singers, the one major exception being the first Berlin production of 21 December 1931. This was put on in a theatre by Aufricht (the producer of *The Threepenny Opera* in 1928 and *Happy End* in 1929) with Brecht himself and Neher as joint directors and a cast of actors and cabaret performers, including Lenya, for whose untrained voice Weill very effectively rewrote Jenny's song in scene 5. The result seems to have been remarkably successful, Theodor Adorno for instance thinking it the best and clearest production to date; it ran for fifty performances. Yet Brecht quickly lost interest, and from then on had no further use for *Mahagonny*, even to the point of forgetting it when making lists of his works.

He was cantankerous at rehearsals and according to Aufricht had to be diverted from these by getting him involved in an almost simultaneous production of *The Mother*, the second of his political pieces with Eisler. This allowed Neher to take over the direction. At the same time it was Neher who wrote the libretto for *Die Bürgschaft* (The Surety), Weill's next work in the theatre, a popular opera or 'Volksoper' with Handelian elements – in other words almost a reversion to pre-*Beggar's Opera* models – which was staged by Carl Ebert the following year at the Berlin Städtische Oper, a thoroughly conventional opera house. However Neher, as we have seen, was not merely part of the triumvirate that had put *Mahagonny* together in the first place but also a primary contributor to all Brecht's theatre, not excluding *The Mother*. This suggests that the differences with Weill (whom Aufricht reports Brecht as having called a 'phoney Richard Strauss' for insisting on the interests of his music at rehearsal) added up not so much to a final split as to a divergence within the team. Certainly Weill and Brecht chose different ways of reacting to the new socio-cultural context, the one trying to consolidate on the basis of the traditional 'apparatus' of opera house and concert hall while the other hoped for its revolutionary overthrow and meanwhile sought alternative channels. Neither however in any way welcomed the context itself or conformed with it as did such lesser artists as Orff and Werner Egk, and when at the end of 1932 Weill was able to establish a new reputation in Paris with performances of *Mahagonny* and *He Said Yes* under his pupil Maurice Abravanel there was nothing to stop the triumvirate from working again, without notable disagreements, on the ballet commission that resulted. This was *The Seven Deadly Sins*, a work of no major significance to Brecht, but one which certainly alienated neither him nor Weill.

By then both men were exiles from the Nazi regime, and afterwards the collaboration ended. It had overlapped the new partnership with Eisler by nearly four years, and although the latter now became Brecht's sole composer till the Second World War they never meant such arrangements to be exclusive. Nor was there any positive reason why the old collaboration should not have been resumed at any time. Indeed both

Brecht and Weill considered the possibility more than once, as we shall in due course see.

* * *

Eisler belonged to the same generation as Weill and Brecht, and his radio cantata *Tempo der Zeit* was performed along with the first two *Lehrstücke* at the 1929 Baden-Baden festival. Like Weill too, he was a severe and fairly regular critic of Berlin concert and operatic life, writing entertainingly about such aspects of the 'apparatus' as the bourgeois concert audience, the over-glamourised conductor and the unintelligible opera text. He differed however in two important respects. First of all, his musical training had taken place in post-war Vienna, where he had been one of Schönberg's most promising pupils after Webern and Berg; and secondly on arriving in Berlin late in 1925 he became closely involved with the Communist Party, whose ex-secretary Ruth Fischer was his sister, while his elder brother Gerhard became a Comintern agent. This commitment, and the new concern with 'alternative' music of a radical popular kind to which it led him, effectively alienated him from his teacher and made him for several years one of the cultural-political leaders of the German Left. In 1927 he became a recognised contributor to the party's paper *Die Rote Fahne* and began composing for the Young Communist agit-prop group 'Das rote Sprachrohr' (The Red Megaphone) under the Reinhardt actor Maxim Vallentin; from September 1928 he was a lecturer at the Marxist Workers' School (or MASch, which Brecht sometimes attended); subsequently he served on the party's joint board for workers' culture (IfA) and headed the International Music Bureau when this was formed in Moscow in 1932 as part of Piscator's International League of Revolutionary Theatres. When Brecht and he began to think of collaborating, therefore, he had by far the greater experience and inside knowledge of Communist affairs of the two. Though he had already set a couple of Brecht poems (notably the 'Song of the Girl and the Soldier' for inclusion in Feuchtwanger's *Kalkutta* play) and must have met Brecht at Baden-Baden if not elsewhere, their serious discussions seem only to have begun in the early spring of 1930. In these, said Eisler long afterwards, 'I functioned as the messenger of the working class movement'.

At the outset this may indeed have been his main role in Brecht's eyes, though his musical and literary understanding very soon made themselves felt, along with his considerable wit. For their first concern was to make a political reality of the 'Einverständnis' theme as set out in *He*

Said Yes by writing a further *Lehrstück* for Hindemith's 'Neue Musik' festival that summer. Their plan, rejected in advance by the organisers, was to take the essence of the original Noh story – the killing of the boy whose weakness endangers an important expedition – and rewrite it in the same expository dramatic form on the basis of Gerhard Eisler's experiences as a Comintern emissary in China, a country whose affairs had a considerable topical interest for the German Left. Exactly what Eisler's brother's activities there had amounted to is not very clear, but he had been one of a group of foreign Communists – along with Heinz Neumann and Besso Lominadze – who took part in the short-lived Canton Commune of December 1927, and he later returned to China as political secretary of the Communist unions in Shanghai. The changing of the expedition in *He Said Yes* into an undercover mission and of the boy into the naïve Young Comrade accordingly has a certain authenticity, and the latter's secret execution in an extreme situation is only too credible. At the same time much of the new strength of *The Decision* came from the composer, whose massively simple choruses drive the story forward with the relentlessness of a crime novel while punctuating it with a number of great political songs. It is almost as if he had approached it as a secular Passion in the tradition of Bach; indeed later he spoke of having played Brecht passages from the St Matthew and St John Passions to convince the poet 'how magnificently Bach can set a report'.[1]

All Eisler's works with Brecht before the Nazi takeover were performed outside the accepted 'apparatus': *The Decision* in a concert hall, by communist choral societies; *The Mother* by a left-wing actors' collective in various Berlin halls and theatres; the film *Kuhle Wampe* initially by one of Münzenberg's companies but ultimately by a collective of those involved, including Vallentin's agitprop group and members of the communist sports movement. All three moreover were built round the actor-singer Ernst Busch (who had sung the opening 'Moritat' in the original *Threepenny Opera*) and the 'Kampflieder' or militant political songs that Eisler was now composing for him, the best of them to texts by Brecht. Busch henceforward not only took part in these major works but also performed the songs at cabarets or political meetings, usually with Eisler accompanying him at the piano. This was a field which Brecht had entered somewhat later than such poets as Tucholsky, Erich Weinert and Robert Gilbert, the successful writer of musicals who wrote some of Eisler's first political songs under the pseudonym 'David Weber'. However, his irregular unrhymed verse with its 'gestic' syncopations and caesuras proved particularly congenial to

Eisler, who was not only a fine orchestrator in the Mahler tradition, and a good second to Weill as a writer of memorable tunes, but also a masterly manipulator of rhythms and accents who could exactly convey Brecht's unique poetic fusion of sense and shape. This was a matter not of subordination but of a growing identification which allowed Eisler not only to propose verbal changes for the sake of the sound but in due course to make useful criticisms of almost any kind of writing by Brecht. 'I see his settings', noted Brecht some years later, 'the same way as a performance is to a play: the test. He reads with immense precision . . .'.

Eisler's deepest and perhaps most lasting contribution to Brecht's work only becomes clear after 1933, when the two men resumed their collaboration in exile. The attempt to explore alternative outlets then proved a good preparation for those practical difficulties which other anti-Nazi refugees found overwhelming; there was an audience for their militant songs, however scattered, and their best performers, like Busch and Weigel and Carola Neher, had likewise emigrated. At the same time, while Eisler had his new function with the International Music Bureau in Moscow, Brecht's decision to settle in the Danish countryside meant that they could work together in comparative isolation, more intimately than they had been able to do in Berlin. Much of 1934 was spent in this way, first in Denmark and later in London, leading Eisler much later to recall

> certain moments in the winter on the Danish island of Fünen by the sea when I would spend the morning in my house composing 'like a wild man', as they say in Vienna, and Brecht like a wild man would write verses.
> Hopeless.
> If some philistine had seen us he'd have said 'those two gents are just mad'.[1]

This was when they wrote the devastating 'Ballad on Approving of the World' (*Poems 1913–1956*, pp. 196–201) for voice and small orchestra and did most of the work on *Round Heads and Pointed Heads*, whose songs are no longer detachable 'Kampflieder' as with the pre-1933 works but 'muckrakers and narks' in the vein of the *Threepenny Opera*. Three 'Kampflieder' followed in the autumn on a commission from Eisler's Moscow headquarters: the 'United Front' and 'Saar' songs and the haunting minor-key 'All of us or none' which much later was taken into *The Days of the Commune*. The 'Ballad of Marie Sanders, the Jew's whore' was written the following year (that of the Nuremberg Race Laws).

With the exception of the second version of *Galileo* (whose music is mostly confined to the linking verses between scenes) *Round Heads and*

Pointed Heads is the last play whose musical setting was composed in such close collaboration and before the script itself had been finished. In 1935 Brecht wanted to tackle the short 'Lehrstück' *The Horatians and the Curiatians* in a similarly collaborative way, but Eisler was unable to oblige and the music remained unwritten till another composer took it up some twenty years later. (This was the last of Brecht's works in 'Lehrstück' form, its predecessor *The Exception and the Rule* having also been left without music, though in that case we do not know what Brecht himself had in mind.) The little Chinese-influenced play appears to have been commissioned by the Red Army,[1] possibly in the spring when Brecht was Piscator's guest in Moscow; however, Eisler was called away from Svendborg to negotiate with the ISCM, on behalf of the International Music Bureau and could not or would not find time to return to Denmark before their joint trip to the United States that autumn. This shook the partnership and may help to explain its apparent inactivity in 1936, though the two men were able to present a solid enough front in New York when it came to criticising the Theatre Union's interpretation of *The Mother*, whose production they had been invited to attend. What does seem clear on that occasion is that Eisler felt much more at ease in American 'progressive' cultural circles than did Brecht; for he had, in Lee Baxandall's words, 'an enormous personal success' in New York,[2] and his lectures at the New School (which began that October) along with his earlier musical travels around the country gave him a footing there which Brecht never enjoyed.

This was important in view of the onset of those 'dark times' which closed down the Moscow international cultural bureaux and soon reduced both men's contacts with the USSR. Both artistically (thanks to the growing worldwide influence of Stanislavsky) and politically, Brecht, Eisler and Piscator were henceforward made even more dependent on one another while their isolation increased. It was Eisler therefore who, having once established himself with the New School, was the first to move his base across the Atlantic, which he did finally at the beginning of 1938. Immediately before this however he had spent the best part of a year in Denmark close to Brecht, working on seven cantatas to words by Silone – a name that had recently become anathema to orthodox Communists because of his condemnation of the Moscow trials – and on his own massive project for a *Deutsche Symphonie*. The latter originated around the same time as Brecht's *Fear and Misery of the Third Reich* scheme and for much the same motives, and it involved the use of a number of Brecht texts. Not that Brecht himself ever cared for large-scale symphonic music, or indeed for any music that was not what Eisler termed 'praktikabel' in the theatrical sense: i.e. firm enough to be used, rather than just admired. From this point of view the most significant aspect of this very productive spell of free composition by Eisler was Brecht's handing him a folder of *Svendborg Poems* to set, from which he chose two of the 'Literary Sonnets' (on Goethe and Schiller), along with the second and third sections of 'To those born later' which he set for voice and piano as 'Zwei Elegien'. When he performed the latter to Brecht, singing them presumably in his wonderfully articulated corn-crake voice, Brecht called the result 'very epic'. Told later that this verdict indicated great enthusiasm on Brecht's part, Eisler said characteristically:

> You know, expressions like 'great enthusiasm' just weren't part of our working equipment.
> We regarded it as usable.
> When Brecht handed me the poem and asked if it struck me as usable I said it was usable.
> A day later when I had set it he said it was usable too.
> That was all we said at the time, and we've said nothing since.[1]

A few months later the first section of this great, usable poem was added. Eisler set it as 'Elegie 1939'. He was then in Mexico City, and the date, according to his editor Manfred Grabs, was 2 September 1939: the outbreak of the Second World War.

∗   ∗   ∗

Though Eisler's departure for the United States in January 1938 saw the beginning of one of Brecht's most productive periods, from then on he had no regular musical collaborator for the next four years. The great plays therefore, from *Galileo* to *Arturo Ui*, were written without any integral musical component; in fact from 1936 to the end of his life no Brecht play bears a composer's name among the 'collaborators' listed after its title. Weill, after one or two indifferently successful musicals (such as *Marie Galante* in Paris and *A Kingdom for a Cow* in London) had gone to New York to work on the Reinhardt–Werfel Jewish pageant *The Eternal Road*, and decided to settle there. Paul Dessau, then in a dodecaphonic phase, wrote some music for *99%*, the first (Paris) version of *Fear and Misery of the Third Reich* – settings of the inter-scene verses which he sang himself to his own accompaniment – but there is no evidence that Brecht ever heard it or was as yet aware of this composer. There were no more Brecht–Eisler 'Kampflieder'; moreover Ernst

Busch, who had sung them on a tour of the USSR with Grigori Shneerson and to the troops in Spain with Eisler, was interned by the French and handed over to the Gestapo in 1940. For his current preoccupations therefore Brecht had to make do with whatever composers he or the relevant producers could find. Thus he discussed the *Mother Courage* songs with the Finnish composer Simon Parmet, giving him the 'L'étendard de la pitié' (or 'Ballad of the Pirates') tune for the theme song and suggesting he model his approach on Weill; then for the Zurich première Parmet's music was ignored in favour of a setting by the Swiss Paul Burkhard. The radio *Lucullus* would have been composed by Hilding Rosenberg if Stockholm Radio had broadcast it as planned, but in the event it too was given in Switzerland, apparently without any music to mention. Apart from *Ui* all the other plays contained songs, but the question of their setting was left open.

When Brecht eventually followed Eisler and Piscator, ostensibly to take up a long-standing invitation to the New School, the former was still lecturing there and had at least another year to go on the long-term Film Music Project for which the Rockefellers had recently given the school $20,000. Weill too was in New York, where he had just scored his great Broadway breakthrough with *Lady in the Dark* (for which Ira Gershwin wrote the lyrics); he had thus started competing in a somewhat different league, and when Adorno wrote to him at Brecht's request about a proposed Black production of *The Threepenny Opera* he wrote back – in English – what Brecht termed 'a nasty letter full of attacks on me and a hymn of praise to broadway'.[1] This was nearly nine months after Brecht had decided to settle on the West Coast; in other words his American gestation period too was spent without any musician to work with. However, only days after the 'nasty letter', Eisler arrived, having apparently decided to write his book on film music in collaboration with Adorno and within range of the studios. 'when i see eisler', wrote Brecht in his journal on April 21st,

> it's a bit as if i had been stumbling confusedly around in some crowd of people and suddenly heard myself called by my old name.

'Wise and witty as ever', Eisler was almost immediately picking out new poems to set and spraying critical comments in all directions, not least about Brecht's theoretical writings, which he found 'too positivistic'. So he was available to write the music for Fritz Lang's film *Hangmen Also Die* (including the setting of Brecht's 'Lidice Song') which got him an Oscar nomination for the best film score of 1943, and several other film jobs followed. He also wrote music, often incomplete, for *Simone*

Machard, *Švejk* (after the collapse of negotiations with Weill), the 1945 New York production of *The Private Life of the Master Race* (the rejigged wartime version of *Fear and Misery of the Third Reich*) and the Hollywood production of *Galileo*. However, he abandoned the effort to set *The Caucasian Chalk Circle* on deciding that Brecht's mental image of a bard-like 'epic' singsong of Homeric proportions was 'a phantom'.[1] At the same time he told Brecht what he thought about the new-style idealised heroines of the first and last of these works, the one too patriotic, the other too good.

Eisler's great achievement during the first two years of their renewed partnership was the setting for voice and piano of twenty-eight more of the poems, all but one of them written since he and Brecht had last met. 'You can only do that sort of thing when you're poor', was Clifford Odets's comment on hearing a first sample of the *Hollywood Songbook* which he began building around them in June 1942. At the heart of this collection stands a genuine collaborative work with Brecht, a set of 'Hollywood Elegies'.[2] These arose in the first place from a shared detestation of what Eisler later termed 'Hollywood's depressingly permanent springtime', which one day made him tell Brecht that it was a classic place to write elegies, somewhat as Goethe had once written elegies in Rome.

> I told him 'We must do something of the sort too. You don't go unpunished in Hollywood. You just have to relax and describe it.'
>
> And Brecht promised to do just that, and in due course brought me eight (I think it was) Hollywood Elegies . . .[3]

These were the six recognised Elegies of the collected poems plus 'The Swamp' and the four-line epigram 'Hollywood'. They were amended – whether by Eisler or by Brecht is not clear – and later augmented by an English-language poem called 'Nightmare', 'The Hearing' or 'Rat Men's Press Conference'. This is Eisler's own:

> The rat men accused me
> Of not liking stench
> Of not liking garbage
> Of not liking their squeals
> Of not liking to eat dirt.
>
> For days they argued, considering the question
> From every angle. Finally they condemned me:
> You don't like stench

You don't like garbage
You don't like squeals
You don't like to eat dirt.

The settings – terse, angular and venomous in a quite new way – seem to reflect not only the two men's contemptuous dislike of the surface beauties and luxuries of the Los Angeles area but also Eisler's long-delayed reconciliation with Schönberg, who was then teaching at UCLA. Brecht was not unaffected by this, for Eisler took him to meet the old man and to hear him lecture, with the result that the poet, while still rejecting the arbitrary melodic leaps characteristic of dodecaphonic writing, came to accept Schönberg himself as a genius, however contorted; and he was pleased when Schönberg complained once 'that there was no musical conceptual material for music', so that its forms had to be described in quasi-physical terms.[1] Along with this return to modernism there was also a marked Schubertian strain in a number of Eisler's songs of the time – for instance in 'Tank Battle' or 'Of sprinkling the garden' or the lovely setting of Goethe's 'Der Schatzgräber'[2] – so that the whole *Songbook* with its almost epigrammatic compression and its balance of classic (Hölderlin, Anacreon/Mörike et al.) and Brecht texts is like a refunctioning of the great German–Austrian heritage to accommodate radical social thinking and gestic use of words. 'We had nothing going for us', Eisler later told Hans Bunge, 'but our insight into the way times would develop'.[3] And he wrote an introductory note to say:

> In a society which understands and loves a book of songs like these, it will be possible to live well and free from danger. These pieces have been written in confidence that such a society will come about.

Of all these 'American' Brecht settings by Eisler perhaps only the 'Song of a German Mother' and the three *Švejk* songs were directly political in the old sense. Yet it is clear from the evidence that the two men's shared convictions were unchanged, and the fact was well known to the FBI and to J. Parnell Thomas's investigators. Thus Brecht's eventual hearing before the Un-American Activities Committee, though presented as part of their investigation of the motion-picture industry, was really linked with the cases of Hanns and, more importantly, Gerhard Eisler. To all intents and purposes Brecht and Eisler were in the same boat, and it is ultimately this that gave them their freedom to develop along such fresh and unexpected lines. At the same time however Brecht always made it clear that he would welcome settings by other composers, and was even interested in the possibility of Stravinsky (yet another who had taken refuge in California) making an opera of *Lucullus*. Roger Sessions too set the radio version of this work for a performance at Berkeley, using Hays's English translation, though the Brechts never gave permission for it to be repeated until very recently. Weill resurfaced in 1943 as a result of Aufricht's plan for a Švejk musical which would repeat the success of *The Threepenny Opera*; so Brecht's play was written with him in view, as was the 'Santa Monica' shortened version of *The Good Person of Szechwan*, a play which Weill thought might make an opera – Lenya being involved anyway in the former, where Brecht intended the Mrs Kopecka part for her. Quite aside from the conflict with Piscator about the rights however (as outlined on pp. 113–14 above), Weill wanted Brecht's *Švejk* script to be adapted (and in effect rewritten) as a 'musical play' in the Broadway convention by someone like Ben Hecht –

> with more openings for music than the present version, as I do not under any circumstances wish to write incidental music.[1]

– while the *Szechwan* plan too depended on signing up an American author, failing which no more work could be done on Brecht's version. These stipulations by the now successful Broadway composer were naturally unacceptable to Brecht, who was not prepared to act (or be paid) as a mere libretto-writer and, while allowing Weill to nominate whoever he liked for the 'lyrics', refused to sacrifice ultimate control over his play. Nonetheless Weill's interest in Brecht's song texts too seems to have reawakened, for he set the 'Song of the Wife of the Nazi Soldier' (later included in *Švejk*) for Lenya, and there was also some question of his composing the long 'Children's Crusade'. Not long before leaving America Brecht approached him again about *Švejk*, and found him willing to meet and discuss writing the music for a German-language production of Brecht's play, though the meeting seems in the event not to have taken place. Weill also retained his interest in an operatic version of *The Good Person of Szechwan*, apparently to the end of his life.

*   *   *

Paul Dessau, who became Brecht's principal musical collaborator after his return to East Berlin in 1948, effectively came to the writer's attention in the spring of 1943, when the two men met during the rehearsals for a Brecht evening in New York.[2] Dessau, who had come to the United States from Paris as a music teacher in 1939, was now working on a New Brunswick chicken farm, and besides the ballad in 99% had only written two Brecht songs. One of them, the 'Battle Song of the Black Straw Hats' from *Saint Joan of the Stockyards*, was to be performed by a certain singer, who rehearsed it with Dessau under Brecht's direction, then walked out. 'In those days', wrote Dessau later,

> we didn't have much idea of gestic singing: a contralto, she could just as well have been singing Amneris in *Aïda*.

So Dessau, at Brecht's suggestion, sang it himself. Judging by recordings, this son of a cantor manqué (Weill likewise was the son of a cantor) had almost as raucous a voice as Eisler, and it seems to have been the delivery rather than the song itself that so impressed the younger man.[1] Straightway, it seems, they arranged to work together; then in the autumn he moved out to California to work on three large Brecht projects, of which only one was completed. This was the *German Miserere*, an oratorio counterpart to Eisler's still unfinished *German Symphony*, using twenty-nine of Brecht's *War Primer* epigrams, seven more of his political poems (including two already perfectly set by Eisler) and one written specifically for this work: 'Mit Beschämung' (*GW* 943). The (roughly) hundred-strong orchestra included twenty-four violas, eighteen cellos and twelve double-bases. Another set of twelve of the same epigrams remained unfinished, while a 'dramatic ballad for music' on the theme of Brecht's short story 'The Augsburg Chalk Circle' was not taken very far, and four songs and about a hundred pages of assorted script are all that survive of *Die Reisen des Glücksgotts*, the opera project on which they began working right away. During 1946 however Brecht gave Dessau a play to read, remarking 'There are some songs that need setting'. And then, wrote Dessau,

> he began reading me the poems, calmly, gently and concentrating on the meaning, more musically perhaps than any writer before him.[2]

The play was *Mother Courage*, which Eisler had had since 1940 but never attempted to set to music, probably because there was no immediate pressure for a production. Dessau promptly composed the songs, and a year later did the same for *The Good Person of Szechwan*.

By the middle of 1949 Brecht, Eisler and Dessau were all re-established in East Berlin. Weill had remained in New York and a year later was dead. So in setting up the Berliner Ensemble with his wife Brecht knew he could call on two composers who were 'usable' and happy to be regarded as such; and the remaining six years of his life repeatedly involved collaboration with one or the other. This did not preclude approaches to outsiders: to Carl Orff, whom he asked to write music for *The Caucasian Chalk Circle* in 1952; to Rudolf Wagner-Regeny for the *Trumpets and Drums* songs, or to the Austrian Gottfried von Einem for the unrealised *Salzburg Dance of Death*; both these last two being friends of Neher's. But with Eisler and Dessau he now knew where he was. Broadly speaking Dessau seemed best suited to the theatre's demands during the first half of this period, starting with the Berlin *Mother Courage* production of 1949: moreover, unlike Eisler, he was extremely productive, enthusiastically committed to the new State and very willing to follow Brecht's suggestions about melodies and even scoring, no doubt because he recognised the immense stimulus which their collaboration had given to his work. More personally but none the less significantly, he had become one of Brecht's extended family-cum-collective by marrying Elisabeth Hauptmann. Meantime Eisler, though certainly a senior member of the cultural-political establishment, found it necessary to justify his position by writing some untypically laboured offical music: a flaccid, almost Bruckneresque 'Rhapsody' for the Goethe bicentenary in Weimar; a National Anthem to words by Johannes R. Becher (first playing its tune to Becher on Chopin's piano during the Polish Goethe celebrations); and two sets of 'New German Folk Songs' – folk music being one of the Soviet leadership's current preferences – to Becher's texts. By contrast his only new Brecht settings, up to the end of 1952, were of 'Children's Songs' (*GW* 970–977; *Poems 1913–1956*, pp. 420–23) written in the poet's 'positive' vein. Of these the Neruda-based 'Peace Song' and 'Die Pappel vom Karlsplatz' can only be described as verbally and musically soppy.

During the early 1950s both composers nevertheless fell foul of the establishment: Dessau with his opera version of *Lucullus* and Eisler with his libretto for a *Johann Faustus* opera. The former work was held to be 'formalist' – i.e. musically too difficult, in the Stravinsky–Bartók tradition – the latter took too 'negative' a view of the national 'cultural heritage'. Dessau accordingly was forced to rework his opera (which Brecht defended, though it hardly accorded with his ideas of musical clarity and gestic singing), but without letting himself be silenced; thus it was not long before he embarked on a cantata version of Brecht's Lysenko poem 'The Training of Millet' for soloist, two choruses, and an orchestra, again, of over 100. Eisler however abandoned his whole plan, was thrown into what Brecht termed a 'crisis of production' and withdrew, quasi-paralysed, to Vienna, whence he was only lured back at the beginning of 1954 by overtures from the East German Academy. By then Brecht had experienced and digested the events of 16–17 June 1953;

his earlier, 'positive' approach to his country's problems had been
abandoned in favour of a new reflective, critical distance, as seen in the
Buckow poems.

At this crucial juncture, the Ensemble's revival of *The Mother*, along
with the Vienna production which followed, may well have reminded
Brecht of the need to re-employ Eisler. It was at any rate after the
autumn of 1953 that Eisler wrote nearly all of his settings for the
Berliner Ensemble – including the completion of the *Švejk* and *Simone
Machard* music which he had started in California – and also returned to
writing 'serious' if relatively simple songs for voice and piano, including
'The Flower Garden', 'The Way the Wind Blows' and the splendidly
non-serious 'Die haltbare Graugans' which he and Brecht hatched from
the old American 'Grey Goose'. Dessau in the same (roughly) three-year
period completed 'The Training of Millet', using allusions to the folk
music of Soviet Asia, followed by the copious incidental music to *The
Caucasian Chalk Circle* – the job Eisler had thought impossible and Orff,
presumably, had turned down – based partly on folk dances from
Azerbaijan. Brecht was not happy about this incidental music, feeling
that it was too strenuous and needed cutting and simplifying; and he
objected to Dessau's absence from the rehearsals.[1] It also looks very
much as if Brecht had no more use for their earlier 'semi-staged' work
Report from Herrnburg, an anti-West German piece for the Free German
Youth, which he wrote 'not least to give [Dessau] a chance to contribute
comparatively simple music'.[2] For he subsequently excluded this from
his plays; nor did the two men collaborate on further songs. Dessau's
plan for an opera version of *Puntila* was known to Brecht before his
death, but it was left to Palitzsch and Wekwerth to write the eventual
libretto.

*   *   *

Today Brecht's words still fascinate composers and challenge them to
write settings, primarily because as he himself said, he was 'always
thinking of actual delivery'.[3] Bound up with this, certainly, is the fact
that, for all his distrust of 'the stupor . . . the mad coma'[4] which even the
finest music can create in its listeners, he was extremely musical, as many
of his friends and collaborators agree. 'His musical taste was quite first
rate', said Hanns Eisler,

– with one flaw.

You have to realise that Brecht saw all the arts, while enjoying equal rights, from the point of view of a playwright, a writer for the theatre.

Art for him only counted if it was practicable. Then he became interested.[1]

His musical ear, just like his critical eye, was thus concentrated on the demands of his theatre; in other words it fused with his concern for 'gestic' performance, to such an extent that his perception took in the two aspects at once. Wherever the gest seemed to him fudged or blurred he found even the greatest composers lacking: Beethoven for instance, Brahms, Strauss and Schönberg (said Eisler, who accordingly never invited Brecht to concerts where his own works were being performed). From the first *Mahagonny* on, Brecht no longer needed to supply the musical component for his theatre himself, since he found composers who were in their differing ways able and willing to do this. But the same close association between phrasing and sound stayed with him, and it affected the shape of whatever he wrote.

He knew what he wanted, musically speaking, and perhaps even better what he did not. And this he made clear to the composers with whom he worked. They in turn seem to have followed his instructions, and sometimes his rhythmic and melodic models, to varying extents. Dessau, coming latest on the scene, was perhaps the keenest to listen; and the most successful of his settings remains *Mother Courage*, where he was still fresh to Brecht's ways. Weill too for some years sympathised with what Brecht wanted and suppressed his more autonomous musical instincts in order to try and achieve it; though Brecht was certainly right in pointing out later that his music for the *Mahagonny* opera is 'not purely gestic'.[2] Eisler, while reserving substantial areas of disagreement where instrumental music and the concert hall were concerned, almost entirely shared Brecht's attitude within the latter's field of theatre, poetry and the communication of non-musical ideas: not least because these were ideas which both accepted. The result in all three cases was certain recognisably common features, and these are due, surely, not to mutual influence or imitation so much as to the three men's experience with Brecht. Among them are the thin, clear, slightly tart orchestration (concentrating on wind instruments and percussion); the use of jazz elements and the 1920s *song* (the only modern folk music Brecht found truly congenial); the vocal writing for untrained singers; the shaping of the melody to fit and underpin the verbal rhythms; the audible importance of punctuation. This was the kind of music that Brecht needed in order to stimulate thought and to make the audience prick up its ears. It must not be heavy but be fun. The more serious the ideas it conveyed the less pretentious it could afford to sound.

When he and Brecht were in New York in 1935 Eisler drew up a table of old/new contrasts that compares interestingly with Brecht's tabulations in the *Mahagonny* notes. It deals with the 'refunctioning' of music for new ends, and among its main points (here greatly shortened) are the following:

[old]	[new]
Dominance of instrumental music.	*Dominance of vocal music.*
Small musical forms: as reflecting the composer's private moods, maybe with formal innovations. Studies to develop and show off technical skills.	Small musical forms: as a chance to try out material and develop musical and logical thinking.
Large musical forms: as expression of a world outlook or religious struggle, also as a depiction of 'pure' forms. Autonomous development of the musical material (ensemble and delight in playing).	Large musical forms: as test of material for varieties of Lehrstück music, film music, etc. Also as utility music for political meetings, also to destroy conventional musical conceptions.
Place: concert hall.	Place: concert hall.
In films: as illustration, to depict moods.	*In films*: as a musical commentary.
Song: performed by a specialist in a concert hall to passive listeners: subjective, emotionally conditioned.	*Mass song, Kampflied*: sung in the streets, at places of work or in meetings by the masses themselves, stimulating action.
Ballad: sentimental or heroic content, mostly with a hero.	*Ballad*: socially critical, often with ironic references to conventional music.
Oratorio . . .	*Lehrstück* . . .
Opera, operetta: combination of same musical forms as in an oratorio, but handicapped by the need to achieve theatrical effects.	*Opera, operetta*: social criticism, genre tableau [*Sittenschilderung*] with destruction of conventional operatic effects.

Theatre music: atmospheric and contributing to illusion no independence.	*Theatre music*: independent element serving as musical commentary.[1]

[etc.]

This table was set out before Eisler came to accept that the 'apparatus' was not going to be transformed, least of all in a country under Stalinist rule (where works like the Goethe Rhapsody would be required). He also changed his mind about the *Kampflied*, reckoning after the war that it would take at least ten years to get march rhythms out of the German system: likewise 'music stimulating action' had been discredited by US advertising jingles. But the views which the table expresses were in no way imposed on Eisler by Brecht; rather they explain why the two men so often saw ear to ear (as it were), and why it is only in Eisler's case that we have no evidence of Brecht hammering out rhythms or suggesting tunes.

At the root of this basic agreement was Eisler's awareness of language: the relation between its obvious purposes and its infinite rhythmic, gestic and stylistic subtleties. Thus in the *Hollywood Songbook* he astounded Brecht by taking Hölderlin and 'shaking the dust off him', and even more by setting Mörike's translation of the Anacreon fragments, which he 'changed around a bit'. Though never so self-destructive as George Grosz, Eisler was a man full of inhibiting doubts, so that after the 'dark times' of the 1930s there are moments when he seems paralysed by the feeling that his whole concept of 'refunctioning music' may have been a mistake, that he had been wrong ever to quit the orthodox path and that all he was now really fit for was to win Oscars or East European official decorations. In the light of such uncertainties, which Brecht recognised in Eisler but never seems to have had himself, Eisler's 'refunctioned' version of the poem which Mörike called 'Delayed triumph' has a special meaning:

> And round his ribs he wrapped a bald ox-hide
> Stiff with filth, an old shield-cover.
> And he had it off with the baker's assistant
> And with the dames who are crazy for men,
> The dirtiest. Unclean too was all his business.
> Often his neck was on the block
> Often too between the spokes.
> And often he was whipped with chastising rods.
> And his head too was defiled and his beard pulled out.
> And now? He is mounting the golden coach.[2]

For at the same time he knew from Brecht's example that works written in emigration 'for the desk drawer', or merely to keep their hand in, might be recognised as masterpieces a quarter of a century or more later. Such *langer Atem* or stamina, he said,

> is not talent, hard work or genius – but the indestructible belief that if you have something right to say it will get through.[1]

At a time when they had little else to do Brecht and Eisler kept this belief alive in one another. There is a fascinating passage in Eisler's first conversation with Hans Bunge, recorded some eighteen months after Brecht's death, which describes his bringing Brecht in wartime Hollywood a book on the punctuation of Shakespeare from the Quartos up to the time of Pope, which seemed to prove that Shakespeare's own use of punctuation must have been 'gestic' rather than grammatically correct. They discussed the matter for hours, leading Eisler to comment:

> When the Russians defeated the Germans at Stalingrad we were still concerned with Shakespeare's use of the dash in the Quarto. Such things aren't inconsistencies but correspondences. And battles were fought so that punctuation marks could be determined.[2]

Far from being a defence of the ivory tower, this is the remark of an exceptionally integrated artist who believes that there is no tower anywhere: that he, in his concern with gestic stresses and rhythms, is fighting for the same aims as the armies who beat the Nazis. Like Brecht he saw formal, technical questions as having a political sense.

What is truly radical with Brecht is his view of the relationship between words, music and the singing voice. And of course it is dictated by the feeling of having 'something right to say'. In traditional song-writing, and even more markedly in grand opera – however advanced the purely musical conventions employed – it is the music rather than the words that has to do most of the saying. 'Modern music', as he noted in 1944 after discussions with Eisler and Dessau, 'converts texts into prose, even verse texts, then poeticises that prose. It poeticises it and at the same time makes it "psychological". The rhythm is dissolved (except with Stravinsky and Bartok).'[3] True enough, poetry has often been squeezed dry for this kind of subjective re-creation, then thrown away apart from some nice but mostly unintelligible sounds, predominantly of pure vowels. Such a demolition of verbal form and sense is then compounded by the use of singers trained to produce pre-determined tonal qualities ('soaring' soprano, 'dark' contralto etc.) and to regard verbal communication as marginal to their professional requirements.

Though perhaps none of the composers with whom Brecht worked rejected these still prevalent principles quite so sharply as he did himself – thus even Eisler could still admire a 'beautiful' voice, much as he would admire a Stradivarius – they all saw the point where the theatre was concerned, and Eisler went a lot further. In Brecht's view any kind of song and any kind of singing that violated them was to be welcomed – whence his liking for sloppy nineteenth-century ballads, genuine folk songs, oriental epics and American jazz; it was all grist to his mill, for these things were broadly speaking 'gestic', communicating not only the meaning of the words but the attitude of the singer. All his composers understood this, whatever else they might choose to do outside the framework of their collaboration. What Eisler managed to do as well however, during the extraordinary interlude in a despised and (at bottom) detested paradise, was to marry a 'gestic' approach and a post-Schönberg technique with a tradition of subtle and beautiful song writing that goes back to Schubert. Brecht wanted effective didactic and theatrical music, and from 1927 on he got it. What he, and we, got over and above that was a corpus of marvellous settings of great modern poetry such as no other collaboration – not Auden and Britten, not Claudel and Milhaud, not Ramuz and Stravinsky, not Cocteau and Poulenc – has been able to provide.

The changing role of politics

There must be something very special about the role played by politics in Brecht's life and work, or it would hardly have bulked so large, for better or worse, in so many people's views of him. Not that most professional politicians would think it of much consequence; for what did it amount to in terms of practical experience? A few months' military service at the end of the First World War, in a hospital, in his home town, generally in civilian clothes. Membership of the Workers' and Soldiers' Council there: brief and, so far as details or hard facts are concerned, nebulous. The honour of being (allegedly) blacklisted by the Munich Nazis, for his satirical 'Legend of the Dead Soldier' a year or so later. Exile in 1933, cancellation of contracts, loss of citizenship. A speech to the Paris International Writers' Congress in 1935. Two visits to Moscow in the 1930s and nominal co-editorship of a German literary magazine published there. A third visit in transit in 1941, on the way from Finland to the United States. Membership in 1944 of a short-lived American-based Council for a Democratic Germany. Interrogation by the House Committee on Un-American Activities in 1947. Return to East Germany at the age of fifty to become an academician, national prize winner and artistic director of a state theatre in the Eastern bloc. A rare public statement on such issues as peace, mostly pretty short; bitter attacks on him in the 1950s in the West German and anti-communist press whenever an opportunity offered. A Stalin peace prize in 1955. A laudatory memorial speech by Walter Ulbricht in 1956, somewhat in defiance of his own request for no ceremonies to be conducted over his dead body. That was about all.

Yet Brecht's politics were, and still are, resented in many quarters with a virulence quite spared to more orthodox communist writers like Aragon or Neruda or Aimé Césaire, earning him a leading place in the Cold War propagandists' Pandaemonium and inspiring even reputed scholars to dishonesties such as those practised in my view (see pp. 227–34) by the late Hannah Arendt. With this went a less overt dislike that tried to play off the early, pre-communist Brecht against the committed writer he was to become in his thirties, arguing that the canalising and concentration of his imaginative powers which took place after *The Threepenny Opera* was a Stalin-inspired disaster. Opposed to this you had a growing feeling now in the West that Brecht was an erudite Marxist, a master of agit-prop in the theatre, eventually becoming a sage whose least sayings merit widespread quotation. Meanwhile, with the appearance of many of his previously unknown writings the Western and Third World interest in his work continued to grow, even though the collapse of Communist governments would cut down his already diminished significance in Middle and Eastern Europe. Then in the nineties a new campaign against him began, based on the growing power of feminism in the US and culminating in Professor John Fuegi's widely reviewed and serialised monograph *The Life and Lies of Bertolt Brecht*, with its central argument that Brecht was a pig of variable sexuality who mastered his women collaborators by seducing them, and thereby got them to write a great part of his works. The aim was openly stated – Brecht was a 'socialist icon' that had to be demolished – and it was openly supported by a dozen or so reputed American foundations, receiving mysteriously generous coverage in the English-language press too: six pages in the *Observer*, for a start, whose critical review only appeared later.

The trouble with such a thesis, which is based largely on guesswork (for instance, Hauptmann's 'eighty per cent' authorship of *The Threepenny Opera*), is that it can appear to be supported by a mass of scholarly-looking footnotes, all of which need to be verified by its critics. This was not done until four independent sceptics (of whom I was one) joined to compile a hundred-page list of 'mistakes, misquotes and malpractices' for the *Brecht Yearbook*, no. 20, published in 1995 by the International Brecht Society for its members. It would, I suppose, have been possible to append that list to the present book, but it would no longer be very interesting, and the real question would remain, which is: why does Brecht get treated in such a resentful way? Partly, of course, because his reputation survived the fall, first of Stalin and then of the Berlin Wall, without his supporters (theatrical, musical, literary, theoretical) making any conspicuous retractions. But one part of the trouble also is that whereas other creative artists in our century, whether inside or outside the communist sphere, have restricted their commitment to particular aspects of their work or even kept their work insulated from it, Brecht systematically made it a part of everything he did. Far more than Picasso or Éluard, or George Grosz or André Malraux, he was all of a piece, fusing political and aesthetic considerations on a whole series of different levels. It is this that makes him seem special to admirers and critics alike, and just because the process was neither easy nor obvious to himself it is a nagging challenge to his interpreters of whatever colour.

Much comes under this heading of politics, ranging from the Brecht–Eisler *Kampflieder*, through the Marxist dialectic, the establishment of an official Soviet cultural doctrine, the administration of justice, the conduct of the Second World War and the occupation of Germany, right down to such apparently trivial matters as the issuing of travel documents; and none of it is without its bearing on what Brecht did, thought and wrote. In this tangle of different factors I shall try to deal with the major elements more or less chronologically, as they came to seem most relevant to him, while allowing for certain overlaps.

So I propose to begin with Brecht's evolution towards Communism in the 1920s and the period of his most intense commitment to the revolutionary cause and the fight against the Nazis; then take up the question of Socialist Realism in writing and the theatre (linked for Brecht particularly with the names of Lukács and Stanislavsky); then try to analyse his attitude to the Soviet Union and its leaders up to mid-1941; then compare his view of the Western democracies and their freedoms; explain his return to East Germany and his variable standing there as these factors became more or less influential; and finally do my best to set out those elements of his political approach which gave his later work its unique character. The ultimate aim is to be able to look at a poem like, say, 'Of sprinkling the garden' and see just how he had become able to take an everyday domestic activity, give it a precise setting and briefly, clearly, simply, bring it to a political point – something that few other committed artists have been able to do.

* * *

Generally the left-wing commitment of the Weimar intelligentsia originated in its opposition to the First World War, and at first reflected the utopian socialism of 1918–19. Thereafter a certain disillusion set in as the non-revolutionary nature of the majority Socialist Party (or SPD) became clear, though many of those who followed the new Communist Party (KPD) and pinned their hopes to Russia did so not out of Marxist conviction but from knowledge that the Bolsheviks had been the only effective pacifists: Piscator being an outstanding example of this. Such men were guided above all by enthusiasm, whether for the utopian ideals of men like Toller, Gustav Landauer and the architect Bruno Taut (on all of whom Whitman and Verhaeren had a powerful influence) or for the heroic new revolutionary society in the East, and at first they very largely constituted the activist wing of German Expressionism in the arts. As we saw in connection with that movement, Brecht was notoriously antagonistic to such romantic feelings: he had not been shaken by any experience of the war front; already at the time of the first version of *Baal* he thought that 'this Expressionism is frightful'; and, while highly critical of his own class, felt himself to be 'a materialist and a lout and a proletarian and a conservative anarchist'[1] without faith in any other. His 'cold route' to his political convictions of ten years later is quite clear, and it distinguishes him from nearly all his contemporaries however radical. He was not swayed, he said, by Eisenstein's films or Piscator's first revolutionary productions (1924–26), but derided the 'Theatre Communist' who staged 'the misery of the masses' in Berlin's West End. Once he walked out of a Munich lecture on the new Russia by Piscator's adviser Alfons Goldschmidt. 'Perhaps', he noted much later, such scepticism

> may have been due to my scientific education (for several years I studied medicine) which made me strongly immune to any kind of influence on the emotional side.[2]

There are two main accounts of his development into the uniquely political artist he became. Both may well be true, and although current mythology tends to concentrate on the first it would not have led very far without the second. On the one hand, then, he became interested in the writings of Karl Marx (starting, it seems, courageously with *Das Kapital*) in the course of his struggles to understand the operations of the Chicago wheat exchange, which he had read about in Frank Norris's *The Pit* and wanted to make the theme of a play. Certainly he was deeply impressed by what he found:

> It wasn't of course . . . that I had unconsciously written a whole lot of Marxist plays; but this man Marx was the only spectator for my plays I'd ever come across.

So in the summer of 1927 we find him asking Helene Weigel to send him 'only Marxist literature. Especially further instalments of the History of the Revolution',[3] while in 1926 and 1928 (respectively) he listed biographies of Lenin and Marx among the best books of the year. What this primarily shows however is that from the summer of 1926 Marx's ideas were becoming part of his concept of an 'epic theatre'[4] which could deal with the economic realities of 'mankind's occupation of the big cities'. This association of Marxism with a purely theatrical problem did not make Brecht an instant communist, though the same year saw him contributing for the first time to a KPD paper – the satirical *Der Knüppel* edited by Heartfield – and writing poems about such subjects as class solidarity, the class war and the 'new man'. Indeed, even after he was already established as one of Piscator's collaborators in a theatre that accepted political control by the KPD he was still some way from being accepted as a party writer. As late as 1928 *The Threepenny Opera* was being viewed in party circles at best as a destructive satire on bourgeois morality, at worst as being itself a piece of bourgeois opportunism which the *Rote Fahne*'s critic said contained 'not a vestige of modern social or political satire'.

But then we have the view of Fritz Sternberg the sociologist, some of whose lectures on Marxism Brecht attended in Berlin, according to which the turning point came on 1 May 1929. Brecht watched the banned parade from Sternberg's flat, and, says Sternberg:

> As far as we could see these people were unarmed. Several times the police fired. At first we thought they were warning shots. Then we saw a number of the demonstrators falling and later being carried away on stretchers . . . When Brecht heard the shots and saw people being hit he went whiter than I had ever seen him before. In my view this was an experience which largely helped to push him towards the Communists.[1]

Chronologically this makes sense, for 1929 was the year of the first *Lehrstücke* and of Brecht's virtual abandonment of *Happy End* and the cannibalisation of that play to make *Saint Joan of the Stockyards*, after which the collaboration with Eisler, the *Kampflieder* and the other mainly political poems all began. What is more, 1929 was a turning point in the affairs of the Weimar Republic itself, in that the world economic crisis (associated particularly with the Wall Street crash of that autumn) led to the rise of the Nazis. Parliamentary government was soon on the verge of collapse, while at the same time the combination of financial stringency and new right-wing administrations largely stifled further experiment in the arts. If ever there was a time for Brecht to set aside his mistrust of personal involvement it was then, and so when Elisabeth Hauptmann applied to join the KPD – as we know she did that year – Brecht could well have done so too. If Hauptmann at that point became a member and Brecht did not, it was seemingly (to judge from his evidence to the Un-American Activities Committee) because the KPD itself decided that he should not be formally admitted. Hanns Eisler's position was similarly equivocal: '1926 February', says an approved East German chronology of his life, 'Application to join KPD, which however is not processed further' – something that did not stop him subsequently filling a number of national and international party appointments. 'Making contact with the KPD', an East German Academy publication calls it. Much would be explained if Brecht was treated in the same way: in particular that mixture of intellectual independence and outward conformity which was to characterise his attitude to the party's policy from 1929 on.

Brecht's new communist convictions are mainly spelt out in the songs to *The Decision* and *The Mother*: (a) Communism is simple, rational and depends on questioning and study; (b) the party is immense, anonymous, and indestructible, and if its policy is wrong it would be still more wrong for the individual to act on his own; (c) altering the world means dirtying your hands; (d) piecemeal reforms are inadequate; (e) the rank and file of the oppressors are not all that different from the oppressed; (f) an unfulfilled life is a worse fate than death. These were genuine beliefs, and neither he nor Eisler could have expressed them so powerfully if they had been anything else. At the same time Brecht had come over to his new allies complete with all his inbuilt scepticism and detachment, which continued to operate even where he was now prepared to override them under principle (b) above, likewise his sharp sense of humour. Thus a figure called Do in the *Me-ti* aphorisms.

> argued that one has to doubt anything one hasn't seen with one's own eyes. Rebuked for this negative attitude, he was not pleased and left the house. After a short while he came back, stopped on the threshold and said: I must amend that. One has to doubt what one has seen with one's eyes, too.
>
> Asked what could set a limit to doubt in that case, Do said: The wish to act.[1]

Given this one antidote to scepticism – which in his own case was not so much the wish to act as the wish to let the party act – Brecht could align himself and his writing with the KPD, yet ignore any attempt by its functionaries to dictate his ideas and methods, while loyally accepting their political objectives. So he continued to discuss Marxism with his 'teachers' Sternberg (who later became militantly anti-Soviet) and Karl Korsch (a former KPD deputy who had been expelled in 1926 for 'left' deviations, then became a law professor at Jena and lectured at the Karl Marx school at Neukölln in Berlin). From Sternberg he seems to have acquired a greater awareness of the social context of the arts generally and his own work in particular; from Korsch much of his understanding of the Hegelian and Marxist dialectic, which Korsch always treated as a critical, empirical tool for the investigation of modern social life. The result was that Brecht too continued to judge Marxism by its usefulness and relevance, and had no hesitation in reading Trotsky, Souvarine, Gide and other writers regarded as dangerously heretical by the party.

In 1930 he, Walter Benjamin and the journalist Bernard von Brentano were planning a critical journal to be published by Rowohlt and devoted to analysing scholarship and the arts from a socially functional point of view; Jhering too was drawn in to this scheme, and discussions also began with Lukács, though they seem to have broken down on the ground that his self-confident dogmatism would have alienated uncommitted readers. Tentatively named 'Crisis and Criticism' this journal never appeared. And though the thinking behind it had been that 'the shattering of their economic basis has made the intellectuals, within limits, prepared to discuss'[1] – i.e. presumably with the communists – there is no real evidence to suggest that Brecht at that time was any more far-sighted than the KPD about the need to join forces with others if Hitler was to be kept out. On the contrary he seems to have shared their view that proletarian revolution was now inevitable and a Nazi government merely the last desperate throw of the ruling class: a brief if unpleasant phase that the KPD could afford to sit through. All his writings of the years 1929–1932 suggest that for him, as for the party, capitalism was then still the main enemy, and the SPD its ally. The 'solidarity' which was the theme of his most successful *Kampflied* with Eisler bore as yet no relation to any united front against Fascism, but was thought of as a straightforward banding together of the world proletariat against its rulers.

In this period he provided the communists with three highly original works – *The Decision*, *The Mother* and the film *Kuhle Wampe* – all three produced and played outside the accepted machinery of the arts. This concept of an 'apparatus', which evidently owes something to his talks with Benjamin and Sternberg (as well as to his experiences with Pabst's *Threepenny Opera* film), did not add up so much to any socio-aesthetic notion of 'alternative' theatre and cinema as to a wishful conviction that the established cultural institutions of capitalism would soon be captured by the workers and their allies, and reorganised on new lines. Together with Eisler, and joined by a new aide from the cast of the Berlin *The Mother* – the working-class communist Margarete Steffin who remained with him for nearly a decade – he gave the KPD some of the materials for this impending change; and if it sometimes disagreed with his message it knew that his individual songs and sketches were not only politically impelling but would be of practical value to its performance groups in the waiting period. At the same time he remained outside the party's own organisations, never joining the BPRS or Proletarian-Revolutionary Writers' League for instance or working with the recognised agit-prop groups. Moreover he only marginally contributed to the party press. Thus the daily *Die Rote Fahne* asked him for a brief statement on the anti-Russian attitude of the German radio and printed a song apiece from *The Decision* and *The Mother* following their respective premières, while of Willi Muenzenberg's enterprises, the *AIZ* included a message from him in its tenth birthday issue and printed the poem 'Coal for Mike'; the Neuer Deutscher Verlag's *Volksbuch 1930* reprinted this; and at the end of 1931 the *Illustrierte Rote Post* published the 'Song of the SA Man'. This was then called 'Song of the SA Proletarian' and appears to be one of the *three* poems about the Nazis which Brecht wrote before January 1933, when Hitler came to power.

*　　*　　*

For all the impact of his major works with Eisler (which for many of the individuals who experienced them was unforgettable) it was the fight against the Nazis that really integrated Brecht and his work with the political, artistic and emotional history of the German Left. His by-passing of the established 'apparatus' now had the advantage that his songs, poems and scenes could be played in the makeshift conditions of the exiled theatre, while his 'epic' use of montage meant that performers could dismantle a play and turn it into cabaret material on the principle of 'each scene for itself'. Leaving the country after the Reichstag Fire moreover, he was much quicker than the KPD leadership to realise that they would need to do more than just wait. So he wrote to Sergei Tretiakov in Moscow a few weeks later that 'for the moment the existence of the party is more hindrance than help' to the exiles because 'everything is centralised, and the centre isn't answering'.[1] He also began pressing Johannes R. Becher, an old acquaintance from student days in Munich, to organise a meeting of the exiled writers, many of whom already foresaw that Hitler was there to stay. To Tretiakov again, who seems to have wondered why Brecht was not subscribing to the various anti-Fascist manifestos, he replied that the time for that sort of thing was past: 'What's necessary now is a patient, relentless, laborious job of enlightenment and study.'[2] So he helped on the preparation of Muenzenberg's first *Brown Book* that summer under the direction of Otto Katz; supported Kurt Kläber and Otto Biha in their efforts to set up a Paris institute for the study of Fascism; wrote his six 'Hitler

Chorales' and several other anti-Nazi poems (*Poems 1913–1956*, pp. 206–218, prints some of these) and grouped them with several of the Eisler songs in the booklet *Lieder Gedichte Chöre* (Songs Poems Choruses) which was published by Muenzenberg's Strasbourg firm Editions du Carrefour the following year. Meanwhile Helene Weigel toured Russia the same autumn; Margarete Steffin set up an agency in Paris to handle stories and articles by Brecht, Anna Seghers and others; and Elisabeth Hauptmann stayed on for some months in Berlin, where her flat enjoyed a certain immunity on account of her Red Army lodger.

At the end of 1933, with the help of his industrialist father and a publisher's advance for his *Threepenny Novel*, Brecht bought the Danish house where he was to live until the eve of the Second World War. 'Danish Siberia' he termed it in a letter to Kläber in Paris, which ironically drew attention to the Comintern Executive's latest interpretation of the situation in Germany under Hitler as being 'a markedly revolutionary one'. Abetted no doubt by the proximity of Korsch, who was a neighbour till he left for America some four years later, he began to develop his own interpretation of the Third Reich, culminating in two dozen or so scenes of *Fear and Misery of the Third Reich* which expose different aspects of that edifice, seen from below. This interpretation was orthodox enough in its continued identification of Fascism with capitalism – hence Brecht's injunction to Muenzenberg's Paris Congress for the Defence of Culture in 1935 to 'study the property relationships' – and its corresponding interpretation of Hitler's anti-semitism as a more or less cynical cloak for this – which is what makes *Round Heads and Pointed Heads* such a hopelessly unreal play. It was less so however in its recognition that Hitler had been voted into power by the German electors, that this policy with regard to supposed 'national interests' was not entirely stupid, and that he had won over a good part of the working class: points that were to determine Brecht's own future attitude to a 'democratic Germany'. At the same time he drew a line between Nazi neo-paganism and the Christian religion, and recognised that German Fascism had specifically German roots.

Even before Hitler came to power the prospective exiles had been preparing a cultural as well as a political base in the USSR, largely through the international secretariats there (like MORT, the IMB and the writers' organisation MORP) and through Muenzenberg's International Workers' Aid. Such men as Piscator, Arthur Pieck, Lukács, and Kurella were already effectively established there, not to mention Brecht's old friends Reich and Lacis who had emigrated in the 1920s. Moreover, Brecht himself had visited Moscow in May 1932 for the première of *Kuhle Wampe* (which was not a great success) and established a working friendship with Tretiakov, Mayakovsky's successor as editor of *New LEF*, who was now bringing out a first translation of his plays: this was when (according to Muenzenberg's paper *Die Welt am Abend*) the two of them collaborated with Eisler to plan an opera for Leningrad on the theme of 'construction of the New Man'.[1]

Over the ensuing four years he was thus able to build up a number of further connections in that country and to start getting his work accepted not just by exiled theatre groups and the Foreign Workers' publishing house Vegaar (which published the *Threepenny Novel* in 1935 and planned to co-publish the subsequent Malik edition of the collected works) but even up to a point by the Russians. Tairov staged *The Threepenny Opera* in 1933; Mikhoels at the Moscow Jewish Theatre considered a production of *Round Heads*, which also figured in the plans of Piscator, Gustav von Wangenheim and other resident Germans, and was accepted for filming by Mezhrabpom-Film. Steffin too, who suffered from tuberculosis, was treated more than once in Soviet sanatoria, while Weigel expected to join first one, then another of the planned German theatres. Most of these hopes of Soviet support rotated around Piscator, following his appointment to the presidency of MORT in November 1934, and it was he who invited Brecht for his two months' visit during the following spring, when the playwright was amiably received by Kun and Knorin of the Comintern and, together with Eisler, was commissioned to write a *Lehrstück* for the Red Army. That year he also saw something of Mikhail Koltsov, leading journalist and head of the Jurgaz publishing firm, who was jointly responsible with Tretiakov for the foreign relations of the Soviet Writers' Union. Koltsov, a fluent German speaker, was then living with Maria Gresshöner, prior to 1933 an editorial assistant in Herzfelde's Malik-Verlag in Berlin and now known under the name of Maria Osten; and soon he became Brecht's main Soviet patron. For it was his firm which in July 1936 published the first number of a new, broadly-based émigré magazine designed to succeed Herzfelde's *Neue Deutsche Blätter*, with Brecht as one of its editors: *Das Wort*.

Unfortunately for Brecht's expectations, this was just the point when things were beginning to change, and from then on both the cultural and the political conjuncture in the USSR became progressively less favourable. On the one hand the new creative formula of Socialist Realism, from being, as it were, a mere banner waved over the big Moscow Writers' Congress in autumn 1934 (which Brecht did not attend or even make any noteworthy comment on) unexpectedly became a stick with which *Pravda*, seemingly in response to Stalin's own views, began beating the avant-garde. First Shostakovitch was attacked for his opera *Lady Macbeth of Mtsensk* (subsequently known as *Katerina Ismailovna*) in a leading article in January 1936, under the heading 'A Mess instead of Music'; then much of March was taken up, again at *Pravda*'s instigation, by a debate on literary Formalism in the course of which the further slogan of 'popularity' was put forward; then Eisenstein's film *Bezhin Meadow* was rejected by the politicians and destroyed; Tairov's theatre was attacked and the Leningrad experimental youth theatre TRAM reorganised on conventional lines, till by the beginning of 1938 Okhlopkhov's and Meyerhold's theatres had both been closed down. Moreover this whole switch to traditional nineteenth-century models in all the arts, with its emphasis on the sanctity of the 'cultural heritage', was entirely in line with the criticisms of Brecht's chief literary antagonist Georg Lukács, who had led the theoretical opposition to montage, agitprop, documentary, the *Lehrstück* and the epic theatre within the German 'proletarian-revolutionary writers' movement ever since 1931. Writing primarily in German, he and his fellow Hungarian Andor Gábor were now settled in Moscow as members of the KPD and had a considerable influence on *Internationale Literatur* under Becher's editorship, Becher himself having finally moved there from Paris in 1935. At the same time Lukács had a footing in *Literaturny Kritik* thanks to his alliance with the Soviet Marxist Mikhail Lifschitz, and it was their view of 'popularity' that won out in the Formalism debate of March 1936. From now to the mid-1950s, Lukács, to Brecht's private irritation and derision, was to dominate German communist thinking about the arts.

On the other hand the arrests also began, and already in the course of 1936 the international organisations – a main source of patronage and of travel facilities for men like Brecht – were closing down and German architects and theatre people deciding to leave. MORP was then supposed to shift to Paris, but fizzled out; MORT likewise; Piscator, with his plans in ruins, decided not to return from Paris to Moscow; Mezhrabpom-Film was liquidated and given over to making children's films; Vegaar's plan to co-publish the Malik Brecht edition was dropped; Erich Wendt, its would-be publisher, was sacked, arrested and sent to the Volga Republic. Reich, Lacis, Alexander Granach, Maxim Vallentin were among the earlier detainees; Ottwalt, Carola Neher, Tretiakov, Kun and Knorin among those who vanished, never to return. Quite apart from the practical effects from Brecht's point of view – and these were all people he knew – the coincidence of such measures with the campaign against formal innovation in the arts was disturbing: 'every one of their criticisms', he said of Lukács to Benjamin, 'contains a threat'.

*   *   *

The control of *Das Wort* by its three editors was never all that easy, even when Bredel was living in Moscow and Maria Osten was active in the Moscow office. The arrangement was that copies of all the material selected should be sent to Brecht and Feuchtwanger the day it went off to be typeset; they would then have some ten days in which to approve, veto or amend. As this never really worked, their influence seems to have been mainly a general one, agreed at occasional meetings in France or during Feuchtwanger's visit, along with the recommendations or otherwise of specific articles by writers who got directly in touch with them, or on subjects the Moscow office thought they should be consulted about. Even so Brecht was unable to secure the publication of Benjamin's now classic essay on 'The Work of Art in the Era of its Technical Reproducibility' and found it easier to keep a contribution out than to get one in. 'At the moment', he told Dudow at the end of the paper's first year,

> there's virtually nothing theoretical appearing [in the USSR] about literature and related matters so far as I can see; I've banned any efforts in that direction up to now, as it would have meant treading on a whole lot of people's toes including mine.[1]

However, Lukács, who had already written his first attack on Expressionism in the rival *Internationale Literatur*, was by then being allowed, said Brecht, to write 'a few rudimentary things about the technique of the novel' in *Das Wort* too. Then with Osten's and Bredel's (and Koltsov's own) departure for Spain in July 1937, Fritz Erpenbeck took over the Moscow office, and although Brecht and Feuchtwanger secured the establishment of a Paris branch office (which Osten ran on her return from the fighting) the 'Moscow clique' (as Brecht termed them) of Lukács, Gábor and the Hungarian playwright Julius Hay began increasingly to affect the paper's policy. From that September till the middle of 1938 Lukács and Alfred Kurella were able to control a running 'Expressionism debate' in its pages that identified formal innovation not merely with 'bourgeois decadence' but even with the rise of Nazi ideology. Brecht finally put in a veto against the appearance of Lukács's closing article in the June issue; but Kurella ignored this after first passing it to 'Walter' (presumably Ulbricht) and admitting to Erpenbeck that 'formally he [Brecht] is right'.[1] Two articles which Brecht wrote in answer to Lukács's arguments that July were not published and may not have been sent, though he told Kurella to expect one of them. Criticised that same month in *Internationale Literatur*, once again by Lukács, he told Bredel that he was not replying 'because I consider such debates to be highly confusing and damaging' at that time. He did however send *Das Wort* a corrective note when Erpenbeck refused to print Hanns Eisler's reply to Lukács's final offensive remarks. This the Moscow office simply shelved.[2]

'It's a disgrace, what they've made of our beautiful scheme'. So Brecht wrote to Maria Osten at the end of 1938. Returning from Spain, Koltsov had been summoned to see Stalin and arrested on December 12th; he was not seen again. At the beginning of March Erpenbeck gave up answering letters; then on the 31st the publishers (now Meshdunarodnaya Kniga) told the editors that the magazine was uneconomic and would have to be fused with Becher's *Internationale Literatur*. Erpenbeck thereupon moved over to the rival outfit, and when Brecht wrote claiming money was still due him at the end of July Erpenbeck replied that this was a technical matter over which he had no control.[3] With the Second World War only nine months away Brecht could sum the position up in the *Journals*[4] which he had recently started:

> koltsov too has been arrested in moscow. my last russian link with that country. no one knows anything about tretiakov, who is said to be a 'japanese spy'. nor about carola neher, who is supposed to have carried out trotskyist commissions in prague for her husband. reich and asya lacis have stopped writing, grete [steffin] is no longer getting any response from her friends in leningrad and the caucasus. béla kun too has been arrested, the only politician i met. meyerhold has lost his theatre but is apparently tolerated as an opera director. literature and art seem to be in the shit, political theory to have gone to the dogs, there's a kind of bureaucratically favoured thin bloodless proletarian humanism. [. . .]. all you hear about political 'democracy' is verbiage, and as to the way in which production is socially organised – nothing. the logical position for marxists outside is roughly that adopted by marx towards german social-democracy. critical, but in favour.

From then on Brecht was living in what he repeatedly called the 'dark times'. His first use of this phrase was in the title of a poem which his editors ascribe to 1937 and which mentions Hitler's defeat of the workers, the coming wars, the alliance of the great powers 'against the workers' and finally 'Why were their poets silent?'. He never actually mentioned the cultural and political changes in the USSR in this connection, clearly because so long as war threatened he felt that he could not publicly attack them; so this is where he remained 'silent' himself. All the same, chronology suggests that they too contributed to the darkness and very possibly also to the change in direction of his work following the Spanish War one-acter *Señora Carrar's Rifles*, the 27-scene version of *Fear and Misery of the Third Reich* and the 'German Satires' and other poems for the communist-run German Freedom Radio. We cannot, in other words, divorce the shifts in Soviet policy from the fact that after 1937 Brecht virtually gave up writing scenes or poems for immediate political use. Significantly, both Eisler and Piscator had begun looking towards New York as a place to work rather than Moscow or (following the fall of the Popular Front government) Paris; and of course all hope of an internal overthrow of the Nazis had long since disappeared.

Brecht's reaction to his disillusionment with Soviet developments therefore had to be a complex one. Outwardly, and even in private conversations with all but his closest intimates, he maintained his acceptance of the party line, though he could sometimes avoid committing himself, as when his two fellow-editors made a statement in *Das Wort* of March 1937 approving the Pyatakov–Radek trial and he abstained. At the same time however he began quietly setting down a number of his doubts and criticisms, most trenchantly where cultural policy was concerned, which he dealt with largely in the *Journals* which he started in 1938; but also in relation to Stalin's leadership, to the show trials, the new Soviet constitution, the growth of Stalin-worship and the persistence throughout the system of 'contradictions' and inefficiency, which are analysed mainly in his *Me-ti* aphorisms. The recipients of his real views on such points we know to have included Benjamin and Korsch, though doubtless he discussed them with Eisler too before the latter left for America at the end of the year.

Me-ti, a loose sequence of aphorisms modelled on the work of the pre-Christian Chinese philosopher known to us as Mo Tse, was never completed or set in order; it remained unpublished till the 1960s, and the dates of its individual paragraphs are generally unknown. But we know that Brecht consulted Korsch about it and showed him parts of it, and he told Korsch that he was about to work on it again around the beginning of 1938. Among the material which seems to date from then are a number of sections which, with one or two other notes from the same time, add up to a coherent picture of his view of Stalin's dictatorship in the late 1930s. Thus he could distinguish Stalin from Lenin, who ruled by convincing people, as follows:

Mi-en-leh [Lenin] could not say that the superiority of his enemies forced him to give orders. It forced him to convince. Ni-en [Stalin] had fewer enemies and gave orders. [*GW* 12, p. 530]

And again:

Mi-en-leh knew everyone's weaknesses and could work with all and sundry. Ni-en could work with very few and didn't know their weaknesses. [p. 536]

Brecht agreed with Stalin against Trotsky that socialism must be built first in one country by building up its industry, and held that this had to be done before socialism could be established anywhere else (p. 495), which meant that therefore foreign communist parties must subordinate their policies to that of the Russians (*GW* 20, p. 99). But he also believed that only the establishment of socialism in other countries would lead to its full achievement in the Soviet Union. Since 'liberation is an economic task, and one that has to be organised' (p. 439) the Soviet peoples were very far from free; indeed 'Me-ti laughed at those who claimed that the individual was free, not to say freer than he ever had been' (p. 540). On the contrary, he suggested,

The decision of the [party] in Su to institute *die Grosse Ordnung* [the great Order, i.e. socialism] weighs on the people of Su like a nightmare. The moves towards progress make them stagger. The bread is hurled at the people with so much force that it knocks many of them flat. The most beneficial arrangements are put into effect by rogues, and a number of virtuous people form an obstacle to progress. [p. 524]

A still more startling note, written independently of *Me-ti* but around the same time, it seems, sets out what Brecht terms 'preconditions for the successful leadership of a movement directed towards social transformation', i.e. of a revolutionary party of the kind that Brecht would have liked ideally to see. Among the points which this puts forward are abolition of the leadership principle within the party, a shift away from centralism, greater ethical concern (to include the application of bourgeois morality), abstention from dishonest tactics, substitution of proof for 'faith', and finally a renunciation of any claim to primacy by the industrial workers in favour of a simple acceptance of the dictatorship of the proletariat as being the easiest and quickest solution. There is not much in common here with the reality of the new Soviet Constitution of 5 December 1936, which Brecht felt had to be seen as a war measure, a 'strengthening of the class of leaders by means of a truce with the led'.[1]

He thought it entirely right that this should be known as the Stalin Constitution:

> It is indeed a constitution that should be laid at the door of the man constituting it. [. . .]. Certain essential elements of *die Grosse Ordnung* have been laid down and are being developed. [. . .]. But the new system, the most advanced in the history of the world, is still working extremely badly and unspontaneously and it needs so much effort and use of force that the individual's freedoms are minimal. Because it is being forced into existence by small groups of people there is force everywhere and no real popular rule. The absence of freedom of thought and freedom of combination, the false professions, the arbitrary administrative measures all show how many basic elements of *die Grosse Ordnung* still have to be realised and developed. [p. 535]

This state of things had largely demoralised the foreign communist parties, where 'it was not the members who elected the secretaries but the secretaries who elected the members'.

> The slogans were laid down in Su and the secretaries paid by Su. When mistakes were made the people who criticised them were punished, but the people who had perpetrated them remained in office. [. . .] Those in Su who were giving the orders no longer got any information because the secretaries had stopped reporting anything that might be unwelcome. [p. 539]

The trouble was at the top, because 'Breaking off discussions in a critical situation, wishing for obedience rather than enthusiasm, mistaking haste for speed, hogging the credit: all adds up to bad leadership' (p. 541). And yet Brecht still thought that 'in several ways Ni-en is a useful person', while criticising the corrupt and degrading flattery of him then prevalent (pp. 467, 491, 536). This usefulness was certainly one factor in his first comments on the trials, where he went no further than saying that Stalin demanded too much confidence. 'If I am asked to believe something that is provable, but without any proof, it's the same as asking me to believe something that cannot be proved. I won't do this. Ni-en may have served the people by removing the enemies in the [party], but he has not proved it' (p. 538). Later, in 1941, the year when he decided to replace the concept of 'die grosse Ordnung' by 'die grosse Produktion', he was less cautious and more cynical:

> When Me-ti passed through Su [. . . he] found it a matter for congratulation that scarcely anyone thought people guilty just because they had been arrested. [. . .] Good surgeons separate the cancer from the healthy flesh, bad ones cut away the healthy flesh too, it was said. Me-ti was amazed at the popular

attitude and remarked: they are treating their policemen as bad, crude, stupid menials; that's something at least. [p. 546]

* * *

Critical, but *for* it. That was still his position as he decided that he too would try to go to the United States for the impending war, then applied himself to writing great but for the moment virtually unperformable plays. He still thought of the Western democracies with contempt, arguing for instance that Chamberlain's objection to the Nazis was that they were overdoing things: thus 'pogroms aren't essential for the survival of capitalism, and can be dispensed with', whereas Britain's ruling class could continue to work through parliament 'because they still have a parliamentary majority'.[1] He was not therefore exactly 'choosing freedom', an abstraction about which anyhow he had doubts. Nevertheless the course of events in the first months of the war certainly did nothing to increase his respect for the Soviet government. First came the German–Soviet pact, by which the USSR 'saved itself, at the cost of leaving the workers of the world without guidance, hopes or help' (*Journals* entry for 9.9.39); then the Soviet invasion of Eastern Poland, which meant for Brecht

> the stripping of ideological pretences [. . .], the abandonment of the principle 'the soviet union doesn't require a single foot of foreign soil', the adoption of all that fascist bullshit about 'blood brotherhood', liberation of the 'brothers' (of slav descent): the entire nationalist terminology. this is being spouted to the german fascists, but at the same time to the soviet troops. [18.9.39]

Finally the Soviet attack on Finland at the end of 1939, in his view, drove too many Finnish workers into the arms of their bourgeoisie, and all three events seemed to involve 'serious political errors such as can only be understood in terms of the internal Russian situation' (1.1.40). Once the Russians had 'won' and settled down to consolidate their gains in peace the Brechts themselves moved into Finland, where Brecht (as he wrote in the poem 'Finland 1940') still saw a 'small door' in the shape of the Arctic port of Petsamo, which the Nazis, however, shortly afterwards occupied. It is typical of the subsequent cold war campaign against Brecht that this remark should be treated as unintended proof that he 'had not even thought of [the USSR] as a possible refuge'.[2]

Brecht's actual passage through the USSR in the following year took place, as it turned out, in the three months' interval between the end of the Finnish war and the start of the 'Great Patriotic War' (as the

Russians call their share of the Second World War) against Germany.
And it would not have been possible without the help of the Soviet
Writers' Union, whose foreign relations secretary Mikhail Apletin
organised the family's tickets and their payment out of sums due, in
roubles and hard currency, from Soviet publishing firms, then saw to
Margarete Steffin's treatment in a Moscow hospital when she had to be
left behind.[1] Maria Osten – who was arrested and disappeared soon
afterwards – helped to look after her; Fadeyev himself signed the
telegram telling Brecht of her death. Thereafter the war seems to have
dominated Brecht's concern with Soviet affairs; his original contributions to the Moscow journals stopped; and in other ways too his political
interests altered. For whereas in Scandinavia Brecht, for all his isolation,
had had continual visitors and held group discussion with exiles of all
trades and classes,[2] in California his circle became more restricted, both
in numbers and in social composition. Unlike Hanns Eisler, who fitted
cheerfully into the American scene and felt comfortable there, Brecht
was determinedly unassimilable by Right and Left alike, as his 'Letters
to a grown-up American' – itself a somewhat contemptuous title – go to
show. In these he confesses that he 'hasn't the least hope of learning
colloquial American', and this not because he lacked either the
vocabulary or the grammar but because his whole character is wrong:

> With some effort I might in due course be able to find American sentences for
> the thought that the sky and the trees in certain American pictures strike me as
> cosmetic, like creatures designed to generate maximum sex appeal. But the
> attitude in which I would have to say so, if the attitude itself is not to seem
> offensive, is something I shall never learn. I'd have to learn to be a *nice fellow*.[3]

As might have been expected from his previous visit, Brecht accordingly
was not accepted by American 'liberals' and 'progressives'. As James
Lyon put it, 'because American Marxists disliked Brecht as a person,
they had no use for his ideological or artistic views'. More than in any
other period of his exile, for the next six years he was a fish out of water
and never became anything else.[4]

Politically his main concern in this period was with Germany and the
resistance to the Nazis. Otherwise his opinions went largely into storage,
though with three significant exceptions: the tacit abandonment after the
battle of Stalingrad of the concept of 'dark times', the dropping of the
idea of *die grosse Ordnung* in favour of *die grosse Produktion*, and the
writing of the great Lucretian *Lehrgedicht* or didactic poem, with its
hexameter version of parts of the *Communist Manifesto*, made in
consultation with Feuchtwanger, Eisler and Korsch. That main concern

had already inspired *Arturo Ui*, which was written just before leaving Europe with a specific eye to the US theatre, and it is also visible in the first three major Californian works. Unlike the earlier *Fear and Misery of the Third Reich*, these were romanticised in their view of the subject and seem tailored, however vainly it turned out, to suit an American audience: thus *Simone Machard* is a tale of patriotic heroism, while both *Schweik in the Second World War* and the film *Hangmen Also Die* are based on a highly unreal view of the Czech resistance. Briefly Brecht hoped to work for the Office of War Information, for whom he got Lenya to record the 'Song of a German Mother' in 1943, but this was not transmitted; nor, seemingly, was the long poem 'To the German soldiers in the east' which he is said to have intended for Radio Moscow. Later that year he found himself disagreeing with Thomas Mann, whom he once or twice met, first about a declaration which both men had signed in support of the embryo Free German Committee in the USSR, then more generally about the notion of German collective guilt which Brecht, ruthless anti-nationalist though he was, could not accept. His (again) unrealistic belief in a German internal resistance, which he claimed was tying down thirty SS divisions on the home front, led him to take part in a New York rally organised by Paul Robeson where he spoke alongside the Communist Party secretary Earl Browder. At the same time he served on Paul Tillich's Council for a Democratic Germany, where he is said to have pressed for communist representation (the ex-socialist union and party functionary Jakob Walcher became a close colleague) and organised various prominent Hollywood names in support. 'Hitler', he had noted after Stalingrad, 'may fall any day'.[1]

It was during 1943 that the FBI transferred Brecht's name (according to Lyon) from 'enemy alien control' to 'internal security'. In the end their file on him consisted of about 1000 pages, including the result of wire-taps authorised on different occasions and a mass of largely gossipy, sneaking and often quite absurd reports of which some are recognisably from American progressives or fellow-refugees. In the opinion of Lyon and others who have studied this material it adds up to little of any security significance. Thought to be a communist 'front' organisation, the Council for a Democratic Germany was petering out by the spring of 1945; Brecht had not shown signs of activity in other ways; and really the only understandable motive the FBI had for continuing to keep an eye on him was his friendship with the Eislers and his occasional contacts with Soviet diplomats, notably the San Francisco vice-consul Grigori Heifetz who was thought to be in the NKVD. The FBI's concern with Gerhard Eisler is a matter of history: denounced by his sister Ruth

Fischer (joint chairman of the KPD 1924–25), he was thought to have
been Comintern representative in the US and thereafter Moscow's chief
agent, acting as a link in the transmission of information about the atom
bomb. Repeatedly arrested and sentenced on minor charges, he
eventually skipped bail in 1949 and got away via Canada and a Polish
liner. Hanns Eisler meanwhile, in the face of protests by the international
musical and artistic world, was 'technically deported'. So although
Brecht's summons by the House Committee on Un-American Activities
in the summer of 1947 was treated by the committee and by the media as
part of its 'investigation of the motion-picture industry' and of
Hollywood's alleged infiltration by communists, in fact its relevance was
to the case of the Eisler brothers. Having made it clear to his Hollywood
fellow-witnesses and their lawyers that he would tell the truth, Brecht
now broadly speaking did so. Yes, he had played chess with Gerhard
Eisler and discussed politics with him; yes, he had been to Soviet
receptions; no, he was not a party member. Only his answer to the
question if he had applied to join rings oddly: 'No, no, no, no, never'.
And on my saying to him nine years later that when questioned about
The Decision he had answered about *He Said Yes* he laughed.

There used to be a school of thought in the West which claimed that
Brecht would have settled permanently in the US but for this hearing,
which was indeed instantly followed by his departure for Europe. This
appears to have been wrong on every count. Brecht never expressed any
intention to stay, or made any arrangements to do so; his attempts to
break into Broadway were uniformly unsuccessful and his assaults on
Hollywood virtually so; while his hopelessly un-American temperament
has already been mentioned. As Lyon has shown, supported by the FBI
evidence, Brecht had spoken of returning to Germany already in 1943,
and in June 1944 he and Hanns Eisler had inquired officially about
getting Czech passports, presumably with some such move in view.[1]
Moreover he even seems to have prepared for it before leaving Finland,
where he was asked authoritatively in 1940–41 – it is not clear by whom,
but presumably by Soviet or KPD representatives – if he intended to
return, and replied yes, after a while.[2] During 1946, then, with Ruth
Berlau recovering from a mental breakdown and the Hollywood
production of *Galileo* impending, Brecht began laying his plans for his
come-back to the German theatre. This would consist roughly of a spell
of a year or more in Switzerland or North Italy, then a takeover of, he
hoped, the Theater am Schiffbauerdamm in some kind of alliance
primarily with Piscator and Caspar Neher. Though the far-sighted
Korsch warned him of the possibility of West Germany becoming a

'reactionary Utopia' backed by American money, there never seems to have been any question of his basing himself there, and he pilloried the occupation forces' distribution of their own brand of democracy quite damningly in the poem 'The anachronistic procession, or Freedom and Democracy' which he sent ahead as a rather gruesome greeting.

* * *

Nothing seems to upset Brecht's enemies more than his association with the Russian-occupied, communist-run Eastern zone of Germany which in due course became the GDR. Yet surely it should have been predictable enough to anyone who had followed his evolution since 1929. Not only his outward political loyalties and his personal links with East German politicians and theatre people affected his choice but so also did his character, as illustrated by Herr Keuner's preference for the town that needed him and invited him into the kitchen, or his earlier remark to Benjamin that one must not build on the good old things but on the bad new ones. Yet Brecht was not going to enter a new and largely unknown set-up uncritically or with his eyes shut, and the experience of Anna Seghers, whom he met on the way through Paris and who reported on the 'intrigues, suspicions, spyings' she had encountered in Berlin, convinced him not only that he must have 'a strong group' working with him there but also that 'a residence outside Germany is essential'.[1] This of course was very much what he had been planning, and so the immediate questions for him in Zurich were how such a plan could be effected and what the travel possibilities would be. Given that he was stateless and that his US papers were about to expire – they were sent to the US for extension and never returned – he was attracted by the idea of settling in the Salzburg area in order to work for the revived Salzburg Festival with von Einem and Neher (who became an Austrian subject at the end of 1948); and from this developed the idea that he too, as husband of an Austrian-born wife, might apply for a nationality that would give him a proper passport and some freedom of movement. 'I don't immediately want to settle permanently in [Germany]', he wrote to Korsch,[2] nor had he much idea how stable the situation there might be.

In September 1948, during the Berlin Airlift, he got the necessary Swiss exit and re-entry permit for his trip to stage *Mother Courage* in Berlin but failed to get clearance from the American Military Government, which meant that he had to travel via Austria and Czechoslovakia. Once there, so he wrote to Piscator later, 'I myself made no public speeches, not anywhere, didn't make any kind of public statement, just got on with my work'. With Weigel he began planning, in between rehearsals, what was to become the Berliner Ensemble, with a view to taking over the Theater am Schiffbauerdamm for the 1949/50 season; however, the SED (successor to the KPD) would not after all release the theatre to him, and the East Berlin mayor Ebert struck him as markedly discourteous. Instead the Brechts were only authorised to form a homeless but officially subsidised company which would perform primarily as guests of the Deutsches Theater; so on returning to Zurich just before his permitted six months were up he began seriously organising the prospective recruits from Switzerland and Austria. One problem was setting up an account in Swiss francs which could be used after his departure for their travel expenses; another was the discovery that Nordahl Grieg's play about the Paris Commune, scheduled to be the company's opening production possibly with Piscator as director, was hopelessly bad and would have to be rewritten by Brecht. To Piscator himself he explained that in East Berlin 'food and lodging is no problem for people like us' and that

> Klemperer, who is an American domiciled in Budapest, conducts in the East
> Berlin Komische Oper without any kind of difficulty.[1]

To Viertel, who was concerned about travel formalities, he suggested that he too become an Austrian subject; and this in due course Viertel did.

In his first reactions to his old city Brecht had once again been realistic, finding a meeting of trade union officials 'clearly on the defensive' about the Soviet blockade of West Berlin – he had arrived during the airlift – and noting that the Germans were taking advantage of the conflict between the occupying powers to ignore the 'powerful impulses' given by the Russians:

> the germans are rebelling against the order to rebel against nazism; few accept
> the principle that socialism to order is better than no socialism at all. the
> takeover of the [means of] production by the proletariat is occurring just at the
> point when the products are being handed over to the conquerors (so that
> many people think this must be its object).

Thus there were nationalised factories which had been got going with the greatest difficulty only to have their machines repeatedly taken for reparations. Moreover there were 'errors due to the very different stage of development' of the Russians, as seen in their refusal to let Felsenstein at the Komische Oper distribute the rations equally among all his workers.[2] Even so Brecht was ready to join in the work of reconstruction, and not merely where the theatre and its standards were concerned. So he had written the 'Aufbaulied' ('Reconstruction Song') and the 'Zukunftslied' ('Future Song') for the new Free German Youth and discussed the wording with their leaders; and Dessau had promptly set the former, though Eisler, whom he pressed to return to the 'vulgar excesses' of their old *Kampflieder*, was more reluctant. Thenceforward for the next three years Dessau was involved in the majority of Brecht's 'positive' works and actions as the poet adjusted from 'the travails of the mountains' to 'the travails of the plains' – to quote the short 'Observation' which he also wrote that first winter. This undoubtedly genuine commitment, particularly to the youth of the new country (itself formally constituted just ten days before the opening of the Ensemble's first season the following November), led to such works as the 'Children's Songs' and the long ballad 'The Training of Millet' of 1950, the inaugural (and over-plugged) 'To my countrymen' which he dedicated to Wilhelm Pieck, the revision and production of Erwin Strittmatter's home-grown play *Katzgraben*, the Open Letter to German Artists and Writers and the Free German Youth's quasi-*Lehrstück Herrnburger Bericht* which dramatised an incident with the West German frontier police for the benefit of the 1951 World Youth Festival. This same 'positive' phase also earned him a National Prize. At the same time it caused Brecht once again to see if he could come to terms with the prevailing official aesthetic, which was still that of Socialist Realism as decreed by Zhdanov, exemplified in the theatre by Stanislavsky, presided over in Berlin by Becher, and most eruditely interpreted for the Germans by Georg Lukács, then at the height of his influence outside his own country.

He therefore made some slight attempt to read these authorities, whom previously he had condemned largely on the strength of occasional articles or from hearsay (though even then he based his picture of Stanislavsky's ideas on Gorchakov's book rather than any study of *An Actor Prepares* or *Building a Character*),[1] and while maintaining his disagreement with that aesthetic did nothing to make his view public. He also stretched his own principles so far as to support the slogans of Socialist Realism, its references to the 'cultural heritage' and to folk music, folk poetry etc., though at the same time twisting these concepts so as to make them bear a more or less heretical meaning by the standards then prevailing. Occasionally, as in the case of the Barlach exhibition of winter 1951/52, he intervened to discourage the doctrine's more philistine effects, using his membership of the new Academy of Arts as a lever. Neither this self-restraint however nor his new positive contributions were enough to offset the hostility, not so much of the politicians, of whom Pieck in particular always seems to have accepted him, but of the cultural politicians and functionaries, the minor critics and, alas, the more orthodox theatre directors. Starting with attacks on his 'negative' attitude to the cultural heritage, as instanced in the Ensemble's productions of *The Tutor* (1950), *The Broken Jug* and Goethe's *Urfaust* (spring 1952) and continuing through the major controversy over Dessau's *Lucullus* opera (1951) – was the music 'formalistic'? was the text too pacifist for a country that might have to defend itself any day? – there was a mounting campaign which culminated in the banning of *Urfaust* by the repertory commission and the summoning of Brecht by the State Commission on Art affairs to attend a Stanislavsky conference in the spring of 1953. This, like the repertory commission, was presided over by Fritz Erpenbeck, the former Piscator actor who had served in Moscow as the manipulator of *Das Wort*.

Brecht by then had improved his personal relations with Lukács, who had been under severe official criticism in Hungary for his indifference to modern Soviet literature; but he always objected to any attempt to lay down formal criteria for realist art, noting repeatedly that to do this, rather than to develop and modernise realism by extending its formal devices, was 'formalism' in the true pejorative sense. He also disliked the communist nationalism that had grown up since the mid-1930s and been helped on by the war; in particular Becher's patriotic poems written in Moscow had disgusted him, making him at one point during the war follow some phrases of Becher's about 'the genius of an eternal Germany' with the comment 'nachbar, euren speikübel!' or, in English parlance, 'pass the sick-bag, Alice'.[1] For Brecht felt that if you talked about German scholarship, German culture and the like you opened the way to talk about German crimes, and at the moment these were rather more in evidence. 'we of all people', he wrote in the next *Journal* entry,

> are the race who should set an example by calling our country country number
> 11 and leaving it at that.

This deep unhappiness about his country's past evolution, which he saw as leading only too logically to the election of Hitler – a development, not an excrescence, he called him – and being able to do so again, runs through many of his notes and makes his various 'Deutschland' poems written over some forty years both fascinating and moving to study; and of course it determined his attitude to the masterpieces of the 'cultural heritage' – even to the very idea of such a thing. He was concerned therefore about the teaching of that heritage to the young, suggesting to the secretary of the Academy (who had been officially consulted) that Flaubert, Stendhal and Maupassant should be added to the approved prose works, along with (on stylistic grounds) the *Communist Manifesto*. But 'neither political judgement nor critical taste can be based only on good examples',[1] so why not give instances of kitsch, comparing for instance Ludwig Ganghofer's prose with that of Tolstoy? – a policy that might have provided some illuminating insights into Socialist Realism.

What Brecht wanted from the party and the government was clear political and social objectives for the arts rather than lessons in artistic form. This is why he accepted their criticisms of *Lucullus*'s text while resisting their attacks on its musical language. The Stanislavsky conference however was different because it was plainly aimed at his whole theatrical approach. Thus an introductory article in the party paper spoke of 'the criminal underrating of the significance of Stanislavsky's method for the development of a German national theatre' and attacked unnamed Berlin productions of the highest quality in which

> Formalism and its twin brother schematism appear in every area, from the choice of the plays to dramaturgy, production conception, direction, stage design and acting method.

See the account in Ernst and Renate Schumacher: *Leben Brechts in Wort und Bild*, Henschel Verlag, East Berlin 1978, pp. 269–271. Their quotation is from the party paper *Neues Deutschland*, 17 April 1953. The remarks of the speakers at the conference itself may have been less sweeping, though there were a number of direct criticisms of Brecht, based less on Stanislavsky than on naturalistic convention; and Weigel and Brecht himself seem apparently to have put up a stout defence. But within a month this first offensive was being followed by three further meetings to discuss Eisler's *Johann Faustus* opera libretto, which like the Ensemble's quite unrelated *Urfaust* production the previous year was held to offend against the 'cultural heritage' part of the official canon. Here not only did *Neues Deutschland* return to the assault, writing that Eisler had 'been badly advised' (clearly by Brecht), but Ulbricht himself too waded heavily in and announced that 'we shall not permit one of the most significant works of our great German poet Goethe to be formalistically violated . . .'.[2] Eisler's sin had been to present the magic doctor (who of course had entered literature well before Marlowe even, let alone Goethe) as a traitor to his peasant origins; Brecht's and that of his young colleagues had been to bring out his ridiculous side. The effect of this post-mortem on the former was to stop his opera from ever being

composed, disorganising him much as *Pravda* in 1936 had disorganised
Shostakovitch. The cumulative effect on the much tougher Brecht was
to make even him promise to set a 'brigade' of the Ensemble to study
Stanislavsky, and meanwhile to use one or two Stanislavskian methods
experimentally in the rehearsal of *Katzgraben* and *The Trial of Joan of
Arc*. That was all. But, taken together, the events of spring 1953 did
nothing to improve the position of the Ensemble as a whole, of which
Brecht had noted in March that

> our productions in Berlin are now getting almost no response. press notices
> appear months after the opening night and contain nothing but a few feeble
> sociological analyses. the audience is the petty-bourgeois audience of the
> volksbühne, workers constitute a bare 7 per cent.[1]

It was indeed a low point in his work.

* * *

Only a few days after the conclusion of the Eisler inquest the situation
was drastically changed as a result of the East German protests and
demonstrations of June 16th and the more general rioting that followed
the next day, when the West Berliners joined in and the Russian
occupation army moved to stop it. Stalin by then had been dead for three
months, but no loosening of the communist bureaucracy and restrictive-
ness had been visible, and now the pot briefly boiled over. For Brecht
this was not only a shock – comparable in its way with that of 1929,
when he had also seen violent events with his own eyes – but a scare, and
not only a scare but a hope. 'For a number of hours', says one of his
comments, 'Berlin was tottering on the edge of a third world war'.[2] Ever
since his return his feeling had been that the German workers, who had
first been expected to throw out Hitler soon after he came to power, then
to be providing a major internal threat to him during the war, were in
fact passive and powerless. Yet here at last they were acting:

> we had the [working] class confronting us, in its most depraved state, but the
> class all the same. all depended on making proper use of this first meeting. it
> was a contact. it came not in the form of an embrace but of a blow with the
> fist, but it was contact none the less. the party was bound to be scared, but
> there was no need for it to despair.[3]

And so he was shocked into two lines of action, both of them
subsequently fruitful for his work. First of all on the public level he was
quick to tell Ulbricht that, while convinced that there must be 'a large-

scale discussion with the masses' about working conditions, he felt bound to express his solidarity with the SED. Secondly however he now abandoned the effort to write 'positively' – i.e. produce encouraging songs and poems for public consumption – in favour of a more reflective consideration of the society around him, poised uncomfortably between Nazism and Stalinism – a development encouraged by his recently-bought house in Buckow east of Berlin, where he wrote the more private 'Buckow Elegies' that August under the impact of events that for him had 'alienated the whole of existence'.[1] In his terminology this meant that he was looking at everything with fresh eyes; hence the plan that autumn for a work about the East German model shock-worker Hans Garbe to be written in collaboration with Eisler, 'in the style of "the decision" or "mother", with an entire act about june 17th'. (Spring 1954 however was given up to rehearsals for the long-delayed production of one of the five great unperformed plays – *The Caucasian Chalk Circle* – so that the new *Garbe*, or *Büsching* as it had previously been called, survives only as a single page of notes.)

While privately he was going over to a new policy of criticism, his public stance on June 17th seems to have altered the official attitude to him almost overnight, even though he thereafter insisted on publicising his reservations about the party's mistakes, which the initial reports of his letter to Ulbricht had not mentioned.[2] So Ulbricht thanked him in a letter of July 8th, addressing him as 'comrade', thanking him for his 'courageous statement of faith'[3] and proposing a meeting to 'discuss one or two questions personally'. One factor here seems to have been that Brecht was so much quicker to react than many other intellectuals. He had been even quicker however in writing Grotewohl a letter from Buckow, dated just one day before the initial workers' demonstrations, to point out that the Volksbühne no longer needed the Theater am Schiffbauerdamm now that its own theatre had been rebuilt, and to suggest it was time for the government to fulfil its original promise by handing it over to the Ensemble. This, he said, 'would be a very clear proof of my association with our Republic' and might also contradict the 'senseless rumours' current in West Germany of friction between the government and himself.[4] During July the handover was agreed in principle and from then on Brecht began exploiting his changed status both privately and publicly by campaigning for the abolition of the troublesome Art and Literature Commissions, with their rigid control by mediocre party officials, in favour of a new Ministry of Culture. In this he allied himself with the East German Academy and with a number of individuals ranging from Becher and Ernst Bloch to the young

philosopher Wolfgang Harich (who later cited Brecht as sympathising
with the oppositional programme for which he became sentenced to ten
years in gaol). Above all the important article 'Cultural Policy and
Academy of Arts' (reproduced in *Brecht on Theatre*, pp. 266–268)
resumes his point of view, while his contempt for the Commissions is
well expressed and defined in two poems published in the non-party
Berliner Zeitung in mid-July.[1]

In January 1954 the Ministry of Culture was set up under Johannes R.
Becher; in March the Berliner Ensemble reopened in its own Theater am
Schiffbauerdamm. In spring of the following year the whole change of
policy and of cultural-political climate was consecrated, as it were, by the
award to Brecht of a Stalin Peace Prize. Pasternak translated his speech
of thanks for him; Fedin and Okhlopkhov were friendly to him;
otherwise (said Reich, who came to Moscow with Asya Lacis for the
occasion[2]), the representatives of the Soviet literary and theatrical world
showed 'amiably correct neutrality' but no particular interest in his work.
In the week which he and Weigel spent in Moscow they made inquiries
about Carola Neher's presumed death (which her son Georg Becker has
now established as being from typhus contracted in prison at Orel in
1942, roughly six years after her arrest), saw to the upkeep of Margarete
Steffin's grave and asked for Reich's own 'rehabilitation' to be speeded
up.[3] All this of course still happened under the name of Stalin and prior
to Khrushchev's revelations at the Twentieth Party Congress, though
afterwards the prize was renamed 'Lenin Peace Prize' (and now figures
retrospectively as such in official accounts of Brecht). But already Brecht
had evidently been aiming at Stalin in some of the 'Buckow Elegies'.
Moreover there are four undated poems, written probably in the last
months of his life, and though they too never mention Stalin by name
they are quite clearly about him. Long included in the Brecht Archive
catalogue they were unearthed by John Fuegi in a Harvard library and
then published in *GW* Supplement 2. The first calls him by the mock-
Soviet honorific title of 'Honoured Murderer of the People' and, in terse
irregular lines, compares his daily brutality unfavourably with that of the
Tsar on Bloody Sunday.[4] It accuses him, in phrases larded with imitation
homage, of having forgotten the *Communist Manifesto* and struck a blow
at Lenin, concluding that anybody who is treated as a god becomes
stupid. The second briefly takes up the theme of 'The Training of
Millet', but is very different from the 1950 ballad; for Stalin, from being
'the great harvest-leader', now becomes simply 'the leader', with the
word for 'leader' being changed from *Leiter* to *Führer*: he leads his
scientists, but it is not at all clear where. The strongest of the batch is the

third, which measures its once divine subject on the scales and says that the weights in both pans are heavy. On the credit side is shrewdness, topped up with cruelty, but the worshippers start wondering what went wrong, the god himself or the quality of their prayers; for they were promised apples but never got bread. Four things are then listed for their (and our) consideration: heavy industry, military success, hungry children, the unheard screams of tortured comrades . . . The last and shortest simply says

> The god has gone mouldy
> The worshippers beat their breasts
> As they beat women's bottoms
> With satisfaction.

*   *   *

In the essay which he wrote on Hanns Eisler in the last days of *Das Wort* – and which like all but one of his articles for that journal was never published in it – Brecht mentioned five artists who had stood up for the German workers.[1] They were Eisler, Brecht, Grosz, Heartfield and Piscator. And indeed, seen against the wider background of committed or political art as it is understood either in the capitalist or in the communist sphere today, they form a special group. For generally speaking the chief such figures in the West during this century have been people who either lent their names and their signatures to the communist movement or portrayed major political themes; while in the Eastern bloc, though artists of all kinds have felt the impact of politics more sharply there than anywhere, the spontaneously committed artist, finding his own themes and his own language, has been virtually unknown since Mayakovsky. In the case of those five however – Brecht and those he acknowledged as his brothers; if there was a sister around it was Anna Seghers – the implications of politics were particularly deep and rich. Brecht observed political events very closely, and had to do so in order to preserve his family and himself through what was indeed a dark time, but it is a mistake to regard him as a political philosopher; for interesting as his insights often are they are the product not so much of a fully worked out theory as of what is now called lateral thinking. Nevertheless he knew more than most poets of the pain and tragedy of politics, whether inflicted by Hitler or by Stalin, and over nearly three decades he also experienced the professional ups and downs due to changes of policy: to the whole principle of cultural policy or *Kulturpolitik* which comes from an acceptance of the somewhat un-English notion that the arts have a social and political role and can make an impact on the world.

So even the small actions of vice-consuls and passport officers have their relevance to his work, let alone the larger decisions of subsidised theatres and state publishing firms or the immense deeds of the parties and their leaders. And because of the commitment which he appears to have undertaken – whether tacitly or in consultation with others – in 1929 he in turn found it natural to make some kind of politics his theme, either directly or indirectly, to influence events or to express his reactions. This already puts him in a category outside the type of criticism practised by the Lukács school, whose approach was an ideological, theoretical one based on a Leninist approach to Marxism; that is to say that Lukács was concerned less with the political usefulness of the work of art, as judged primarily by considering its aims and its subject, than with its relation to philosophical idealism and the degeneration of ideology in bourgeois society from the nineteenth century on. For Lukács moreover, and for orthodox Soviet criticism too whatever its differences with Lukács in other respects, there were two overriding criteria which were due not so much to his particular ideology as to his upbringing; and these were, first, that a work of art must not only be realistic but must form an undivided whole, and secondly that it had to fit into what he (from an educated Austrian point of view, formed before 1910) saw as the great Western tradition. Brecht's idea, which he shared with Tretiakov as well as with Yeats, Pound and Claudel, that the 'cultural heritage' could also embrace the works of non-European civilisations, was as alien to Lukács as it would have been to Alfred Rosenberg and his 'Militant League for German Culture'. Even in Stalin's multi-national Union the non-Russian cultures were effectively relegated to the zone of folk art.

But Franço Fortini is right, and this conviction of Brecht's – to which we owe most obviously the *Lehrstücke*, *Me-ti*, the Confucius opera plan and the outward trappings of *The Caucasian Chalk Circle* and *Turandot* – is related to a more fundamental attitude of his, which led him, somewhat uncharacteristically for a communist, to see the peasants as quite as important as (and if anything more interesting than) the industrial proletariat, and to look at political life generally from the underdog's point of view. Hence the 'plebeian', 'earthy' emphasis of so many of his works; hence the impact made on his theatre by the elder Brueghel; hence his dislike of any 'popular' art that was dictated from above or engineered by revivalists; and hence too the phrase in his Stalin Prize speech warning that 'a future for mankind can only be seen "from below", from the standpoint of the oppressed and the exploited'.[1] This preference for base company, which his imagination, like Kipling's, carried right back even into classical times (the slaves and fishwives, the plebeians in *Coriolanus*, the 'Questions from a worker who reads' about Thebes and Atlantis), may have had its roots in his south German youth (see his short stories about 'The Unseemly Old Lady' and the Augsburg judge who developed into Azdak), but it also seems to relate to his sympathy for the Chinese. As his (always qualified) esteem for Stalin sank beyond recall so his admiration for Mao and the Chinese peasantry rose; thus his re-titling of the poem 'On sterility' 'Mao's song' after it had earlier been earmarked as Stalin's;[2] and thus too his recommendation of Mao's pamphlet *On Contradiction* as the best book of 1954. In 1949, at the time of the Chinese revolution, Eisler had been given a German version of Mao's poem 'Thoughts while flying over the Great Wall', which Brecht turned into one of his own 'Chinese Poems', most of the rest having been adapted from Waley's versions in the late 1930s or in 1944. There was even a report from one of his friends in the 1950s that 'Brecht is talking of Chinese exile', which the usual friendly interpreters took to mean that he was thinking of leaving the GDR. Chinese exile was the internal exile of a poet like Po Chü-I which Brecht could reasonably compare with his own growing isolation.

Another basic element of Brecht's make-up which became absorbed into his work to an exceptional extent was his understanding of dialectics. This conceptual method, which Marx developed almost into a communist secret weapon from Hegel's non-materialist version, came into the forefront of Brecht's theorising at two stages in his life, first around 1931 when he was studying Marxism and began writing a work on 'Dialectical dramaturgy'. His argument here was that the early epic drama had been designed for the existing bourgeois 'apparatus' and audience. Unconsciously dialectical, by its success it brought out the message inherent in its (social and economic) subject-matter, thus allowing later playwrights to use dialectics more purposefully. Then in the last two years of his life he came to the conclusion that 'epic' was too neutral a term and began replacing it by 'dialectic' and 'dialectical', as in his last collection of theoretical notes.[3] These outward uses of the term however were much less important than the encouragement given to Brecht's natural way of seeing things by the very notion of a continual clash of opposing factors leading to a situation where everything was in a state of qualitative and quantitative change. A world in motion was congenial to him, a world of contradiction, inconsistency and paradox even more so. Dialectics then not only helped him, as a dramatist, to understand the conflicting elements in people's interests and to put such conflicts of motivation clearly and sharply on the stage; it also made him laugh, whence his somewhat unexpected assertion that nobody could understand the Hegelian dialectic without a sense of humour.

Hegelian was it? Or Marxist? He certainly read and admired both writers, but there was also a strongly dialectical aspect in the writing of an earlier author whom we know he read and annotated very throughly; and that was Mo Tse. Though Waley had even less use for Mo[1] ('feeble, repetitive . . . unentertaining . . . lack of psychological subtlety') than for the 'Buckow Elegies', there are aphorisms of Mo's which read remarkably like Brecht's *Me-ti*, and Antony Tatlow has cited such quasi-paradoxical statements as 'Wherever there is an "is" there will also be an "isn't" ' to argue that Mo could sometimes anticipate Hegel. Indeed, just as Brecht seemed to base other aspects of his mature persona on the classical Chinese – the emphasis on courtesy and *Freundlichkeit* (friendliness), the aesthetic preference for lightness and 'ease', the idea of quiet subversion (as in the great Lao-tse poem) and the Heraclitan flux of things – so Mo Tse proves to have been strikingly close to him in character, at least as presented by his editor of 1922. For Mo, in the latter's foreword,

> was a pugnacious arguer; he was fond of antitheses and sharp points. Like Christ he had a way of taking his parables and examples from everyday life . . .[2]

If dialectics were an analytical tool to Brecht, and sometimes an aid to stylisation and sharpness – the latter being a sought-after quality in a society that still admires aggressiveness – the executive tool corresponding to this was the gestic principle. Everything in Brecht's work was saying something – every sentence, every movement, every musical phrase or pictorial element in the set – and saying not only its surface meaning but the attitude underlying and possibly conflicting with this; each episode, each scene, each poem had its overall attitude; and so, finally, did each work as a whole. All this had to be identified and conveyed so as to make clear the contradictions and the irregular forward movement of their resolution. This progression was something very different from the traditional encapsulating 'plot' of the 'well-made play' or from the kind of totality admired by Lukács. It involved not so much an overall grasp of reality – a forcible wrenching of it into artistic shape – as a careful dissection, presented in dismembered form without any imposed links or unities, on the assumption (as early notes on 'Dialectical Dramaturgy' put it) that 'the modern spectator' does not want to be patronised and raped, but simply to have human material tossed before him so that he can *put it in order for himself.*[1]

Often there was a bit too much of this do-it-yourself material, and the play consequently dragged; but in principle Brecht wanted it set out economically, with a minimum expenditure of words, temperament and other resources (orchestral scoring, stage set). This economy, like the intelligibility and ease of execution that went with it, was not special to Brecht but was one of the socially-grounded principles of *Neue Sachlichkeit*, though few handled it with such elegance and strength as he. It was partly a reaction against the verbal and emotional wastefulness of Expressionism and the inflated egos that went with it. And so, if Brecht was exceedingly lucky in his musical and artistic collaborators – whose acceptance of the same principles added so greatly to his achievement – the ideal of a self-effacing collectivity was also part of the socio-political climate of the time.

Brecht believed in a new age, an age of new ideas and technologies when everything would be subject to change and nothing would be left unquestioned, an age of productive doubt, very much the kind of age he makes Galileo experience in the marvellous great speech at the beginning of the play. Between 1929 and the mid-1930s he seems to have seen this coming through Communism; then he realised that he himself was not going to experience it. Thus the middle section of 'To those born later', written perhaps as early as 1934, reports that

> Our forces were slight. Our goal
> Lay far in the distance
> It was clearly visible, though I myself
> Was unlikely to reach it.

Evidently it had become less clearly visible by the time Brecht wrote the various forewords to *Galileo*, with their vivid picture of what it means when such expectations come to nothing – a picture that seems not to have been painted with his usual detachment. And yet at the end of the play he still, in the last version, made the old scientist say a laconic 'Doch' to Andrea's assumption that he no longer believes in a new age at all. 'Doch', a curtly affirmative denial like the French 'Si', a single word for 'on the contrary'. This in my view was Brecht's own position and it represents that obstinate, contradictory element in his character which led him always to accept change, development, innovation even if it came as a 'bloodstained harridan' or a pregnant whore. It was not just a political conviction but also an attitude to artistic techniques and movements: whatever he might say to condemn particular works or to shock particular people he was alert to anything new, and ready to think whether he could use it. So he looked at new media and new technologies (as at the Neue Musik festivals in the 1920s, or as exemplified in his sparse but original writing about the radio), and he never gave up his view that as times changed so must the artistic language.

What do we find then if we look at 'The Fishing-tackle', a poem which he wrote in 1943?[1] Formally it is in his own very gestic irregular free verse – which could be read as prose, but must not be because it is the placing of key words in relation to the punctuation and to the slight pauses at the end of each line that gives them, and the succeeding information, their importance. Its first half consists of a report, in concrete, easily visualised images, hardened by the hard consonants used. ('The truth is concrete', he used to quote from Hegel.) Then two lines of comment, restating his 'labour theory' of beauty: the evidence that this tackle has been used by a working man over a long time. Then Brecht's sympathetic leap to the situation of the interned Californian Japanese in the Second World War – 'enemy aliens'; the German phrase 'verdächtige Fremdlinge' with its less familiar ring makes the racial point better – which only seriously began to worry the American conscience a generation later. And finally the sudden widening of the focus to show, in the background, so many other great human problems looming: unsolved, but not insoluble. Sixteen lines: economical, vivid, down-to-earth, moving from a precisely described object to a human tragedy of those times, then onward and outward. It is political. It is poetic. Neither aspect interferes with the other; it is perfectly fused, right down to its elements. This is what Brecht could do. Could anybody else?

12

Two political excursions

a: Brecht, Stalin and Hannah Arendt

Hostile criticism of Brecht in the Cold War era effectively began with an article by Herbert Luethy in the Congress for Cultural Freedom Berlin magazine *Der Monat* in May 1952. Sneeringly entitled 'Vom armen Bert Brecht' after the poem 'Of poor BB',[1] it was reprinted in *Encounter* and others of that CIA-subsidised body's publications. It evidently stung Brecht enough for him to ask Geneviève Serreau to take it out of the bibliography of her short book on him (published by L'Arche, Paris in 1955), saying 'I am not happy to have this gentleman as one of my referees'.[2] Normally Brecht neither answered nor even visibly reacted to such criticism, much of which was entirely parochial. Indeed in West Germany for some years there was so much hostility to his work, much of it official or semi-official on one level or another, that the Rhineland theatre critic André Müller could devote an entire book to charting the ebbs and flows of the various campaigns mounted there at different times.

Then in the 1960s an international heavyweight joined in when Hannah Arendt, currently at the height of her reputation as a political philosopher, wrote a long 'profile' of Brecht in the *New Yorker* which stated, among other things, that he had written 'odes to Stalin'. Thinking that this needed some clarification, I took the steps which in due course led to my retailing the following story in *The Times Literary Supplement*, for whom I was still working.[3]

* * *

Some four years earlier in the *New Yorker*, Professor Hannah Arendt, Fellow of the American Academy of Arts and Sciences and of the Deutsche Akademie für Sprache und Dichtung, had published an unusually posthumous 'Profile' of Brecht. Its thesis, as she herself put it,

was 'that a poet's real sins are avenged by the gods of poetry', the central
sin in Brecht's case being 'his ode to Stalin and his praise of Stalin's
crimes, written and published while he was in East Berlin but mercifully
omitted from the collection of his works'. In revenge for the Communist
political commitment of which this unidentified 'ode' (referred to
throughout the rest of the essay as 'odes' plural) was symptomatic, on
Brecht's return to East Berlin after the war 'his poetic faculty dried up
from one day to the next'. He came to realise that he could not write in
East Berlin, so he bought a house in Denmark and thought of moving to
Switzerland: 'all he planned for when he lay dying was exile'.

Most of this was news to me when I read the article a few months
later, so I wrote a long letter to the *New Yorker* to say

(i) that I knew of no such 'ode' or 'praise of Stalin's crimes' and would like to
know titles and sources.

(ii) that Arendt had mis-dated a number of the early poems, identifying them
with Brecht's supposed feeling of release after the First World War,
though in fact they had been written before or during his military service
in 1918.

(iii) that it was wrong to count Brecht's stay in America before his return as
'creatively the best years of his life', since in six years there he wrote only
one major play, no theoretical work of any consequence and no major
poem. That is, apart from his verse rendering of the Communist
Manifesto, which Arendt dismissed as 'an almost total failure'. The
drying-up process, in fact, had not been a sudden one, but had begun
around 1941, when there was not yet the immense distraction provided by
his work with the Berliner Ensemble, for which Arendt made no
allowance. (Brecht to von Einem, January 7 1951: 'Trying to build up a
new theatre has deprived me of the time needed to write for it.')

(iv) that the Danish house had been bought for a friend [Ruth Berlau], but
that I would like to know the evidence for the Swiss story and if Arendt
had any other reason for claiming to know what was in the dying poet's
mind.

The *New Yorker* acknowledged this letter and said they would return it
if they couldn't publish it. That was on 1 December 1966.

The following April I again wrote to them to enquire progress,
stressing that I was genuinely anxious to know Hannah Arendt's
explanation. 'Has she', I asked, 'in fact had access to poems of Brecht's
with which I am not familiar? If so it would help me in my own work to
know what they are. Or has she simply got hold of the wrong end of the

stick? In that case I would say that both she and you owed the readers some rectification.'

This second letter was not answered at all. However, towards the end of the year I was approached by the *New York Review of Books* to write them a general article on Brecht, and in refusing (because I was already engaged to do such an article elsewhere) I inquired whether they would publish my queries about the Arendt essay. Instead the editor gave me her address, suggesting I write to her direct and saying that he would be interested to know what happened. I did so, quite briefly, in March 1968, and on 25 May she replied.

The following were my three principal questions and Hannah Arendt's answers:

Q: What have you in mind when you speak of an 'ode' or 'odes' to Stalin?

A: It is indeed difficult today to find Brecht's odes to Stalin because they are not included in his Collected Works. I would suggest to you to look through the old issues of *Sinn und Form* [organ of the East German Academy] and also East German newspapers. If you look at *Sinn und Form* II:5 (1950), page 128, you will find one example of what I allude to in my essay.

Q: Where does Brecht praise Stalin's crimes?

A: If you know Brecht's prose works, especially *Me-Ti* which was published posthumously, you will see that Brecht praises Stalin as the 'useful one', which refers to the well-known old Communist theory that Stalin's crimes were necessary and useful for the development of socialism in Russia as well as, by implication, the world revolution.

Q: What is the evidence for saying that at the end of his life he thought of living in Switzerland?

A: You'll find the evidence in the Brecht monograph which appeared in the Rowohlt Verlag.

I already knew Brecht's contributions to *Sinn und Form*, but on getting Arendt's letter I checked her references and five days later wrote back to her:

I have looked up the *Sinn und Form* printing of Brecht's *Erziehung der Hirse* ['The Training of Millet'], to which you referred me, and find that apart from one or two points of punctuation and the rewording (not affecting the sense) of one line – not on p. 128 – it is identical with the text as printed in the Collected Works. I have always shared your dislike of this poem, but I must say that one reference in a 53-verse poem to Stalin as 'des Sowjetvolkes grosser Ernteleiter' [the Soviet people's great harvest-leader] doesn't seem to me to make it exactly an ode to Stalin. Unless there is anything that we have all missed in the E. German press – and at one time or another I have checked all the unfamiliar [i.e., not self-explanatory] references to it in Walter Nubel's Brecht bibliography – I cannot think of any published poem that would fit your description.

Again, I wouldn't have thought that calling Stalin 'the useful one' – which incidentally, like the other reference, is about as low on the scale of Stalin-flattery as you can get – constituted praise of his crimes. This quite apart from the questioning of many aspects of Stalinism which one also finds in *Me-Ti*, and which is presumably what has so far stopped that work appearing in East Germany. [It appeared later.]

Marianne Kesting's book on Brecht [the monograph referred to] reports the fact that he bought the house in Denmark, but says nothing about any possibility of living in Switzerland or any intention of going into exile. I would be very interested to know where these two suggestions originated, and just what weight should be attached to them.

I had already pointed out my special interest as co-editor of the English and American editions of Brecht's selected works. But once again there was no answer.

Two years passed, and the same essay reappeared in a book published under the title *Men in Dark Times* (itself a phrase borrowed from Brecht). So far as I could see it was unchanged, even the word 'recently' being still used of events that had been recent four years earlier. It continued to maintain that Brecht wrote an 'ode' or (three pages later) 'odes' to Stalin and 'praise of Stalin's crimes'; that he dried up overnight on returning to Berlin; that he 'considered moving to Switzerland' and that 'all he planned for when he lay dying was exile'. The early poems were still mis-dated (suggesting to me that the writer had not looked at Hans Otto Münsterer's recollections of Brecht in 1918), the years of exile in California still counted among his most productive; in short the writer had decided to change nothing. All that had been added was some footnotes giving sources, though not of the alleged odes. The crucial note referring to them read:

Brecht's praise of Stalin has been carefully eliminated from his *Collected Works* [i.e., the old forty-volume edition, which Arendt referred to throughout]. The only traces are to be found in *Prosa*, vol. V, the posthumously published *Me-Ti* notes ... There Stalin is praised as 'the useful one' and his crimes are justified (pp. 6off. and 100ff.). Immediately after his death, Brecht wrote that he had been 'the incarnation of hope' for 'the oppressed of five continents'.

(*Sinn und Form*, vol. 2, 1953, p. 10). Cf. also the poem in *op. cit.*, II, 2, 1950, p. 128.

Every one of the items cited in this note could already be found, unexpurgated, in the *Collected Works*. The poem actually says no more about Stalin than the phrase already quoted; the message on Stalin's death (*GW* 20, p. 325), which I had referred to in my first *New Yorker* letter, that

> The oppressed of five continents, those who have already freed themselves and all who are fighting for world peace must have felt their heart stop beating when they heard that Stalin is dead. He was the embodiment of their hopes.

– i.e., not necessarily of Brecht's. As for *Me-ti*, which was of course neither written nor published 'while he was in East Berlin' but dates from a decade earlier and only appeared after his death, there is *no* mention of Stalin's (or Ni-en's, as Brecht calls him) crimes in the passages cited. Elsewhere in the book there is indeed such mention, but not in any laudatory sense: e.g. on pp. 125–6, where Trotsky's criticisms of the trials and death sentences are summarised, or on p. 141 (*GW* 12, p. 538) where Brecht gives Me-ti's, i.e. his own, views as cited on p. 208 above, going on:

> trying them without proof he has harmed the people. He should have taught the people to insist on having proof, particularly from him, who is in general so useful.

Writing this around 1937, Brecht made it very clear that 'Me-Ti was on Ni-en's side' (*GW* 12, p. 195) particularly because he had built up Soviet heavy industry – something that (I suggested in my *TLS* article) was indeed to prove useful to us all in the Second World War. But wherever 'praise' of Ni-en was concerned Me-ti is made to appear extremely sceptical. Thus, on the first page cited by Arendt (i.e. *GW* 12, p. 467), 'Me-ti said: Ni-en's reputation is tarnished by bad praise. So much incense that one can no longer see the picture, and says "They're trying to hide something".' And even the reference to Ni-en's 'usefulness' which follows (ibid.) seems double or triple-edged, starting as it does

> Me-ti suggested that Ni-en should always be called not the Great, but the Useful one. But the time was not yet ripe for this type of praise. Useful people had been for too long without any reputation, so that saying a man was useful no longer inspired confidence in his ability to lead. Leaders had always been identified by their knowledge of how to be useful to themselves.

At the very least, I said, it was clear from such paradoxical, half-camouflaged musings that they add up to nothing so straightforward as any 'well-known old Communist theory', let alone a fulsome tribute to Stalin.

I didn't want to embark on the complex question of Brecht's exact relation to Stalinism, which would involve writing at some length, but was concerned only with the accuracy of Arendt's premises. There, with regard to the three questions which I asked her, it was quite clear that

   (i) she had not identified any ode or odes to Stalin;
  (ii) she had not specified any praise of his crimes;
 (iii) she had not substantiated, or even accurately attributed, the story that Brecht wished to move to Switzerland.

For two years she had been aware of her failure to do these things, yet she still chose to republish her essay in its original form, speaking for instance of the 'odes' as sounding 'as though they had been fabricated by the least gifted imitator Brecht ever had', so that the reader might imagine her to have the texts before her or to know them off by heart. There was not even a footnote to suggest any doubt concerning the foundations on which her 'thesis' rests. Possibly, I said, she might be convinced that the evidence existed somewhere, and would in due course turn up to substantiate her dramatic and undoubtedly memorable picture of an abruptly punctured poetic talent: of the great writer who, after twenty years of close association with the Communist movement, 'crossed the line marking what was permitted to him' by deciding to settle in East Germany, and was retributively stripped of his gifts. Pending its appearance, however, I thought it should be made clear what her scientific standards were (she claimed to be writing as a 'political scientist', not as a literary lady). For this kind of allegation sticks in readers' minds, who will remember that Brecht wrote 'odes to Stalin' even if they remember nothing else about his work.

* * *

George Steiner, I remember, warned me that Professor Arendt was a formidable controversialist and thought I was being rash to say such things. However, no doubt because the *New York Times*'s London office was immediately above that of the *TLS*, so that its then correspondent (later an editor) Antony Lewis took a friendly interest in our paper, my piece of lèse-majesté was reported in New York two days later after its office there had telephoned Arendt and two other professors for their comments. The former was reported as once more claiming that 'several Brecht poems and prose writings laudatory of Stalin had been suppressed during the de-Stalinisation period in East Germany', though possibly the crucial 'odes' might have been reissued *since* her letter to me of May 1968, 'in view of the partial rehabilitation of the Soviet dictator'. She was supported by a (to me unknown) Brecht scholar called Professor J.P. Bauke who attacked 'radical leftists across the globe' for accepting a line 'established by the keepers of the Brecht Archives'. Professor Frederick Grab, who had recently been working there, seemed to disagree.

Thereupon Arendt wrote a letter to the *New York Times* alleging 'revision, suppression and misrepresentation of facts' – by me or by the Brecht Archive? I wasn't quite clear – and saying that Brecht's public attitude to Stalin was unambiguous (which wasn't ever at issue), that calling him 'the useful one' was high praise and that 'the spiritual and material weapons' which Brecht had given him credit for providing were known elsewhere as his 'crimes'. Finally she referred to 'what seems to me to be the only important issue in this whole matter', which proved to be a new and unexpected one: the alleged unwillingness of someone, it was not clear who, to invite her friend W.H. Auden 'to help in the publication of Brecht's collected works in English under the editorship of Mr Willett'. So I wrote again to the *TLS* repeating that what she termed 'odes to Stalin' had all been published by the autumn of 1967 and saying that though there *were* 'suppressed' (or still unpublished) poems they were of a different nature and might even include anti-Stalin material. Indeed they did, for these poems, written probably after Stalin's death, have since been published (e.g. in *Bad Time for Poetry*) and are summarised on pp. 220–1.

My letter went on:

> That Brecht for many years supported Stalin is not contested by anyone, even though there seem to be only three instances (one of them unpublished in his lifetime) of his doing so in print and by name. In my view, however, Miss Arendt is far too myopic about the nature of such 'praise'. 'Useful' was indeed a considerable tribute from the highly critical Brecht, but it was not unqualified and it has to be compared, not with the terms which Miss Arendt would have liked him to use about Stalin, but with the terms that other poets like Becher, Eluard, Neruda and Guillén (for a start) actually did. That, and the Soviet Stalin-worship of that time, is the scale of Stalin-flattery I had in mind, not Brecht's idiosyncratic range of grudging compliments. As for the 'material weapons', there is a less tortuous interpretation of those words: the

Red Army has been put to some pretty discreditable uses since Brecht wrote, but it can hardly be classed as one of Stalin's crimes, while before then Hitler would not have been beaten without it.

About the question of Auden's involvement in our edition I had to explain that the UK and US editions of the plays were different – as had actually been stipulated by the Brechts at the outset – but that I had more than once asked Auden if he would translate some of the poetry (as described earlier on pp. 64–6). The British edition of the plays moreover now includes, as I had always wanted it to, his collaborative versions of *The Caucasian Chalk Circle* – which I had been partly instrumental in unearthing – *Mahagonny* and *The Seven Deadly Sins*. What I did not include was his translations of the *Mother Courage* songs, for the simple reason that my own versions are closer to Brecht, more accurate and fit Dessau's music; but he did publish them himself and I was able to include five in *Poems and Songs from the Plays* (along with Isherwood's translation of two songs from the *Threepenny Novel*). This and the *Duchess of Malfi* passages were all Auden ever did in the way of translating Brecht, as far as I know, though, as I said in my letter,

> Quite apart from my own feelings about his poetry, which are akin to Miss Arendt's, he is the one poet whom Brecht's wife, son and daughter have all at different times told me they would like to see translate Brecht's verse.

Subsequently I noticed in the Brecht Archive catalogue that, apart from Eric Bentley who figures in a number of pictures with Brecht himself, Wystan Hugh Auden is the one foreign writer of whom Brecht seems to have kept a photograph. It is in one of the *Duchess of Malfi* files, the one that also contains an English-language version of the opening scene of *Man equals Man* in Brecht's handwriting: another item that we included in the English edition; though I doubt if Auden had anything to do with it.

b: Brecht, Alienation and Karl Marx

I have said virtually nothing yet about Brecht's theatrical theories, partly because it is so easy to cause confusion with them – sometimes with unhappy effects in the theatre itself – and partly because I have nothing fresh to say. But I thought it might be useful to put in this fairly short résumé of his doctrine of Alienation which I wrote in 1980 for a special issue of *Studio International* edited by Jasia Reichardt. The very fact that

I was asked to write on this when the other contributors were dealing with the quite different variants of Alienation discussed by Hegel and Marx seemed a challenge to try and clear this particular confusion up. It is, as I said, a confusion peculiar to the English language which, thanks largely to Eric Bentley and myself, now uses the same word to translate the *Ver*fremdung of Brecht and the *Ent*fremdung of Hegel and Marx. People think that because Brecht was a Marxist he must be meaning it in Marx's sense. But he is not.

The actual history of Brecht's concept of *Verfremdung* is curious. Almost from the outset of his career as a writer his instinct was to shatter illusion and stop the reader or spectator from getting swept away by the story, the characters, the actors who represented them on the stage, and/ or the naturalistic devices with which that stage set out to make their representation truly life-like. Explicit counter-measures were prescribed in the notes to his plays and productions from 1922 on. In addition there was the perpetual irony and undercutting implicit in all his work, its sense of parody and startling paradox and its tendency to pick remote or imaginary settings and situations, ones that would be unfamiliar to the German (especially the Bavarian) public.

This deflating, detached attitude, associated by many critics with lack of emotional warmth on the writer's part, is basic to Brecht from start to finish. Of all his forty or so plays only four deal directly with the contemporary world; while only one (*Señora Carrar*) follows the Aristotelian conventions of what he termed 'empathy drama', whose audience is expected to identify with the hero. And because Brecht was an incorrigible theorist as well as a resourceful practitioner of theatre he devoted the notes to his plays from the later 1920s onwards to trying to expound, codify and coordinate the various methods which he adopted – or wanted to see adopted – in order to keep his readers and spectators at a distance: cool, critical, uninvolved.

The methods in question were partly those of the 'theatrical theatre' as practised by the pre-1914 avant-garde whose outstanding figure was Meyerhold: devices to remind the audience that it is in a theatre and not taking part in real life. These made use of purely theatrical resources in order to break the illusion and upset the traditional suspense of the cunningly-told story. In Brecht's case they involved song (from *Baal* on); even, non-atmospheric lighting and a new type of curtain (as in *Edward II*); inscriptions or projections (see the *Threepenny Opera* notes on 'literarisation of the theatre'); elements of knockabout and music-hall (as in *Man equals Man*); analogies with the staging of sporting events (as in *Mahagonny*); and deliberate measures by the actor to prevent himself and the audience from becoming caught up in his part. Brecht came to subsume all these under the heading of 'epic theatre', a formula which he shared with Piscator, though the two men never understood it in exactly the same sense.

But it was not until 1935 that he actually began to speak about alienation – or rather *Verfremdung*. So far as we know he first used the term after seeing a private performance by the Chinese actor Mei Lan-fang, who had been invited to Moscow seemingly under the auspices of the Society for Cultural Relations as then represented by Sergei Tretiakov. Brecht too was in Moscow that spring, and on returning home he wrote a long descriptive analysis of Mei's acting, with its renunciation of any kind of illusion or empathy, under the title 'Alienation Effects in Chinese Acting'. This new phrase, the *Verfremdungseffekt*, appears to be a precise translation of Viktor Shklovsky's term *Priëm Ostranenniya* – 'the device [or trick, theatrical effect] of making strange' – which formed part of the corpus of Russian Formalist literary theory evolved in the First World War and the early 1920s. Tretiakov would certainly have been familiar with this, as would Eisenstein (who also met Mei and knew Brecht); and there seems to me every reason to accept the view of Bernhard Reich, who said in his memoirs that he first heard the term *Verfremdung* used that year by Tretiakov, with Brecht present, and concluded that this inspired Brecht to adopt Shklovsky's formulation as a description first of the Chinese methods and then of his own.[1]

Reich, who had taken Soviet citizenship, was later arrested in the purges. Tretiakov, friend and in some measure successor to Mayakovsky, was arrested and shot as a Japanese spy. Both were subsequently 'rehabilitated', the one dead, the other alive. But their long spell as un-persons, along with the official condemnation (still theoretically in vigour) of Formalism as a politico-aesthetic heresy, has hitherto prevented East European critics from admitting that Brecht could have derived one of his key concepts from such a source. Even to suggest this possibility is seen at best as a 'speculation'.

* * *

Recent German lexicographers treat the verb *Verfremden* as a neologism (along with its *-ung* noun and its *-effekt*) and give it its Brechtian sense. It is however to be found in Grimm's great dictionary – the German equivalent to *OED* – which cites one or two mentions of it in mediaeval legal documents. But these show a very different meaning: either

Verfremden intransitive, to become an alien, or else *Verfremden* transitive, to bring under alien ownership. In any case the word is certainly not of Marxist-Hegelian descent, any more than is its Russian prototype; Shklovsky himself, for that matter, was not a Marxist, and it is not irrelevant that he only just escaped trial for counter-revolutionary offences in 1922. Obviously *Verfremdung* sounds like *Entfremdung*, and the etymological relationship – the root *fremd* is common to both words, meaning, like *strann* in *ostrannenie*, strange, foreign or alien – is close enough for Brecht once or twice to have used the earlier term in the same sense as the later. But this sense itself had nothing to do with the political-philosophical-psychological aspects of *Entfremdung* or 'Alienation' as used by other writers. For Brecht it was a matter rather of perception and understanding: or gaining new insights into the world around us by glimpsing it in a different and previously unfamiliar light.

This is a concept which can be traced back for at least a hundred years before the Russian Formalists, and it must have been around a lot earlier than that. Its basic idea is of art as a means of productive reorientation, making 'familiar objects to be as if they were not familiar', as Shelley said of poetry, or 'the strange familiar and the familiar strange' as Wordsworth wrote in the preface to *Lyrical Ballads*, and thereby permitting one, in Schopenhauer's words, to 'completely alienate oneself from the world and from things so that the commonest objects and incidents appear quite new and unknown'. In other words it comes close to what is meant by the common clichés 'to shed a new light on', 'to look with fresh eyes at', or 'to open one's eyes to', and it may well be wondered why Brecht devoted so much effort to explaining and establishing it as part of his theatrical theory.

From his point of view its value was not only that it justified his love of breaking through the spectator's illusion, of consciously getting away from the commonplace, the acceptable, the everyday: it also lay in the positing of specific devices, tricks or effects by which such alienation of the audience could be achieved. Repeatedly thereafter we find him in his theoretical writings putting his finger on particular 'A-effects' – in the theatre of different nations and periods, in the cinema, in the paintings of Brueghel, in everyday life. Nothing illustrates his concept of alienation more clearly indeed than some of his most everyday examples, for instance 'To see one's mother as a man's wife one needs an A-effect; this is provided, for instance, when one acquires a stepfather', or again:

An alienation of the motor-car takes place if after driving a modern car for a long while we drive an old model T Ford. Suddenly we hear explosions once more; the motor works on the principle of explosion.

It is one of the great delights of art that, by artifice, it can create 'alienations' as sharply revealed as these.

As for the debatable translation of the term: literally speaking, Alienation comes about as close to *Verfremdung* as *Verfremdung* itself does to *Ostrannenie*. But it has some unfortunate overtones even apart from its Marxist-Hegelian use – it suggests, for instance, the alienating of somebody's sympathies or affections, or simply putting-off or 'off-putting' – and I myself would have preferred some less mystifying English term such as 'detachment'. There is also the accepted concept of 'aesthetic distance' or 'distancing'; indeed the French often translate *Verfremdung* by *distanciation*. The trouble however was that when I came into the Brecht business (or Brecht industry as we now call it) 'alienation' was so widely in use as a rendering of Brecht's term that I felt it would be too confusing (not to mention laborious) to attempt to change it. I just hope that the ambiguity doesn't do any harm.

13
After-notes

The first conception of this book, as agreed between the publishers and myself, was that it should be a straightforward selection of some of my lectures and articles about Brecht. It didn't turn out that way, because not only did I find myself rewriting those items which I wanted to include but I also found that I had to write entirely new chapters to fill the huge gaps which they left, and this went on until I had written what is almost entirely a new book. Then, after having thrown out most of the material I had looked out for it – notably a number of long review articles for the *TLS* – I realised that I did want to put in some much shorter notes, some of them almost jottings, which for the most part had never been intended for publication. So here they are: notes on performance of Brecht's plays, which I hope will give some idea of what their impact was like when it was still fresh; notes on meetings with Brecht and some of his closest collaborators, which I now of course greatly regret not having made fuller at the time; a word on translation; and a section on practical realisations in the media in the early 1980s.

The performance notes with which I start are of varying kinds, and the first three of them deal in more detail with some of the early experiences mentioned in the opening chapter. I hoped *Horizon* might print the one about Burian, but they did not. The notes on *Life of Galileo* were made for Elisabeth Hauptmann in the hope of securing some modifications in the production; I recall only that the boys' songs were later heard as a recording. The review of *Ui* was printed in the *Guardian*. I am not sure how far I would agree with any of them if I saw the performance in question again; I now like Dessau's *Courage* music much better, and I certainly feel much more indulgent to Ernst Busch now that I know more about him, though the memory of his acting still sometimes makes me wince. Schall and Erni Wilhelmi were in their very different ways quite unforgettable.

Perhaps any unevennesses, not to mention inconsistencies with my present views, will be acceptable in the cause of light relief. This

miscellaneous chapter should be seen as a form of hors d'œuvre, placed
(for a change) at the end of the meal.

a: Notes on performances 1945–1960

(i) *The Threepenny Opera* directed by E.F. Burian, Prague, 1945

D46 certainly is one of the outstanding theatres of the world, whether
one likes it or not, and like *The Threepenny Opera* itself, may have great
influence on the theatre of the future. Technically its productions are
almost perfect in every respect, so that the most revolutionary tricks do
not jar as they do in highbrow theatres elsewhere. Costumes, very simple
settings and continually changing lighting; you will never see better. The
acting is excellent, and the quality of the whole thing is shown by the
fact that one can sit as I did through any of Burian's productions without
knowing a word of Czech, and be continually interested and impressed.
This of course also indicates the style of production: any play when
Burian produces it becomes a rounded-off theatrical work in which
lighting, movement, acting play as important a part as do the words. For
this reason Burian has no scruples about altering the text (e.g. in his
current *Romeo and Juliet*), and it is in a way a criticism of him that he
could probably make a wonderful thing out of the most rubbishy play.

So *The Threepenny Opera* was certainly not quite the *Threepenny
Opera* of Brecht and Weill. It was played on a permanent set, with the
curtain up the whole time and two pianos in lieu of orchestra. After the
overture the whole cast, in lovely late nineteenth-century costumes and
brilliantly made up, trooped through a door on the left of the
auditorium, marched round the audience singing the Moritat [or 'Mack
the Knife'] at the top of their voices, up on to the stage, and danced an
excellent rampageous ballet to set the play going. The various scenes, all
differently lit, with lovely use of coloured lights – nothing but spotlights
in this theatre – were broken by fresh verses of the Moritat, sung by a
tough and dirty old beggar to the accompaniment of a (presumably)
specially-made hurdy-gurdy manipulated by himself. During these
breaks the electricians would come, unselfconscious and matter-of-fact,
on to the stage and arrange the lights for the next scene. For example,
before the scene where Polly, after a slanging by her mother, sings the
'Barbara Song' to explain how she came to marry Macheath, an
electrician brought out a spotlight and laid it on the stage to shine
upwards, up the stairs of the permanent set and away from the audience,

so that the scene could be played with the three characters on the stairs, lit from below by a warm yellow light. When the lights were fixed the electricians would return to their posts, jumping over the furniture and running up ladders, a brightly-dressed sailor would come on with a gong, beat it; so would the beggar, and the next scene would begin.

The two most remarkable scenes: first, the bordello in Tonbridge. Wonderfully-dressed tarts; a girl flopped on the keyboard of an out-of-tune piano at the left of the stage with a drunk sprawling across her, the sailor (without his gong) sitting in a matter-of-fact way at a small table. At the back of the stage some kind of translucent hanging covering the ground floor of the permanent set: green lighting behind. Macheath comes on in his grey bowler and Max Miller coat, and at the front of the stage he and Jenny, a wonderful old whore in black, sing Brecht's version of the 'Ballade de Villon et de la grosse Margot':

> Vente, gresle, gelle, j'ay mon pain cuict!
> Je suis paillard, la paillarde me duit.
> Lequel vault mieux? chacun bien s'entresuit.
> L'ung l'autre vault: c'est a mau chat mau/rat.
> Ordure amons, ordure nous affuyt.
> Nous deffuyons honneur, il nous deffuyt,
> En ce Bourdel ou tenons nostre estat . . .

They are accompanied by the girl at the piano, which is deliberately old and out of tune. (The versatility of Burian's actors is noteworthy. This girl plays a tart and the piano; the electrician returning to his switchboard leaps like Nijinsky; everyone can sing and dance. So is the trouble taken over details: the special hurdy-gurdy, the out-of-tune piano.)

The second memorable scene is for the song based on Villon's Epitaph [in scene 9], which Brecht intended to be sung by Macheath in his condemned cell. Burian goes closer to the Villon original. Three men, draped in long white sheets which cover the chairs on which they are standing, cock their necks sideways and twist and turn exactly like bodies dangling from the gallows: viz. certain drawings by Pisanello. They are lit by a faint white light with very concentrated green spotlights picking out their faces, and sing the song in unison.

The course of the play then changes. Brecht, like Gay, made it finish with a farcical happy ending, pointing the moral that happy endings are not normal in real life. Burian cuts all this out; no reprieve comes, and Macheath is waiting to be hanged as the play ends with what Brecht intended to be the second-act finale: possibly the most forceful song of them all, and one which is particularly true for central Europe today, where you get an overwhelming impression that nothing can matter till people are adequately fed:

> You who set out to teach us good behaviour
>
> . . .
>
> Must learn for all time how the world is run:
> However much you twist, whatever lies you tell
> Food is the first thing, morals follow on.
>
> . . .
>
> How does man keep alive? Because his fellows
> Are persecuted, tortured, plundered, strangled and die.
> Man only keeps alive because he well knows
> How to forget his own humanity.
> For once you must try not to shirk the facts:
> Man only keeps alive by bestial acts.

– a song which in 192[8] may have seemed gloomy and unpleasant, but now, to audiences who knew the SS and the concentration camps and are spending every day fighting starvation, if necessary by dishonest and unscrupulous means, is just plain fact.

And yet although this is an astonishing production of a very fine and important work there is something wrong with it. I think it is because the breaks between the scenes are too marked and because too many of the songs have been omitted. *The Threepenny Opera* should not be so leisurely, and it should not fall apart. The whole point about it is that it is a new and strongly effective type of opera. Burian, keeping the content, has rather altered the form, and in the case of this work it is the form which is of importance.

(ii) *Mother Courage* directed by Brecht and Engel at the Deutsches Theater, East Berlin, 1949

Mutter Courage, still sold out after over fifty performances, is a big success, yet without the tension between audience and stage which usually characterises one. I think for most people it must be the quality of the production, not the uncompromisingly unstagey play which attracts them. This quality you notice immediately the lights go down: the little orchestra in one of the boxes, the thin music, the drab dusty tattered family dragging its cart forward on the revolving stage, singing with fire and looking as if it had been rolled in dirt. The setting gives the minimum of help; the lighting is bright and straightforward irrespective of times and seasons. But at once you see these are a group of real people who have been right to the raw, miserable primitive bottom of an endless war, and at the same time that they are actors with their hearts in the play. A tremendous air of conviction.

What in the play calls out these qualities? I suppose above all, Brecht's seriousness and directness, and the ascetic simplicity which, because it is so unGerman, it takes a German to show. Item one: this is a play tackling a huge theme, the hateful implications of war. Item two: Brecht is approaching his audience in a wholly original way, showing them one thing after another without ever appealing for their sympathy. Item three: there is neither turgid language here nor muddled thinking. And the whole sceptical, dispassionate nature of his argument – the lack of emotion and the final 'take it or leave it' – is a vital corrective for the Germans, if not for others too. The play grips the actors, I would say, and the actors grip the audience. It is far from thrilling or pleasing in the orthodox way; you watch intently, but you never forget where you are. Yet there is something very strenuous and worthwhile about it which orthodox plays seem to lack. It is tough, without being difficult to understand: a highly simplified essay on profound themes.

This in itself is refreshing, and although the play is not 'entertaining' it sticks in the mind as a more notable experience than most of those which are. Cutting out all the theory, that is in effect what Brecht's idea of non-Aristotelian drama boils down to. The interest of a plot, the self-identification of audience with actor, the compulsion of a strongly dramatic scene: these are the standard theatrical weapons which Brecht chooses to do without, and the play itself is as bare and unrelieved as the empty stage and whitewashed cyclorama on which, with Mother Courage's wagon and a few rags and scraps of scenery, the whole action is thrown. Concentration on the bare minimum, but a loving, scrupulous concentration which brings that minimum somehow to life.

There is so much that is prickly here that it is hard to grasp. What one has to accept however, before discussing the play's weaknesses, is that this is a justifiable way to use the theatre, and that it can create an appeal as forceful, in an entirely different manner, as the orthodox. What it loses in tension and atmosphere it gains in honesty and economy. It may be depressing, it may be tiring, but it is never cheap; at the worst it is like one of those fat stodgy books which no one wants to read, yet everyone who has read finds satisfying. Such a play is not poured into you in an effortless way, but the effort is worth making.

This is a basis from which Brecht may do great things, and sometimes, as in *The Mother* and *Fear and Misery*, he has brought it off.

But *Mother Courage* has some drastic faults. First of all, Brecht has not really a great deal to say about war, and one feels that his own history has not associated him closely enough with it for him to develop any great understanding of its implications. Second, the unrelieved grey flatness of the play and the rejection of a plot are all very well, but something is needed to compensate if it is not to become an indigestible jumble of episodes and a torture for the audience as they wonder how long it is to the interval. This play lacks shape; one feels that the author has made no effort to cut or tighten up the individual scenes; there is no rise and fall apart from the one climax of Kattrin and the drum, and there is very little apparent reason why the whole pack of cards should be dealt in this particular order; you could stage the play almost equally well back to front. Whatever one's views of the plot as a help or hindrance to the development of a theme, some sort of formal unity and sequence are needed. As in music, there must be a structure if the work is to stand.

Third, Brecht compensates for his asceticism by a bunch of affectations which are extremely irritating and in no necessary connection with the core of his theory. The captions which have to be thrown on the screen between scenes: these don't belong to the theatre but to youthful memories of the silent cinema in the 1920s. The lowering of lights and a posy of old musical instruments to hover above the actors' heads every time a song is sung: what is the point of this piece of ceremonial? Is it an effort to make up for the arbitrary way in which the songs are slung willy-nilly into the text? Like the almost overdone emphasis on rags and tatters it verges on the merely quaint. And the music itself is pretty childish. The thin, acrid orchestration would be all right but for the drawing-pins which some bright chap has thought of putting into the hammers of the piano; this gives not a brittle but a tinny effect. Dessau's music has neither the nostalgia of Weill's nor the verve and conviction of Eisler's, and in trying to capture something of both it misses the simplicity of either. It is an old principle: songs must have tunes if their words are to come across. Here a lot of good poetry is flung away on a succession of desert airs.

For a German writer it is easy to wrap up such affectations in a mass of theory and present them as a justifiable part of his system. This is a type of dishonesty and inverted modishness which simply doesn't go with the bald dramatic statement at which Brecht aims. It is excellent in *Mother Courage* to see him paying more attention to his individual characters and giving them – above all to the central figure herself – a life of their own; and this humanisation of his approach will give his works immensely more weight and power. But no audience will be able to get to grips with them if he hems them in with the ugly exotic little cactus hedge of his own fads. This is his great danger, and it would be good to see him overcome it. After all, he is one of the few real playwrights we have.

(iii) *Herr Puntila und sein Knecht Matti* directed by Hans Schweikart at the Kammerspiele, Munich, 1949

Mr Puntila and his man Matti however is a very different affair. Here the pretensions are less, the scale is smaller; there is a firm logical shape; the affectations are reduced to the cinema captions only, and even these are shorter and more to the point. But like *Mother Courage* this is produced with a loving, thoroughly practised hand; it may be true of all playwrights whom, being unfashionable, it needs a particular belief and effort to put across, but Brecht commands the devotion of his actors and producers. If anything this performance in the Munich Kammerspiele was better than [*Courage*] in Berlin; Puntila himself was magnificent, and the smallest roles were exceptionally well done.[1]

The brilliance of this play is that you ride through four scenes (half the play) of rollicking full-blooded comedy, with the drunken red-faced farmer Puntila staggering about the stage and committing the friendliest extravagances. Then, with a minimum of warning, you have the Hyde to this jolly Elizabethan Jekyll, this Finnish Toby Belch – Puntila sober is a grasping, unscrupulous soreheaded fat thug, as testy as a debauched brigadier and as brutal as any monopolist in the Moscow comic papers. Not only that, you have the typical effect of this behaviour: the four women whom he has cheered up by inviting them drunkenly to his daughter's engagement party, and has then soberly and unexpectedly thrown out, come to highly bolshy conclusions as a result; and the crux of the play is in the stories which they then tell. And then immediately after this, the most political and least easily digestible scene, you get two excellent climaxes, pointed, dramatic, yet comic. Both very typical of Brecht's play-within-a-play method of construction. First, Matti the chauffeur to whom, after throwing out her foreign office fiancé, Puntila in a fit of bottled amiability engages his daughter, examines her in wifehood by acting out with her various domestic situations while the rest of the party look blearily on. (Answer after several tests: she wouldn't make a chauffeur's wife, because on the whole she can't take working-class hardships and anyway she doesn't like being slapped on the bottom.) Second, Puntila and Matti, piling up chairs and tables, conclude the party alone by pretending to climb a mountain; there they

stand swaying on top of the pile, shouting and singing away, with a good
roistering whack of poetry and a sharp moral: that the beauties of nature
look different to possessors and possessed. So this means that the play
has the progression and balance which in *Mother Courage* are lacking.
And the individual scenes (like the individuals in another sense) are
much tighter.

That *Verfremdung* at which Brecht normally aims is missing here,
though this may be due to the fine acting. Not only, as in *Mother
Courage*, the central figure but all the characters are alive and human; the
audience develops strong sympathy for many of them, and an active
interest in the wayward half-joking, half-real love affair between Matti
and Puntila's scarcely adult daughter. The difference between this and
Mother Courage is quite striking; the play becomes smoother and offers
less resistance to the audience, and yet *Mother Courage*, for all Brecht's
ignorance of war, has a size and sweep which this hasn't got. Brecht was
not so far wrong when he picked the name 'epic theatre' for his non-
Aristotelian, anti-plot approach; there is something epic about his bigger
works. But what one wonders after seeing *Puntila* is whether he gains or
loses by it. Puntila could and should be a successful play (though this
was the twenty-fifth and last performance here) in many countries; its
colour and life should bring it to audiences who would never see or
stomach one of Brecht's didactic dramas. And its moral is at the same
time pretty plain: neither love nor booze, for all their powers, can bring
different classes permanently together, and their humanising effects are
of little use if incomplete. Yet will this sink in? Or will the audience soon
forget the selfish antisocial farmer, the brutal employer, and remember
only the Rabelaisian drunkard with his friendliness and remorse?

It is an interesting comparison with Zuckmayer's *The Devil's General*
because the genial back-slapping relationship of General Harras to his
subordinates is not unlike that of Puntila drunk, and it is obviously what
many people admire. Ah, I could work for a jolly chap like that, even if
he's a bit strict at times. How many people, after seeing *Puntila*, will look
that jollity more closely in the eye, as Brecht, unlike Zuckmayer, intends
them to do? How many people will begin to see that geniality can be a
pose? The more normal style of *Puntila* makes such conclusions more
easily acceptable, yet it smears them over. The epic style makes them
clearer, but it has many elements which frighten, irritate or bore.
Zuckmayer of course shirks the moral issue, creating merely an
impressive character and a most entertaining play. I think *Puntila* is a
good compromise between this and the thin gruel of *Mother Courage*.

There is one serious weakness in this production which I don't think is Brecht's fault necessarily, even though much the same happens in *M.C.* That is the great gaps between scenes, where one stares in rustling, coughing silence at the low white curtain, waiting for the next caption to appear, while pieces of scenery and backcloth can be seen hanging suspended or whisking up and down in the half-dark over the top. It matters more here because the scenes are more concentrated and the general *Schwung* of the play more rapid. Admittedly the scenery was quite decent, especially the village with its rose-coloured timber houses and telegraph pole. But something simpler and/or more mobile would have helped the production better.

(iv) *Der Kaukasische Kreidekreis* directed by Brecht at the Paris International Theatre Festival, 1955

The Caucasian Chalk Circle is in some ways one of Brecht's best works. At least when one reads it. It has very good scenes; its language is superb; its theme a noble one, interpreted with originality. And there are two first-rate characters: Grusha the servant girl, and the eccentric judge-malgré-lui Azdak. The simplicity of the writing, the twists given to story and moral, the epigrammatic short sketches are all typical of the author, but there is often a humanity and depth which are relatively new. The girl who looks after a baby in the civil war when its mother has abandoned it, the debauched judge who turns the law into a farce, but an oddly just one: these are universal human figures, not Marxist puppets, and the point of the play is similarly universal. Only the angle of vision, the technique of analysis, the whole way of seeing and expressing that point are communist; and that surely is how it should be. Politics and philosophy are methods of dealing with essentials; the essentials themselves – like love, hunger, laughter – go deeper.

Shortly, the story is of a bloody coup d'état in Georgia at some indeterminate time apparently before firearms were invented. The Governor's Wife, fleeing, leaves her baby, which Grusha adopts and takes into the country to her farmer brother's, where she pretends that it is her own and, although engaged to another man, feels bound to marry in order to give it respectability. But the soldiers who have been pursuing her at last track her down, and she is sued for the return of the child by its 'proper' mother. Before Azdak the judge they perform the old Chinese test of the chalk circle: the child is seated within a circle drawn on the floor, and the two claimants try to pull it out. But this time it is Grusha, not the rival mother who lets go of the child's arm, rather than hurt it by pulling. The legend is altered, and with it the moral. For

Grusha gets awarded the child, on the concluding principle that everything should go to those who treat it best and make best use of it. A conclusion that has been foreshadowed in the prologue, where two Soviet collective farms are shown discussing which should take over a certain valley.

All this is told in a succession of short scenes linked together by the comments of a narrator, who acts as compère-cum-chorus. There is a lot of fine verse in his part, and the whole sequence of Grusha's flight into the country is both touching and dramatic, with the wonderful comic scene of her marriage by a drunken monk to a supposedly dying man as its climax. But even in the printed play there are weak and tedious passages, and these were accentuated in Brecht's production where perhaps a more detached producer would have excised or at least concealed them. Brecht makes many demands of his players and sets a high standard, but he seems to have no idea of timing and momentum. And he somehow fails to fill the stage, so that the tremendous vitality which impelled Erich Engel's *Mother Courage* is here lacking.

The trouble is twofold. In the play the character of Azdak is built up at much too great length, and the story held up while this happens: only a sudden spurt of speed and craziness could make these scenes fit in. It might have been anyway better if part of their material could have been woven into the main story and the rest scrapped. And, as still too often happens with Brecht, the villains of the piece, doomed to be such by their social position, are the silliest of dummies. This was badly emphasised by the production, which stylised their movements and hid their faces behind masks; you could in fact pick out the Good characters from the Bad simply by seeing who wore a mask and who did not. In particular the production confirmed that Brecht has no understanding of soldiers; as in *Man equals Man* they were presented as impossible inhuman monsters, here masked and vastly padded out, with a curious crouching walk and a liking for two-gallon wooden tankards of wine. If Brecht cannot say more about the military than that he cannot say much about war. Fascination and disgust, even hatred; but none of the insight which is needed if wars are to be avoided.

These faults become more striking after the half-way mark, where the story stops just short of the final court scene and the play doubles a long way back on its tracks to introduce Azdak. This Azdak, who ought to be an immensely funny and vital character, a cross between Sir Toby Belch and Harpo Marx, becomes something of a bore. And this was undoubtedly made worse by a bad piece of miscasting: Ernst Busch as Azdak. It was doubly bad, because Azdak's crazy and Rabelaisian sides quite elude this revolutionary hero grown middle-aged, this model of the German communist worker. And alas, Busch does not seem to fit in the Brechtian theatre at all: he is far too conscious of his audience and inclined to play up his own personality. An admirable Narrator, he upset the whole play as soon as he took up the part of Azdak, and the second half of the performance was unnecessarily trying.

This is a case where more *Verfremdung* would have been a help. It is odd that in this production, directed by Brecht himself, there was less deliberate attempt to alienate and hold off the audience, a less detached attitude of the players, than in the others I have seen, and much less than he in theory demands. The element of demonstration, of 'look, this is how it happened', lies entirely in the construction of the play, with its linking narrative, not in its presentation and performance. Perhaps as a result, there is a lack of that sharpness and clarity that seem essential to Brecht's whole method, and this was aggravated by Dessau's often tediously repetitive mock-Caucasian music, which makes nonsense of many of the Narrator's finest passages. The original intention, according to the printed text, was that the Narrator should have his accompanying musicians on the stage with him, and I am sure this simpler approach would have been better than the Berliner Ensemble's arrangement of three singers on stools at the side of the stage, with the instrumentalists in a box. Given the fussiness of the score and the awkwardness of the melodic line a great part of their words would have been better delivered without music. Such a composer is the wrong partner for Brecht.

The production might also have been more lively and forceful if there had been more colour on the stage. Presumably because the original legend was Chinese, and because Brecht himself has a profound interest in China, the silk backcloths imitated Chinese landscape paintings, soft and monochromatic. This seemed pointlessly inapposite, and in the later, Azdak scenes there was that scarecrow element of which Brecht has long been overfond: the old dingy rags and tatters. It should all have been gayer, and the first and last scenes more crowded.

It misfired. Enough work had gone into the production, and Angelika Hurwicz's performance as Grusha was compelling enough to have put over any normal play. But Brecht's plays are so out of the ordinary that they can only come over with a bang or not at all. This time there was no bang.

(v) *Leben das Galilei* directed by Engel at the Theater am Schiffbauerdamm, East Berlin, 2 March 1957

1. The production succeeds in conveying the quality of the play. This is
tremendously impressive.

2. One fundamental mistake: guying the church. To judge from the
photos, the New York production was not free of this fault; but Brecht
did expressly warn against it. It not only cheapens the play (and
incidentally the company); it wrecks the sense. The clerics' hostility to
Galileo's ideas is shown by Brecht with great intelligence; seen from
their own standpoint, or from that of the nobility, their arguments are
quite convincing. The point is that within the limits of their position
they are being clever and even reasonable: it is the position itself that
emerges as wrong. It cannot do this if they are caricatured. The spectator
then feels 'there's more to it than that', and so dismisses a main part of
the play.

3. In detail: the laboured distinction drawn between the Pope and his
uniform; the unsuitable cardinals (far too young); the old cardinal's
overdone decrepitude; the semi-military movements of the Pope's
attendants; the failure to justify the lavish costumes by getting the
ceremonial, or even the colours, at all correct. The dressing of the Pope
seems like a pantomime, where it should be impressive and slightly
frightening. Nobody would think of this church as a huge political-
ideological body with a 1600-year tradition: probably the greatest force
in the world of that day.

4. Setting and costumes. There are two ways of dealing with this play:
utmost simplicity, designed to *explain* (so that the chief items of the
setting become the diagrams and the instruments), or else a vivid
recreation of the time and spirit of the counter-reformation in Italy.
Neher chooses neither. The copper box is an irrelevant piece of
opulence; the costumes clash, but the colours have no life; clerics and
noblewomen look historically unconvincing without achieving any other
quality; there is a certain element of fancy dress.

5. This is emphasised by the production. Women and clerics alike are
unrealistic, not because they are stylised, but because they are utterly
wrong – casting; manners; movement. As a result the most ambitious

scenes, such as the ball in Rome or the dressing of the Pope, are the least effective. They look expensive; but they don't look right.

6. Virginia is not a comic character. She really is in an abominable position, and acts intelligently within her own interests and limitations. The fact that these are very different from her father's is not her fault; after all, who was it brought her up? It is wrong to guy her, just as it is wrong to guy the church. Treat her seriously, and she helps to illuminate Galileo; it is part of his character that he is an appalling parent.

7. Given that he is so far from any conceivable academic or intellectual type, Busch's performance is surprisingly good. A lot of the sense comes through, and still more might have emerged if the production as a whole had been more expository, so that casting by type really became as unnecessary as Brecht always claimed it was. But he sets the wrong tone for the figure at the start; the business of the telescope becomes a cheap swindle, and sly winks at the audience imply that Galileo is an intellectual crook. Personally I forgot this dreadful introduction as the play and the character developed; but for anyone coming to the work for the first time it could well distort them both: the recantation could seem a trick, and Galileo emerge not as a historically decisive tragic figure (at once a warning and an explanation for our time) but as a man who managed to live and work under an ideological dictatorship, uncomfortably perhaps, but with ultimate success. And to anyone seeing the play this way the conclusion must be that oppression doesn't really matter: sooner or later Truth Will Out.

8. The children would be better if they were heard and not seen, and if they sang in tune. An accurate recording would be preferable to what we went through.

(vi) *Der aufhaltsame Aufstieg des Arturo Ui* directed by Peter Palitzsch and Manfred Wekwerth at the Paris International Theatre Festival, June 1960

I have just come back from seeing one of the most extraordinary performances in the history of the Paris International Theatre Festival: Ekkehard Schall playing Arturo Ui. This Ui, a caricatured, parodied, yet always frightening fusion of Hitler and Al Capone (with a dash of Richard III), is the central figure of a blank-verse play which Brecht wrote in a few weeks in 1941. Schall is a young actor whom he appointed to the Berliner Ensemble shortly before his death; we have seen him in London as a violent, yet mannered Eilif in *Mother Courage* and as an over-stylised ADC in *The Caucasian Chalk Circle.* He is certainly not dull, but his acting has often seemed too tense and at the same time contrived; too reminiscent of the Japanese film and the methodical violence of Brando and Dean, and, behind that, of the disciplined horrors of the Third Reich.

One might well wonder what this actor would make of this particular part. For although *The Resistible Ascent of Arturo Ui* (to give it its full title) is a play of great verve, in its mock-Elizabethan way, it is by no means one of Brecht's masterpieces, and it seems trivial beside the monstrous realities which it is supposed to reflect. The author was cocking a snook at the Nazis, rather as Chaplin did in *The Great Dictator*, at a time when half Europe was fighting and monsters like Himmler, Kaltenbrunner and Eichmann were making the street-fighting and concentration camps of the 1930s look like a Sunday School outing. Because he was satirising Hitler's rise to power, from 1932 to the annexation of Austria, his satire was already out of date. It would surely be very wide of any mark today.

And yet at the Théâtre Sarah Bernhardt both actor and play were uproariously justified. Two of Brecht's East German pupils, Peter Palitzsch and Manfred Wekwerth, in a big, raw, rowdy production, have turned this Chicago allegory from a superficially shallow parody of Nazism into a forceful commentary on the present cult of violence. The setting, the atmosphere, the ear-splitting music are all drawn from the pin-table saloon and the juke box; debased tunes looted from Liszt or Chopin (specified in Brecht's text) boom out over the loudspeakers; naked electric light bulbs frame the stage, like in a fair; peals of happy gangster laughter fill the brief black-outs in the central trial scene (with its obvious references to the Reichstag Fire) as justice is crudely mocked and fooled. The machine-guns rattle; the gangsters slouch across the blood-spattered revolving stage; and you no longer feel, as the author originally intended, that the Nazis were just petty criminals, blown up to huge proportions by the gale of history. Instead you begin to feel scared that our current brand of senseless brutality could produce such genuine monsters once more.

Against this background we have Schall at first sitting staring and silent in a corner of the stage. Here is something very rare: an actor who can be a great clown, and at the same time a blood-curdling maniac; who can make the audience howl with laughter without forgetting or under-estimating the horrors in which he is taking part. There he slumps, a moody unsuccessful petty gang-leader on the verge of ruin, dressed in a mackintosh and a dirty soft hat, with ghastly red-ringed eyes, ginger hair and a nailbrush moustache. He is a truly pathetic figure as he appeals to the avuncular but corrupt mayor (i.e. Hindenburg) to save him from the police; it seems like some pitiable form of madness as he mutters and grovels and blurts. Then the threats begin – blackmail, offers of 'protection', spoken demagogically over a growling accompaniment on the brass, with sudden unpredictable switches back into a whining or normally conversational tone. The first murders quickly follow: his first short, bloody, but still half-ridiculous appearance in public affairs.

It is a gradual crescendo. The loudspeakers blare; the stage rotates; and Ui stands there in a dinner-jacket, taking a necessary lesson in deportment and declamation from a broken-down Shakespearean actor. Staggering with his head thrown back, pawing the air for a handhold, he learns to walk in the heroic style; to clasp his hands in front of himself, as if caught without trousers; imperiously, if still ineptly, to fold his arms. He practises such motions in front of the mirror, discussing them coldly with the old actor and the cynical, slit-mouthed henchman who represents Goebbels; a short distant burst of tommy-gun fire punctuates his remarks. Then, clumsily following the actor at first, imitating his tones and trying to copy his gestures with one hand as he holds his Shakespeare in the other and squints down at it, he declaims 'Friends, Romans, countrymen . . .' with a mounting conviction which verges on hysteria, dropping back to the ridiculous now and again as he stumbles on a word like 'Lupercal', or strains, like his fellow-ham, to squeeze an authentic tear for 'Caesar hath wept'. It seems like a brilliant (and brilliantly-written) 'turn', but even as the audience is applauding the stage spins round again; the Liszt theme roars out; and there is Ui speaking to the crowd, yelling 'Murder! Butchery! Blackmail! Violence! Rape!' through a brassy amplifier, promising 'protection' against these self-invented disorders, and rasping an officer of 'peace and quiet and safety'. He is applying, with occasional comic uncertainty, the lesson and even the gestures which he has just learnt.

One cannot remember or describe it all. There is Ui again, in his hotel room after the trial, cursing and cajoling his lieutenants as they quarrel, cowering as they come to blows, imploring their confidence – their 'Glaube' or faith – in a series of hysterical gulps. Guns are drawn; the furniture bounces and clatters across the stage; there is a half-hypnotised, wholly mawkish reconciliation; and Ui is left alone to rehearse his next speech. 'Friends', he begins, as he clasps his hands in virginal modesty. He moves back a few paces, and begins again . . . No good. Back further, up a long carpet to a square, ugly, modernistic and unusually springy arm-chair. He sits in it. 'Friends! . . .' He stands up in it. He straddles on top of it, but finds the position too precarious, and steps gingerly down on to the seat again. 'Friends!' he cries. 'With sorrow I have learnt/That treacherously, behind my back . . .' and at this point somersaults backwards, in an apparent loss of balance, and disappears suddenly behind the chair.

Fresh start. He gets as far as 'behind my back', then peers cautiously behind him over the chair in each direction, as if defying the same dark forces to pull him over again. He holds his ground and goes on. Some of those closest to him, he shouts, have plotted to betray him. They are hand in glove with big business. 'No, that won't do', he mutters, and drops down promptly into the attitude of Rodin's Thinker. 'I've got it: hand in glove with the Police!' And he bounces excitedly up and down in the chair, working himself into a rhetorical frenzy until an interruption makes him quickly curl up, very small indeed, between its padded arms.

The murder of Hitler's lieutenant Röhm, to which this is all leading, is paralleled in a scene that might have come from one of the classic gangster films: the melancholy gunmen in oilskins, waiting behind an armour-plated garage door that grinds and whirrs convincingly as it is raised or lowered. Steady rain; nerves and nostalgia, broken by the first loudspeaker warnings from an outpost. 'Police car down Church Street . . . moving on.' 'Two cars coming round the corner without lights.' The two cars contain Ui and others of the gang, who in the best Shakespearean tradition butcher all of those present, so that the bloodstained stage can spin on to its next scene: a parody of the garden scene in *Faust*, where Ui, now sedate in top hat and tails, and his faithful Goebbels walk peacefully round a flower shop (well stocked with wreaths), talking in rhyming couplets with Mr and Mrs Dullfeet, whom Ui is about to treat as Hitler did Austria on the eve of the war.

Next, inevitably, Dullfeet's (or Dollfuss's) funeral, black and solemn as some painting of the 1860s, while the hypocritical mourners wind past in silence, shaking and furling their umbrellas before entering the church. And then the final triumphal public meeting, where Ui harangues the cowed citizenry from a rostrum with all the methods and madness of the mature Hitler, the surviving businessmen supporting him, and on either side, diagonally across the stage, the gangsters lounging with their guns.

The epilogue, delivered quietly by Schall in front of the curtain, as the applause suddenly snaps off:

Learn how to face the facts you tried to shun
And how to act, where once you idly slept.
That's how the world was going to be run!
The nations duly mastered it, except
(In case you think the battle has been won) –
The womb is fertile still from which *that* crept.

Garish, strident, savage, the play is over and a stunned audience is left to cheer and perhaps to think. Full marks to the producers, and for Appen's setting and Hosalla's music. Full marks for Schall's marvellously controlled virtuosity. A special cheer for a company whose younger members can carry on a great tradition with such freshness and force, and can incidentally recruit such a very remarkable newcomer as Hilmar Thate, who takes the Goebbels part. A wish that this may help to revitalise our way of staging the Elizabethans. A new respect for Brecht's less good plays. A hope that this production will be seen in London next year.

b: Notes on meetings 1956–1973

(i) Visit to Buckow, 17 June 1956. [Comments 1982 in square brackets]

Bentley suggested Auden do verses of *KKK*: A. agrees if he can alter metres and rhymes: Brecht says fine, Dessau must then try to make music fit. (But Brecht knows nothing of Auden's since 1939.) [Confusion by me? Dessau hadn't written the music of *The Caucasian Chalk Circle* when Auden translated those verses, so perhaps this related to some question from me about using the Auden–Stern version.]

Generally B. thinks music subordinate to sense: e.g. when I suggested having *KKK* narrative in English [for the impending London season] he was ready to drop music – unlike H[elene] W[eigel]. And when I said my *GM* [*Szechwan*] verses were not quite identical he said 'schliesslich ist der Dessau noch am Leben' ['Dessau's still alive'] and he can adapt. Obviously against slavish translation.

And against slavish productions. E.g. re an offer to stage *GM* on Broadway and who could [direct] it, he suggests Welles, because Welles is not dull. 'Alles, nur nicht langweilig'. If it's a balls-up, well and good.

Meyerhold. He saw *Camelias*, *The Forest*, *Roar China* and others in Moscow in 1930s [and/or on the company's Berlin visit in spring 1930]: wonderful, aber nicht auf den Sinn gespielt [not played for the meaning]. Really expressionist. Meyerhold a great man: he was murdered of course.

Vakhtangov [made] most use of *Verfremdung* – because paid more attention to sense. Saw *Turandot, Dybbuk*: these productions kept going long after V's death (just as a 1902 or so production by Stanislavsky he saw – kept absolutely fresh: this a gt Russian gift).

Present vulgarity due to people coming fresh to art. That is what he tells the E. German authys, that they know nothing about it. What's more, they take no interest. Not one. Nobody e.g. comes to the theatre except for galas.

[Elisabeth] H[auptmann] spoke night before of intelligence of Dymschitz, Sov. Lt-Col. Brecht said Semeonov [Soviet High Commissioner], whom he obviously liked, came twice to *Courage*, then said, 'Genosse Brecht, you must ask for anything you want. Obviously you are very short of money.' B. said no; what made him think that? 'But it all looks so poor. No rich decorations, and that's what the people want to see.' S. himself was originally a metal-worker.

For the first time something has begun to appear in Russian press – on the lines of 'Why are our producers so unenterprising? oughtn't they to try some of this stuff?'. And there is a question of the B[erliner] E[nsemble] going there next year. [They did so.]

Poland is that country where they were a huge success. And their visit unleashed a controversy re socialist art etc. The former culture minister, now dethroned, told B. 'You have upset the whole of our cultural policy'.

Hptm. says that for about the last two years B and the Ensemble have been solidly est[ablished]. But before that they were looked askance at. Now (this emerged in genl. talk) the Erfurt theatre has been able to do *KKK*, though originally the Party there were against it – on the simple ground that the bourgeois in Paris thought it was good.

Hptm. said B. wd be delighted to talk about his finances in exile, and obviously was so herself, as she straightway plunged into it with him after lunch.

> Left Germany on money borrowed from Suhrkamp, which Hptm. got his father to repay.
> Denmark at first chez K. Mich[aelis], then bought a fisherman's cottage. On royalties fm *DGO* [*Threepenny Opera*] piled up in Switz. [And money from his father.]
> 7 *Deadly Sins* for Balanchine/Losch/Ed[ward] James
> Advance on play for Royal Th, Copenhagen, never written.
> R[undköpfe] und Spitz[köpfe]. [*Round Heads and Pointed Heads*]
> Advance on *DG Roman* [*Threepenny Novel*] from de Lange.

Sweden. Earned nothing. Danish house sold for what it cost.

Finland. Journey through Russia to Vlad[ivosto]k, paid out of royalties in S[oviet] U[nion] – *Wort*. So was boat Vlad – California (Swedish-Russian mixed line) and earlier Stockholm-Helsinki. [See p. 209–10. Brecht's subsequently published letters suggest that he hadn't got this entirely right.] US. Money raised when abroad by com[mittee] incl Dieterle, Homolka et al. *Hangmen Also Die* script. Three treatments sold. [Some confusion about these categories, probably mine.] Enough to buy a house (later sold at profit) and live modestly.

KKK for Luise Rainer.

'I gave up psychology a long while ago' (ich hab auf das Psychologische seit . . . verzichtet).

Wilder pinching idea of *J. Cäsar* [*Julius Caesar*], then writing offensive letter.

[In pencil, re *Lucullus*] P[ar]ty told Dessau (member) too formal[ist] – on gr[ound] statements of other composers. D. told B. B. said, well, it's nothing to do with me. I'm no party member, and I'm not going to withdraw my text. D. wanted [?him to]. B. referred to contract, said he would take it to the courts, and if nec[essar]y sue the C[entral] C[ommittee], the State or anyone else.

He had contract w[ith Ernst] Legal of Staatsoper.

Same occurred w. Kulturpolitik[?er]. All right: forbid it – I'll say nothing.

B. and Dessau to attend Ministerrat [Council of Ministers] Sat. 9 a.m. 3½hrs, w. Pieck, Grotewohl and all. G'wohl pointed out places where B. made changes. Upshot, go ahead. But if very bad notices, then w'draw. [Brecht's letters and the relevant notes show that this meeting was on 24 March 1951, i.e. a week after the trial performance.]

When asked [by me] why not pol[itical] plays, says, if I put in U[lbricht]'s policy, then that must be criticised. I don't write for U. as an actor, I write for him to be in the audience and learn s[ome]th[in]g.

[Scrappy pencil jottings. Brecht on his influences?] Chaplin Eis[enstein] and Pud[ovkin].

Shakes[peare] via Büchner Woz[zeck] – first perf. by Steinrück after '18/'19 rev[olutio]n. Made [Brecht] read Shakes.

C[om]p[are] *Baal* to Sh.

die 2 Mantelhälften. Chin[ese] play [of] that time.

fm '22 [surely can't be right] Ev[enin]g classes Marxist.

Fleischhacker – [he found he had] to describe cornering wheat Chic[ag]o.

F. J. Bonn, Berlin
Brentano, Munich   economists: he asked
Intro fm Berlin Bank pres to wheat broker fm Chico, Vienna. flew (2
   interpreters). [Broker says:] 'You get in – and then something tells
   you to get out' – I.e. he didn't understand.
So B.
43,000 G[old] M[arks] spent on a mittlere Marxistische Bildung
   [moderate education in Marxism].
pvt. lessons too
dieser scheussliche Stalinismus [this ghastly Stalinism] wasted 20
   years in development.
Shakespeare as thief.
Rostock dress rehearsal [of *The Good Person of Szechwan* in Besson's
   production] 40 masks bought.
DGO [*Threepenny Opera*] to earn money.
[*In pen*] Ustinov cd do Galileo.

(ii) Note ?1957

Bunge tells me B. read very little: he used to buy him books. He only
read serious modern stuff when someone recommended it; and few did.
Mainly he bought him Greek classics in good translations: Molière etc
too. Otherwise he read detective stories etc.

(iii) Conversations with Elisabeth Hauptmann and Helene Weigel, ? October 1963.

Elis. said (24.x.) that *Messingkauf* was a Begriff [concept] to B. like
['On a non-aristotelian dramaturgy'] – that he shoved things into that
category at various times.
   26.x. Re the mass of unpublished material: that B was not at all vain.
Another job came up; work was interrupted, might or might not be taken
up later. E[lisabeth] found the essays 'Weite und Vielfalt' and (which
other? from *Wort* time), and thought them most important to publish in
Versuche [series] in the '50s, because of bearing on current controversies.
B. had entirely forgotten them, but was glad to see them appear. [These
may have been the items in 'Die Truhe'].
   Re *Das Wort*. B. very anxious E. should write them something about
WPA etc. [i.e. the Federal Theatre Project] in America, and the various
left-wing artistic experiments. He said 'I can still get almost anything
into *Das Wort*, but I can't keep everything out.' I.e. he didn't entirely
agree with its line.

The notes 'On a dialectical dramaturgy' date from between 1930–33, about when B. was working on *The Mother*.

Seems to have been no reaction to his invitations to form a Diderot Soc. B. very keen on Diderot, and frequently recommended him to younger B[erliner] E[nsemble] members.

How much Wodehouse B. read in exile. Also [Stevenson's] *The Master of Ballantrae* was a favourite work.

Helli [Weigel] (26.x.) emphasising haphazard nature of arrangements in archive files, said she would often clear the table, and simply bundle up all the papers there, whatever they happened to be, tie them up and label them. She bought a number of grey folders before they left Scandinavia, and shoved the things in them.

The US consul in Helsinki was very disagreeable. At a late stage they went to him to see about their papers, and he looked through the dossier. 'Yes, you seem to have got everything. Except that es fehlt eine Sittenbestätigung' [a certificate of morals]. (From the Berlin Police, for Helli.) Impossibility of getting such a thing in wartime. So H. wrote off without much hope. And back it came almost at once from the Innenministerium, posted privately by some unknown official. She's always wondered who he was.

Elis. (24.x.) said how B. had written to her to prepare his trip to Hollywood. It was she who went round Lorre, Dieterle, Feuchtwanger etc. collecting money. Then a wire from Vladivostok announcing Grete Steffin's death. Then nothing.

She [Elisabeth] helped on *Duchess of Malfi*.

The reason why so little theoretical writing in US. The need to earn money, the lack of outlets for publication (a German and an Austrian émigré paper, both poor), the demands on time. Hollywood: the distances, and the hours spent discussing.

(iv) Meeting with Rosemarie Hill (undated)

[Rosemarie Hill was a friend and neighbour of Elisabeth Hauptmann, and helped her in the editing of Brecht's poems.]

Elis. made about 5 wills, still not proved. But was very firm about wanting her books and papers to go to DAK [the East German Academy, who now include the Brecht Archive]. Lately she had become much more concerned about her own share in B's work: annoyed, e.g., that it wasn't clear that she translated *Dom Juan* with Besson, also Pauken [*Trumpets and Drums*], & only showed to B. when complete: his changes were made mainly in course of (or as a result of) rehearsal. She would kick herself for not having insisted more on her contribution to HJ, A&R etc. [i.e. *Saint Joan of the Stockyards* and *The Exception and the Rule*], nor getting proper share of royalties. Frau H[ill] wd. tell her she *would* have it that way. That was all right while B. lived . . .

c: Some factors in translating Brecht, 1967

When I first went to New York along with Ralph Manheim to discuss setting up the Random House edition of the Collected Plays I was asked by Erika Munk to write something about translation for the second special Brecht issue of *TDR*. Why she didn't use it (or, so far as I recall, pay for it) I never knew. It was written at a moment when I was discussing translation a good deal, not least because Stefan Brecht, with whom I was staying, was very insistent that the Random House edition must use only American translations and the corresponding Methuen edition 'British' translations; this, he said, was because each theatre had its own modes of speech, and translations could not cross the Atlantic. I think he said it had also been his father's view.

I was already thinking about the poetry edition (to which this proviso did not apply, since no dialogue was involved), which is probably the real reason why I discussed the translation of poetry first. Reading the piece through I think I still agree with all that I said. As follows:

With the poems I think it's essential to preserve rhyme and metre, and would rate this higher than strict accuracy, so long as the general gist and flavour of the German is carried over into English. This is because Brecht was a masterly technician. His command of different verse forms needs to be communicated, particularly now that so few poets of any serious pretentions are attempting them.

Where poems are meant to be delivered or sung the English version must help this, or at least put no positive obstacles in the way. There must be none of those awkwardnesses that shout 'translation' at you, and if possible the quality of sound must be matched; i.e. it shouldn't be softened or given a wholly different rhythm.

Even in Brecht's unrhymed, rhythmically irregular verse the form is more important than some translators appear to think. As he himself explained, the caesuras determine the emphasis and direction of what he is saying – the 'gest', to use his technical term for it. This isn't something to be copied exactly, but the translator needs to follow the same principle, using the rhythmic breaks in such a way as to give weight to the words, images or ideas that Brecht wanted stressed.

I've put poetry first because it's also involved in the plays, and the verse is the weakest part of some translations. With the prose dialogue the chief problem is one of character: it's awfully easy to translate the dialogue correctly and fluently, yet in such a way as subtly to change the character of the person who is speaking it and defined by it. This can be very damaging to a play. Accordingly the way each of the play's figures speaks must convey the same characteristics as does the original German. It is a matter of rhythms, of sentence lengths and progressions, as well as (obviously) of the social implications of his choice of words.

It's a mistake, in my view, to try to 'improve' Brecht's dialogue by chopping up sentences, giving it extra punch or making it in any way more colourful. It's also dangerous to assimilate it too closely to the currently accepted language of the Anglo-American theatre. It has got to be delivered, yes, and an actor has got to speak it. But what seem like awkwardnesses and unfamiliarities may be awkward and unfamiliar to German actors too, yet very necessary to the characters and the individual linguistic climate of the play. A specific instance: *Mother Courage*, where the vitality of the artificial language that Brecht uses is the main dynamic force in an otherwise flat chronicle. The translator's task is then to devise an equivalent vitality in English. (Has anyone done this yet? Not as far as I know.)

I need hardly say that I'm even more against 'adaptation'. That is: I think cutting and changing is the director's business rather than the translator's, and that the translator should render the text as Brecht wrote it before any changes are made. This is particularly so if the text is to be printed. The reader must have what Brecht wrote, not what his translator thinks he ought to have written. Nor is there any excuse for additional stage directions to show how the translator visualises the play. We aren't interested in the translator's ideas but in Brecht's: if these are unclear or ambiguous it is for the reader, not the translator, to sort them out.

Then there are the prose essays and stories. There is one general problem here and one specific. General: the rendering of Brecht's prose style, which is very individual and to my mind very fine, direct, comic often. Rhythm again is important; certainly the pace of the writing shouldn't be altered by breaking sentences or trains of thought. As for the specific problem of Brecht's theoretical vocabulary I would like to think that the terms I used in *Brecht on Theatre* were fairly widely acceptable, but I just don't know. The one thing that's plain is that a tangle of competing equivalents would be fearfully confusing.

Finally there is the question of 'British' or American translations. Personally I don't in the least agree with the school of thought that holds American translations to be unsuitable (for performance and/or publication) in Britain and vice versa. These things have to be judged on their merits, and it's hard enough to find translations that meet the requirements I've outlined without having to complicate matters by a nationality test. Certainly our joint language is a tremendously varied one, but not to the point of mutual unintelligibility; the whole delight of it is that as it stretches – as the West Indians, the Nigerians, the Australians come along with their typewriters and make fresh dents and bulges in it – so does our comprehension. And anyway what about those West Indians, Nigerians, Australians: are they to have their Brecht in British English or American English? No, no, it's nonsense: all that's needed is for publisher or producer to change a word here and there, transmuting sidewalks to pavements and vice versa, wherever he thinks it would jar.

Brecht looks easy to translate because of the clarity of his writing; moreover the Anglo-Saxon element in his style brings him close to us. Yet good translations are rare. Why? I'm not sure, but I have seen a lot of the translations that have been made and it might be useful if I summarised the commonest faults. In no particular order they are:

1. Germanisms
2. Distortion of the characters
3. Impossible verse (specially songs)
4. Incongruous dialects, slang etc. (They *can* be congruous.)
5. Wrong speech rhythms
6. Failure to match Brecht's use of styles (E.g. his contrasting of heightened and ordinary speech.)
7. Tinkering with the tempo by breaking sentences up or stringing them together
8. (Result of 5, 6 and 7) Flatness
9. Improvements

I don't count ordinary inaccuracy, mistranslations etc., which are easily enough remedied in revision if only the basic style is right. The same goes for such English or American expressions as can't cross the Atlantic without embarrassment.

d: Brecht for the media, 1981–82

Early in 1981 my Brecht agenda for the rest of the year looked interesting but manageable. For the Eyre Methuen edition I had to complete the preparation of a volume of the short stories, which Antony Tatlow and Hugh Rorrison had translated; this would entail a visit to Berlin to gather material for the notes. Otherwise the main job would be the long-delayed rehearsal and recording of a first album of Brecht songs in English by the Australian singer Robyn Archer, who had arrived just before Christmas to spend a year in Europe. I had first worked with her in 1975 when she sang Jenny in Wal Cherry's Adelaide production of *The Threepenny Opera* with New Opera, South Australia (the enterprising nucleus of the present state opera company). Two years later we were both involved, with Dominic Muldowney as musical director, in a National Theatre programme called *To Those Born Later*, since when she had added to her Brecht repertoire on various occasions in both Australia and England under the guidance of Michael Morley and Muldowney respectively. The plan for a full-scale recording supported by the Australian Music Board had been in the air some time, and now it was settled that it would be made in England by EMI. Muldowney would conduct and accompany, and the band would be the excellent London Sinfonietta.

In the spring Archer and her manager Diana Manson went off to the European mainland on a trip that was to take in visits to the Berliner Ensemble and to Georg Eisler in Vienna as well as one of the Goethe-Institut language courses at Prien. I went on a short visit to Philadelphia to see the graduate acting students of Temple University perform my version of Lenz's *The Tutor* under Carl Weber's direction. While I was away my wife was quite unexpectedly telephoned by the English film director Alan Clarke to say that he had been asked to direct *Baal* for BBC television and would be interested to talk to me about the 1926 *Life Story of a Man Called Baal* of which I had given a brief account in the notes to the Manheim/Willett edition. What had drawn him to this shortened and somewhat deromanticised version of Brecht's first play, so it turned out, was the notion that it might have a more technological, mid-twenties, slightly *Neue Sachlichkeit* flavour in keeping with the austere toughness of some of his own productions. We talked in the office given him at the BBC Television Centre, where I gathered that he was intending to record the play in the biggest studio, making use of gauzes for the outdoor scenes and a split-screen technique for the inter-scene titles. I wasn't instantly clear what these ideas might mean, but

Clarke himself was refreshingly straightforward and free from bullshit,
and I decided that the best thing I could do would be to take what I'd
put in my notes and turn it into a full translation of the 1926 text. He
and the BBC producer and script editor (Louis Marks and Stuart
Griffiths) could then decide if it was suitable or not.

On going back to the German (in Dieter Schmidt's *Baal. Drei
Fassungen. Materialienband*, edition suhrkamp no. 170) I found of course
that the *Lebenslauf* version wasn't as technological as all that. So on
sending in the complete translation – which was a slightly inelegant
collage of extracts from the published notes and some handwritten pages
– I added a separate commentary, starting with a discussion of where and
when the *Life Story of a Man Called Baal* should be set. Thus, I wrote:

> I see it isn't the mid-twenties after all, since BB sets it very specifically
> between 1904 (at the start) and 1912 (Baal's death). And it is half urban, half
> countryside.
>
> If we stick to 'Baal the abnormality trying to come to terms with the
> twentieth century world' then this is ok, I think. It is a meeting between pre-
> 1914 Bavaria and the new technology . . .
>
> I'm for setting it visibly in Germany, and south Germany at that. But with
> 'Mr' and 'Mrs' rather than 'Herr' and 'Frau' . . .
>
> From halfway through the play the countryside dominates: woods, trees and
> those marvellous great German landscapes. And right through, from start to
> finish, a great variety of skies.

The Baal Hymn (or *Choral*), I then pointed out quite unoriginally, could
be used for the opening and closing titles and also to link the different
scenes:

> With it one should sometimes see Baal's face, but always at some point the
> sky. Skies of all sorts and colours: sunny, stormy, windy, starry, pre-dawn,
> sunset etc. Perhaps with the odd technological hint: telephone wires, an
> airship. Or a flight of birds, suddenly shot.

Unlike anyone else involved at that stage, I had seen the West German
TV version of 1969, which Volker Schlöndorff had filmed in natural
Bavarian settings, always with a hint of modern industrial life in the
background – cooling towers on the horizon, or a distant autobahn with
great articulated lorries trundling by. Though Wolfgang Gersch has
criticised this for 'de-historicising' Brecht and failing to show the
'asocial' nature of the social framework, I have never understood why the
Berliners so objected both to the film itself and to Fassbinder's powerful

performance in the title part. I thought we'd be lucky if we could do as well.

The 1926 text was instantly accepted as a basis, photocopied and retyped with some additional material. Clarke wanted to include the discarded episodes with two more women, first Ekart's red-haired girlfriend among the young hazel bushes (and the scene leading up to this), then the peasant girl whom Baal meets after Ekart's murder and who, alone among the five of them, is impervious to his charisma because she sees that he has grey hairs. Meanwhile I for my part wanted to bring back 'Death in the Woods' (*Poems and Songs from the Plays*, no. 4) as a chain of verbal imagery dragging across Baal's mind while Ekart observes him sleeping immediately before the murder scene. Together, too, we agreed to add the two *Landjäger* (rural policemen) who go over Baal's criminal (and other) record as they trudge uneasily after him in the last scene but one of the final version. All this was duplicated as the first draft script on 22 May. I then went through it making amendments and adding suggestions for the action, many of which Clarke took over into the stage directions of the second draft a week later; this then had to be amended and corrected once more. Such a process was highly instructive for anyone who, like me, now and again has to compare different scripts and stages of a play in order to try and reconstruct a dramatist's thoughts. For not only is one apt to overlook the most obvious infelicities and inconsistencies, but absurd mistakes keep insinuating themselves into the work of the expert copyists, sometimes at quite a late stage. Thus 'a vast waitress in costume' in one of my stage directions became 'vast waiters in costumes'; 'the man in question is about to clear out' became 'the man in question is to clear out'; while Baal's historicising statement in the first scene was half turned into a stage direction, to wit: '*Baal*: In the year 1904. *Joseph Mech offers Baal a light for his cigar.*' In fact almost anything may happen at any stage, and the writer has to keep very wide awake if ineradicable misunderstandings are not to arise.

From the second draft we hammered out what was in effect the final version of our text. The two extra women, having added little to the story, were now dropped again, though we kept the policemen since their summary of Baal's career just before his death seemed useful. 'Death in the Woods' too was included after Ekart's monologue over the sleeping Baal (scene 9 of the 1926 version). Otherwise the structure was almost entirely that of the *Lebenslauf des Mannes Baal* which Brecht and Homolka had directed for the Junge Bühne – the only version of the play ever to have been directed by Brecht himself. Its great advantage from a television point of view was that it was both shorter and clearer than Brecht's 'definitive' (but unperformed) version of 1953 which Manheim and I had had to use for our edition. Its only lapse in clarity – the failure to spell out Johanna's suicide before the oblique allusion in the 'Drowned Girl' song – could be remedied by a shot of her walking by the river to the accompaniment of some chords from the song or maybe a glimpse of Millais's *Ophelia*. To set against that it had a number of passages which we greatly liked: the Ichthyosaurus monologue, Baal's comments on our planet, his concerns with 'the devising of an evil deed', his ignorance of (and indifference to) Sophie's pregnancy, his dialogue with Ekart about the vanishing countryside and Ekart's subsequent remarks about the human potentialities implied in the tall buildings of Manhattan – these and others like them would, we thought, more than make up for the loss of some of the stranger sub-episodes in the pre-Berlin versions, such as the selling of the bulls and the theft of Teddy's schnapps. For we thought we saw a well-defined line running through the *Lebenslauf* which the prodigal inventions of the earlier texts would have confused rather than strengthened.

The pattern as I set it out in some notes at the end of May was one of steady decline from the social and domestic high point represented by the opening scene. This, I wrote:

> shows the bourgeois world of early Wilhelmine Germany, which (like the Federal Republic after 1948) was outstripping England economically and seemed headed for the leadership of a brave new technologically advanced Europe. What mattered was industry, inventiveness, enterprise; but along with these things went good design – so that people like Mech were far more design-conscious than their English or French opposite numbers – and also, by tradition, increased patronage for the arts. Paintings and poetry became a visible justification of the money-making process, and parasites like Piller acted as a useful means of access to them. This still holds good (and not only in Germany), so that the scene offers a chance to underline certain incompatibilities between moneyed good taste and real creativeness. It also sets things up for the nemesis that comes after the second pub scene.

The 'small swinish café' scene was a climax: noisy, dirty-minded and jovial-sadistic in the worst Bavarian tradition, with the drunk customers ready to lynch the Soubrette when she sings the Marseillaise (all wrong, starting 'Allons, enfants de la batterie'). Either side of this, and eight years apart in time, the two scenes in the pub were lesser peaks, with the crowd in the second all raring to tear Baal limb from limb only a few moments after his singing. I was thinking, I'm afraid, of Munich 'die

Hauptstadt der Bewegung' a decade or two later, and accordingly wanted the woodcutters in the last scene to be

akin to the rustic element of the crowd in the pub and swinish café scenes. Only now they are relaxed, mocking, indifferent rather than actively brutal. They are the types whom the Nazis put forward as models of rural blood-and-soil Nordic authenticity, and who at the same time happen to be very much the pious Christian peasantry approved by many decent, high-principled and normally tolerant traditionalists.

Before the 'swinish café' scene the element of contrast lies in Baal's three episodes in the garage: those with Johannes, with Johanna and with Sophie (the uprooted descendant of the actress in the 1918 version). Afterwards it comes with the break out into the countryside and 'a succession of more even and reflective (if windblown and morally shabby) episodes follows'.

These should be suffused with one kind or another of south German rural beauty, so that all the time the (at most) three figures are secondary to the vastness of the landscape and the elements. In these episodes – which cover three years at least – Baal and Ekart must get browner and more weatherbeaten, their clothes tattier but also more practical . . . They are never in a hurry, though the swift recitation of the 'Death in the Woods' poem as Baal lies motionless shows how quickly time is really passing and how fast the images flicker across Baal's apparently inert mind.

Interspersed throughout the play were the songs. Using Brecht's own tunes wherever I could, I had radically reworked the words for singability from the earlier translations which I had (unattributedly) grafted on to Peter Tegel's and William Smith's versions of the dialogue in our edition. Such was the case with the 'Ballad of the Adventurers' (in the second café scene), 'The Drowned Girl' (for which we would use Weill's beautiful setting) and the 'Baal Hymn' (where we envisaged using three verses for the opening titles, one or possibly two at the end, and the rest individually between the scenes). For the 'ballad' sung by Baal in the first café scene, where the standard version has 'Orge's Song', I suggested we should use 'Remembering Marie A.', which Oskar Homolka had once told me was sung in the 1926 production, along with its sentimental fin-de-siècle tune. For the dirty song in the swinish café, where the 1926 text specifies nothing and the definitive version is useless, we went back to the 1918 version's 'If a woman's hips are ample' which had been translated by me for the notes in our edition and sung in the Papp/Foreman New York production of *The Threepenny Opera*.

Even this was hardly shocking enough by modern standards to justify
the ensuing hullaballoo, so I later added the two obscene epigrams which
Ekkehard Schall performs in his one-man shows (and which are now
published in *Gedichte aus dem Nachlass*, pp. 33 and 46). Finally we felt
that Savettka, the soubrette in the swinish café scene, should be seen and
heard doing her act, so I gave her three verses of 'Song of the ruined
innocent folding linen' in Lesley Lendrum's translation and proposed
that she also do a dramatic dance to that epitome of 'Immortal Art',
according to *Mahagonny*, the nineteenth-century piano piece called 'The
Maiden's Prayer'.

By this point, which was reached in early June, a number of important
steps had been taken towards the actual production. To start with,
Clarke and the BBC's designer Tony Abbott had worked out the basic
settings and use of studio space. Up against Studio 1's four walls would
be four naturalistic sets showing early twentieth-century German
interiors: Mech's nouveau-riche apartment, the doctor's garage with
Baal's squalid quarters leading off it, the pub of scenes 3 and 10 in the
1926 text (suitably refurbished in the intervening eight years), and finally
the swinish café with its small stage and dressing-room and toilet at the
back (subsequently replaced by the woodcutters' hut). There would be
four cameras for each scene, but not much camera movement, so that the
prevailing view would be of the set seen square-on right across the whole
length or width of the studio. Gauzes would be used to cover these sets
for all the exterior shots, which would generally show the actors – Baal
and Ekart, and at first Sophie, then in the penultimate scene the two
country policemen again and again – walking the whole length of the
studio towards the camera. Right from the start, it seems, there had been
no question of filming in South Germany, not even to get views and
skies for projection. The only chance then to show the sky at all would
be in the split-screen interludes when the verses of the Hymn would be
sung and the next scene title shown ('Baal on the run. 10° East of
Greenwich' and so on, as in Brecht's text). I argued as strongly as I could
that we should in that case show details of paintings, preferably by Hans
Thoma, who would have been most apt on various counts, or at a pinch
some of Constable's sky studies. But this would have meant additional
work and expense and it was felt that the BBC graphics department
could run up adequate substitutes.

Clarke and Louis Marks the producer were already in touch with
various actors and their agents; erudite pieces of equipment like a
nickelodeon for the pub, a mechanical organ for Mech's drawing room
and an early motorcycle on which Baal was originally to make his

entrance were all being hired. Catalogues of these specialist hire firms lay around Clarke's office along with fascinating but potentially misleading casting directories. For the more frightful-looking Bavarians – Barbarians, one of our typing errors had called them – he had turned to an agency named Ugly, which sets out to provide peculiar-looking people; but too often the peculiarity was merely one of height or age and the photos provided were disappointing. There remained the problem of Baal himself, the central figure who has to carry the whole improbable and ultimately quite juvenile play on his shoulders. Clarke clearly felt strongly inclined towards Steven Berkoff, a powerful if slimly built East End London actor with an obsessive dislike of the peculiar English class system – something that I felt might be a distraction in Brecht's play. I suggested the great Australian comic Barry Humphries, who can produce a certain chilling demonic quality even in his classic female impersonations and would make a convincing genius, though one rather older than envisaged by Brecht. This intrigued Marks, who evidently hadn't thought of looking outside the straight theatre and cinema, and he jumped at my next suggestion, which was David Bowie. Bowie I knew of course as a charismatic singer, but he had just been acting in New York as the Elephant Man (which suggested that he was seeking to exend his range even to the point of looking hideous), and I inferred more or less by guesswork that he might be interested in pre-1933 Germany and even in Brecht. As it turned out this was indeed so. Marks and Clarke looked at whatever they could find of Bowie on film or in the BBC's archives, approached his agents and in mid-July arranged to spend a day with him in Switzerland to discuss details. When they came back we had our Baal.

Meantime I was spending four days closeted in the EMI Abbey Road studios, where Robyn Archer was now recording her album; a fifty-minute selection of Brecht songs of all kinds and periods, all of them in English and for the most part translated by me.[1] She had returned from her travels not long before in excellent heart and voice, and the clarity of her words was stunning. We only had the orchestra for two of those days however, so that it was a quite remarkable achievement on the part of Muldowney (who is normally thought of as a composer rather than a conductor) not only to fit in the rehearsal of some ten songs largely unfamiliar to the players, but to get performances of such vitality. There were a number of Eisler's songs to piano accompaniment, which Muldowney played on EMI's very beautiful best Steinway, while the remainder were for small combinations, notably involving our saxophonist friend John Harle who acted as a valuable adviser and helper throughout the whole recording. At the end of each session we had a replay with Diana Manson and John Mordler, the record's producer, at which it was quickly and amiably decided what needed re-recording and how the final version of each song should best be put together. It was up to Mordler and his colleagues to complete the editing before we got down to the difficult problem of the exact composition and running order of the two 33 rpm sides, which would in due course be pressed in Australia. Muldowney then was more or less free, so far as his National Theatre job allowed, and I persuaded Marks and Clarke to engage him as our musical director for *Baal*. This would entail a good deal of work with Bowie – who was to play the banjo, having never previously done anything of the sort – setting the 'Ruined Innocent' song for Savettka, finding music for Emilie's mechanical organ performance and for background noise in the pub scenes, and equipping the swinish café scenes with a small but typical Bavarian band. We called the latter 'Lohengrin und seine Lederhosen' and painted the title in gothic letters on their drum, though I am not sure how many of the eventual audience were able to read it.

A much thicker script now came off the duplicators, headed impressively 'THE SENDING OF THIS SCRIPT DOES NOT CONSTITUTE AN OFFER OF A CONTRACT FOR ANY PART IN IT'. Tacitly (and I think now wrongly) the 'Life Story' title had been dropped in favour of the single word *Baal*. This was the Rehearsal Script, and on 13 July we began working on it with the first members of the cast at the BBC's rehearsal rooms in North Acton, an area of West London which is mainly given over to industrial buildings. The actors, thank goodness, saw nothing all that alarming in the thought of performing Brecht, nor was there any of that discussion of alienation or other special techniques which can bedevil over-ambitious productions. Clarke was friendly and matter-of-fact, Bowie serious and unassuming. At the opening session I tried to suggest that the key to this play, even more than to others by Brecht, lay in his poetry, and persuaded Marks to give copies of the paperback *Poems 1913–1956* to any of the actors who were interested. There were to be four weeks of rehearsal altogether before moving into Studio 1 on 9 August, i.e. around the middle of the school holidays. We also learned, more or less indirectly, that Bowie's involvement was not to be made publicly known until he and the BBC wished it. Even the title of the play was not to be put up on the board in the entrance hall (which simply announced us as 'Classic Play'); no outsiders were to be allowed in; what's more, one of Bowie's two aides was always on guard inside the rehearsal room door. At the same time morale seemed high all through, and this was due surely to Bowie's professionalism and to Clarke's

equable firmness. Muldowney, who had attended many more temperamental opening rehearsals at the National Theatre, was slightly amazed.

How far the other actors were worried by Bowie's rather unusual
approach to the job I never knew, though I must have attended about
half the rehearsals and could talk easily enough to them except where
their performances were concerned (which I could discuss only with
Clarke). The rest of us were pretty impressed. Right from the start he
knew virtually the whole part, except for 'Death in the Woods' which he
never securely mastered, so that in the end this poem had to be cut. He
understood the play and had thought about it, and it was my impression
that he knew more about Germany as a whole and Brecht's ambience in
particular than anyone except possibly Marks and myself. As a collector
of Expressionist graphics, he at once grasped the relevance of Masereel's
intensively poetic *Mein Stundenbuch*[1] whose final pages I had thought
might help shape Baal's end: the skull-headed protagonist strolling
nonchalantly through the stars and planets. He was also marvellously
equipped for the songs, imposing the sense and rhythms of the words on
Brecht's recitative-like tunes, which he rightly compared to plainchant.
But where he was so unlike an actor was in his inability to build up a
performance from the most tentative beginnings, adding a little at each
rehearsal till it starts to take shape. With him each rehearsal was like a
performance, often a very interesting one but not necessarily a direct
development from what he had done the time before. His speech was
sometimes less clear than his singing voice, and once background noise
was added it wasn't always easy to follow. But at any rehearsal whatever
he said had meaning – the meaning of the part and of the play: nothing
he said was routine. I remember in particular one discussion about Baal's
attitude to the Mechs and their guests in the opening scene: he was
trying to score off them and show his contempt for them, and was this a
class attitude or what? I argued that it was trivialising the poet to make
him *mind* so much about people: he would be secure enough in his own
genius to remain detached from them. 'Detached?' said Bowie. 'Don't
tell me to be detached, or I'll be so detached you won't know I'm there.'

Another image: Bowie on the last day of recording in Studio 1. This
was to be devoted to the recording of the Baal Hymn, the 'Drowned
Girl' and 'Death in the Woods' and the accompanying split-screen
images with no one on the floor but Bowie, Muldowney, a guitarist and
the cameramen and managers. It was 11 a.m. on a Thursday. Bowie was
right at the end of nearly five weeks of highly concentrated and
disciplined work during which he had had to carry a pretty difficult play
on his shoulders. He began singing the first three verses of the Hymn,

which would be crucial for the start of the play and for that matter for his own commitment to it, when suddenly there was a tremendous banging through the studio wall. Everything stopped while someone was sent round to Studio 2 to tell them to be quiet. Studio 2 turned out to be locked. Telephoning produced no answer. Clearly this was some quite different part of the BBC machine at work, so Marks got on to some superior administration and the noise suddenly stopped. Bowie began singing again, but the noise restarted. Marks again telephoned up through the hierarchy. Noise stopped. Bowie sang a few lines. Noise began again, this time from somewhere up in the roof. Marks back to the telephone. Clarke all the time amazingly unruffled, as indeed he was throughout the whole five weeks; I take my hat off to him. Then silence, Bowie once more started to sing. Noise. Telephone. And so on – I forget how many times. Finally Bowie strode out into the centre of the studio floor saying 'I know how to stop it'. He then put his hands to his mouth, looked up at the roof and shouted 'Lunch!'. It didn't work, I fear, but as a one-man demonstration of how to keep one's cool it really wasn't bad.

This whole process of rehearsal and recording was otherwise very smoothly managed, and my own role became increasingly that of a privileged onlooker. The actors didn't seem to have much trouble with their dialogue, not even with Baal's long and deliberately stilted sentences to Emilie just before he sings 'The Ballad of the Adventurers', which were easily and intelligently managed by Bowie. Now and again an actress would mildly hanker after the longer and more familiar version of the play, but in the event very little had to be reworked, or even argued over. Johanna's 'Leibchen' in her seduction scene was a bit of a problem; I had inexpertly translated it first as 'vest', then 'tummy-band' (a childhood memory), then after consultation 'liberty bodice'. Nobody was satisfied, so we settled for 'corset', which at least didn't jar on the ear and looked interesting when Tracy Childs as Johanna got out of her bed to fetch it. Sophie too had difficulties in her scene on the road, when she tells Baal 'Es ist sicherlich ein schöner Abend, der dir gefällt. Aber es wird dir nicht gefallen, dass du einmal ohne einem Menschen verrecken sollst'. I had made this 'I know it's a beautiful evening and you like it. But you won't like it one day . . .' etc. Zoë Wanamaker found this artificial verbal transition rather awkward, but in the end she delivered it as written and I don't think it jarred more than Brecht meant it to. Another passage which gave me trouble myself was the whole story arising out of Baal's remark in the second pub scene that he felt 'noch immer gesund' – the story about the man who went off into the woods. I tried various expressions for this: 'perfectly well', 'perfectly all right', then (in the final Camera Script – a massive document on multi-coloured paper with many technical details and the scenes rearranged in order of shooting –) 'perfectly healthy'. This last didn't work – whether for Bowie or for Jonathan Kent as Ekart I don't remember – so we changed it back to 'perfectly all right'. Where I did feel I had slipped up was in not attending the first rehearsal of the final scene with the woodcutters, where one or two minor changes had crept in during my absence and became too deeply engrained to be corrected. These were in the direction of 'normalising' the men's language and were in my view a mistake, though I don't suppose that anybody else noticed them.

Most of the time, however, I was able to watch fascinatedly as the various elements of the show began to come together. Numbers of additional extras (or 'Supporting Artists' as the script termed them) would appear to thicken up the crowd in pub and swinish café which Clarke had rehearsed first with the leading actors only, then with a select group of ringleaders from the crowd and finally with the whole mob. Polly James as the Soubrette sang the song which Muldowney had composed for her, finishing on a kind of coloratura flourish that had the ringleaders blocking their ears and groaning, then went on to interpret 'The Maiden's Prayer' in a solemnly Isadora-like dance involving a rather stiff dummy baby. I had to write a few words with which Mjurk could introduce this tear-jerking number, also a complete verse of the Marseillaise for her to sing in the mangled French suggested by Brecht ('Allons, enfants de la batterie' etc.); these were not really to be heard. After the initial rehearsals the whole swinish café scene was taken apart, so that eventually it was shot twice over: once to show whatever was going on onstage and among the clientèle, then again so as to concentrate on events backstage – each time with the noises from the other part of the set ensuring synchronisation. Here and in the country walking scenes it was a matter of recording the raw material for subsequent editing; likewise the shots for the split-screen interludes left a variety of options open. This 'video fx', as the script cryptically termed it, was in the hands of a technician with a special gadget which could record on one part of the screen in such a way as to combine with other pictures or graphics on the rest of it. With these exceptions, however, it was possible to get a fairly good idea of the eventual result from watching the recording in Studio 1's central room, since Clarke had specified the camera angles to be used and any unforeseen changes could be carried out then and there. Most of us, I think, were enthusiastic about what we saw, though some of the more hardened BBC technicians preferred to spend their time in the neighbouring cabin where one screen was given up to cricket.

For the moment that was that, and we went off on our various occasions. For me this meant (among other, sadder things) thinking about the final composition of Robyn Archer's album, whose tapes had now been very skilfully edited by John Mordler to make what was clearly going to emerge as a most impressive performance. Australian EMI were insistent that the selection should open with the 'Alabama Song', on the grounds that this would already be familiar to the customers from a forthcoming Australian Opera production of *Mahagonny*. There were also commercial reasons for not starting with the voice and piano songs: the Sinfonietta's presence must, as it were, be felt from the outset. So we hammered out an order giving roughly 25 minutes on each side, and in due course the edited tape went off to Australia, leaving it still unsettled whether the record was going to be issued anywhere else. There were at this time a number of contractual loose ends, not least because EMI wanted Muldowney to commit himself to an undertaking not to make Brecht recordings for anyone else. Bowie however (who records for RCA, not EMI) was keen to make an EP (or 45 rpm) record of the Baal songs, partly, I think, because he genuinely loved them and sang them so well and partly to stop his fans taping them from their TV sets. And he had asked Muldowney to work with him on this. Accordingly there was a recording session in West Berlin under the supervision of Bowie's highly gifted record producer, Tony Visconti, where some fifteen musicians (as against the nineteen used by the Sinfonietta) were conducted by Muldowney in new arrangements of the five songs. I greatly welcomed this, since only 'The Drowned Girl' would overlap with Archer's album and otherwise the two recordings would complement one another; and shortly drove off to the Brecht Archive to complete my work on the short stories. While there I was taken to a café in the Dimitroffstrasse (of all inappropriate names) which convinced me that our café customers and woodcutters in *Baal* had not been nearly nasty enough. As I wrote to Marks, I had been told that this was an old Nazi *Lokal* from which (before 1933) brawls had been mounted against the SPD across the way and the *Roter Frontkämpfer-Bund* further down the street. On certain evenings, it was said, the old believers gathered there and the band played the old songs. Sure enough they were there that night, along with a crowd of younger followers, and we were turned away with no pretence of amiability – something that has never happened to me before. Not so inappropriately this time, the place was called 'Hackepeter' or 'Mincemeat'.

In September the publicity and public relations machine started rolling. 'The new Bowie – warts and all', said the headline to a centrepage spread in the *Daily Express*; 'Pop goes Bowie's image', said the *Daily Mail*. 'ROCK star David Bowie', began the story in Rupert Murdoch's *The Sun*, 'gets a grubby new look for his TV acting debut . . . as a hell-raising singer, poet and womaniser.' And the *Daily Mirror*, clearly working from the same PR handout, 'He plays a singing poet with a huge appetite for sex and wine called Baal by German' (*sic*: at this point words evidently failed). The BBC's competition with commercial television is thus a two-edged process: on the one hand it has made that old body a good deal more enterprising, on the other it has reduced it to playing the personality game. So eventually the date for the showing of *Baal* was decided by the availability of the front cover of the corporation's programme magazine *Radio Times*, which was to bear an excellent colour photograph of an unshaven, gap-toothed Bowie caressing the beautiful art-deco banjo which an admirer had perceptively given him; this also appears on the sleeve of his record. The original idea was that the play would be shown during the first available week in January 1982, but the editing took longer than expected, and the rival demands on the relevant BBC facilities – another hierarchical limitation – meant in the end that the date would have to be postponed to 2 March, some six months after the actual recording. I was asked along to see the first consecutive edit, which I found effective and quick-moving: this normally rambling play actually took only five minutes over the hour, though I was unexpectedly worried by the dingy uniformity of the colour. The trouble with such massive and highly professional organisations is that they tend to have a routine answer for everything, so that our early twentieth-century *Baal*, from the look of it, could equally well have been Gorky's *The Lower Depths*. Next the remaining sound effects were added, including the mechanical organ, the fragment of Ekart's fugue and the music in the pub. Finally there was a kind of trade show for critics and others in a projection theatre in Wardour Street. Here again I came and answered questions and thought, I must say, that the play seemed quite good.

Yet sitting a week later and watching the actual transmission like any other viewer I was disappointed. Partly this may have been because I knew there was an important new play on the commercial channel – John Mortimer's play about his father, acted by Laurence Olivier, which had been cunningly timed to start half an hour earlier than ours. Partly it was the titling of the play *David Bowie in Baal*, which I think was a bad mistake by the BBC whether or not it was their idea: it got the priorities wrong from the start. Partly it could have been the fact that neither play nor production stood up to repeated viewing, and my appreciation of it was by then wearing a bit thin. But there was also another factor which I have noticed before in other contexts, and this was the curious contagion which occurs as soon as one becomes part of an audience, even if there is no communication whatever between its individual members. Willy-nilly some kind of *Verfremdung* sets in, and one suddenly sees the work through other eyes. As a result I went to bed that night none too cheerfully, despite one or two approving telephone calls, and was not surprised by the very mixed verdicts which I read or heard over the next few days. Some, like the BBC's own team of critics, were truly enthusiastic about Bowie's performance, and there were reviews of his songs which welcomed them as something new and strong. Generally, however, the TV critics devoted themselves to Mortimer's play instead, and there was a certain tendency to dismiss *Baal* as scarcely justifying its production. Discussing it with a group of 'A'-level drama students not long after, I found that they too felt the lack of a 'story' and were baffled by the protagonist's apparent freedom from any kind of emotion. Right up to the end, said one girl, he 'showed little vulnerability – which he should have had'.

   In the subsequent calculation of audience figures, so Marks told me, we were reckoned to have had $3\frac{1}{2}$ million viewers; the Mortimer play had done better. All the same it would have taken about sixteen years of full houses at Brecht's Theater am Schiffbauerdamm six nights a week to achieve even this total, and a lot of people must have seen *Baal* who would not normally think of looking at a play by Brecht. This fact has to be set against all my gloomier afterthoughts, which were concerned in particular with the hybrid style of our production. Clarke, I felt, had originally envisaged something much starker and simpler, and this would perhaps have appealed better to the critics, who doubtless expected something recognisably 'Brechtian', reflecting the *Neue Sachlichkeit* of the mid-twenties Berlin or even the angularities and exaggerations of *Dr Caligari*. However, I had helped influence the naturalistic setting of the main scenes, while all the exteriors had been shot in the non-naturalistic, recognisably theatrical mode of the initial conception. My thinking here had been that TV audiences are used to naturalism, and that by placing the events firmly in pre-1914 Bavaria we could explain Baal's urge to break out of that society, while at the same time showing the latent nastiness of the peasants and pub habitués who would be hunting down Communists and Jews two or three decades later. As it turned out we failed to do this for various reasons; so maybe the whole approach had been wrong. This didn't apply to the casting of Bowie, whose performance was always interesting and sometimes inspired, nor (with the exception of the failure to convey Johanna's death) to the 'alienating' division of the episodes by the split-screen presentation of titles and the singing of verses of the Hymn which seemed to achieve Brecht's intended effects without affectation. The square-on, longshot emphasis in the shooting also worked, giving the audience a slightly formal, remote view of the naturalistic scenes, though it was a pity that the predominantly brownish colours made the effect quite so old-masterly. But despite the tightness of the editing we never achieved anything like the edge and power that the play needs if its immaturity is not to jar.

The most interesting of the press reactions, to my mind, came in an article in the *New Musical Express* (27 March 1982) where a contributor by the evocative name of Biba Kopf (Chris Bohn) wrote about the relevance of Brecht as playwright and song writer to the avant-garde pop music world served by the magazine. The writer's thesis, already outlined in a more general article several months earlier, was that the allegiance of that world had been shifting from the Nazi and SS nostalgias evident in the work of certain pop groups to the more forward-looking Weimar culture symbolised by the Bauhaus (now the title of one British group) and even the *AIZ*, the Communist illustrated weekly (whose logo is used by another). Bowie's EP record had made the charts – it then stood at number 26 in the United Kingdom – even though, as the article puts it with eighty per cent accuracy, 'Baal has no Kurt Weill tune to disguise its vibrant dirtiness or whiff of Weimar decadence to perfume its filthy smells'.

> Bowie might be responsible for introducing Baal into your home, but having done so he leaves him standing there alone in all his threatening nakedness.

Certainly for me the most successful aspect of the whole operation was this short record, which had been exceptionally well presented by RCA and showed Bowie as one of the most gripping Brecht singers of all time, sounding even more committed to the material than in the play, and helped now by Muldowney's very clever and compelling arrangements. The Baal Hymn in particular comes brilliantly together as a long ballad given shape and variety by occasional stanzas in an Eislerish marching rhythm with semitone shifts of key. Perhaps the 'Drowned Girl', with its oddly staccato delivery, comes over less well than in the play (and, I'd say, less well than on Archer's record) but there is at least one unforgettable moment in the 'Ballad of the Adventurers' such as no other singer could have given us, and after the BBC's over-selling of Bowie it was cheering to find that the pop magazine had got the order right. For the familiar quizzical face of Brecht looks out at us across three columns of the *NME* from Gerda Goedhart's old photograph, towering over the smaller faces of Bowie, Bobby Darin and Jim Morrison of The Doors, the three singers who had got works by Brecht into the charts. Of all his possible candidates for this honourable and commercially useful position *Baal*, as Kopf rightly says, 'is his unlikeliest and therefore the one he'd probably love best'.

If I'm pleased about this I'm even more so by the Archer album which, unlike our BBC production, stands up to repeated replaying. What is so special here, aside from the quality of performance, is first of all the range of material covered – from the very early 'Ballad of the Pirates', through familiar and unfamiliar settings by Weill, 1930s songs by Eisler, and Dessau's very tricky 'Ballad of the Girl and the Soldier', right up to Eisler's Hollywood and post-Hollywood songs. Not only has no other singer, to my knowledge, attempted such a catholic selection even in German, but the whole thing makes up a Brecht anthology of exceptional richness which is bound together by what can only be identified as the poet's genius. This will, I hope, emerge all the more clearly because, secondly, the meaning of his texts (and therefore of the songs themselves) comes across intelligibly to the non-German listener, something that is largely due to the singer's commitment and ability to make each word and each phrase comprehensible. Archer has of course been involved with this material – and for that matter with Muldowney for the music and myself for the English words – a great deal longer than Bowie, but she too owes her ability to perform it to her experience as a popular entertainer (starting at the age of six in the family pub in Adelaide, and working up via football club dinners and young businessmen's outings) and also to her initial lack of conventional voice training. One only has to listen to Teresa Stratos's beautiful but quite unintelligible singing of the Kurt Weill songs to realise what an advantage this supposed handicap can be. Trained singers, as Muldowney told an audience at the National Theatre in the course of our work, only sing the vowels: consonants are somehow regarded as unmusical. At worst this makes it impossible for the listener even to identify the language used, let alone to pick out what is being said. And this is ultimately due to the traditional concept of the composer's role. As Brecht so perceptively suggested, the words are usually seen as a disposable inspiration to the composer, who transfers their emotional meaning to the music, using the vowels as sound, and then throws the empty consonantal husks away. If anything still needs to be communicated it can be done in that lowest form of musico-literary life, the programme note.

At the end of a year spent thus dabbling in the media I remained fascinated (and of course hopeful about the financial rewards, though without any very solid reason). What still seems very clear to me is that the songs are the most immediately convincing way into Brecht, and not only into his other writings and ideas but into the whole future relationship between music and words. Accordingly Muldowney and I hoped to plan some kind of practical inquiry which would suggest some of the new possibilities implicit in what we had learned, and help perhaps to extend the horizon of the popular entertainer and his or her audience even further. Already this has begun to encompass some of the more interesting experimental video work – an important area – nor can anybody now believe that easily accessible words and music must always be banal, because Brecht has shown otherwise. Whether a comparable post-mortem on the televising of *Baal* would be as potentially constructive I don't know, for what is at issue there is the manner of working in large, well-greased and smoothly functioning machines, where the crucial decisions may have been taken in advance and much can hinge on apparently non-artistic factors such as budgeting and publicity. Much then has to be left to people with clearly defined jobs where unsolicited advice is not welcomed; when everyone is treated as a specialist a system of 'divide and rule' grows up almost unthinkingly. Does this mean that the lesson in such cases is that one should steer clear of the machine altogether unless one is prepared to stick within the limits of one's own immediate task? Brecht, I'm sure, wouldn't have said so, though his own experience was of course with less tightly and efficiently organised, unionised and compartmentalised apparatuses. But he never got very far in Hollywood, did he?, and all his most telling critiques were of the kind of apparatus he knew in Berlin. What we need to know more about in this context is the true history – administrative and financial as well as artistic – of those occasional original masterpieces which despite everything are still to be seen on TV. The problem still is how to present Brecht to the viewers so convincingly – not that he is seen as a television playwright, which he wasn't – but that his basic socio-artistic approach can be absorbed.

Notes

p. viii   1. John Fuegi, *The Life and Lies of Bertolt Brecht*, HarperCollins, London, 1994.

p. 12   1. See note above.

p. 18   1. *Collected Plays 2i: Man equals Man*, p. 117.

p. 19   1. These influences are more fully analysed in Patty Lee Parmalee's *Brecht's America*, Miami/Ohio State University Press, 1980.

p. 20   1. *GW* 15, p. 119.

        2. *GW* 10, pp. 1051–2.

p. 21   1. *Journals*, 28 Nov. 1944.

p. 22   1. Letter 333, Svendborg, end of July 1937.

        2. *GW* 18, pp. 34–5.

        3. *GW* 19, p. 451.

p. 23   1. Letter 287, to Lee Strasberg, New York, 27 Jan. 1936.

        2. See the full account in Lee Baxandall's article 'Brecht in America', 1935, in *TDR*, vol. 12, no. 1 (T37), New York, Fall 1967.

p. 24   1. Constant Lambert, *Music Ho!*, Faber, London, second edition 1937, pp. 159–160.

        2. Letter 334, Svendborg, August 1937.

p. 25   1. Letter 296, c. July 1936.

        2. See James K. Lyon, *Brecht's American Cicerone*, Bouvier, Bonn, 1978, for an account of Brecht's relations with Reyher and their correspondence.

p. 26   1. *Journals*, 5 March 1939.

        2. *Journals*, 25 July 1945.

p. 27   1. *Journals*, 8 Jan. 1941.

        2. *Journals*, 19 Aug. 1940.

p. 28   1. *Journals*, 16 Jan. 1942.

p. 29   1. *Journals*, 17 Nov. 1944.

p. 30   1. *Collected Plays 5i: Life of Galileo*, p. 165.

p. 31   1. Letter 544, from Santa Monica [August–October 1947].

        2. *Journals*, 5 Sept. 1944.

p. 32   1. *Poems*, p. 367.

        2. *Poems*, p. 384.

        3. *Poems*, p. 384.

        4. *Journals*, Oct. 1943.

        5. BBA 192/182–4.

p. 34 1. *Poems*, pp. 472–7.

p. 35 1. In *Germanisch-Romanische Monatsschrift*, Neue Folge, X, pp. 451 ff.

        2. *Poems*, pp. 57–8.

p. 36 1. *Poems*, p. 348.

p. 37 1. Michael Morley, 'The Light that Shineth More and More' in *Modern Language Notes*, 88, April 1973.

        2. James K. Lyon, *Bertolt Brecht and Rudyard Kipling*, Mouton, The Hague, 1975.

p. 41 1. Reprinted in *Abaft the Funnel*, B. W. Dodge & Co., New York, 1909, p. 262.

p. 45 1. *Poems*, p. 13.

p. 47 1. *Poems*, p. 233.

p. 48 1. *Poems*, p. 447.

        2. *Poems*, p. 423.

p. 49 1. Alas, the German text of James Lyon's book mistranslates this word (which it cites from me) as '*snob*'.

p. 53 1. Letter from Auden to me, 2 March [1957].

p. 54 1. Letter from Auden to me, 18 Aug. [1958].

        2. Ditto.

        3. Ditto.

        4. *A Certain World*, Faber, London, 1971, p. 371.

        5. No. 1, 1966, pp. 163–172.

p. 55 1. See Michael J. Sidnell, *Dances of Death*, Faber, London, 1984.

p. 56 1. Letter from Rupert Doone to John Johnson, 18 December 1934, communicated by Robert Medley, 6 May 1983.

        2. See letters 229 to Helene Weigel, 13 October 1934, and 235 to Margot von Brentano.

        3. Britten himself had heard the first English performance of *Die Massnahme* (*The Decision*) that March and found 'many fine things in this work, and it is splendidly dramatic'.

        4. Auden to Margrit Hahnloser-Ingold, dated 9 Aug. In *Brecht in Britain*, TQ Publications, London, 1977, p. 68.

p. 57 1. Brecht to Auden, August 1936 (BBA 1396/36).

p. 58 1. See *Brecht on Theatre*, pp. 153 ff.

p. 59 1. *Journals*, 20 Sept. 1943.

        2. Christopher Isherwood, *Diaries, Volume One: 1939–1960*, Methuen, London, 1996, p. 312

        3. Ditto, pp. 318–20.

        4. Ditto, p. 340.

p. 60 1. Brecht to Auden, undated (BBA 210/13).

        2. Act 2, scene 1 of the *Duchess of Malfi*, in *Collected Plays 7*, where the notes contain my own completion of this translation to match Brecht's fuller German version.

p. 61 1. Auden to the Sterns, postmarked 7 Aug. 1944.

2. Ditto, 11 Aug. 1944.

3. Brecht to James Stern, postmarked 13 Dec. 1944.

4. Letter 501, to Ruth Berlau, undated.

p. 62   1. Auden to T. Spencer, 17 Nov. 1945.

2. Letter from Auden to me, 18 Aug. [1958].

p. 63   1. Hanns Eisler later said that he felt unable to supply the kind of setting for a Homeric epic that Brecht wanted. So Paul Dessau wrote the music when the Berliner Ensemble staged the play in 1954.

2. Auden to James Stern, 13 Oct. 1959.

p. 64   1. Letter from Auden to me, 6 Sept. 1971. For Hannah Arendt's suggestions about my attitude to Auden see p. 233.

p. 65   1. Letter from Auden to me, 2 Nov. 1971.

p. 66   1. Letter from Charles Monteith to me, 29 Aug. 1975.

2. Air-letter from Ed Mendelson to me, 11 March 1977.

p. 67   1. A fuller text is in Michael Turner (ed.), *Just a Song at Twilight*, Michael Joseph, London, 1975, p. 89.

p. 68   1. See note 1 for p. viii.

2. Elisabeth Hauptmann, *Julia ohne Romeo*, Aufbau-Verlag, Berlin, 1977.

3. Sabine Kebir, *Ich fragte nicht nach meinem Anteil: Elisabeth Hauptmann's work with Bertolt Brecht*, Aufbau-Verlag, Berlin, 1997.

p. 77   1. Ditto, pp. 168 ff.

p. 78   1. Ditto, p. 186.

p. 82   1. Kebir points out that this cannot have been the composer, who died in 1924.

p. 96   1. *GW* 19, p. 304.

p. 103   1. *Poems*, p. 112.

p. 105   1. 'Rechenschaft' from a speech of 25 March 1929, included in Piscator, *Schriften* 2, Henschelverlag, East Berlin, 1968, p. 50.

p. 108   1. Bernhard Reich, *Im Wettlauf mit der Zeit*, Henschelverlag, East Berlin, 1970, p. 372.

p. 109   1. Letter from Steffin to Benjamin, 18 Feb. 1936, in *Exil in der Tschechoslowakei, in Grossbritannien, Skandinavien und Palästina*, Reclam, Leipzig, 1980, p. 489.

2. Letter 298, 12 Oct. 1936.

p. 111   1. Letter 411.

p. 112   1. Letter 431, to Piscator.

2. Louis Shaffer (Labor Stage) to Piscator, cited in James K. Lyon, *Bertolt Brecht in America*, Princeton University Press, 1980; Methuen, London, 1983, p. 100. Lyon suggests that the fault lay in the play, but it is worth noting that America was not yet at war.

3. Cited by Lyon in *Brecht in America*.

p. 113   1. Letter of ? Jan. 1942, not included in *Briefe* but translated by Hays in *Poems*, p. 517.

2. Letter in the Morris Library, University of Southern Illinois. Cited in *ICarbs*, Carbondale, vol. 1, no. 2, Spring–Summer 1974, p. 88.

p. 115 1. Letter of 29 May, cited in *ICarbs*, Carbondale, Spring–Summer 1974, pp. 90–91.

2. Letter 502, 2 June 1945.

p. 116 1. *ICarbs*, as above, pp. 91–2.

2. Letters in the Morris Library, University of Southern Illinois.

p. 119 1. Cited by Herbert Knust in Siegfried Mews and H. Knust (eds.), *Essays on Brecht*, University of North Carolina Press, Chapel Hill, 1974, p. 67. Likewise my own *The Theatre of Erwin Piscator*, Eyre Methuen, London, 1979, p. 189.

p. 120 1. *Théâtre Populaire*, Paris, 1956, no. 19.

p. 121 1. Joseph Gregor, *Das Zeitalter des Films*, Reinhold-Verlag, Vienna–Leipzig, 3rd printing, 1932, p. 143.

p. 122 1. Hans Bunge, *Fragen Sie mehr über Brecht*, Rogner und Bernhard, Munich, 1972, p. 233.

2. George Lellis in *Screen*, London, vol. 16, no. 4, Winter 1975/6, p. 138.

3. Editorial in *Screen*, vol. 15, no. 2, Summer 1974, p. 6.

p. 123 1. *Diaries 1920–1922*, 27 July 1920.

2. Ditto, 14 Feb. 1921.

3. In *Texte für Filme*, I, 1969.

p. 125 1. *Diaries 1920–1922*, 29 Oct. 1921.

p. 126 1. Programme for *Die rote Zibebe*, Munich Kammerspiele, 29–30 Sept. 1922, note on Valentin by Brecht.

2. *GW* 18, p. 138, partly quoted in *Brecht on Theatre*, p. 50.

p. 127 1. In conversation with me in Budapest, spring 1967.

p. 130 1. Short extract under heading 'The Film, the Novel and Epic Theatre' in *Brecht on Theatre*. Full German text in *GW* 18, pp. 139–209.

p. 131 1. *GW* 18, p. 210.

2. *Poems*, pp. 185–6.

p. 132 1. This was on 9 April, but is not recorded in Kessler's diary.

p. 133 1. Note BBA 464/51.

p. 135 1. Cited by James K. Lyon in *Bertolt Brecht in America*, p. 50.

p. 136 1. Gersch, *Film bei Brecht*, Henschel, East Berlin, 1975, pp. 205–6.

p. 137 1. Lyon, *Bertolt Brecht in America*, p. 51.

2. *Texte für Filme*, II, p. 654.

3. Ditto, p. 538.

p. 138 1. In the pages of *Theatre Workshop* magazine.

2. *Journals*, 19 Oct. 1942.

3. Lyon, *Bertolt Brecht in America*, p. 54.

p. 140 1. *Texte für Filme*, I, p. 264.

2. Gersch, *Film bei Brecht*, p. 288.

p. 146 1. Letter 514. Kasack, formerly Brecht's editor at the Kiepenheuer Verlag, was a reader for Suhrkamp and also a novelist. Gustav Hartung had been among the leading Expressionist theatre directors.

2. See Letters 567, 572 and 576.

3. *Poems*, p. 145.

p. 147   1. Beth Irwin Lewis reports that Wieland Herzfelde claimed to have been told this by Brecht in the 1950s. See her *George Grosz: Art and Politics in the Weimar Republic*, University of Wisconsin Press, Madison, 1971, pp. 77–78.

p. 149   1. George Grosz, *Briefe 1913–1956*, edited by Herbert Knust, Rowohlt, Reinbeck, 1979; letter 7 July 1936.

p. 150   1. GW 20, pp. 42–3.
         2. *Brecht on Theatre*, p. 17.

p. 152   1. Notes in the *Threepenny Opera*, 1931; *Brecht on Theatre*, p. 46.
         2. *Brecht on Theatre*, pp. 57–8.

p. 153   1. *GW* 15, p. 463.
         2. *GW* 15, p. 441.
         3. *GW* 15, p. 450.
         4. *GW* 15, p. 455.
         5. *GW* 15, p. 453.
         6. *Brecht on Theatre*, p. 213.

p. 154   1. *GW* 8, p. 386; *Poems*, p. 192.
         2. *Brecht on Theatre*, p. 91.
         3. 'Alienation effects in the narrative pictures of the elder Brueghel', *Brecht on Theatre*, pp. 157–9.

p. 155   1. *Brecht on Theatre*, pp. 158–9.
         2. Translated from 'Aufblickend vom Studium der Weltgeschichte', which is printed with two other epigrams in the Neue Münchner Galerie catalogue *Bilder und Graphiken zu Werken von Bertolt Brecht*, Munich, 1964, p. 85.

p. 156   1. *Brecht on Theatre*, p. 166.
         2. Ditto, p. 167.

p. 159   1. *GW* 12, p. 385.
         2. *GW* 12, pp. 483–4.
         3. *Poems*, pp. 248–50.
         4. *GW* 19, pp. 517–19.
         5. *GW* 18, p. 269.

p. 160   1. *GW* 19, pp. 511–16.
         2. *GW* 19, p. 522.
         3. *GW* 19, p. 528.

p. 161   1. *Brecht on Theatre*, p. 269.
         2. Letter, Becher to Heartfield, 19 June 1951, printed in Roland März (ed.), *John Heartfield. Der Schnitt entlang der Zeit*, Verlag der Kunst, Dresden, 1981, p. 437.
         3. Ditto, p. 439.

p. 162   1. *Poems*, p. 431.
         2. Wieland Herzfelde, *John Heartfield. Leben und Werk*, Verlag der Kunst, Dresden, 2nd edition 1971, p. 99.

p. 163   1. Reproduced on p. 79 of *The Theatre of Bertolt Brecht* and there mistakenly identified as 'The Doubter'.

2. *GW* 18, p. 279.

p. 165   1. *Poems*, p. 89.

p. 166   1. These can be found in the original German editions of *Die Taschenpostille* and *Die Hauspostille*, and in Eric Bentley's bilingual edition, *Manual of Piety*, Grove Press, New York, 1966.

        2. Carl Zuckmayer, *Als wär's ein Stück von mir*, S. Fischer, Frankfurt, 1966, p. 375.

p. 168   1. 'Zeitoper' in *Melos*, March 1928, Jg. 7, nr. 3. Reprinted in Kurt Weill, *Ausgewählte Schriften*, ed. David Drew, Suhrkamp, Frankfurt, 1975, pp. 37–40.

        2. 'Über den gestischen Charakter der Musik' in *Die Musik*, March 1929, Jg. 21, nr. 6, p. 419 f. Reprinted as above, pp. 40–5. Translation by Erich Albrecht in *The Tulane Drama Review*, New Orleans, Autumn 1961, pp. 28–32.

p. 170   1. From 'On the use of music in an epic theatre', written c. 1936: *Brecht on Theatre*, pp. 85–6.

        2. *Musikblätter des Anbruchs*, Vienna, Jan. 1929, Jg. 11, nr. 1, pp. 24 ff. Reprinted in Weill, *Ausgewählte Schriften*, pp. 54–6.

        3. 'Introduction to the prompt-book of the opera' in *Collected Plays 2iii*, pp. 93–4.

p. 173   1. *Versuche* 2, 1930, p. 148. (Note to the *Badener Lehrstück*.)

        2. Interview in *The London Magazine*, May 1961.

p. 177   1. Hans Bunge, *Fragen Sie mehr über Brecht*, Rogner und Bernhard, Munich, 1972, p. 18.

p. 178   1. Ditto, p. 193.

p. 179   1. Letter 267, Brecht to Eisler, 29 Aug. 1935.

        2. Lee Baxandall, 'Brecht in America 1935', *TDR*, vol. 12, no. 1 (T37), New York, Fall 1967, p. 70.

p. 180   1. Bunge, *Fragen Sie mehr über Brecht*, pp. 222–223. The poem is on pp. 318–20 of *Poems*.

p. 181   1. *Journals*, 15 April 1942.

p. 182   1. Bunge, *Fragen Sie mehr über Brecht*, p. 241.

        2. The *Hollywood Songbook* has never been published in full, but items from it are on pp. 72–156 of Eisler's *Lieder für eine Singstimme und Klavier*, Leipzig, 1976. The Elegies occupy pp. 102–113. See also *Poems*, pp. 380–2 and the relevant notes.

        3. Bunge, *Fragen Sie mehr über Brecht*, pp. 19–20.

p. 183   1. See *Arbeitsjournal* entry for end of October 1944, following a dinner party at Schönberg's with Dessau and the Eislers.

        2. See respectively pp. 119, 151 and 116 of *Lieder für eine Singstimme und Klavier*.

        3. Bunge, *Fragen Sie mehr über Brecht*, p. 193. Jürgen Schebera, *Hanns Eisler. Eine Bildbiografie*, Henschel, East Berlin, 1981, p. 123.

p. 184   1. Letter, Weill to Brecht, 5 Dec. 1943, quoted in introduction to

Collected Plays 7.

2. It is not clear whether this was the New School's programme of 6 March in Brecht's honour, or the 'Tribune' programme of 24 April in which Brecht himself took part. Fritz Hennenberg gives the former date.

p. 185   1. See Dessau's recollection in Fritz Hennenberg, *Dessau-Brecht Musikalische Arbeiten*, Henschel, East Berlin, 1963, p. 541.

2. Cited in Fritz Hennenberg, *Paul Dessau. Eine Biographie*, Deutscher Verlag für Musik, Leipzig, 1965, p. 55.

p. 187   1. See letters 792 and 793, Brecht to Buckwitz and Dessau respectively, March 1955.

2. *Journals*, 3 July 1951.

3. See his essay 'On rhymeless verse with irregular rhythms' in *Brecht on Theatre*, p. 116, and *Poems*, p. 465.

4. *Journals*, 16 Aug. 1944, following a private recital by Salka Viertel's brother, Eduard Steuermann.

p. 188   1. Bunge, *Fragen Sie mehr über Brecht*, p. 213.

2. In 'On the use of music in an epic theatre'; *Brecht on Theatre*, p. 87.

p. 190   1. '[Gesellschaftliche Umfunktionierung der Musik]' (Music's Purposes in Society) from Eisler, *Musik und Politik. Schriften 1924–1948*, Deutscher Verlag für Musik, Leipzig, 1973, pp. 372–374.

2. Eisler, *Lieder für eine Singstimme und Klavier*, pp. 129–30. Text only: Bunge, *Fragen Sie mehr über Brecht*, p. 25.

p. 191   1. Bunge, *Fragen Sie mehr über Brecht*, p. 193.

2. Ditto, p. 28.

3. *Journals*, 6 Nov. 1944.

p. 196   1. Letter 33, Brecht to Neher, June 1918.

2. *GW* 20, p. 46.

3. Letter 126, Brecht to Weigel, August–September 1927.

4. *Brecht on Theatre*, pp. 24–5.

p. 197   1. Fritz Sternberg, *Der Dichter und die Ratio*, Sachse und Pohl, Göttingen, 1963.

p. 198   1. 'Über den Zweifel' in *GW* 12, p. 504.

p. 199   1. Letter 156 (unfinished), to Lukács, end 1930/beginning 1931.

p. 200   1. Letter 170 [Carona, Switzerland, April 1933].

2. Letter 193 [c. December 1933].

p. 202   1. See Manfred Grabs, 'Eisler's Versuche', cited in *Musik bei Brecht*, p. 584.

p. 204   1. Letter 332, dated [Skovsbostrand, July 1937].

p. 205   1. See David Pike, *German Writers in Soviet Exile 1933–1945*, University of North Carolina Press, Chapel Hill, 1982, p. 293.

2. Letters 365 to Kurella and 366 to Bredel, dated 17 June and c. July/ August 1938. Lukács's criticism is in the original version of his 'Marx and the Problem of Ideological Decay' in his *Essays on Realism*, Lawrence and Wishart, London, 1980, where the words 'as in certain

plays by Brecht or novels by Ehrenburg' followed 'in such cases' on p. 154, line 2. Brecht's corrective concerning Eisler, 'Kleine Berichtigung', is in *GW* 19, p. 337; Eisler's own reply finally appeared in *Die Neue Weltbühne* on 15 December and is now in his *Musik und Politik. Schriften 1924–1948*, pp. 433–4.

3. See Pike, *German Writers in Soviet Exile 1933–1945*, p. 276, Brecht's letter 394 to Erpenbeck from Sweden dated 25 July 1939, and the account given by Simone Barck in the collectively written *Exil in der UdSSR*, Reclam, Leipzig, 1979, p. 203.

4. See entry for January 1939.

p. 207 1. *GW* 20, p. 101.

p. 209 1. *GW* 20, p. 245.

2. Martin Esslin, *Brecht: A Choice of Evils*, Eyre and Spottiswoode, London, 1959, pp. 144–5; third edition, Eyre Methuen, London, 1980, pp. 148–9, citing an article by Herbert Luethy in *Encounter*.

p. 210 1. Letters 420 and 427, to Apletin, [Helsinki] 20 Nov. 1940 and Moscow, 30 May 1941.

2. See Hans Tombrock's drawing of August 1939 showing a 'Discussion about the defeat of the Spanish Republic at Brecht's house in Lidingö near Stockholm', reproduced in *Bilder und Graphiken zu Werken von Bertolt Brecht*, p. 80.

3. *GW* 20, pp. 298–9. The italicised words are in English.

4. James K. Lyon, *Bertolt Brecht in America*, Princeton University Press 1980; Methuen, London, 1983, p. 288.

p. 211 1. *Journals*, 7 Aug. 1943.

p. 212 1. Lyon, *Bertolt Brecht in America*, p. 309, marshals these and other clues.

2. Letter 506, to Ruth Berlau [Santa Monica, Aug. 1945].

p. 213 1. *Journals*, 4 Nov. 1947; letters 548 and 549 to Ruth Berlau from Paris, 3 Nov. and Zurich, 5 [Nov.] 1947.

2. Letter 558, dated Zurich, April 1948.

p. 214 1. Letter 579, dated from the Deutsches Theater, 9 Feb. 1949.

2. *Journals*, 6 Nov. 1948 and 9 Dec. 1948.

p. 215 1. Kathe Rülicke-Weiler, *Die Dramaturgie Brechts*, Henschel Verlag, East Berlin, 1968, p. 264.

p. 216 1. *Journals*, 10 Nov. 1943.

p. 217 1. Letter 681, dated 29 Nov. 1951.

2. *Neues Deutschland*, 14 May 1953. Walter Ulbricht, *Zur Geschichte der deutschen Arbeiterbewegung*, vol. 4, East Berlin, 1954, p. 604.

p. 218 1. *Journals*, 4 March 1953. This is the last entry for nearly six months. When the typescript restarts it does so in another file.

2. *GW* 20, p. 327.

3. *Journals*, 20 August 1953.

p. 219 1. Ditto.

2. Letters 725 and 726 are those which Brecht wrote on 17 June respectively to Ulbricht and Grotewohl the premier. In *The Theatre of*

Bertolt Brecht, 1959, I referred to three further statements; and there
are indeed three in the Brecht Archive which are reproduced without
comment on pp. 326–8 of *GW* 20. The other statement which I
quoted there on p. 202 of my book came however from the letter of 1
July to Peter Suhrkamp, now published as letter 728.

3. Cited in the note to letter 725 in the Suhrkamp edition of 1981.
4. Letter 724. The reply of 22 July is summarised in the relevant note.

p. 220 1. *Poems*, p. 436.

      2. Reich, *Im Wettlauf mit der Zeit*, Henschel Verlag, East Berlin, 1970, pp. 386–7.

      3. Pike, *German Writers in Soviet Exile 1933–1945*, p. 345.

      4. *Gedichte aus dem Nachlass 1913–1956*, pp. 437–8. English translations of all four of these are in Bertolt Brecht, *Bad Time for Poetry: 152 Poems and Songs*, ed. John Willett, Methuen, London, 1995, pp. 127–8.

p. 221 1. *GW* 19, p. 336.

p. 223 1. *GW* 20, p. 344.

      2. *Poems*, p. 276.

      3. See *Brecht on Theatre*, pp. 281–2.

p. 224 1. Waley, *Three Ways of Thought in Ancient China*.

      2. Alfred Forke (ed. and trans.), *Me Ti, des Sozialethikers und seiner Schüler philosophische Werke*, Berlin, 1922, p. 34.

p. 225 1. *GW* 15, p. 221.

p. 226 1. *Poems*, p. 386. 'Das Fischgerät', *GW* 857.

p. 227 1. *Poems*, pp. 107–8.

      2. Letter 785, dated 9 Feb. 1955.

      3. *TLS*, 26 March 1970.

p. 236 1. Reich, *Im Wettlauf mit der Zeit*, pp. 371–2.

p. 245 1. Puntila was Adolf Gondrell; Eva, Erni Wilhelmi. The latter's, very delicately balanced, is one of the acting performances I still remember a third of a century later.

p. 269 1. *Robyn Archer Sings Brecht*, EMI, Australia, 1981, OASD 4166.

p. 271 1. *Mein Stundenbuch*, Kurt Wolff Verlag, Munich, 1926.

Notes on sources

Some chapters of this book incorporate material and ideas which originated as follows:

2. 'Anglo-American forays' is to some extent a synthesis of lectures given at Rutgers University (and published as 'The poet beneath the skin' in the *Brecht Yearbook*, 1972) and to the City Literary Institute (in May 1974, subsequently developed into the introduction to *Brecht in Britain*, TQ Publications, London, 1977) along with an article which I wrote for the South Australian English Teachers' Association journal *Opinion*, Adelaide, February–March 1976.

3. 'The case of Kipling' includes parts of a review of Charles Carrington's Kipling biography and Alan Bold's *Penguin Book of Socialist Verse* which appeared in *The Poetry Review*, London, vol. 62, no. 1, Spring 1972.

4. 'The case of Auden' is a revised version of a paper on Brecht and Auden read informally to members of the Humanities Research Centre, ANU, Canberra, mid-winter 1979 and subsequently included in Ian Donaldson (ed.), *Transformations in Modern European Drama*.

5. 'The role of Elisabeth Hauptmann' is a revised version of my article entitled 'Bacon ohne Shakespeare?: The Problem of Mitarbeit', which appeared in the *Brecht Yearbook*, vol. 12, 1983, Wayne State University Press, Detroit.

6. 'Brecht and Expressionism' is translated and slightly revised from a paper originally written in French, read at an Expressionism conference at Strasbourg University in November 1968 and subsequently edited by Denis Bablet as part of the volume *L'Expressionisme dans le théâtre européen*, CNRS, Paris, 1971.

7. 'Brecht and Piscator' derives originally from a lecture given for City University, New York and the New York Goethe Institute in October 1974.

13(d). 'Brecht for the media, 1981–82' is reprinted from my article which appeared in the *Brecht Yearbook*, vol. 11, 1982.

Other sources will be largely evident from the detailed Notes above, but I would like in particular

to say how much I profited from the pioneering work of Wolfgang Gersch, James K. Lyon and Patty Parmalee;

to acknowledge my debt to Robert Medley, Edward Mendelson, Michael Sidnell and James Stern for permission to refer to unpublished work and reproduce letters from Auden and Rupert Doone;

to thank the many others who helped me in various ways, notably Sir Isaiah Berlin, John Calder, Patrick Carnegy, Gabriel Carritt, Sir William Coldstream, Georg Eisler, Thomas Elsaesser, Christopher Isherwood, Charles Monteith, Michael Morley, Fiona Searle, Sir Stephen Spender, Eric Walter White and Basil Wright;

and finally, to honour the memory of Denis Bablet, Wal Cherry, John Cullen, Bernard Dort, Elisabeth Hauptmann, Hans Hess, and Ralph Manheim.

Index

General index

Abbott, Tony, 268
Abravanel, Maurice, 175
actors: associated with Brecht and Piscator, 105; as singers, 170, 174–5
Adamic, Louis: *Dynamite*, 19
Adorno, Theodor Wiesengrund, 1–2, 29, 175, 181
agit-prop, 97, 107, 177, 194, 200; in *Kuhle Wampe*, 132
Aitken, Max, 50
AIZ (Arbeiter-Illustrierte-Zeitung), 150, 200, 277
Albers, Hans, 139
'Alienation'/'Alienation effect' (*Verfremdung/Verfremdungseffekt*), 36, 86, 164, 234–8, 246, 249, 256; differs from 'Entfremdung', 235, 237; Kafka and, 88–9; Piscator and, 120; 'A-effect', 95, 107; and Russian Formalism, 236
Allio, René: *La Vieille Dame indigne*, 142
Anacreon, 183, 190
Anbruch (magazine), 170
Anderson, Hedli (Mrs MacNeice), 57
Anderson, Sherwood: *Poor White*, 19
anti-Nazi writing by Brecht, 200–2; *see also Resistible Rise; Fear and Misery*; 'German Satires'; *Round Heads and Pointed Heads*
Apelman, Maya *see* Bentley, Maya
Apletin, Mikhail, 210
'apparatus', the, 123, 177, 199, 200; and film-making, 128, 133, 138, 141; of opera, 19, 171, 176; similarity of in

East and West, 141, 190
Appen, Karl von, 151, 157, 255
Aragon, Louis, 38, 51, 97, 99, 193; and Brecht, 38, 51, 97; and Becher, 97
Arbeiter-Illustrierte-Zeitung see AIZ
ARBKD (Association of Revolutionary Artists), 151
Archer, Robyn, 11, 263; *Robyn Archer sings Brecht*, 43, 263, 269–70, 274, 277, 278
Arendt, Hannah, 64, 66–7, 98, 193, 227–34; *Men in Dark Times*, 230–2
Arnold, Matthew, 26–7
art: Chinese, 163; non-figurative, 153, 159
Ashcroft, Peggy, 8
Askin, Leon, 116
'Asleep on the Deep', 67, 167
Asso (Association of Revolutionary Artists), 97, 151, 157
atom bomb, the, 212
Auden, W. H., 16, 25, 32, 38, 53–67 *passim*, 100, 134, 143, 192, 233; Brecht poem on, 65; *The Duchess of Malfi*, involvement, 30, 60; and his translations of Brecht's works, 20, 53–4, 60–6, 234, 255; *The Ascent of F6*, 58; *A Certain World*, 54; *City Without Walls*, 64; *Coal Face*, 56, 67; *The Dance of Death*, 55, 56; *The Dog Beneath the Skin* (with Isherwood), 56; and *The Duchess of Malfi*, 30, 60; *Letters from Iceland*, 57; *Night Mail*, 56; *The Poet's Tongue*, 67; 'Victor', 53
Aufricht, Ernst Josef, 106, 117, 175;

Index of Brecht's works